Office 97 Small Business Edition Shortcuts
Word 97 Shortcuts for Common Tasks

Action	Button	Shortcut
Copy text or graphics	📋	Ctrl+C
Cut text or graphics	✂	Ctrl+X
Highlight a word		Double-click the word
Highlight a sentence		Triple click a word in the sentence
Highlight entire document		Ctrl+A
Move to beginning of document		Ctrl+Home
Move to beginning of line		Home
Move to end of document		Ctrl+End
Move to end of line		End
Open a document	📂	Ctrl+O
Paste text or graphics	📋	Ctrl+V
Print a document	🖨	Ctrl+P
Save a document	💾	Ctrl+S
Undo last action	↩ ▾	Ctrl+Z

Excel 97 Shortcuts for Common Tasks

Action	Shortcut
Apply currency format	Ctrl+Shift+$
Calculate active worksheet	Shift+F9
Calculate all worksheets	F9
Complete cell entry	Enter
Display Format Cells dialog box	Ctrl+1
Edit the active cell	F2
Enter the date	Shift+;
Fill down	Ctrl+D
Fill right	Ctrl+R
Fill selected range with current entry	Ctrl+Enter

Using Microsoft Office 97 Small Business Edition   *Copyright© 1998 by Que® Corporation*

Outlook 97 Shortcuts for Common Tasks

Action	Button	Shortcut
Create a contact		Ctrl+Shift+C
Create a mail message		Ctrl+Shift+M
Create an appointment		Ctrl+Shift+A
Find		Ctrl+Shift+F
Open the Address Book		Ctrl+Shift+B
Reply to mail message		Ctrl+R
Switch to the Inbox		Ctrl+Shift+I

Publisher 98 Shortcuts for Common Tasks

Action	Shortcut
Group or ungroup objects	Ctrl+Shift+G
Nudge to left	Alt+←
Nudge to right	Alt+→
Nudge up	Alt+↑
Nudge down	Alt+↓
Delete text frame	Ctrl+Shift+X

Using

Microsoft® Office 97
Small Business Edition

Tom E. Barich

Julia Kelly

Laurie Ulrich

A Division of Macmillan Computer Publishing, USA
201 W. 103rd Street
Indianapolis, Indiana 46290

Contents at a Glance

Using Microsoft® Office 97 Small Business Edition

Copyright© 1998 by Que® Corporation

All rights reserved. Printed in the United States of America. No part of this book may be used or reproduced in any form or by any means, or stored in a database or retrieval system, without prior written permission of the publisher except in the case of brief quotations embodied in critical articles and reviews. Making copies of any part of this book for any purpose other than your own personal use is a violation of United States copyright laws. For information, address Que Corporation, 201 W. 103rd Street, Indianapolis, IN, 46290. You may reach Que's direct sales line by calling 1-800-428-5331.

Library of Congress Catalog No.: 98-84089

ISBN: 0-7897-1570-8

This book is sold *as is*, without warranty of any kind, either express or implied, respecting the contents of this book, including but not limited to implied warranties for the book's quality, performance, merchantability, or fitness for any particular purpose. Neither Que Corporation nor its dealers or distributors shall be liable to the purchaser or any other person or entity with respect to any liability, loss, or damage caused or alleged to have been caused directly or indirectly by this book.

99 98   6 5 4 3 2 1

Interpretation of the printing code: the rightmost double-digit number is the year of the book's printing; the rightmost single-digit number, the number of the book's printing. For example, a printing code of 98-1 shows that the first printing of the book occurred in 1998.

Composed in Janson Text, Formata, and MCPdigital by Macmillan Computer Publishing.

Printed in the United States of America.

Trademarks

All terms mentioned in this book that are known to be trademarks or service marks have been appropriately capitalized. Que cannot attest to the accuracy of this information. Use of a term in this book should not be regarded as affecting the validity of any trademark or service mark.

Screen reproductions in this book were created using Collage Plus from Inner Media, Inc., Hollis, NH.

Credits

Executive Editor
Lisa Wagner

Acquistions Editor
Jamie Milazzo

Development Editor
Jan Snyder

Technical Editor
Sherry Kinkoph

Managing Editor
Thomas F. Hayes

Project Editor
Gina Brown

Copy Editor
Malinda McCain

Indexer
Tim Tate

Book Designers
Nathan Clement
Ruth Harvey

Cover Designers
Dan Armstrong
Ruth Harvey

Production Team
Lissa Auciello-Brogan
John Bitter
Jena Brandt
Jerry Cole
Toi Davis
Sean Decker
Linda Quigley

Contents

About the Authors

Tom E. Barich, a former editor, has finally become a productive member of society. He now writes computer books, develops and produces *CD-ROM*s, and acts as a consultant. He has written a number of computer books on a variety of subjects including Office 97, Outlook, Quicken, and others.

Julia Kelly, cybergirl in cowspace, ex-jet jockey, and former mad scientist, has also done time as a stable cleaner, hardware-store cashier/barrista, theme park candy girl, veterinary cat-holder, Caribbean pilot, and teacher of diverse topics. She currently lives on her farm in Idaho, where she writes books, teaches classes, builds databases, chops wood, and shovels snow.

Laurie Ann Ulrich started life as an artist, working her way up from finger paints to watercolors and sculpture. When the art world didn't run to her with open arms upon her leaving college and entering the world of work, she fell into a computer job in 1981. That job and her love of telling people what to do led to computer training—first as a training manager for a large computer reseller, and then to the establishment of her own firm, Limehat & Company, in 1992. Since then, Laurie has been teaching and writing training materials for universities and computer training organizations throughout the PA, NJ, and NY areas. She is the author of *Using Word 97*, published by Macmillan in October of 1997, and a contributing author to several books, including Que's *Windows 95 6-in-1* and *Works 6-in-1* books. She can be reached at `limehat@aol.com`.

About the Technical Editor

Sherry Kinkoph has authored over 25 computer books for Macmillan Publishing over the past five years, including books for both adults and children. Her recent publications include *The Complete Idiot's Guide to Microsoft Office for Windows 95*, *Easy Microsoft Word 97*, *Microsoft Office 97 Small Business Edition 6-in-1*, *The 10 Minute Guide to Lotus Organizer 97*, and *The Big Basics Book of Microsoft Office 97*.

Sherry started exploring computers back in college and claims that many a term paper was whipped out using a trusty 128K Macintosh. Today, Sherry's still churning out words, but now they're in the form of books, and instead of using a Mac, she's moved on to a trusty PC. A native of the Midwest, Sherry currently resides in Fishers, IN and continues in her quest to help users of all levels master the ever-changing computer technologies. You can email Sherry at skinkoph@inetdirect.net.

Dedication

From Thomas Barich:

This book is dedicated to Kathy Ivens for getting me started as a writer. She began by driving me crazy when I was her editor, thus motivating me to find a new vocation. Then, experiencing pangs of guilt, she gave me my first opportunity to write as a co-author on one of her books. Last but not least, I want to thank her for providing me with a seemingly endless supply of straight lines.

Acknowledgments

As is the case with most successful projects this one could not have come to fruition without the efforts of quite a few people. Julia Kelly and Laurie Ulrich contributed outstanding material without which we would never have been able to meet the strenuous deadlines imposed upon us by the nature of the business.

The team at Que provided the support, expertise and direction that kept us working and striving to put our best foot forward even as we dealt with last minute beta and impossible deadlines. I'm especially grateful to Jamie Milazzo for her support, guidance, professionalism, and downright perkiness. Not only did she do a great job as the team leader, she even remained pleasant and professional no matter how cranky I got. Jan Snyder developed this book with professionalism, personality, and a cat-o'-nine-tails. To be fair I guess I should add that she only beat us when we deserved it. The technical accuracy of this book is largely due to the skills of Sherry Kinkoph, our technical editor. Gina Brown, our project editor, managed to keep the stream of manuscript flowing smoothly, while putting up with my frequent, and on rare occasion, cantankerous requests to review material again. Finally, if after reading this book you conclude that I actually understand the rules of grammar and punctuation, it will be the result of the diligent efforts of our copy editor, Malinda McCain.

We'd Like to Hear from You!

Que Corporation has a long-standing reputation for high-quality books and products. To ensure your continued satisfaction, we also understand the importance of customer service and support.

Tech Support

If you need assistance with the information in this book or you have feedback for us about the book, please contact Macmillan Technical Support by phone at 317-581-3833 or via email at support@mcp.com.

Orders, Catalogs, and Customer Service

To order other Que or Macmillan Computer Publishing books, catalogs, or products, please contact our Customer Service Department:

Phone: 1-800-428-5331

Fax: 1-800-882-8583

International Fax: 1-317-228-4400

Or visit our online bookstore: http://www.mcp.com/

MICROSOFT OFFICE 97 SMALL BUSINESS EDITION is, without a doubt, a powerful tool for both home and business use. Harnessing all that power is also no simple matter. The sheer number of applications and features available in the Office 97 Small Business Edition make it difficult to put the product to use quickly and efficiently through the old trial-and-error method. Unless you're fascinated by software and enjoy tinkering, exploring, and getting your fingernails dirty in the process, you'll probably want to get right to work.

That's where *Using Microsoft® Office 97 Small Business Edition* comes in. Why bother reinventing the wheel if you don't have to? Here you'll find information to get you up and running in no time and able to accomplish most of the common Office tasks in short order, with a minimum amount of hassle.

Don't get me wrong—there's no magic here. You're going to have plenty of work to do, but you'll be able to concentrate on results instead of figuring out the best way to get them.

Features in This Book

This book has been designed to provide you with the information you need, in a way that enables you to use it efficiently and effectively.

- *Real-life experience*. This book is the result of years of experience in using Microsoft Office products, making mistakes, digging around in the software, and searching out the tips and tricks other users have found. In all that time I've discovered—sometimes by happy accident, sometimes from the experience of others, and occasionally by my own leap of logic—the quickest and easiest ways to get things done. If it's possible to learn from the experience of others, you've come to the right place.

- *Sidenotes.* Throughout the book you'll discover margin notes that have useful or interesting information (or, hopefully, both). Most of the time, the notes are set apart because they aren't a basic element in the topic under discussion, but they are relevant and will add to your knowledge base. Sometimes they take the form of a tip or a warning, and sometimes they have background information that can make the big picture clearer.

- *Step-by-Step.* I have a confession to make—I'm incorrigibly lazy. As a result, when I have something to do, I like to do it quickly, and I like to do it right the first time. I hate having to go back and do the same job twice. That's why you'll find that the step-by-step procedures in this book walk you through each task, using the most efficient method for getting the job done.

What's Covered in This Book

Because this book deals with four major Office 97 Small Business Edition applications (Word 97, Excel 97, Outlook 97, and Publisher 98) and a couple of minor ones (Expedia Streets 98, Small Business Financial Manager 98, and Internet Explorer 4.0), I was limited in how much I could squeeze between the covers. Therefore, I've made an effort to include the kind of information that will help you get up to speed on the most common tasks for which the various programs are used.

Part I: Getting Started with Office

Part I includes some simple things to get you off on the right foot. I imagine you're going to be eager to start using the software, so Part I gives you some information on launching the various Office 97 Small Business Edition applications and on getting help when you need it. I see no point in getting bogged down in a lot of theory or repeating information you're going to get when you start working with the applications.

Part II: Using Word to Increase Productivity

The Word 97 section covers the basics, plus a lot more, so you can get started with word processing right away. You'll learn to create, format, dress up, and print documents in no time. If you want to use styles and templates, add graphics, create tables and numbered lists, and more, look here. The real secret to getting the most out of Word 97 is customization, so you'll find plenty of tips scattered throughout the Word section, as well as an entire chapter on getting Word to work your way. Do you want to create form letters or mailing labels? Word's Mail Merge makes it a snap.

Part III: Using Excel to Track Your Finances

Using Excel 97 can be somewhat intimidating if you just open it up and find yourself staring at a blank worksheet. Check out the Excel section to get everything from the basics of opening and closing worksheets to building formulas and ranges. You'll discover how easy it is to analyze your data, create charts, and forecast for the future.

Part IV: Using Outlook to Organize Your Email and Your Time

Outlook 97 is a suite of mini-applications in its own right. It contains an email program, a contact manager, a scheduling program, and more. You can put this section to use immediately to send and receive email, track your appointments, and organize your contact information. You can even keep track of all your phone calls, correspondence, and documents with the Journal feature.

Part V: Using Publisher to Get Your Message Out

Publisher 98 is a powerful graphics program that can help you with projects from making a birthday card to creating an entire marketing campaign. Part V walks you through the things you need to know to design professional publications, no matter what they are.

Part VI: Using SBE Extras

Learn how to use Expedia Streets 98 to plan your business trips or your vacation trips. Put the Small Business Financial Manager 98 to work analyzing your accounting data. If you're not on the Internet yet, you will be sooner or later. Here's your chance to get the lowdown on getting connected with Internet Explorer 4.0.

Conventions Used in This Book

The Using series has some conventions that control the formatting of text and are used to help you distinguish between generic information and a discussion about a dialog box or menu you're viewing on your screen.

- *Menu and dialog box choices.* Words that appear in a menu or a dialog box are printed in bold type. For example, you might see text that says "Choose **Color**, and then select a new background color from the palette."

- *Hotkeys.* We underline references to hotkeys, which are underlined letters in menu commands and dialog boxes that you can use with your Alt key instead of employing the mouse.

- *Stuff you choose and stuff you type.* Whenever there's an instruction for you to select a menu, a menu command, or an option within a dialog box, the name of the menu, command, or option appears in bold. Whenever there's an instruction for you to type something into a text box, it appears in a monospace font. Here's an example: If you want to exclude records where the state is Florida (FL), select **Not equal to** in the **Comparison** drop-down list and type FL in the **Compare to** text box.

- *Combination keys.* We use a plus sign (+) to indicate that keys should be used together. For example, you may see "Press Ctrl+A to select everything."

- *Cross-references.* If the book has information elsewhere that's connected to the topic you're currently reading, we tell you which chapter has it. You can go look at this information to learn more about the subject or take the next step in building the project at hand. Here's an example:

SEE ALSO

➤ *To access application commands, see page 220*

- *Glossary terms.* Words that have technical or special computer meanings are italicized. This means we know you might not be familiar with them, and it's a signal that the definition can be found in the glossary.

- *Tips, tricks, warnings, and sidebars.* Sometimes I want to give you a hint to make something work better, or a tip about a clever way to use a particular feature. By giving these valuable notes explicit titles and placing them in the margin, we've made them handy and easy to find, without breaking up the text that explains the procedure you're currently working your way through.

Getting Started with Office

Working with Office Applications

Getting Started with Office 97 SBE

Most introductory chapters on Office suites start off by telling you how to use the features that the Office applications have in common—how to open menus, use toolbars, save documents, and so on. For the life of me, I can't figure out why you'd want to come back to this chapter to get that information after you begin using the Word or Excel section. I suppose I could do what some of the other Office books do and repeat the information in both places. Again, I can't come up with a good reason, other than that's the way everybody else does it. For my money (actually, *your* money), it just doesn't make sense.

Therefore, this introductory chapter is going to be short and sweet. Rather than waste your time repeating stuff that belongs elsewhere in the book, I'm going to provide you with some information and advice to help get you off to a running start with Office 97 Small Business Edition.

Here's what we'll cover in this chapter:

- Ways to launch (start) the various Office programs from Windows 95.
- A solution to the annoying mess that the Office 97 Small Business Edition install leaves when it dumps all its shortcuts on your **Programs** menu.
- How you can make the Office applications work together to increase your productivity.

So without further ado, let's get to work.

Launching Applications

Office 97 Small Business Edition is all about productivity. However, unless you get the programs up and running, you won't be very productive. Although it's a relatively simple matter to open an Office application there are a number of ways to do it and, depending on what you're attempting to accomplish, you might be better off using one method over the other.

Because only Outlook and the Small Business Financial Manager place shortcuts on the desktop during install, you have to either use the **Start** menu or create your own shortcut to open the rest of the SBE applications. Actually, I guess that's as good a place to start as any.

Creating Application Shortcuts

A *shortcut* is a Windows 95 device that provides easy access to a file from any number of different locations, without having to move or copy the original file. Because many executable files are quite large, it would be a waste of disk space to place full-size copies in the various places from which you might want to use the file. A shortcut, on the other hand, only takes up 1KB of disk space (actually a little more—how much depends on your file system) and gives you instant access to the file at the same time.

Creating Office application shortcuts on the desktop

1. Right-click on a blank spot on the taskbar and select **Minimize All Windows** from the shortcut menu that appears (see Figure 1.1). You can ignore this step if you're already at the desktop.

FIGURE 1.1

Use the taskbar shortcut menu to unclutter your desktop.

2. Right-click anywhere on the desktop background to open the desktop shortcut menu (see Figure 1.2).

FIGURE 1.2

You can reorganize your desktop and create new items from the desktop shortcut menu.

3. From the **New** submenu, select **Shortcut** to open the
   Create Shortcut dialog box (see Figure 1.3).

FIGURE 1.3

Use the **Browse** button to
locate the application targeted
by the shortcut.

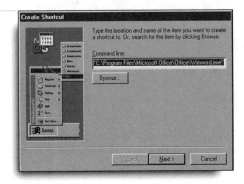

4. Enter the path and filename of the file that runs the application, or click the **Browse** button and use the Browse dialog
   box to find it. If you browse, select the file and then click
   OK to return to the Create Shortcut dialog box.

TABLE 1.1   Office 97 Small Business Edition executable files

Office Application	Executable File	Default Location
Word 97	Winword.exe	C:\Program Files\ Microsoft Office\ Office
Excel 97	Excel.exe	C:\Program Files\ Microsoft Office\ Office
Outlook 97	Outlook.exe	C:\Program Files\ Microsoft Office\ Office
Publisher 97	Mspub.exe	C:\Program Files\ Microsoft Publisher
AutoMap	Automap Streets Plus.exe	C:\Program Files\ Microsoft Reference\ Automap

5. Click **Next** to open the Select a Title for the Program dialog box (see Figure 1.4).

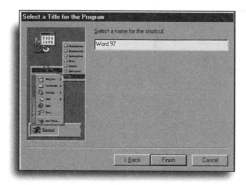

FIGURE 1.4

Make the name short, descriptive, and easy to recognize.

6. Click **Finish** to create the new shortcut, as shown in Figure 1.5.

FIGURE 1.5

Windows 95 adds an icon to the shortcut and places it at the spot on the desktop where you first right-clicked.

Anytime you want to open the application, double-click the shortcut.

Launching Office Applications from the Start Menu

The truth of the matter is, the Office 97 Small Business Edition install does create shortcuts; it just doesn't put them on the desktop. It places them on the Windows 95 Start menu and on the Programs submenu. The two shortcuts that it places on the Start menu are called **New Office Document** and **Open Office Document** (see Figure 1.6).

FIGURE 1.6

The **Start** menu provides easy access to many applications as well as a number of Windows 95 settings.

How to open one or more documents with a desktop shortcut

When I write, I usually have multiple Word documents open at the same time—the chapter I'm working on, my outline, and my chapter schedule. I could open Word first and then each of the documents separately; however, I find it much easier to open everything at once. Because I always have the Windows Explorer running I open the folder with the documents and drag all three to my Word 97 desktop shortcut. As soon as I drop them on the shortcut, Word 97 opens and immediately loads each of the selected documents.

Opening a new Office document with the Start menu shortcut

1. Click the **Start** button on the Windows 95 taskbar to open the **Start** menu shown in Figure 1.6. Remember, your **Start** menu will appear somewhat different, depending on the programs you have installed.

2. Click **New Office Document** to open the New Office Document dialog box (see Figure 1.7).

3. Select the appropriate tab to find the document type you want to open.

4. Double-click the document type to open the application associated with that document type. A new document or a wizard (an easy-to-follow set of steps) of the selected document type appears in the application.

FIGURE 1.7

The New Office Document contains wizards and templates for all kinds of Word, Excel, and Outlook documents.

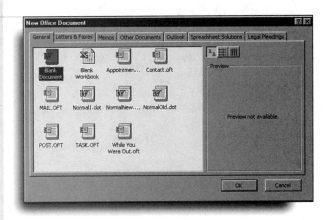

You can begin working as soon as the application finishes opening.

If you have existing Office documents, you can use the Open Office Document shortcut to open the existing document and the associated application at the same time.

Opening an existing Office document from the Start menu

1. Click the **Start** button on the Windows 95 taskbar to open the Start menu.

2. Click the **Open Office Document** shortcut to open the Open Office Document dialog box shown in Figure 1.8.

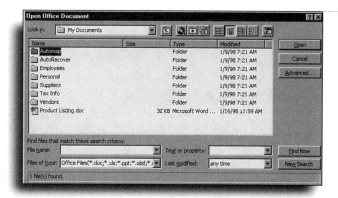

FIGURE 1.8

Use the Open Office Document to locate the existing Office document you want to work on.

3. Use the **Look in** drop-down list to locate the document you want to open.

4. Double-click the file to open the Office application associated with the file type and load the file at the same time.

As soon as the application and the document finish loading, you're ready to go to work.

Using the Programs Menu

Unfortunately, the Office 97 Small Business Edition is not entirely well mannered, and it haphazardly drops shortcuts to the individual Office applications on the **Programs** submenu of the **Start** menu, as shown in Figure 1.9.

FIGURE 1.9

The Office 97 Small Business
Edition **Programs** menu
shortcuts are wandering
around on the loose.

① SBE shortcuts

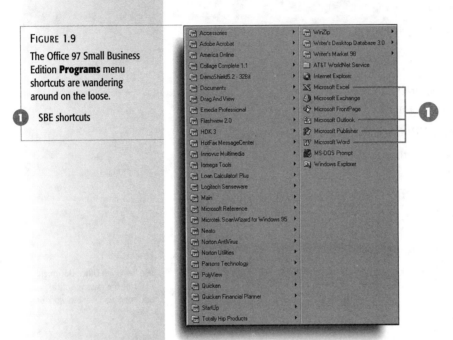

As always, keep in mind that your **Start** menu will appear somewhat different, depending on the programs you have loaded on
your system.

To open any of the programs, click the **Start** button and select
Programs. Clicking the shortcut that carries the name of the
Office application opens the program of the same name.

Cleaning Up After the Office 97 Small Business Edition Install

As you can see, the Office 97 Small Business Edition, unlike
most other Windows programs that add shortcuts, does so in an
unruly and—to my mind—exasperating fashion. As a matter of
fact, if you look closely at Figure 1.9, you'll see that the only
shortcuts without a folder of their own are all Microsoft
products.

Now, I don't know if this is arrogance or carelessness on the part
of the Microsoft programmers, but one thing I do know is that

it's unnecessary and annoying. Most other Windows programs automatically create a folder for shortcuts they place on the **Programs** menu. It's neater, it takes up less valuable menu space, and it's easier to find a particular application your looking for. The solution? Simple. Create your own folder and put those pesky little SBE shortcuts in their place.

You could create a folder and stick it on the **Programs** menu. However, if you use the Office 97 Small Business Edition applications a lot, you'll probably want to add it directly to your **Start** menu. That's what we're going to do in the following exercise.

Corralling the Office 97 Small Business Edition shortcuts

1. Right-click the **Start** button on the Windows 95 taskbar and select **Open** to open the Start Menu window (see Figure 1.10). This is another instance where your Start Menu window may not be identical to mine but will have the same basic elements.

FIGURE 1.10

The Start Menu window contains most of the items that appear on your **Start** menu.

2. From the **File** menu, choose **New, Folder** to create a new folder in the Start Menu window (see Figure 1.11).

3. Type over New Folder with a short, easily identifiable name for the folder. I called mine Office 97 SBE.

4. Press Enter to save the new name.

5. Double-click the **Programs** folder in the Start Menu window to open the Programs window.

6. Minimize (click the minus sign in the upper-right corner) all open windows *except* the Start Menu window and the Program window.

FIGURE 1.11

The new folder appears at the bottom of the Start Menu window.

7. Right-click a blank spot on the Windows 95 taskbar and select **Tile Vertically** to enlarge and reposition both open windows (see Figure 1.12).

FIGURE 1.12

With both windows sitting side by side, dragging the contents from one to the other is a snap.

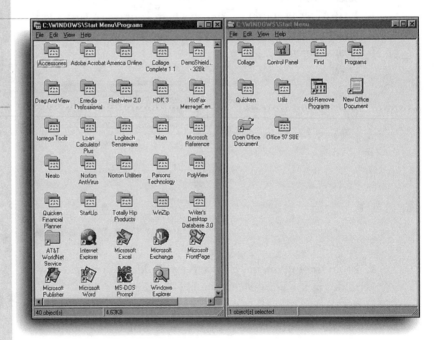

8. Find the SBE shortcuts in the Start Menu window. Then hold down the Ctrl key and click the Microsoft Excel, Microsoft Word, Microsoft Outlook, and Microsoft Publisher icons (keeping the Ctrl key down the whole time) to select them.

9. Let go of the Ctrl key, place your mouse pointer over any one of the selected icons, and drag it (the rest will automatically follow) to the Start Menu window. Be sure to use the left mouse button so you move the shortcuts rather than making copies.

10. Drop the selected icon(s) on the new folder you just created to move them from the Programs window to the new folder in the Start Menu window.

11. Click the **Start** button on the Windows 95 taskbar and select **Office 97 SBE** (or whatever you named the new folder) to see the new location of the shortcuts as shown in Figure 1.13.

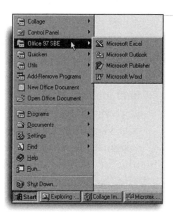

FIGURE 1.13

Now the Office shortcuts are taking up less space, are out of the way, and are more easily accessible.

12. Now you can go back and close any windows you opened during this operation by selecting the window and pressing Alt+F4.

You can use this method to create any number of folders and include any shortcuts you want (or even other folders). If you add folders to a folder, they become submenus of the parent folder when it appears on the **Start** menu.

Sharing Data Between Applications

The fact that the Office 97 Small Business Edition applications work well together is one of their most useful assets. Utilizing an Excel spreadsheet to drive home a point in a Word budget report is invaluable. Dropping a Word 97 document into Publisher and creating an effective piece of marketing literature is a great way to save yourself a lot of work.

Linking

Two of the most effective means of sharing information between Office applications are linking and embedding. Both appear to do the same thing, but below the surface, they are actually quite different.

Linking information is a great way to include all or part of another document in an Office document while maintaining a connection (link) to the original file. The earlier example of including an Excel spreadsheet in a Word report could be accomplished by linking the spreadsheet (or just a part of it) to the Word report. Because linked objects retain contact with the original file, any changes made to the original are reflected in the linked portion. In other words, if new figures were added to the Excel spreadsheet in the example above, they would automatically be included in the Word budget report as well. Very handy indeed.

Editing an embedded object

If you want to make changes to an embedded object, you can quickly open the originating program by double-clicking the embedded object. Then make edits, using the original program's commands.

Embedding an object in another document produces what appears to be the same result as linking—the selected object appears at the insertion point. To the naked eye, there is no difference. However, after you embed an object, all contact with the original file is lost, and the embedded object becomes one with the destination document. The advantage to embedding over linking is that it freezes the object in time. If you're producing a report on last year's sales, you don't want the January figures for the new year to appear, which is precisely what will happen when they're added to a linked spreadsheet.

Linking can be accomplished in one of two ways—either by using the **Edit** menu's **Copy** and **Paste Special** commands or by selecting the **Insert** menu's **Object** or **File** (Word only) commands. Embedding can be done only with the **Insert Object** or **Insert File** (Word only) commands.

Using Paste Special to link objects in Office documents

1. Open both documents—the document with the object to be linked and the document to receive the linked object.

2. Highlight the object or portion of the object you want to link, and press Ctrl+C to copy it to the Clipboard.

3. Switch to the destination document (the one that receives the linked object).

4. Place the insertion point where you want the linked object to appear.

5. Open the **Edit** menu and select **Paste Special** to open the Paste Special dialog box shown in Figure 1.14.

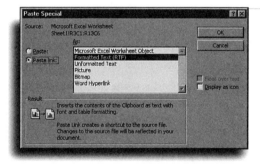

FIGURE 1.14

The Paste Special option enables you to select the formatting applied to the pasted object.

6. Click **Paste link** to create the link between the pasted object and the original file.

7. Select the format for the pasted object from the **As** list box.

8. Click **OK** to insert the linked object and return to the active document.

For embedding and handling bigger linking jobs, from the **Insert** menu choosing **Object** or **File** (Word only) is the ticket.

Using Insert to embed or link objects in an Office document

1. Open the destination document and position the insertion point where you want the object to appear.

2. From the **Insert** menu, select **Object** to open the Object dialog box (see Figure 1.15).

FIGURE 1.15

You can create a new object or use an existing file.

3. Select an object type from the **Object type** list on the **Create New** tab if you want to create a brand new object in the current document. There's nothing to link to a new object, so you can only embed it.

4. To link or embed an object from an existing file, click the **Create from File** tab.

5. Enter the name and path of the existing file you want to use, or click the **Browse** button to search for it.

6. Place a check mark in the **Link to file** check box if you want to link the object. To embed it, leave this box unchecked.

7. Click **OK** to create the link and return to the active document.

In addition to the **Insert** menu's **Object** command, you can also use the **Insert** menu's **File** command to link or embed a file in Word 97 or in Excel 97.

Using Special Commands

Special commands are another way the Office applications interact. These commands, shown in Table 1.2, are not found globally throughout Office but appear in the individual applications.

TABLE 1.2   **Special commands to make Office applications work together**

Office Application	Command	What It Does
Word 97	MailMerge	Creates form letters, labels, and more, using data from Excel, Access, or Outlook
Word 97	**Insert, Database**	Inserts information from Access or another database into your document as a table
Word 97	**Insert, Microsoft Excel Worksheet**	Inserts an Excel spreadsheet in the active document
Word 97, Excel 97	**File, Send To, Mail Recipient**	Opens Outlook, creates a new email message, and inserts the current document as an attachment
Word 97	Microsoft Access	Opens or switches to Microsoft Access
Word 97	Microsoft Excel	Opens or switches to Microsoft Excel
Word 97	Microsoft Mail	Opens or switches to Microsoft Outlook
Word 97	Microsoft Publisher	Opens or switches to Microsoft Publisher
Word 97	PresentIt	Opens PowerPoint and loads the current Word document
Outlook 97	Use MS Word as the email editor	Utilizes Word to create and edit email message text

Some of these commands can be found on menus or toolbars, and others have to be added to the existing menus or toolbars. All the available commands can be found on the **Commands** tab of the Customize dialog box in either Word 97 or Excel 97. To open the Customize dialog box, double-click a blank spot in the toolbar area.

SEE ALSO

➤ *To access application commands, see page 220*

Getting Help When You Need It

Using the Office Assistant

Have you noticed lately that everyone and everything seems to be "proactive"? It's not just enough to deal with a situation as it develops—you've got to be on top of it before it occurs. Well, the Office 97 Help system is right in step with this new philosophy with a new feature called the Office Assistant, which stars a cute animated paper clip called "Clippit." By default, Clippit regularly interrupts your work to offer unsolicited help in an attempt to anticipate your needs (see Figure 2.1).

FIGURE 2.1

The Office Assistant tries to be helpful whenever possible.

As cute as Clippit is, he's not always right, and his advice can sometimes be more nuisance than assistance. Fortunately, there is a way to prevent him from offering his two cents (unless you ask for it) by changing the Office Assistant options. See the "Customizing the Office Assistant" section later in this chapter.

That having been said, some aspects of the Office Assistant are quite handy. You can present Clippit with plain-English questions, and, in return, he will often provide you with just the help you need. Try it and you'll see.

Getting help by asking the right question

1. Click the Office Assistant button 🔲 on the Standard toolbar to activate the Office Assistant (see Figure 2.2).

You also can access the Office Assistant by opening the **Help** menu and choosing **Microsoft Word Help**.

FIGURE 2.2

Clippit shows up and asks you to type your question in the text box.

2. Type right over the existing text in the text box and enter your question in plain English (see Figure 2.3).

FIGURE 2.3

Being ever attentive, Clippit takes notes while you type in your question.

3. Click **Search** to find the answer to your question (see Figure 2.4).

FIGURE 2.4

The Office Assistant presents Help topics that it believes will provide an answer to your question.

4. Click the Help topic that most closely relates to your question to see the associated information (see Figure 2.5).

FIGURE 2.5

A Help Topic window appears with information related to your selection.

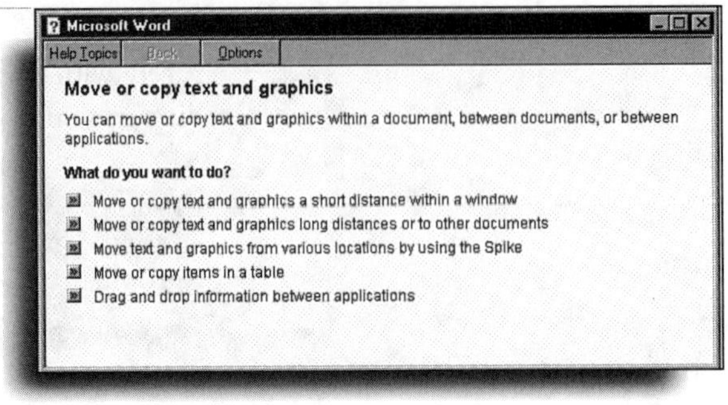

Move or copy text and graphics

You can move or copy text and graphics within a document, between documents, or between applications.

What do you want to do?

- Move or copy text and graphics a short distance within a window
- Move or copy text and graphics long distances or to other documents
- Move text and graphics from various locations by using the Spike
- Move or copy items in a table
- Drag and drop information between applications

   5. Click on icons in the Help topic to see more information. When you're finished, click the **Close** button (x in the top right corner) or press Alt+F4 to close the Help topic and return to the active document.

   6. Click the **Close** button on the Office Assistant if you don't want him hanging around anymore.

If you choose to leave the Office Assistant where it is, you can click anywhere on it to bring up the question box and enter a new query. If you ignore the Office Assistant long enough (five minutes), it will eventually go away. Don't worry about causing it any emotional trauma—it comes back as perky as ever, no matter how many times you ignore it or tell it to go away.

Customizing the Office Assistant

Whether you love the Office Assistant or hate it, you'll want to take advantage of the customization options available. The first thing to keep in mind is that the Office Assistant is available only in Word, Excel, and Outlook. In addition, installing or uninstalling the Office Assistant for one of those applications affects the other two. In other words, it's all or nothing. You can't decide that you want the Office Assistant in Word, but not in Excel or Outlook. As soon as you've adopted Clippit, he's yours. The other thing to keep in mind is that changes you make to Office Assistant options in any one Office application carry over to the other two Office applications in which the Office Assistant hangs out.

Turning off the Office Assistant

To hide the Office Assistant, right-click the Assistant to open the short-cut menu and then choose **Hide Assistant**.

Modifying the Office Assistant's Behavior

Although you can't get rid of the Office Assistant entirely without uninstalling it, you can see that it behaves according to your rules.

Setting the Office Assistant options

1. Click the Office Assistant button on the Standard toolbar to activate the Office Assistant.

2. Click **Options** to open the Office Assistant properties sheet shown in Figure 2.6. You can also right-click on the Office Assistant and select **Options** from the shortcut menu.

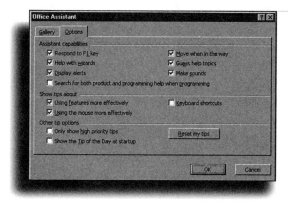

FIGURE 2.6
The Office Assistant options let you control the way the Office Assistant works.

3. Place a check mark next to an option to enable it, and remove the check mark to disable the option. To see the available options and what they do, check out Table 2.1.

4. Click **OK** to save the option settings and return to the active document.

Table 2.1   Office Assistant options

Options Tab	Option	Resulting Action
Assistant capabilities	**Respond to F1 key**	Deselect this option if you want the standard Help system to appear when you press F1; otherwise, the Office Assistant appears.
	Help with wizards	With this option selected, the Office Assistant automatically appears when you're working with an Office wizard.

continues...

TABLE 2.1   Continued

Options Tab	Option	Resulting Action
Assistant capabilities	**Display alerts**	Select this option if you'd rather have the Office Assistant present information usually displayed in a regular dialog box.
	Search for . . . programming	If you're working with VBA, selecting this option results in help from the Office Assistant on the topic involved and on VBA.
	Move when in the way	If you select this option, the Office Assistant moves out of the way as you type or when dialog boxes appear. In theory, this option also causes the Office Assistant to disappear if you don't use it for five minutes. My own experience has been that it doesn't take the hint and hangs around anyway. Go figure.
	Guess help topics	This is the one that causes Clippit to stick his nose into your business without waiting for you to invite him. Deselect it if you don't want unsolicited advice.
	Make sounds	Select this one to hear sounds associated with the Office Assistant.
Show tips about	**Using features more effectively**	If you're unfamiliar with many application features, turning this option on will show tips about using features.
	Using the mouse more effectively	If you're a pro at using the mouse, you can turn this option off.
	Keyboard shortcuts	Select this one to get tips on how to use shortcut keys to get the job done.
Other tip options	**Only show high priority tips**	This one's rather subjective. It displays only those tips that somebody at Microsoft decided are important.
	Show the Tip of the Day at startup	Select this if you want to be greeted by a random tip every time you start an Office application.
	Reset my tips	Click this button to reset tips so that ones you've already viewed will appear again.

Giving the Office Assistant a Face-lift

Just in case you find Clippit, the default Office Assistant, a little too cute—or not cute enough—you can trade him in for a different Office Assistant model.

Changing the Office Assistant character

1. Click the Office Assistant button on the Standard toolbar to activate the Office Assistant.

2. Right-click the Office Assistant and select **Choose Assistant** from the shortcut menu to display the Office Assistant **Gallery** (see Figure 2.7).

FIGURE 2.7
The Gallery includes the available Office Assistant characters.

3. Click the **Next** button to see the only other Office Assistant character included with Office 97 Small Business Edition (see Figure 2.8). It's the Office logo.

FIGURE 2.8
If you're a devoted Office fan, this is the character for you.

Adding more characters to the Gallery

Unfortunately, Microsoft decided to leave the most personable Office Assistant characters off the SBE CD-ROM. However, you can get them quite easily and add them to the Gallery if you'd like. Simply fire up your Internet connection and your Web browser, and head for `http://www.microsoft.com/msoffice/office/enhancements/assistants.asp`. Follow the download instructions and make a note of the installation instructions.

4. Stop at the character of your choice and click **OK** to install it as the new Office Assistant.

As soon as you click **OK**, you're returned to the active document, and the Office Assistant immediately assumes its new identity.

Finding Basic Help Information

If you find the Office Assistant too intrusive or cute for your taste, you can set its options for minimal intervention and use the standard Help system. The standard Windows application Help system consists of a large database of helpful information with a couple of different ways to get just the help you need.

As you can see in Figure 2.9, the main Help system is a three-in-one package called Help topics.

FIGURE 2.9

You can search for help by using the method you find most convenient.

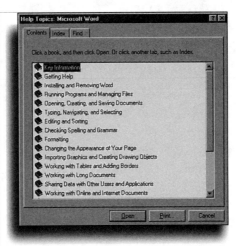

Contents

The **Contents** tab of the Help Topics window provides a series of Help topics in a table of contents format. Each topic has several subtopics, which, in turn, may have subtopics of their own.

Using the Contents tab of the Help Topics window

1. Open the **Help** menu and choose **Contents and Index** to open the Help Topics window shown in Figure 2.9.

2. Click the **Contents** tab if it's not already selected.

3. Scroll through the list of topics until you find the topic of interest.

4. Double-click the book icon just left of the topic you want to learn about. Its list of subtopics expands. Repeat this process until you reach a desired topic with a question mark icon to the left (see Figure 2.10).

FIGURE 2.10
Drill down through the Help topics until you find exactly what you're looking for.

5. Double-click the question mark icon to open the associated Help topic, as shown in Figure 2.11.

6. When you're finished viewing the Help topic, either click the **Help Topics** button to return to the **Contents** tab or click the **Close** button (x in top-right corner of the topic window) to return to the active document.

The **Contents** tab provides a great way to find overview and general information. For more specific help, you might want to try the Index or Find features.

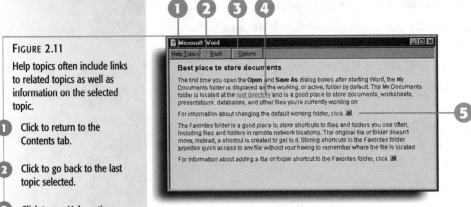

FIGURE 2.11

Help topics often include links to related topics as well as information on the selected topic.

1 Click to return to the Contents tab.

2 Click to go back to the last topic selected.

3 Click to see Help options.

4 Click for an explanation of the term or phrase.

5 Click to see related information.

Index

Not surprisingly, the **Index** tab of the Help Topics window is much like a book index. It is arranged alphabetically, with each entry referencing a specific Help topic, but unlike a book index, you can type a word into the text box and have Help find the index item for you. It's quite handy, assuming the subject you need help on has been indexed.

Searching the Help topic index

1. Open the **Help** menu and choose **Contents and Index** to open the Help Topics window (see Figure 2.12). Then click the **Index** tab.

2. Type a word or phrase in the text box to find a related Help topic. The automatic search begins with the first letter you type and finds matches for each additional letter you enter. As you can see in Figure 2.12, it was only necessary to type hel to access the Help entry in the Index.

3. Double-click the entry of your choice to see the specific Help topic. If the Index contains other entries related to the topic, it will first display a list of the topics (see Figure 2.13).

4. If double-clicking on the Index entry brings up a Topics Found dialog box with more choices, double-click one of them to see a Help topic.

FIGURE 2.12

Except for the lack of page numbers, the Help Topics **Index** tab resembles a book index.

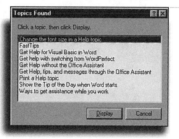

FIGURE 2.13

The Index search sometimes results in a mini-index of related topics.

5. Click the **Help Topics** button to return to the **Index** tab, or click the **Close** button in the Help Topics window to return to the active document.

For general purpose help, I find the Index to be the most useful. When I need help on one of the less common Office features, I turn to the Help Topics **Find** tab.

Find

The third tab of the Help Topics window is called **Find** for a very good reason—its job is to find every instance (in the Help files) of the word or phrase you type in the search text box. This is called a full text search, which requires a database that includes every word in the Help files. Because such a database is rather large, it is not created until the first time you use the Find feature. The reasoning is that if you never use the Find feature, there's no reason to utilize the disk space.

Other database building options

The **Maximize search capabilities** option includes all additional search options not enabled when you select Minimize. **Customize search capabilities** enables you to select which additional options you want to include.

Using the Help Topics Find tab

1. Open the **Help** menu and choose **Contents and Index** to open the Help Topics window.

2. Click the **Find** tab to use the Find feature. If you've already created the database, skip to step 5; otherwise, use the Find Setup Wizard (see Figure 2.14) to create the database.

3. Select **Minimize database size (recommended),** and click **Next** to begin the process.

FIGURE 2.14

The Find Setup Wizard walks you through the database creation.

4. Click **Finish** to build the database and return to the **Find** tab (see Figure 2.15).

FIGURE 2.15

The Find tab searches for individual words and finds related Help topics.

5. In text box 1, type the word(s) for which you're looking for help.

6. From the list in display area 2, select the word(s) related to the topic for which you need help.

7. Double-click the appropriate Help topic in display area 3 to open the related Help Topic window.

8. Click the **Close** button in the top-right corner of the topic window to close it and return to the active document. You can also press Alt+F4 to close the window.

To make the **Find** tab even more powerful, you can set options to customize the search. Click the **Options** button on the **Find** tab to open the Find Options dialog box (see Figure 2.16).

FIGURE 2.16

You decide how to conduct the Find search by setting the appropriate options.

You can set the following options in the Find Options dialog box:

- **All the words you typed in any order**. With this selected, your search digs up every topic that includes all the words you typed, regardless of the order in which you typed them. In other words, if you type adding columns to Word tables, the search will come up with any topic that includes all five words in order, not in order, together, or separate.

- **At least one of the words you typed**. With this option selected, the above search for adding columns to Word tables will return any topic that contains one or more of the five words typed in.

- **The words you typed in underline{e}xact order**. This option is disabled unless you built the database with **Ma<u>x</u>imize search capabilities** or **<u>C</u>ustomize search capabilities** selected. If it's available, use it to find only those Help topics that contain the words exactly as you typed them.

- **Display matching <u>p</u>hrases**. Used in conjunction with **The words you typed in <u>e</u>xact order**, this option results in the search results displaying the words in the Help file that actually follow the word or phrase you entered in your search.

- **<u>S</u>how words that**. Use this option to narrow your search by typing in a word or a couple of characters and indicating where in the search words they should appear. In other words, to find any Help topic that contains the word "mark," enter mark in the text box, click the **<u>O</u>ptions** button, and select **contain the characters you type** from the **<u>S</u>how words that** drop-down list. This will display a list of topics including everything from Automark to Watermarks, and a lot in between.

- **After you click the Find <u>N</u>ow button**. With this option selected, Find won't begin searching for a match to the word(s) you enter in the text box until you click the **Find Now** button.

- **<u>I</u>mmediately after each keystroke**. Select this option so that the search begins as soon as you start typing characters in the text box.

- **<u>W</u>ait for a pause before searching**. You can use this option to hold off the immediate search until you pause in your typing.

- **<u>F</u>iles**. Most of the Help databases are made up of more than one file. Click this button to select which Help file(s) you want to include in the present search.

When you've set all your options, click **OK** to return to the **Index** tab and continue your search. To return to the active document without performing a search, click the **Cancel** button on the **Index** tab.

What's This?

Glad you asked. **What's This?** is a handy little feature that gives you a brief description of just about anything you point at and click. You'll find it on the **Help** menu of Word, Excel, and Outlook. When you select the **Help** menu and choose the **What's This?** item, your cursor acquires a large question mark. Simply point at an item and click to see a description or explanation of the object. If there's no associated Help topic, you get a message telling you so. You'll find a mini version of **What's This?** on most dialog boxes. It's the question mark button that appears in the top-right corner, to the left of the Close button. Click it, point at a text box or option in the dialog box, and click to see a description of the item.

Getting Help on the Web

In addition to the Help files available with each of the Office 97 Small Business Edition applications, you can also find quite a bit of help on the Internet. You'll need an Internet connection, a modem or network connection, and a Web browser. With all three, you're ready to get help on the Web. Help on the Web is available with Word 97, Excel 97, and Outlook 97.

Getting online help

1. From the **Help** menu choose **Microsoft on the Web** to open the submenu of Help on the Web options (see Figure 2.17).

FIGURE 2.17

It should come as no surprise that a wealth of Help information is available on the Web.

2. Select an item from the **Microsoft on the Web** submenu to open your default Web browser and activate your Web connection.

3. As soon as you connect to the Internet, you are taken to the site associated with your menu selection.

Here are the choices for online Web assistance:

- **Free Stuff**. Select this item to go to the Microsoft Office Update page, where you'll find links to downloadable freebies for Office.

- **Product News**. Click this item to visit the Microsoft Web site dedicated to the particular Office application you're in when you select this menu item.

- **Frequently Asked Questions**. This one currently takes you to the Microsoft Office Update Web site.

- **Online Support**. Click this one to be taken to the Microsoft Technical Support Online Web site.

- **Microsoft Office Home Page**. Once again, you'll be whisked away to the Microsoft Office Update page.

- **Send Feedback**. This also takes you to the Microsoft Office Update Page.

- **Best of the Web**. For links to other sites of interest on the World Wide Web, click this item.

- **Search the Web**. Click this menu item to visit the Microsoft Web page that contains a large number of Internet search engines and services.

- **Web Tutorial**. This Microsoft Web site contains an easy-to-follow tutorial on getting around on the Internet.

- **Microsoft Home Page**. This takes you to the Microsoft Home Page, which is the place to start if you want to discover what Microsoft is all about and what it has to offer.

4. Switch from your Web browser back to the Office application from which you started, and make another selection to visit another site.

5. When you've seen enough on the Internet, close your Web browser, disconnect from the Internet, and return to your Office application to continue working.

Keep in mind that the Microsoft Web site, like the rest of the Internet, is in constant flux. Therefore, by the time you read this, the Web sites you visit may be entirely different from those described previously.

Using Word to Increase Productivity

Creating and Editing Documents for Home and Business

Taking a Tour of the Word Window

Whether you're writing letters to the family, creating your small-business correspondence, or producing complex reports for the corporate CEO, you are in the driver's seat with Word 97. You can pick and choose the tools and features you need, and ignore the ones you don't.

The first thing you'll want to do is get acquainted with the basic layout of the Word 97 window. When you open Word 97 for the first time, you're greeted with a window containing a blank document, a menu bar, a couple of toolbars, a ruler, two scrollbars, and a status bar (see Figure 3.1).

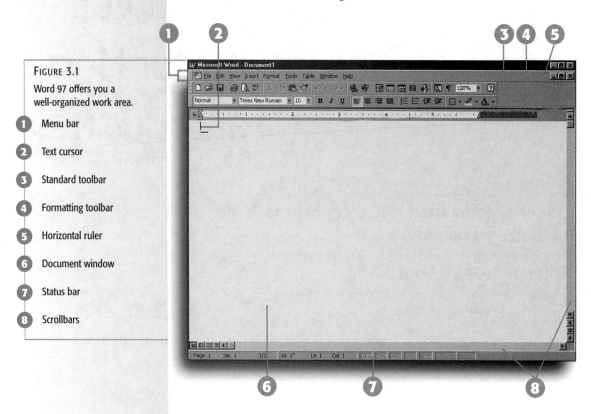

FIGURE 3.1

Word 97 offers you a well-organized work area.

1 Menu bar

2 Text cursor

3 Standard toolbar

4 Formatting toolbar

5 Horizontal ruler

6 Document window

7 Status bar

8 Scrollbars

You'll want to familiarize yourself with each of these items because they are the basic tools you need to harness the power of Word 97.

- *Menu bar.* The menu bar contains most (but not all) of the commands you will generally use while performing common word processing tasks.

- *Standard toolbar.* The Word toolbars are handy devices that place individual commands at your fingertips so you can activate them with a single mouse click. The Standard toolbar contains such useful items as New (document), Open (file), Save (file), Print, Cut, Copy, Paste, and more.

- *Formatting toolbar.* Another toolbar with frequently used commands. This one contains—you guessed it—formatting commands, such as font, font style, and font size, just to name a few.

- *Horizontal ruler.* You can set tabs, margins, indents, and column widths with your mouse by dragging the appropriate markers on the horizontal ruler.

- *Document window.* The document window is the area that houses the active document(s). Word opens with a single, blank document in the document window.

- *Text cursor.* The blinking vertical line indicates the point at which anything you type will appear.

- *Scrollbars.* Located at the right and bottom of the document window, the scrollbars enable you to move through the document by dragging the scroll box or clicking the arrows.

- *Status bar.* The status bar not only provides a continuous flow of information relating to the current document, but it also houses indicators and toggle switches for some of Word's favorite features.

SEE ALSO

➤ *To learn more about opening Word, see page 2*

Creating Word Documents

Now that you've got the basic Word components under your belt, it's time to get down to business. And the business of a word processor is, of course, creating documents. As you start producing letters, memos, and reports, you'll begin to understand the basic building blocks that make up a Word document.

Working with Text

The best way to understand a document is to create one. Word opens with a blank document; let's start there. The first thing you notice is the blinking cursor, or insertion point. Start typing and you'll see your text appear at the insertion point. The blinking cursor keeps moving ahead of your text as you type, always indicating the location for the next character. Keep typing past the end of the first line, and your text automatically "wraps" around to the next line. There's no need to press the Enter key until you're ready to start a new paragraph. Pressing the Enter key actually accomplishes two things. It inserts a carriage return (or a hard return), which indicates the end of a paragraph, and it moves the blinking cursor to the beginning of a new line so you can start the next paragraph.

If word processing were simply a matter of entering text, we'd all still be using typewriters. The reason we're not is that the real power of word processing lies in the capability to manipulate the text after you enter it into your document. Here are just a few of the text-handling features you'll find in Word:

- Delete the character to the left of the insertion point by pressing the Backspace key.
- Erase the character to the right of your insertion point by pressing the Delete key.
- Deleting an entire word to the right of the insertion point is as easy as pressing Ctrl+Delete.
- Changing the typing mode from Insert to Overtype causes text you enter to replace any text directly ahead of it, one character at a time.
- Move the insertion point to the beginning of the next word in a sentence by holding down the Ctrl key and pressing the right-arrow key. Move to the previous word by pressing the left-arrow key.

These examples are just the tip of the iceberg when it comes to the text-handling functions available in Word 97. As you spend more time working in Word, you'll discover more of them. You'll also find that many of these features become second nature, and wonder how you ever got along without them.

Navigating the Word Document

When you first begin creating your document, you only have to worry about typing your text and correcting your mistakes. As your document grows, however, and passes the bounds of a single screenful of text, you will have to learn how to get around in the document. As you fill the current screen with text, the word-wrap feature adds a new line to the bottom of the document, automatically moving the entire document up one line at a time. That's easy, but how do you get back to the top?

Well, how you move around will probably depend on a number of things such as the length of the document, how you structure your document, and whether you prefer to use the mouse or the keyboard.

Scrolling Around

With the advent of the Windows graphical interface, the mouse came into its own. Once the tool of choice for graphic artists and Macintosh users only (in the old days, "real" PC computer geeks wouldn't be caught dead using a mouse), the mouse is now a common sight on every desktop, used by expert and novice alike.

Therefore, it should come as no surprise that one of the most popular ways to navigate a Word document is by using the mouse to operate the two scrollbars located at the right and bottom of the document window. You can either drag the scroll box that appears between the arrows of the scrollbar, or you can click the arrows themselves. The basic concept is the same, no matter which method of scrolling you choose—click the arrow or drag the box in the direction you want to go. In other words, if you want to reach the bottom of the document, click the down arrow on the vertical scrollbar or drag its scroll box toward the bottom of the screen. Using the scroll box provides an added benefit in that a small text box appears (a ScreenTip) informing you of the page numbers as you scroll through them. If you want to move to the right side of the document, use the horizontal scrollbar and click the right arrow, or drag the scroll box to the right.

Scrolling automatically

Scrolling can be rather tedious. Fortunately, Word 97 can scroll automatically for you. Open the **Tools** menu and choose the **Customize** command to open the Customize dialog box. Click the **Commands** tab and scroll down the **Categories** list box. Click **All Commands** to display the entire list of available commands. Scroll down the list of commands until you reach **AutoScroll**. *Highlight* **AutoScroll** and drag it onto any toolbar currently displayed in Word. You should now have an AutoScroll button on your toolbar. Click **Close** to shut the Customize dialog box and return to the active document.

Click the AutoScroll button. The document begins to scroll. To regulate the speed and direction in which your document scrolls, move your mouse pointer to the vertical scrollbar, which has now changed into an AutoScroll bar. When the pointer is placed at the halfway mark of the bar, the scrolling stops. Move the pointer up or down, to begin scrolling again. To return your mouse pointer to its normal state, move the pointer to the middle of the AutoScroll bar and click.

You can use the scrollbar a few more ways to move through your document. If you click just above the scroll box, or just below it, you can move up or down one screen at a time. You can also scroll beyond the left margin in normal view by holding down the Shift key and clicking the left scroll arrow.

SEE ALSO

➤ *To learn more about views, see page 112*

Using the Keyboard

As easy as the mouse is to use, sometimes the keyboard provides a quicker means of getting around in a document. For instance, to move to the end of a line, all you have to do is press the End key, and it instantly transports you to the end of whichever line your cursor is on. Certainly you could use your mouse to move the insertion point. However, it's a lot easier as you're typing to hit the End key once than it is to move from the keyboard to the mouse, position your mouse pointer, click, and return to the keyboard so you can resume typing.

Here are some of the navigational keystrokes you can use in Word:

- *Page Up*. Move up one screenful of text at a time. Because the Page Up and Page Down keys are actually scrolling keys, you experience the same document movement that occurs when using the scrollbars.

- *Page Down*. The opposite of Page Up, Page Down moves you down one screenful of text at a time. As with Page Up, the actual movement of the screen is in the opposite direction you're moving.

- *Arrow keys*. To move left or right one character, press the left- or right-arrow key. To move up or down one line, press the up- or down-arrow key.

- *Home*. Press the Home key to move the insertion point to the beginning of the line on which it currently rests.

- *End*. Go to the end of the current line.

- *Ctrl+Home*. This key combination takes you to the beginning of the document.

- *Ctrl+End*. This key combination takes you to the end of the document.

Printing your own list of Word shortcut keys

A lot more key combinations (sometimes called *shortcut keys*) exist for getting around in Word. You can even make your own "cheat sheet" by printing out the complete list from the Word Help file. Open the **Help** menu and choose the **Contents and Index** command. Click the **Index** tab and type shortcut in the text box labeled **1**. Double-click **Shortcut keys for selecting text and graphics** to open the **Select text and graphics** Help topic. Click the second selection, **Select text and graphics by using shortcut keys**. This opens the **Keys for editing and moving text and graphics** Help topic. Click the **Options** button and select **Print Topic** to print the list of shortcut keys. When you finish printing, press Alt+F4 to close the Help Topics window.

- *Ctrl+right- or left-arrow key.* Move to the beginning of the next (right) or last (left) word.
- *Ctrl+Page Up or Page Down.* Move up (Page Up) one paragraph or down (Page Down) one paragraph.

Navigating with Browse

One of the handy new features of Word 97 is the Browse function incorporated into the vertical scrollbar (see Figure 3.2).

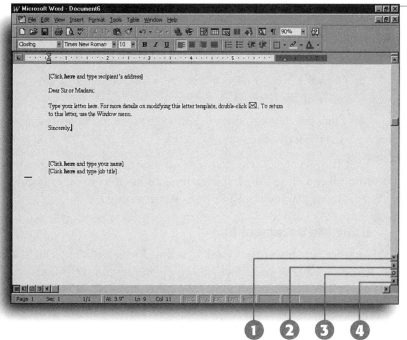

FIGURE 3.2
The new Browse feature is neatly tucked away on the vertical scrollbar.

1. Scroll [down] button
2. Previous browse object
3. Select browse object
4. Next browse object

The Browse function, allows you to select a Word object—such as a page, heading, graphic, or table—and jump sequentially through the document from one selected object to the next. For example, say you have a long newsletter loaded with graphics and you want to make a quick check of all the captions to ensure they match the pictures. All you have to do is use the Browse function and select "graphic" as the Browse object. Clicking the Next button now takes you to the next graphic inserted in your document. Clicking the Previous button jumps you to the preceding graphic.

Using the Browse feature

1. Click the Select Browse Object button to open the **Select Browse Object** menu. As you highlight each object, its name appears on the menu above the icons (see Figure 3.3).

FIGURE 3.3

The Browse function offers you a wide variety of Browse objects from which to choose.

2. Select a Browse object from the **Browse Object** menu.

If the object selected is present in your document, you are immediately taken to the next occurrence of that object.

3. Click the Next browse button to move to the next occurrence of the selected object.

4. Click the Previous browse button to move to the preceding occurrence of the selected object.

Your Browse object selection remains intact until you change it or until you close Word. It even remains in effect in other documents that you have open or open subsequently.

Using the Document Map

Another new feature in Word 97 is the Document Map, which creates a table of contents by using the headings in your document. The document window then splits and displays the table of contents in a small pane to the left of your document (see Figure 3.4).

The nice thing about the Document Map is that all the entries in the table of contents are actually hot links to the headings in the document. In other words, you can move through your document from one heading to the next by clicking the entries that appear in the Document Map pane. To activate the Document Map, click the Document Map icon 🔳 in the Standard toolbar. You can click the Document Map icon again to hide the Document Map.

Because the browsing feature uses the heading styles (a predefined set of formatting instructions that determines the

Using the Go To or Find commands

If you select Go To or Find you are presented with the corresponding dialog box, which you will have to fill out in order to proceed. To use the Go To feature, select the item from the **Go to what** list, but leave the **Enter page** (section or whatever) **number** box blank. For Find, type in the word or phrase you want to find. After you enter the information and use either feature the first time, you can click **Close** or **Cancel** to return to the document. From that point forward, using the Next and Previous browse buttons activates the Go To or Find instructions you indicated in the dialog box.

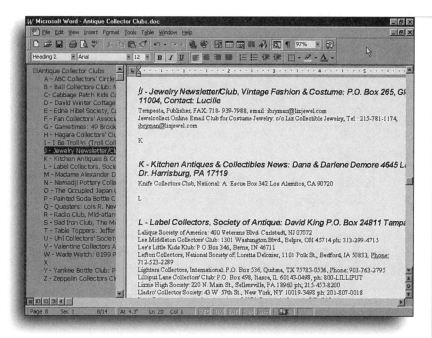

FIGURE 3.4

The Document Map displays all the headings in your document.

appearance of the heading or paragraph) to create the table of contents, your document must contain headings, or the Document Map will be blank. Changing styles is relatively easy, so it might be worthwhile to add headings to a document just for the purpose of creating a working Document Map—which is precisely what I did in the example in Figure 3.4. I downloaded an alphabetical list of collector clubs from the Web. Unfortunately, it was rather long, so it was a bit of a hassle getting around and finding what I was looking for. The solution, however, was simple. I moved to the first entry in each letter group (A, B, C, D, and so on) and changed the style to a heading. As a result, I now have an alphabetical table of contents that allows me to jump to whatever letter I choose with a single mouse click.

Saving Word Documents

One of the most important things you can do when working in Word or any other software application is save your work—frequently. Fortunately, most programs today offer some form of automatic save feature, just in case you forget. However, it's a good idea, to make a habit of saving regularly, regardless of whether or not auto backup is turned on. If your system crashes and you lose five or ten minutes worth of work, you'll be amazed at how much you got done in that short time, especially as you're retyping it and trying to recall those literary gems that are no longer there.

Save As

The **Save As** command allows you to save a new document or an existing document with a name and/or location different from the one it currently has. The first time you save a new Word document, the feature invoked is **Save As** even if you attempt to use the **Save** command. The reason is that Word does not consider the default document names of Document1, Document2, and so on real filenames. They are merely placeholders used until you give the document a name; therefore, a document without a name must be "saved as" something else.

Using the Save As command

1. Open the **File** menu and choose the **Save As** command to open the Save As dialog box as seen in Figure 3.5.

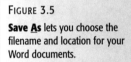
FIGURE 3.5

Save As lets you choose the filename and location for your Word documents.

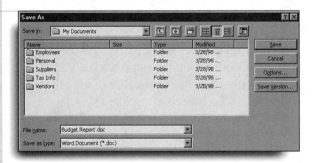

When you install Word 97, it automatically creates a folder called My Documents in which all your documents are stored unless you indicate otherwise. To accept My Documents as the location for the document you are about to save, skip steps 2 and 3 and proceed to step 4.

2. Click the down arrow in the **Save in** drop-down list to display a list of folders on your computer.

3. Select the folder in which to save the active document.

4. In the **File name** drop-down list, enter the filename you want to give this document.

5. Click **Save** to store a copy of the document in the location selected, with the name entered.

Although saving your document is a simple matter, there are a couple of things to think about. You should give serious consideration to the names and locations of the documents you save. When you start out with Word and only have a handful of documents, it's relatively easy to find them. However, as you create more and more documents finding what you're looking for becomes increasingly difficult unless you adopt a logical naming and saving system.

The first thing you can do to ensure that you can find your documents with ease is create separate folders for each document type or each project on which you're working. For example, you might have a Vendors folder for all vendor documents, a Suppliers folder for suppliers, and a third called Personal for your personal stuff.

Creating a new folder when you use the Save As command

1. Open the **File** menu and choose the **Save As** command to open the Save As dialog box.

2. Make sure you are in the correct folder—use the **Save in** drop-down list to select the correct folder.

3. Click the **Create New Folder** button to open the New Folder dialog box as seen in Figure 3.6.

Changing the default save folder in Word

If you would like to change the default folder that Word uses to save documents, you can do so by modifying one of the Word options. Open the **Tools** menu and choose the **Options** command. In the Options dialog box, click the **File Locations** tab. In the **File types** display box, highlight the **Documents** listing and click the **Modify** button. Choose a new folder in the Modify Location dialog box and click **OK** to return to the Options dialog box. Click **OK** to save the new default folder, and return to the active document.

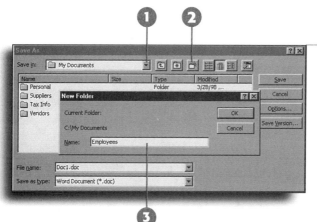

FIGURE 3.6

Organize your documents by creating new folders.

1 Click to open the **Save in** drop-down list.

2 Create New Folder button

3 Enter a name for the new folder.

4. Type the name of the new folder in the **Name** text box and click **OK** to return to the Save As dialog box. The new folder appears in the Save As display window.

5. Double-click the new folder to open it.

6. In the **File name** drop-down list, enter the name of the document to save.

7. Click **Save** to store a copy of the document in the new folder.

The next thing to think about is the name of the document. Because Word sorts by filename when you use the Open feature, you should consider using similar filenames for similar documents. Suppose you create a folder called Vendors for all your vendor correspondence. It would make it easier to find things if you include the vendor's name at the beginning of each document name. Then when you want to open a document in the Vendor folder, you would see all the correspondence listed alphabetically by vendor. By the way, you can get creative with your filenaming because Windows 95 now allows you to use up to 255 characters (path and filename included) for a filename.

Save

After you save a document with the **Save As** command, you can use **Save** to store any subsequent changes you make. This stores the active document in its current form, using the name and location you used the first time you saved it. Several ways to invoke the **Save** command are

- *Menu bar.* Open the **File** menu and choose the **Save** command. To save all open documents at once, hold down the Shift key, open the **File** menu, and choose the **Save All** command.

- *Shortcut key.* Press Ctrl+S.

- *Toolbar (Standard).* Click the Save button (floppy disk icon).

Version

This is a great tool for keeping track of a changing document. It doesn't matter whether several people are making the changes or just one. If you want to see who's doing what, or if you want to be able to retrieve an earlier version of the document, you'll need some way to save it in various stages of its development. Before Word 97, your only choice was to periodically save the document with a different name. It worked, but it also created confusion and ate up a lot of hard-disk space by adding a whole bunch of new files. Not any longer. Word 97 incorporates a new feature called versioning that does the job for you.

Creating a version

1. Open the **File** menu and choose the **Versions** command to open the Versions in [*document name*] dialog box as seen in Figure 3.7.

FIGURE 3.7

You can create as many versions of the document as you need.

2. Click **Save Now** to open the Save Version dialog box.

3. Type a comment in the **Comments on version** display window and click **OK** to return to the Versions in dialog box. Make the comment a descriptive phrase or note to help you identify this particular version at a later time.

4. Click **Close** to return to the active document.

Another thing to be aware of is the fact that versioning only works as long as you are saving your document in the Word 97 format. If you're saving to any other format, the versioning feature is disabled, and you will have to resort to saving each version of the document as a new file, with a new filename.

Automatic Save Options

Word 97 contains a number of automatic save features you can take advantage of by setting the appropriate option. To find these options, all you have to do is open the **Tools** menu,

Caution—Don't count on the version AutoSave feature

The Versions in [*document name*] dialog box has an option to automatically save a version upon closing the current document. Although it's a great idea, it also happens to be a non-functioning option. This is a Word 97 bug. Regardless of whether or not you place a check mark next to the option, Word will *not* save a version of the current document unless you click **Save Now**.

How much AutoRecover is enough?

Being overly cautious can also have its downside. If you set your AutoRecover option for a relatively short period of time, you'll rack up quite a few temporary files if you work on the document for any length of time. As a test, I changed my AutoRecover save time to every 1 minute while I worked on the same document (this chapter) all day. By the end of the day, I had over 50MB of temporary files sitting on my hard disk. Because AutoRecover only saves after you've made some change in the document, it won't matter if you just leave the document open without working on it.

choose **Options,** and click the **Save** tab. The options include the following types of automatic saves:

- **Always create backup copy.** Check this option to create a backup copy of the document each time you save it. What actually happens is the old version is saved as the backup copy, with a .wbk extension.

- **Allow Fast Saves.** To speed up the save process, fast saves store only the changes made since your last save, not the entire revised document. However, this option cannot be used in conjunction with **Always create backup copy** because backups require a full save to work.

- **Save AutoRecover info every *xx* minutes.** Word saves your document information periodically if you check this option. You can then set the number of minutes between the automatic saves. However, this is not a true document save. Your document information is saved in a temporary file in case of a system crash. In the event your system goes down, Word uses the *AutoRecover* file to restore your document. However, when you close the document normally (regardless of whether you save), the temporary files are deleted.

File Formats

One more important issue to consider when saving is the format of the Word documents you save. If you plan to share any of your documents with others, you must be sure the format in which you save is compatible with whatever word processor they are using. The Word 97 format (which is, of course, the Word 97 default save format) is not even compatible with earlier versions of Word.

Changing the format of a Word 97 document

1. Open the **File** menu and choose the **Save As** command to open the Save As dialog box.

2. Select the location in which to save the document.

3. Enter a name for the document in the **File name** text box.

4. Click the down arrow next to the **Save As type** drop-down list to display the list of available format types (see Figure 3.8).

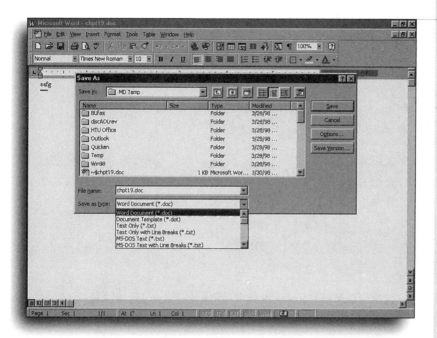

FIGURE 3.8
Word 97 provides a variety of format types so that you can share your documents with others.

5. Scroll through the list and highlight the desired format type. As soon as you choose a format type, Word automatically changes the extension of the filename you entered to match the new file type.

6. Click **Save** to store the file in the selected format. Keep in mind that if you save a document as a text file of any sort, all formatting (such as styles, bold, italic) will be lost.

This allows you to save individual documents in a format other than the standard Word 97 format. However, if you are doing most of your document exchanges with people who are using an earlier version of Word (or a different word processor altogether), you may want to change the default Save As format type.

Changing the default Save As format type

1. Open the **Tools** menu and choose the **Options** command to open the Options dialog box.

2. Click the **Save** tab to view the Save options as seen in Figure 3.9.

When is a .doc file not a .doc file?

Although Word 6.0/95 is one of the Save As format types available, it's actually not a true Word 6.0/95 format. Using this option merely saves the document as an RTF (Rich Text Format) file with a .doc extension. Although neither Word 6.0 nor Word 95 have any problem reading an RTF file, saving in this format does have a drawback—the files become unnecessarily bloated, especially if they contain a lot of graphics.

Microsoft has released a true Word 6.0/95 converter that you can download. If you are sharing files with users of Word 6.0 or Word 95, it will be worth your time to download and install the converter from the following Microsoft Web site:
`http://www.microsoft.com /officefreestuff/word/dl pages/wrd6ex32.htm`.

FIGURE 3.9

Save options enable you to
customize how and when
Word saves your document
information.

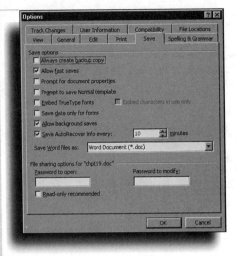

3. Click the down arrow next to the **Save <u>W</u>ord files as** drop-down list to display the list of file format types.

4. Highlight the file format type you want Word to use as the default Save As file type.

5. Click **OK** to save the new setting and return to your active document.

The next time you use the **Save <u>A</u>s** command, Word 97 automatically assigns the new default file type to the document.

Editing Word Documents

After you've created your document and saved it to guard against accidental loss, the next step is to polish it up. It's rare that you will create a document that doesn't require some fine-tuning. Whether it's a single change or a total rewrite, you'll need to learn some basic editing techniques.

Fixing Your Mistakes with Undo

One of the handiest editing features in Word is the Undo feature. This wonderful little utility keeps track of what you do and allows you to reverse your actions, one at time or in groups, beginning with the most recent and working your way back.

For example, if you type a sentence and change your mind, using Undo will delete the sentence. If you bold a word, cut and paste a piece of text, and then delete a graphic, Undo will first undelete the graphic, then remove the piece of text from its new location and put it back to where it was, and finally unbold the word. Unfortunately, what you can't do is selectively undelete actions, except for the last action. In other words, in the previous sequence of events you could not unbold the word without also replacing the piece of text and undeleting the graphic.

You have three options when using Undo. You can open the **Edit** menu and choose the **Undo [*action*]** command, press the Ctrl+Z shortcut key, or click the Undo button on the Standard toolbar. Using any of these options will undo the last action you took in Word.

Undo multiple actions

1. Click the down arrow next to the Undo button to open the recent action drop-down list as seen in Figure 3.10.

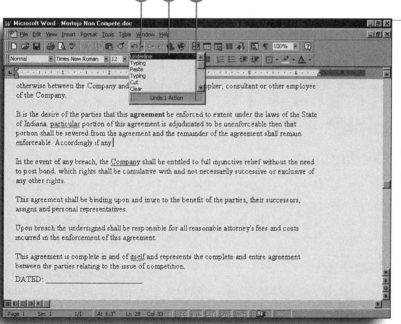

FIGURE 3.10

The Undo drop-down list contains all the actions you've performed since opening this session of the document.

① Click to open the action drop-down list.

② Most recent action

③ Number of actions selected for Undo

2. Highlight the actions you want to undo. Remember you can only undo actions beginning with the most recent and working your way back. As you highlight actions, Word indicates how many actions you are about to undo.

3. Click the earliest action you want to undo and Word will immediately undo all the highlighted items.

Undoing your Undo with Redo

Occasionally you have second thoughts about the corrections you make. What seemed like a good idea at the time may look or sound awkward on a second reading. Not to worry because Word has another useful feature that will restore your corrections to their original state—it's called Redo. Redo reverses the results of Undo. Let's say I want to emphasize the word "reverses" in the last sentence by bolding it. However, when I take another look at it, I decide it wasn't necessary after all, so I press Ctrl+Z to undo the bolding. But being a conscientious writer, I reread it one more time and realize it really should be bold. All I have to do is click the Redo button on the Standard toolbar and—voilà—"reverses" is once again bold.

Redo works the same way Undo works. You can redo a correction by opening the **Edit** menu and choosing the **Repeat** [*action*] command, by pressing the shortcut key Ctrl+Y, or by clicking the Redo button on the Standard toolbar. As with the Undo feature, you can also redo multiple corrections by selecting them from the action drop-down list (on the Redo button).

Selecting Text

Because Word has no way of knowing what character, word, or paragraph you want to change when you're editing, you must first let it know. The way you communicate your editing intentions to Word is by selecting (highlighting) the text you want to change. The only editing actions that don't require selecting text are those that work on the basis of insertion-point location (such as the Backspace or Delete keys or applying styles) and the **Undo/Redo** commands

When it comes to selecting text, you can use your mouse, the keyboard, or a combination of the two. Like most operations in

Word, there are a number of things you can do and a variety of ways to do them, so experiment and find the ways that work best for you.

Table 3.1 shows a few of the text-selection methods available in Word 97.

TABLE 3.1   Text selection in Word 97

Item(s) to Select	Mouse Method	Keyboard Method
Any amount of text	Position the mouse pointer, hold down the left mouse button, drag over text	Position insertion point, hold the Shift key down, press the appropriate arrow key
A single word	Double-click the word	Position the cursor at the beginning of the word, press Shift+Ctrl+right arrow
A single line of text	Move the mouse pointer to the selection bar (invisible column) on the left side of the document window and click	Place insertion point at the beginning of the line, hold down the Shift key, and press End
A single sentence	Hold the Ctrl key down and click anywhere in the sentence	None
An entire paragraph	Move the mouse pointer to the selection bar and double-click	None
The entire document	Move the mouse pointer to the selection bar and triple-click	Press Ctrl+A

If you're like me and sometimes create a short table by using the Tab key to create pseudo columns (rather than actually creating a table), you'll find that you can't format just one of the columns. When you try to select the text, it wraps to the beginning of the next line and highlights everything. However, if you place your cursor at the beginning of the column you want to highlight, hold down the Alt key, and drag the pointer over the column, you can highlight as wide a vertical swath as you want (see Figure 3.11).

FIGURE 3.11

Press Alt and drag the mouse pointer to highlight text vertically in Word 97.

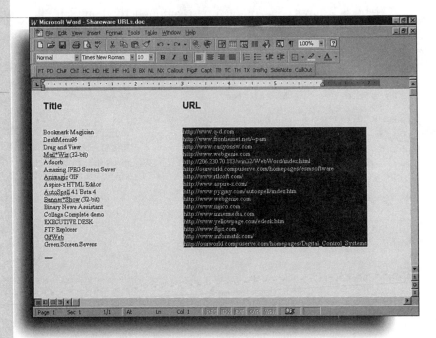

As you can see, you have a number of options for selecting text. As you work with documents and perform editing operations, you'll discover the quickest and easiest method for you.

Replacing Existing Text

One of the most common editing tasks you will perform is replacing existing text with new text. You may decide to replace a single word, a sentence, or a whole paragraph. The way you do it depends on a number of things. If you are replacing a single occurrence of a word or phrase, you might just type over the existing text. If you are replacing multiple occurrences of a word or phrase, you will probably want to use Find and Replace. If you want to replace one chunk of existing text with a different existing block of text, your best choice would be a cut (or copy) and paste operation.

Typing Over Text

The simplest and most direct way to replace text is to just type right over the existing text. You can either highlight the entire block of existing text and begin typing the new text, or you can change from Insert mode to Overtype mode. To employ the first option, use one of the text-selection methods described earlier in this chapter and choose the text you want to replace. As soon as you begin typing the new text, the old text is deleted and the new text is entered in its place.

The second option for replacing text is also implemented quite easily. Double-click the grayed-out OVR box, which appears between EXT and WPH on the status bar. As soon as you double-click it, the Overtype mode is enabled and the OVR title appears (as seen in Figure 3.12).

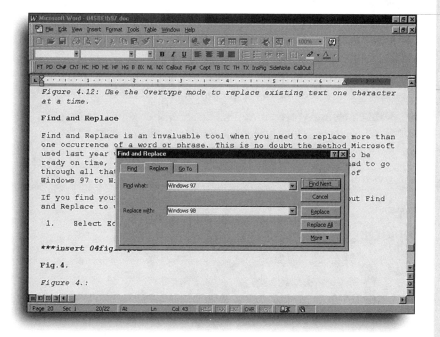

FIGURE 3.12

Use the Overtype mode to replace existing text one character at a time.

Using Find and Replace

Find and Replace is an invaluable tool when you need to replace more than one occurrence of a word or phrase. This is no doubt the method Microsoft used last year when they realized Windows 97 wasn't going to be ready on time and was really going to be Windows 98. Somebody had to go through all that marketing literature and change every instance of Windows 97 to Windows 98.

Using Find and Replace

1. Open the **Edit** menu and choose the **Replace** command to open the Find and Replace dialog box as seen in Figure 3.13.

FIGURE 3.13

Tell Word what to find and what to replace it with, and it will follow your instructions to the letter.

2. In the **Find what** text box, enter the existing text you want to replace.

3. Tab to the **Replace with** text box, and type in the text you want to use to replace the existing text.

4. Click the **More** button to add specific conditions to expand the Find and Replace dialog box (see Figure 3.14). This is where you add specific conditions to the Find and Replace operation.

FIGURE 3.14

You can limit the Find and Replace operation by adding special conditions.

5. Set the special conditions by placing a check mark next to the desired option or by clicking one of the buttons at the

bottom of the menu and making a selection from the menu that appears.

6. Click **Find Next** to locate the next occurrence of the text you entered in the **Find what** text box. Word stops and highlights the occurrence.

7. Click **Replace** to switch the text or **Find Next** to leave it as is and move on to the next occurrence (for example, that Microsoft employee charged with updating all the literature might want to leave in a mention that the program is no longer called Windows 97). If the Find and Replace dialog box gets in your way, just grab it by its title bar and drag it out of the way.

8. Click **Replace All** if you're confident that you don't want to preserve any instances of the selected text. Word will then automatically find each occurrence and replace it without any prompting from you.

9. Click **Cancel** when you're finished and want to return to the active document. If you used the **Replace All** command, Word will notify you when it's finished, give you a count of the replacements made, and wait for you to click **OK** before returning you to the Find and Replace dialog box.

Using the special conditions to customize your Find and Replace operation provides you with an extremely powerful editing tool. Some of the conditions you can set include

- **Match case**. You'll love this option if you have a tendency to be inconsistent with your capitalizing. Enter a word that should be capitalized (without the capital) in the **Find what** text box. Then enter the capitalized version in the **Replace with** text box, and select the **Match case** option. Word only finds instances of the word without the capital and replaces them with the properly capitalized word.

- **Find whole words only**. Suppose you want to replace every instance of "auto" in your document with "car." Nice and simple you say—just use Find and Replace. You're right; however, there's one small problem. Word 97 will not only replace the word auto with the word car, but it will also turn automatic into carmatic, automobile into carmobile, and so on. To prevent this from happening, select **Find whole words only**.

- **Format**. Use this button to locate instances of formatting rather than specific words. If you want to find all the instances of Windows that have been bolded and make them italicized instead, this is the button for you. Enter Windows in the **Find what** text box, click the **Format** button, and select the **Font** tab. In the **Font style** list, choose **Bold**. Click **OK** and do the same for the Replace text, this time choosing **Italic** in the **Font style** list. If you leave both the **Find what** and the **Replace with** text boxes empty of text but set the formatting options, Word replaces the formatting regardless of the text involved, changing to italics every piece of text that is currently bold.

- **Special**. This button provides a menu of special characters you can use in either the **Find what** or **Replace with** text boxes. Place the cursor in the desired text box, click **Special**, and choose the character from the menu.

- **No Formatting**. After you select a formatting option, it remains in effect until you click the **No Formatting** button. This button is disabled until the first time you set a format option.

Cutting, Copying, and Pasting Text

When you start moving whole blocks of text around, you'll find that your favorite editing operations are cut, copy, and paste. These three features allow you to designate any amount of text you want, remove it (cut) from the document or just make a copy (copy), and insert it (paste) anywhere in the document you want. The behind-the-scenes partner in all this is the Windows Clipboard, which holds items that are cut or copied until they are called for again or replaced by something new.

Moving a block of text by using the Cut, Copy, and Paste features

1. Highlight the text to be moved or copied, using one of the text-selection methods described earlier in this chapter.

Searching for simple formatting

To find simple types of formatting such as bold, italics, and underlining, you can highlight the text in the **Find what** or **Replace with** text boxes and click the appropriate button on the Formatting toolbar, or you can use one of the shortcut keys (Ctrl+B for bold, Ctrl+I for italics, or Ctrl+U for underline).

2. Open the **Edit** menu and then either choose **Cut** to cut the selection or choose **Copy** to copy the selected text. In either case, the text is copied to the Windows Clipboard.

3. Move the insertion point to the new location.

4. Open the **Edit** menu and choose **Paste** to insert the text in the new location.

To make your cut, copy, and paste operations go more quickly, you might want to use the shortcut keys or toolbar buttons, as shown in Table 3.2.

TABLE 3.2 **Cut, copy, and paste shortcut keys and toolbar buttons**

Action	Shortcut Key	Toolbar Button
Cut	Ctrl+X	✂
Copy	Ctrl+C	📋
Paste	Ctrl+V	📋

Entering Text with AutoText

One of the things that makes computers so handy is their capability to automate those time-consuming and tedious tasks that we all hate but have to do. The Word *AutoText* feature takes advantage of that capability and enables you to automate text by storing a selection of text, graphics, or both for instant retrieval at a later time. It's great for personalized letter closings, contact information, or special instructions that you frequently include in correspondence. It can be anything from a simple phrase to an epic novel (system resources allowing).

Creating an AutoText entry

1. Select the text or graphics you want to include in the AutoText entry.

2. Open the **Insert** menu, point to **AutoText**, and choose **New** (or press Alt+F3) to open the Create AutoText dialog box as shown in Figure 3.15.

Moving text without using Cut, Copy, or Paste commands

I hate it when I cut something and then realize I need to move another piece of text before continuing. Now I've got a dilemma on my hands—if I cut or copy the second block of text, it will replace the first block on the Clipboard. I don't want to lose the first block since it's been removed from the document (I cut it), and I don't want to have to paste it where it doesn't belong. There are two neat tricks that will enable you to move text without replacing the contents of the Clipboard. First, you can highlight the text and drag it to a new location. Option number two comes in handy when you're moving the text any distance from its original location. Highlight the text you want to move and press F2. "Move to where?" immediately appears in the status bar. Now move to the new location, place the insertion point where you want the text moved, and press Enter. The text is pasted at the insertion point without replacing the Clipboard contents. If you want to copy the text rather than move it, press Shift+F2 instead of F2.

FIGURE 3.15

Give each AutoText entry a unique name so that you can identify it later.

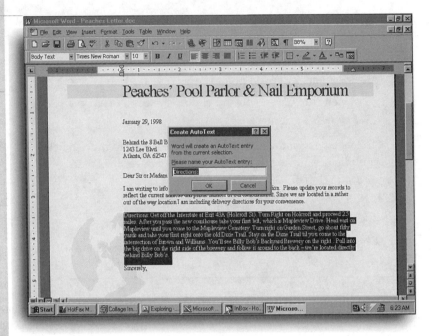

3. Enter a descriptive name for the AutoText entry.

4. Click **OK** to store the entry and return to the active document.

Word automatically creates a menu item for each AutoText entry you save and places it on the **Insert** menu's **AutoText** submenu. It uses the paragraph style of the selection as the menu heading.

To use an AutoText entry, all you have to do is place the insertion point where you want the entry inserted. Then select the entry from the appropriate AutoText submenu. For example, to use the entry created in Figure 3.15, you would open the **Insert** menu, highlight **AutoText**, highlight **Body Text**, and choose **Directions** (see Figure 3.16). "Directions" was the name we gave to the entry, and Body Text was the paragraph style.

You also can insert an AutoText entry by opening the **Insert** menu, highlighting **AutoText**, and choosing the **AutoText** command. Then highlight the entry in the AutoCorrect dialog box and click the **Insert** button.

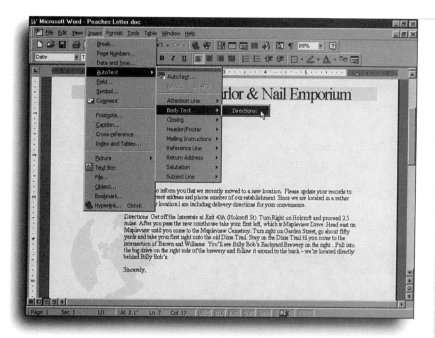

FIGURE 3.16
The new AutoText entry
is added to the AutoText
submenu.

Editing with AutoText

Although AutoText does a great job of automating text entry, it
also contains a useful editing tool called the *Spike*. The Spike,
allows you to gather multiple items from various locations within
the document or even from different documents and then paste
them as a group wherever you choose.

Using the Spike

1. Select the first object and press Ctrl+F3 to place it on the
   Spike. Remember, this is a cut operation, so the selected
   item is removed from the document.

2. Move to the next object and press Ctrl+F3 to place it on
   the Spike. Continue this process until you've collected all
   the items you want.

3. Move the insertion point to the new location for the items
   collected on the Spike.

4. Press Ctrl+Shift+F3 to paste the contents of the Spike at the
   new location. The items are pasted in the order in which
   they were collected. In other words, the first one "spiked"
   is at the top of the group, and the last one "spiked"
   is at the bottom of the group.

In addition to pasting everything, Ctrl+Shift+F3 also empties the contents of the Spike. You can also paste the contents and still retain a copy of everything on the Spike.

Keeping the Spike contents after pasting

1. Collect items on the Spike by highlighting and pressing Ctrl+F3.

2. Move the insertion point to a new location where you want to insert the Spike.

3. Open the **Insert** menu, highlight **AutoText** in the submenu, and then choose the **AutoText** command to open the AutoCorrect dialog box (see Figure 3.17).

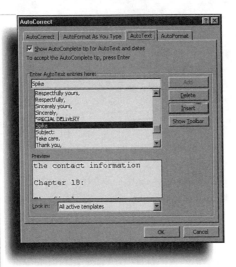

FIGURE 3.17

The Spike is actually an AutoText feature.

4. Scroll through the **Enter AutoText entries here** list box and highlight **Spike**.

5. Click **Insert** to paste the Spike contents at the insertion point. The text is inserted and the AutoCorrect dialog box closes.

When you select **Spike** from the **Enter AutoText entries here** list box, you can also view some of the Spike contents in the **Preview** box. Unfortunately, you cannot scroll through the contents, so if you have more than one or two entries, you won't be able to see them all.

Designing Document Settings

Changing the Page Setup

Form and function are really two sides of the same coin. How your document looks, to a great extent, determines how well it does its job. Not only should it appeal to the eye, but it must also present information in a manner that is convenient and useful to the reader. From designing the basic page layout to selecting the right paper type, putting some thought and effort into your document's appearance is important. That's what this chapter is all about.

The way you set up the opening page of a document determines how the entire document will appear (until *you* change it). Therefore, when you begin a new document, the first thing to think about is the basic page layout. Considerations such as margin size, whether or not to include headers and footers, how the document should be oriented, and even the use of page numbers, should all be thought out ahead of time and implemented before you type your first character.

Although Word comes with a preset configuration that works fine for most common word processing tasks, you may find your needs are just a little different. Fine-tuning is actually relatively easy when you use the Page Setup features, starting with margins.

Setting Margins

Considering your printer when setting margins

Margins are important not only for appearance but also to accommodate the fact that most printers cannot print to the edges of the paper. Consequently, the minimum margin sizes you can set are determined by your default printer. If you set them too low, Word alerts you and offers to fix them by setting them to the correct minimum for your printer.

To impose some initial order on your document, you have to set limits by creating margins, or boundaries, within which the body text of your document must remain. Although margins are often blank borders surrounding your document on all four sides, they can contain text. Headers, footers, page numbers, and footnotes, when present, all reside in the margins of a document.

Word offers you two ways to set margins:

- Use the Page Setup dialog box.
- Use the rulers while working in your document.

Both ways have advantages and disadvantages. Whereas the rulers offer speed and convenience, the Page Setup dialog box offers precision and more options.

Using Page Setup

You can change the following margin settings from the Page Setup dialog box:

- **Top**, **Bottom**, **Left**, and **Right**. These are the easy ones. Each option represents the distance the body text of your document will begin or end from the margin. Note, however, that the top and bottom margin settings can be overridden by header and footer settings.

- **Gutter**. A document's gutter is the space kept empty for binding. If you plan to bind your document, you will need to leave some room between the edge of the paper and the margin so the clips, staples, or other binding tools you use won't interfere with the text.

- **Header**. Headers include text or graphics that appear at the top of the page, independent of the body text. They are generally used for date information, company logos, and such. Use this setting to indicate how far from the top edge of the page you want the top of the header to appear. This number should be less than the Top margin setting. If you set it to a larger number, it will force the Top margin to begin below the bottom of the header, regardless of the margin setting.

- **Footer**. Like the header, the footer contains nonbody text. Set this margin to reflect the distance between the bottom edge of the page and *bottom* of the footer. This setting should be less than the Bottom margin number. And, like the Header setting, a larger number will take precedence over the Bottom margin setting.

- **Mirror margins**. If your printer supports printing on both sides of the paper, you can use this option to ensure that the margins for facing pages are symmetrical (inside and outside margins equal). In other words, the right margin (inside) of the left page will be the same as the left margin (inside) of the right page.

Binding books

If you print on both sides of the page and bind your document, you've created a book. The gutter and outside margins for the odd and even pages must be mirrored. Word provides a feature called Mirror margins to accommodate this. If you are numbering pages, put the page number for the even pages on the upper-left corner, and use the upper-right corner for the odd pages.

Adjusting the size of the margins by using the Page Setup dialog box

1. Open the **File** menu and choose **Page Setup** to open the Page Setup dialog box as shown in Figure 4.1.

2. Click the **Margins** tab to access the margin settings.

FIGURE 4.1

FIGURE 4.1

Page Setup provides plenty of tools for good page design, including precise margin settings.

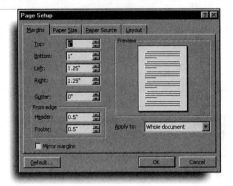

3. Select the margin setting you want to adjust, and enter the number of inches (unless you changed the default unit of measurement) you want the text to begin from the edge of the paper.

To help you in determining the margins that are right for you, Word provides a **Preview** area with a small sample document. As you change the margin settings, the preview document changes to reflect the new margins.

4. Repeat the process until all the margins are set.

5. From the **Apply to** drop-down list, select the portion of the document you want affected by these changes.

Your choices are

- **Whole document**. If you select this option, any margin changes you make will apply to the entire document, including any new pages you create.

- **This point forward**. To change the margin settings from the insertion point forward, select this option. A Next Page section break is created, and all text to the right of the insertion point is placed in the new section, starting on a new page. The new margins affect all text, from the section break on.

- **Selected text**. This option appears only if you highlight a block of text. When you choose **Selected text**, a new page is created with a pair of section breaks, and the selected text is placed between the section breaks. The new margin settings are applied only to the selected (highlighted) text.

- **This section**. If your document contains sections, this option becomes available. Any margin changes you make will be limited to the section in which your cursor rests when you make this selection.

- **Selected sections**. If you highlight text across more than one section break, you can use this option to apply the margin changes to all sections covered by the highlighted text. This option is available only if your document contains sections.

6. Click **OK** to apply the margin changes and return to the active document.

If you plan to use the new margins for all your documents, you can set them as the default margins for all new documents. You do this by clicking the **Default** button in the **Margins** tab of the Page Setup dialog box. If, on the other hand, you decide you don't like the new margins and want to revert to Word's default margins, you'll have to close Word, go to Windows Explorer, locate normal.dot, and change its name to anything but normal.dot (for example, oldnormal.dot). The next time you open Word, a new normal.dot is created, complete with all the original settings (including page margins). The only problem with this solution is that it also removes all toolbar, macro, and menu customizations you have implemented because they too are retained in the normal.dot template.

Using the Rulers

Although the Page Setup dialog box offers you more margin options, you may find it more convenient to set the basic page margins by using the horizontal and vertical rulers in the Page Layout or Print Preview document view. Although the horizontal (but not the vertical) ruler appears in other views, setting even the left and right margins is only allowed in the Page Layout and Print Preview document views. If your horizontal ruler is not visible, you can display it by selecting the **View** menu and choosing **Ruler**. The vertical ruler can be turned on and off in certain views by enabling or deselecting the **Vertical ruler** check box found on the **View** tab of the Options dialog box (from the **Tools** menu, select **Options**).

Quick access to the Page Setup dialog box

If you're in Document view and decide you'd rather use the Page Setup dialog box to change the margins (or any other Page Setup options), double-click a blank spot on the end of either ruler to open the Page Setup dialog box. Be careful about double-clicking the rulers themselves. The Page Setup dialog box will open, but you might also end up with a new tab set at the location you click.

Setting precise margins

To set the margins with a greater degree of precision, hold the Alt key down while dragging the margin boundary, and you'll see the exact margin settings.

Setting margins in Page Layout or Print Preview

1. Position your mouse pointer over the desired margin boundary until the pointer changes to a double-headed arrow (see Figure 4.2).

2. Drag the margin boundary to increase or reduce the margin size.

One thing to keep in mind when changing margins with the rulers—Word will not warn you if the margins are too small for your printer. However, Word will alert you the next time you open the Page Setup dialog box and close it.

SEE ALSO
➤ *To learn more about Print Preview, see page 211*

Using Section Breaks

Very often when creating a large document, you incorporate various elements, each requiring a different type of layout. Try creating a three-column newsletter with a title that spans all three columns, and you'll see what I mean. It just doesn't work. You can have one or the other, but not both—unless you create separate sections for the two elements (see Figure 4.3). True, you could add a text box (a container for text that is unaffected by page layout and paragraph formatting), but a section is so much easier and more flexible that there's no contest.

As you can see in Figure 4.3, the top document, which has a section break dividing the title from the body, allows a single-column format for the section containing the title line and a three-column format for the section containing the rest of the document. The bottom document, which has no section break, forces the title line to conform to the three-column format of the document.

Creating Section Breaks

By creating a section break, you let Word know the layout rules are changing. What applies to one side of the break may or may not apply to the other. Any layout settings you change apply only to the section in which you make them, unless you indicate otherwise.

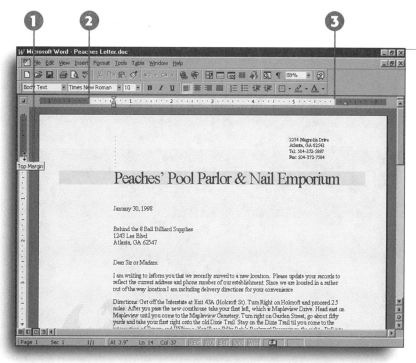

FIGURE 4.2

Drag the margin boundary to increase or decrease the desired margin.

1 Top margin boundary

2 Left margin boundary

3 Right margin boundary

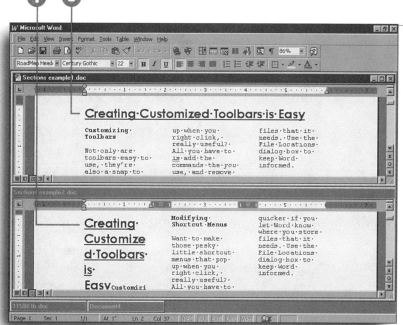

FIGURE 4.3

With section breaks, you can control the layout of any part of your document, whether it's a line, paragraph, page, or the rest of the document.

1 Title without a section break

2 Title with a section break

Creating a section break

1. Place the insertion point where you want the break to occur.

2. Open the **Insert** menu and choose **Break** to open the Break dialog box as shown in Figure 4.4.

3. Select the section break you want to insert.

   The available section breaks include

FIGURE 4.4

Word offers you a number of break options.

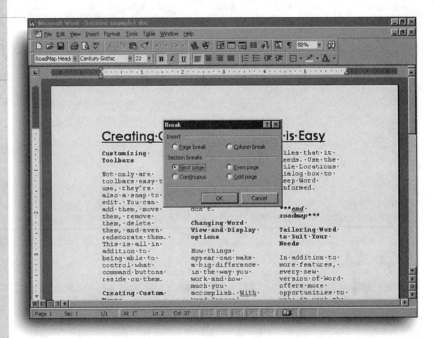

- **Next page**. This option creates a new section and a new page at the same time. Text immediately following the insertion point is moved to the new page.

- **Continuous**. Select **Continuous** to create a new section, starting immediately to the left of the insertion point. This is the section break I used to create the newsletter title in Figure 4.3.

- **Even page**. Creates a section break and a new page at the next even page number. In other words, if you place the insertion point on page three and insert an even-page section break, you will create the new section on page four. However, if your insertion point is on page six when you create the even-page section break, the new section will be created on page eight, and page seven will be blank.

- **Odd page**. The same as the even-page option except it creates the new section on the next odd page.

4. Click **OK** to insert the section break and return to the active document.

After you create a new section, you can change the page layout to suit your needs by making the necessary changes and applying them only to the new section.

You can also create a section break by using the **Section start** option on the **Layout** tab of the Page Setup dialog box. Place the insertion point where you want a new break to occur, open the **Layout** tab, select the section break type from the **Section start** drop-down list, and select **This point forward** from the **Apply to** drop-down list.

Copying and Deleting Section Breaks

If you want to use section breaks effectively, you should know a couple of things about them. As handy as they are, you'll probably want to get rid of one at some point. And one thing that's very convenient—copying the break and all its layout settings.

Deleting Section Breaks

Eliminating a section break is as simple as placing your cursor on the break and pressing Delete. But wait a minute before you reach for that Delete key. Remember that as soon as you delete the section break, all its layout information disappears as well. Everything in the section preceding the deleted break joins the next section and conforms to its layout.

Copying and Moving Section Breaks

Changed your mind about where you want that section break? No problem, just pick it up and put it where you want it. Or perhaps you like it so much that you want to use it somewhere else. Nothing to it. Copy it and paste it in another location. One thing to be aware of when copying and moving section breaks is that they carry the formatting information for the section that precedes them, not the one that follows the break.

Moving or copying a section break

1. Highlight the section break you want to copy or move.

2. Press Ctrl+C to copy the break or Ctrl+X to cut it. You can also use the Cut, Copy, and Paste buttons on the Standard toolbar.

3. Move the insertion point to the location for the new section, keeping in mind that the layout information will apply to the section *before* the section break, not after.

4. Press Ctrl+V to paste the section break in the new location.

Because the section break contains all the layout information, the section preceding the new break is immediately formatted with the same settings as the original section from which the break was copied or moved.

Using Headers and Footers

Headers and footers are handy for including supplemental information that doesn't intrude on the regular body text but is available consistently throughout the document. They're great for including date information, page numbers, the author's name, or the title of the document.

Adding headers and footers

1. Open the **View** menu and choose **Header and Footer** to access the header frame of the page on which your insertion point is resting (see Figure 4.5). Because you can only view headers and footers in Page Layout or Print Preview, Word switches you to Page Layout if you're in another view (even if you're in Print Preview). In addition, the Header and Footer toolbar appears.

2. Type the header information you want to appear at the top of each page of your document into the header. You can use the commands from the Header and Footer toolbar to insert the date, page number, and such. The **Insert AutoText** button even contains a selection of preset header/footer

FIGURE 4.5

Enter the header information in the Header frame, and use the toolbar to switch between the header and footer.

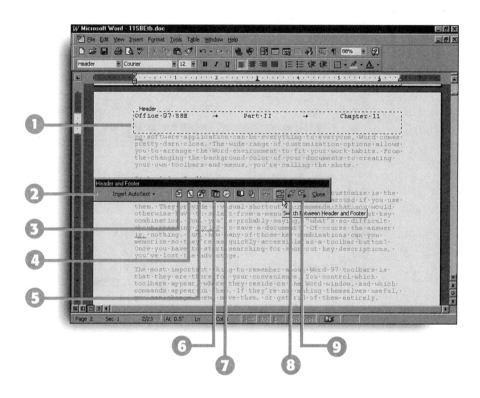

1   Header frame

2   Header and Footer toolbar

3   Insert page number

4   Insert number of pages

5   Format page number

6   Insert date

7   Insert time

8   Show Previous (section)

9   Show Next (section)

information as seen in Figure 4.6.

3. Click the Switch Between Header and Footer button on the toolbar to open the footer frame.

FIGURE 4.6

Use an AutoText selection to create a quick header or footer.

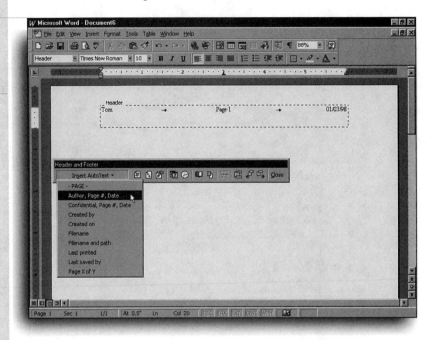

4. Enter the footer information.

5. Click **Close** to return to the active document.

The same headers and footers that you create on any page of your document appear on all other pages of your document. As a matter of fact, you can't create a separate header or footer for each page unless you first insert section breaks or use one of the two header/footer options available in the **Layout** tab of the Page Setup dialog box.

When creating headers and footers for different sections, use the Show Previous and Show Next buttons on the Header and Footer toolbar to move from section to section.

Accessing headers and footers in Page Layout view

If you are in the Page Layout view, you can quickly open the header or footer by double-clicking the grayed-out header or footer.

Modifying the Layout Options

The Page Setup dialog box **Layout** tab (see Figure 4.7) offers several options that enable you to fine-tune your document layout with a minimum of trouble.

Here you can create special headers and footers, change the

FIGURE 4.7
The Layout options give you more control over your page design.

current break type, add line numbers, and even make the new settings the defaults for the document.

Section Start

If, after you create a section break, you find that it is not performing its job well, you may decide to change the break type to better suit your needs. You can use the **Section start** option in Page Setup to change an existing section break from one type to another.

Converting a section break from one type to another

1. Place the insertion point in the section you want to change.

2. Open the **File** menu and choose **Page Setup** to open the Page Setup dialog box.

3. Click the **Layout** tab to access the layout options. The **Section start** drop-down list already displays the section type of the existing break.

4. Click the down arrow next to the **Section start** drop-down list. Select the new type for the existing section.

5. Click **OK** to apply the change and return to the active document.

As soon as you return to the document, the existing break is converted to the newly selected break type, and any layout changes dictated by the new break are affected. For more information on section break types, refer to the "Creating Section Breaks" segment earlier in this chapter.

Headers and Footers

The standard Word headers and footers are identical throughout each section of your document. When you create a header or a footer on any page of a section, it appears on all other pages of that section. The only way to create different headers and footers for individual pages is to create a new section or use one of the header and footer options found in the **Layout** tab of the Page Setup dialog box.

If you have more header or footer information than will comfortably fit in a single set of headers and footers, you can utilize the **Different odd and even** option. This option enables you to create two sets of headers and footers that appear alternately, on odd and even pages of your document.

Creating odd and even page headers

1. Open the **File** menu and choose **Page Setup** to open the Page Setup dialog box, and then click the **Layout** tab.

2. Place a check mark in the **Different odd and even** check box.

3. Click **OK** to return to the active document.

4. Open the **View** menu and choose **Header and Footer** to open the header or footer of the page where you currently have the insertion point.

5. Click the Switch Between Header and Footer button on the Header and Footer toolbar and then fill in the header/footer information.

6. Click the Show Next button on the Header and Footer toolbar to move to the next header or footer. If you're on an even page, it will take you to the header or footer of the next

How Word assigns odd and even headers and footers

Word assumes you always want a header or footer to appear on the first page of your document. Therefore, when you apply the **Different odd and even** option, the existing header or footer (if you have one) is automatically assigned to the odd pages.

odd page, or vice versa.

7. Fill out the header and footer information for the second set of headers and footers.

8. Click **C**lose to return to the active document.

For those times when you want to include one header and footer for the first page and a different header and footer for the rest of the document, you can use the **Different first page** option. In this case Word assign an existing header and footer to the document and assumes you want to add a new set to the first page.

Vertical alignment

For those times when you want all the text aligned between the top and bottom edges of the page (a title page, for instance), use the **Vertical alignment** option. You can choose **Top**, **Center**, or **Justified**. This is great if you want to call attention to an important piece of information by isolating it in the middle of a page or if you want to bring text to the top of the page to make room for a graphic at the bottom. Since **Top** is the default setting, you only have to change it if you previously modified this option.

Like the other Layout options, this one works by applying the change either to the entire document or to some portion of it. The only way it can be applied to part of the document, such as a single page or block of text, is to create a separate section for that portion. Therefore, when you use vertical alignment, be sure to select the correct break type from the **Section start** drop-down list. Then when you choose **This point forward** or **Selected text** in the **Apply to** drop-down list, the correct section break will be inserted.

By the way, just so you don't think you've lost your mind, the Preview window doesn't work for this option. It's another one of those bugs that Microsoft loves to call features.

Line Numbers

Line numbers are great for software programmers, lawyers, and others who need to number each line of a document. If your document (or some portion of it) needs to be numbered, this option will take care of it quickly and efficiently. You could even create a numbered list (no item longer than a single line) by typing it in and using line numbering.

Adding line numbering to your document

1. Open the **File** menu and choose **Page Setup** to open the Page Setup dialog box, and then click the **Layout** tab.

2. Click the **Line Numbers** button to open the Line Numbers dialog box shown in Figure 4.8.

FIGURE 4.8
You can add line numbers, position them, and even designate the number by which they are incremented.

3. Set the line numbering options to suit your needs.

The available line numbering options include

- **Add line numbering**. Without this one checked, none of the other options are available.

- **Start at**. Enter the first number to use for the line numbering. If you're like the bank, you may want to start with 101.

- **From text**. Enter the distance the numbers should be from the line of text.

- **Count by**. This one's a little confusing. The number you enter here is used to increment all the line numbers; however, it negates the entry you make in the **Start at** text box. Therefore, if you enter 2 in the Count by text box, the line numbering starts at 2 and continues 4, 6, 8, and so on, not 1, 3, 5, 7, which would be the logical progression based on a 1 in the **Start at** text box.

- **Numbering**. Indicate whether you want the numbering to start over at the **Start at** number, restart at the beginning of each section, or continue nonstop throughout the entire document.

4. Click **OK** to return to the Page Setup dialog box.

5. Click **OK** to apply the line numbering and return to the active document.

Other Layout Options

The remaining options on the **Layout** tab of the Page Setup dialog box include

- **Suppress endnotes**. *Endnotes* are footnotes that appear at the end of the section rather than the end of the page. To force endnotes into the next section, select this check box.

- **Apply to**. Selects the part of the document to which you want to apply the dialog box settings.

- **Default**. Saves the settings in this dialog box as the new default settings for the current document and its template.

As with the other **Layout** tab options, click **OK** to save your changes and return to the active document.

Changing Paper Settings

The paper size, orientation, and type you use for your document all make a big difference in how the document is laid out. Paper settings are particularly useful in Page Layout view, which displays your document as it will print. In the Page Setup dialog box you have two sets of paper options, paper size and paper source. The choices you have for both these options depend entirely on the paper-handling features of your default printer. To see the paper settings, from the **File** menu, choose **Page Setup,** or double-click a blank spot on either end of the horizontal ruler.

Choosing a Paper Size

The **Paper Size** tab includes the paper size and orientation. You can select a preset size from the **Paper size** drop-down list or create your own custom size by filling in the **Width** and **Height** spin boxes. Your Orientation choices are **Portrait** and **Landscape**. **Portrait** orients the paper so it's taller than it is wide. For example, the dimensions for a letter-size piece of paper with portrait orientation are 8.5" (wide) × 11" (long). **Landscape** on the other hand, turns the page so it's wider than it is long (11" × 8.5").

Choosing a Paper Source

The **Paper Source** options enable you to select the source of the paper for the first page and for all subsequent pages. This is very nice if you use a preprinted letterhead for the first page and plain paper for the rest of the document. If you have more than one paper tray, you can place preprinted letterhead in one and plain paper in the other.

Paper-handling options

No matter what kind of printer you are using, it probably has some form of automatic paper feeding. A laser or ink jet printer usually has a paper tray that can hold anywhere from 50 to 500 sheets of paper, depending on the printer make and model. Dot-matrix printers have pin feeds that draw the paper through the printer. Most printers also enable you to manually feed paper into the printer for the occasional envelope, form, or letterhead that doesn't belong in the main paper source.

Using Page Numbers

Did you ever try having a discussion about the contents of a long document that doesn't contain page numbers? You end up spending half the discussion trying to help everyone figure out which part of the document you're talking about. It's so much easier if you can say, "Hey, turn to page 34 and take a look at the first paragraph." Or what happens when you print it out and drop it on the floor? That's right, you've got to spend the next ten minutes reading the first and last paragraph of each page, trying to match them up. Next time you're creating a document, do everyone (including yourself) a favor and include page numbers. If you use headers and footers, page numbering is included by default.

Adding Page Numbers

Inserting page numbers

1. Open the **Insert** menu and choose **Page Numbers** to open the Page Numbers dialog box shown in Figure 4.9.
2. In the **Position** drop-down list, select the location on the page to place the page numbers. Your choices are **Top** and **Bottom**.
3. In the **Alignment** drop-down list, select the alignment for the page numbers.

FIGURE 4.9

Page number options include location, alignment, and formatting.

Page number alignment options include:

- **Left**. Places the page number at the left edge of the header or footer frame.
- **Center**. Inserts the page number in the center of the frame.
- **Right**. Places the number flush with the right edge of the frame.
- **Inside**. This option is used to position the page numbers close to the binding on facing pages. With **Inside** selected, the number will be to the left on one page and to the right on the next.
- **Outside**. Similar to **Inside**, this option positions the page numbers on the outside edges (away from the binding) of facing pages. This will result in the page number appearing to the right on one page and to the left on the next.

4. Deselect <u>**S**</u>**how number on first page** if you want the first page to be numberless. This is useful if you're including a title page, which generally does not have a page number.

5. Click **OK** to add the numbers and return to the active document.

Now when you view the header or footer you will see the page number inserted in the spot you selected. If your header or footer previously included page numbers, using the above method will not add another set of page numbers. It will simply modify the existing numbers if your choices are different here.

Formatting Page Numbers

You can make page numbers as simple or as complex as you want. The instructions above provide the simple version.

If you want to get fancy with your page numbers, you can take advantage of the formatting options that Word makes available.

Formatting page numbers

1. Open the **Insert** menu and choose **Page Numbers** to open the Page Numbers dialog box.

2. Click the **Format** button to open the Page Number Format dialog box shown in Figure 4.10.

FIGURE 4.10

You can use numbers, letters, or Roman numerals for your page numbers.

3. Set the desired number-formatting options, choosing from the following options:

   - **Number format.** From the drop-down list, select the type of numbering you want to use. Your choices include numbers, upper- and lowercase letters, and upper- and lowercase Roman numerals.

   - **Include chapter number.** If you use heading styles for chapters, you can select this option to include the chapter number with the page number. The first option is for the heading style to use. The second option lets you select the separator character.

   - **Page numbering.** If your document contains sections, you can choose **Continue from previous section** to keep the page numbers flowing continuously. Deselect this option if you want to restart the numbering with each section. Use the **Start at** option to indicate the starting number to use at the beginning of each section.

4. Click **OK** to return to the Page Number dialog box.

5. Click **OK** to save your page number settings and return to the active document.

The page numbers appear in the header or footer, with the new formatting applied.

Formatting Text and Paragraphs

Paragraph formatting

Using line and page breaks

Setting tabs

Using AutoFormat

Formatting text

Implementing character spacing

Animating text

Introducing Paragraph and Text Formatting

After you build a solid framework for your document, using all the setup and layout features Word has to offer, it's time to start dressing it up with the formatting tools. With paragraph and text formatting, you can fine-tune your document by making changes to individual paragraphs, blocks of text, and even characters. You may decide to change the line spacing or indent a single paragraph. Or perhaps the font you're using appears rather dull and lifeless. Why not change its size, color, or style to liven it up? Formatting gives you the opportunity to do all these things and more.

Paragraph Formatting

Although most of us think of a paragraph as a string of sentences tied together by a common idea, Word considers a paragraph anything that ends with a paragraph mark (¶). Word doesn't care if it's a blank line, a single character, or the contents of the Encyclopedia Britannica—as long as it has a paragraph mark at the end, to Word, it's a paragraph. With that in mind let's take a look at some of the ways you can format a paragraph. To see paragraph marks in your document, click the Show/Hide button on the Standard toolbar ¶ .

Creating Paragraph Indents

Indents are to paragraphs what margins are to sections—the distance between the edge of the page and the text. Whereas margins apply to the entire document or to sections of the document, each paragraph can contain its own indent settings.

You can create indents in one of several ways—by using the horizontal ruler, shortcut keys, the **Paragraph** command, or the Increase Indent button ▤ on the Formatting toolbar.

Using the Paragraph command to create an indent

1. Place the insertion point in the paragraph you want to indent.

2. Right-click and select **Paragraph** from the shortcut menu. This opens the Paragraph dialog box shown in Figure 5.1. You can also activate the Paragraph command by opening the **Format** menu and choosing the **Paragraph** command.

3. Click the **Indents and Spacing** tab to view the indents and spacing options.

FIGURE 5.1

In addition to setting indents, you can also change alignment and spacing options.

4. Move to the **Indentation** section and enter a number in inches (unless you've changed the default unit of measurement) for the **Left**, **Right**, or both indents you want to create.

5. Select a special indent from the **Special** drop-down list if you want, and enter the indentation amount in the **By** spin box.

The special indents available are

- **First Line**. A First Line indent automatically adjusts the first line so you don't have to press the Tab key each time you start a new paragraph (if you like the first line of each paragraph indented).

- **Hanging**. The Hanging indent is just the opposite of the First Line indent. It indents everything but the first line of the paragraph, by the amount specified.

Going where no margin has gone

To extend text beyond either the left or right margin of the page, you can enter a negative number in the Left or Right indent field. Because indents are measured from the margin, an indent of –.5" in the Left indent field results in an indent that is half an inch to the left of the left margin.

6. Click **OK** to create the indent and return to the active document.

To create indents by using the ruler, place the insertion point in the paragraph you want to indent (or select multiple paragraphs). Then drag the appropriate indent marker on the horizontal ruler (see Figure 5.2) and drop it on the ruler at the position where you want the indent to begin.

Access indents and spacing options with a double-click

You can access the **Indents and Spacing** tab of the Paragraph dialog box by double-clicking any of the indent markers on the horizontal ruler.

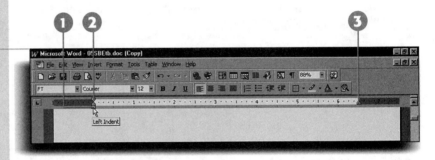

FIGURE 5.2

You can create indents by dragging and dropping the indent markers on the horizontal ruler.

1 Hanging indent

2 First-line indent

3 Right indent

Hold down the Alt key to see the precise position of the marker while you're dragging it.

Aligning Text

Although text alignment is not technically the same as indenting, the two are related and perform similar functions. They both reposition paragraphs in relation to the page margins. You can align a paragraph by positioning the insertion point in the paragraph to align and then clicking the appropriate alignment button on the Formatting toolbar. To align more than one paragraph at a time, select all the desired paragraphs before clicking the toolbar button.

Your alignment choices on the Formatting toolbar are shown in Table 5.1.

TABLE 5.1   **Paragraph alignment**

Toolbar Button	Alignment	Description
	Align Left	Positions each line of the selected paragraph flush with the left margin. As a result, the right edge of the paragraph is uneven. This is the default alignment.
	Align Center	Positions each line of the selected paragraph midway between the left and right margins.
	Align Right	Positions each line of the selected paragraph flush with the right margin, resulting in a ragged left edge.
	Justify	Stretches each line of the selected paragraph so it is flush with both the right and left margins. Word does this by inserting spaces between words. If you only have one line of text, which does not reach the end of the line (right margin), it will not justify unless you enter a soft return (Shift+Enter).

You can also align text by using the **Alignment** drop-down list on the **Indents and Spacing** tab of the Paragraph dialog box.

Spacing

Although you might use this term to refer to what your teenagers do while you're talking to them, Word has an entirely different meaning for it. To Word, spacing refers to the distance between lines in a paragraph and between paragraphs.

In case you're still unclear about spacing, think back to when *you* were a teenager and had to write a ten-page paper. What was the first thing you thought of? "Can I double-space it?"—right? At double-space you got twice the mileage out of the same amount of text. Five pages of single-spaced text filled up ten double-spaced pages. That's what line spacing is all about.

Setting Word spacing options

1. Select the paragraph(s) for which you want to set the spacing.

2. Right-click and select **Paragraph** from the shortcut menu to open the Paragraph dialog box.

3. Click the **Indents and Spacing** tab to view the Spacing options (see Figure 5.3).

FIGURE 5.3

Keep your lines and paragraphs at a safe distance from each other with Word's spacing options.

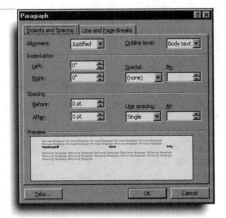

4. Under the **Spacing** options, indicate the amount of space you want to precede the selected paragraph(s) by entering the number in the **Before** spin box.

5. Indicate the amount of space you want following the selected paragraph(s) by entering the number in the **After** spin box.

6. From the **Line spacing** drop-down list, select the line spacing you want to use in the selected paragraph(s).

Your choices for **Line spacing** include

- **Single.** Determined by the size font you use, this option provides enough space for each line of text in that font, plus a little more to keep the lines apart.

- **1.5 lines.** One and a half times the size of single.

- **Double.** Twice the size of single spacing.

- **At least.** This option enables you to set a minimum amount of distance to be used for each line. It also provides flexibility to expand when a font larger than the specified size is used.

- **Exactly**. Line spacing that is no more and no less than you specify, regardless of the size font used.

- **Multiple**. For more precise line spacing, you can stipulate a multiple of single-spacing to be used. For example, 1.1 is ten percent larger than single-spacing, while 2 is twice the size, or double-spacing. You can even reduce the line spacing to something smaller than single by entering a number that is less than one.

7. Enter the **At** number if your **Line spacing** choice requires it.

8. Click **OK** to apply the new settings and return to the active document.

If, after setting the line spacing, you find that part of your text appears to be cut off at the top of each line, you need to readjust your spacing to accommodate the size font you're using. A 12pt font in a 10pt line-spaced paragraph just doesn't work.

Line and Page Breaks

Controlling the flow of text in your document is an important task. The line and page breaks available give you the tools you need to keep your text from getting out of hand.

Line Breaks

For most of my writing I set the paragraph spacing so there's a 12pt space between the end of one paragraph and the beginning of another. Consequently, the lines within the paragraph are closer together than the last line of one paragraph and the first line of the next.

You're probably thinking that's the way it should be so you can distinguish one paragraph from another. I agree. However, there are times when I want to create a quick list a few short lines long and want the lines close together. The trouble is, unless I type to the end of the line and let Word wrap for me, I end up with that pesky 12pt space (as soon as I hit the Enter key and insert a paragraph mark, Word treats each line as a separate paragraph). I really don't want to have to change the spacing settings for a couple of lines, so what do I do?

Glad you asked. I insert a line break, or soft return. By pressing Shift+Enter, you can start a new line and continue the existing style just as it is, without creating a new paragraph. It also comes in handy if you have a style that automatically changes the next paragraph to a different style. By using a soft return, you can move to the next line and continue without changing styles.

Page Breaks

Controlling the way text flows between pages is the domain of page breaks. Normally, when you reach the bottom margin of the page, Word inserts a break and places the balance of the paragraph on the next page. This usually works fine, but occasionally the way Word breaks up the text interrupts the smooth flow that enables a reader to easily follow your train of thought. Straggling lines at the top or bottom of pages, or opening paragraphs without their headings, can jar readers and force them to stop and reread information.

Consequently, Word provides you with a number of options for managing the flow of text between pages, including

- **Widow/Orphan control**. When the last line of a paragraph doesn't fit at the bottom of the page and is carried over to the top of the next page, it is called a widow. An orphan, on the other hand, is the first line of a paragraph that ends up stranded at the bottom of a page, all by itself. Because both can be disruptive and annoying to the reader, you may want to prevent them from occurring by selecting this option. When you select this option, an automatic page break is inserted at the beginning of the widow's paragraph so the whole paragraph is carried to the top of the next page. In the case of the orphan, a page break is inserted before the orphan so it too is carried over to the next page with the rest of the paragraph.

- **Keep lines together**. If you don't want your paragraphs broken up at all, selecting this option prevents Word from inserting a page break anywhere within a paragraph. When a paragraph reaches the bottom of the page and doesn't fit, the whole paragraph is moved to the next page. If your paragraph has a heading that should go with it, you may want to use this option in conjunction with the **Keep with next** option to ensure that they stay together.

- **Keep with next**. If you have two paragraphs (or a heading and a paragraph) that must remain on the same page, select this one.

- **Page break before**. When you want a certain paragraph to start at the beginning of a page, you can select this option to insert a page break before the paragraph.

Keep in mind that all these options apply only to the paragraph(s) selected at the time you set the option.

Setting page break options

1. Place the insertion point in the paragraph to format, or select multiple paragraphs.

2. Open the **Format** menu and choose **Paragraph** to open the Paragraph dialog box.

3. Click the **Line and Page Breaks** tab to view the **Pagination** options as shown in Figure 5.4.

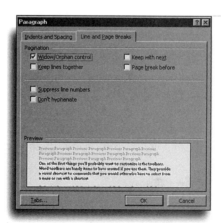

FIGURE 5.4
Controlling text flow is easy with line and page breaks.

4. Select or deselect check boxes for the option(s) you want to set.

5. Click **OK** to apply the changes and return to the active document.

Regular page breaks with options are great until you decide you want to start a new page before you reach the end of the current page. Or perhaps you've set certain page break options for the whole document but decide you want to override them for a single page. When this happens, you can insert a manual page break immediately to the left of the insertion point, which totally ignores all the page break rules you've set.

Inserting a manual page break

1. Position the insertion point to the left of the text you want moved to the top of the new page. Everything to the right of the cursor will be moved.

2. Open the **Format** menu and choose **Paragraph** to open the Paragraph dialog box.

3. Click the **Line and Page Breaks** tab to view the **Pagination** options.

4. Select **Page break before** to indicate you want a page break placed before the insertion point.

5. Set any of the other desired options, keeping in mind that they will apply only to the paragraph in which the insertion point rests.

6. Click **OK** to create the page break and return to the active document.

Actually, the easiest way to insert a hard page break is by positioning your cursor where you want the break to occur and pressing Ctrl+Enter. You can also insert a hard page break by positioning your insertion point where you want the break and opening the **Insert** menu. Then choose **Break** from the Break dialog box and choose **Page break**.

Setting Tabs

Tabs are handy little critters that enable you to move through a paragraph a preset number of spaces at a time. To use tabs, you must first set tab stops along the horizontal ruler. Tab stops indicate the position to which each subsequent pressing of the Tab key will transport your cursor. You can use tabs to indent a line, separate a word or phrase from its meaning, or create columns for a quick table.

Word comes with default tab stops set $^1/_2$-inch apart. Unless you set your own stops, pressing the Tab key will move you along each line .5 each time. As is the case with many of the Word paragraph formatting features, you can use a dialog box or the horizontal ruler to create tab stops; however, to change the default tab stops you must use the Tabs dialog box.

Creating tab stops by using the Tabs dialog box

1. Open the **Format** menu and choose **Tabs** to open the Tabs dialog box as shown in Figure 5.5.

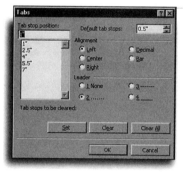

FIGURE 5.5

After you set tab stops, they appear in the **Tab stop position** list.

2. Enter the distance from the left margin to the new tab stop in the **Tab stop position** text box. To move an existing tab stop, highlight the stop and enter a new measurement for it.

3. Select the alignment type for the new tab stop.

   The types of tab stops available are

   - **Left**. Text starts at the tab stop and extends to the right.
   - **Center**. The midpoint of the text is positioned at the tab stop.
   - **Right**. Text ends at the tab stop and extends to the left.
   - **Decimal**. If text contains a decimal point, the decimal is positioned at the tab stop. For non-decimal text, this is the same as a right tab stop.
   - **Bar**. This option places a vertical bar at the tab stop location.

4. Choose a leader type if you want one. Leaders are lines that appear to the left of the text to fill the empty space created by a tab (see Figure 5.6).

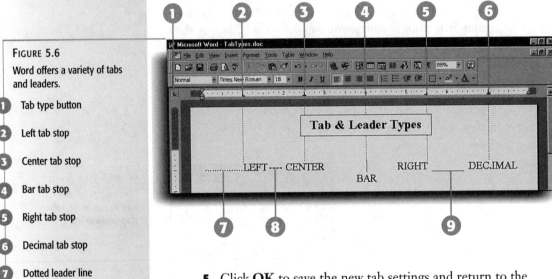

FIGURE 5.6

Word offers a variety of tabs and leaders.

1 Tab type button

2 Left tab stop

3 Center tab stop

4 Bar tab stop

5 Right tab stop

6 Decimal tab stop

7 Dotted leader line

8 Dashed leader line

9 Solid leader line

5. Click **OK** to save the new tab settings and return to the active document.

Of course, to take advantage of your new tab stops all you have to do is press the Tab key and your cursor jumps to the next tab stop. You can clear tab settings in the Tabs dialog box by highlighting them and clicking the **Clear** button, or, to eliminate them all at once, the **Clear All** button.

Setting tab stops using the horizontal ruler

1. Select the paragraph in which you want the tab stops to appear.

2. Click the tab type button on the left side of the horizontal ruler until the tab type you want appears.

3. Click the desired position on the horizontal ruler to set the tab stop.

In addition to adding them on the ruler, you can also reposition tabs by dragging them to different locations on the ruler. You

---

A quick way to open the Tabs dialog box

You can open the Tabs dialog box by double-clicking any tab on the ruler; however, be careful that you don't accidentally add an extra tab. If you do, highlight the accidental tab and click **Clear**. If you wait until you see the ScreenTip, your chances of not creating an unwanted tab will be greatly improved.

can even delete them by dragging them from the ruler and dropping them in the document window.

AutoFormat

AutoFormat is one of those features you either hate or love. It can make your life easy or miserable, depending on the type of word processing you do.

If you create a lot of documents that utilize common writing elements, you'll want to name your firstborn after the Microsoft programmer who designed AutoFormat. If, on the other hand, you use a lot of custom styles and create documents that don't fit any standard mold, you'll be cursing that same programmer (at least until you figure out how turn AutoFormat off).

Here are just a few of the changes AutoFormat makes:

- Creates a numbered list when you type a number followed by any one of several characters (period, hyphen, right parentheses, or greater-than symbol), a space or tab, and finally, text.

- Creates a bulleted list when you type one or two hyphens, an asterisk, or a greater-than symbol, followed by a space or a tab and some text.

- Changes fractions to fraction characters and ordinals to superscript.

For a complete listing of all the AutoFormat changes, activate the Office Assistant, and type AutoFormat in the query text box. Then click **<u>S</u>earch**. Click **What types of automatic changes does Word make?**. At the bottom of the Help Topic window that opens, click **Learn about AutoFormat changes Word makes**.

AutoFormatting an entire document

1. Open the **F<u>o</u>rmat** menu and choose **<u>A</u>utoFormat** to open the AutoFormat dialog box as shown in Figure 5.7.

2. Select the method of AutoFormat you want to use. **AutoFormat now** formats the entire document without any prompting from you. **<u>A</u>utoFormat and review**

each change formats the document and then lets you review the changes and accept or reject each one.

FIGURE 5.7

You can review each AutoFormat change before Word makes it.

3. From the drop-down list, select the document type you're formatting. This enables AutoFormat to make better informed decisions about the changes it implements. Your choices are **General document**, **Letter**, and **Email**.

4. Click **OK** to begin the AutoFormat procedure and close the dialog box.

You also can apply AutoFormat options to set certain features independent of the others. From the **Tools** menu, select **AutoCorrect** to open the AutoCorrect dialog box. Click the **AutoFormat** tab to view or change the AutoFormat options, including the settings to different Word elements, such as headings, lists, and automatic bulleted lists. You can also access the AutoFormat options by choosing the **Format** menu and selecting **AutoFormat**.

Setting AutoFormat options

1. Open the **Format** menu and choose **AutoFormat** to open the AutoFormat dialog box.

2. Click the **Options** button to open the AutoCorrect dialog box.

3. Click the **AutoFormat** tab to view the AutoFormat options (see Figure 5.8).

4. Select the check boxes for the options you want turned on, and deselect those you want turned off.

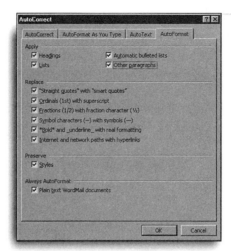

FIGURE 5.8
Let AutoFormat handle the formatting tasks you assign it.

5. Click **OK** to close the AutoCorrect dialog box.

6. Click **OK** again to return to the active document.

As you become more familiar with Word, you'll discover the
options that work for you and those that just make you crazy.
Fortunately, you can take advantage of what you like and discard
what you don't.

Formatting Text

Formatting isn't just for paragraphs, it's for individual characters
as well. As a matter of fact, it's probably character formatting
that most of us are likely to think of when the word formatting is
used. Character formatting encompasses all the changes you can
make to the appearance of a single character and therefore, by
extension, to all the text in your document. You can format characters in Word by changing the font or the spacing or by adding
animation.

Changing the Font

Basically a character is a character. By that I mean the letter A
is still the letter A, no matter how you gussy it up. However,

appearances are important, and just as you wouldn't think of going to a formal dinner in a pair of shorts and sandals (or would you?), you probably wouldn't print your wedding invitations in a font that looks like this. And even if you did, it would be because you wanted to convey the idea that this isn't going to be a typical wedding. Fonts, which are primarily the styles in which you dress your text, enable you to use the appearance of the text to carry part of your message.

Changing the font

1. Select (highlight) the text you want to format. It can be anything from a single character to the entire document.

2. Open the **Format** menu and choose **Font** to open the Font dialog box. Then click the **Font** tab to view the Font options as shown in Figure 5.9.

FIGURE 5.9

You can adjust everything from the size to the color of the font.

3. In the **Font** drop-down list, choose the font to use on the selected text.

4. Add the attributes you want the font to have from the other options available.

    You can set the following options to change the appearance of a font:

    *   **Font style**. Most fonts are limited to Regular, **Bold**, *Italic*, and ***Bold Italic***.

- **Size**. The size of the font, measured in points. In case you're wondering—a point is equal to 0.01384 inches, which, at about 72 to the inch, is pretty small.

- **Underline**. Need I say more?

- **Color**. You'll have to use your imagination.

- **Effects**. You can create all kinds of effects with these options. Even things like ~~Strikethrough,~~ Double strikethrough, superscript, subscript, shadows, Embossing, Engraving, SMALL CAPS, ALL CAPS, and (if you could see it, it wouldn't be called Hidden, now would it?).

You can see the effect your changes are having on the selected text by checking out the **Preview** area at the bottom of the **Fo_n_t** tab.

A quick alternative to using the Font dialog box is to use the Formatting toolbar. Refer to Table 5.2 for a description of the character-formatting toolbar buttons.

TABLE 5.2 **Character-formatting buttons**

Toolbar Button	Effect	How to Use
Arial	Font	Highlight the character(s) and select the font to apply from this drop-down list.
14	Font size	Highlight the character(s) and change the font size by making a selection from the **Font Size** drop-down list.
B	Bold	Highlight the character(s) you want to bold and click this button.
I	Italic	Click this button to italicize the selected character(s).
U	Underline	Select the text to underline and click this button.

Quite a few shortcut keys are also available for character formatting.

Looking under the formatting hood

To see the exact formatting of a particular character, open the **Help** menu and choose **What's this?** Point to the character whose formatting you want to see, and click to display a text balloon showing all formatting details. Press Esc to go back to the normal pointer.

Printing a list of character-formatting shortcut keys

1. Open the **Help** menu and choose the **Contents and Index** command.

2. Click the **Index** tab and type keys in the first text box.

3. Double-click **shortcut keys** in the listing of topics under **keys** to open the Topics Found dialog box.

4. Double-click **Keys for formatting characters and paragraphs**.

5. Click the **Options** button and select **Print Topic** to print a listing of the shortcut keys.

Although character formatting can add impact and appeal to your document, it can just as easily add clutter and confusion if it's overdone, so be sure to use it judiciously. A good rule of thumb when using mixed font types is to limit yourself to three different types in the same document. The same goes for styles. Bold, italic, and underline are great for emphasizing text; how-ever, when used on every other word or phrase, the styles quickly lose their effectiveness.

Character Spacing

Character spacing is one of those formatting features that often gets overlooked. Everyone loves the glamour of fonts, with all their styles, colors, and special effects. By comparison, character spacing seems rather dull and uninteresting. Besides, Word takes care of it automatically, doesn't it? Yes, but . . .

It's true that Word puts a 3pt space between each letter to give your text a consistent appearance. However, at times, you want to squeeze more text in the same amount of space and other times you want to expand the existing text to fill up the space you have. This is when you'll appreciate the character-spacing tools Word offers. And just for the record, you can also do some character positioning with the character-spacing tools.

Using the character-spacing feature

1. Select the character(s), word, or block of text for which you want to change the spacing. Regardless of how much text

you choose, you must include at least one space. As a matter of fact, you can even change the spacing for a single space.

2. Open the **Format** menu and choose **Font** to open the Font dialog box.

3. Click the **Character Spacing** tab to view the character-spacing options (see Figure 5.10).

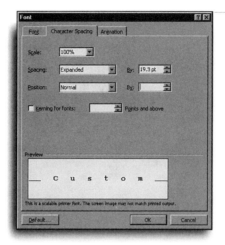

FIGURE 5.10

You can adjust the space between characters by as little as a tenth of a point at a time.

4. Set the spacing or positioning options you want.

The following options are available for your character-spacing and positioning pleasure:

- **Scale**. Increasing or decreasing the percentage in this option is a quick way to change the spacing and the width of the selected text at the same time. The height of the text is not affected, but spacing and width are changed proportionally.

- **Spacing**. Use **Spacing** to keep the characters the same size and change only the size of the spaces between characters. To increase the spaces, choose **Expanded**. To decrease the size of the spaces, choose **Condensed**. After you make your selection, indicate the amount of the change in the **By** spin box.

- **P**osition. You can have selected text appear above or below the baseline (the invisible line upon which each line of text sits). Select **Raised** if you want the text above the baseline and **Lowered** if you want the text below the baseline. Then indicate, in the **By** spin box, the amount by which to raise or lower it. Note that regardless of your paragraph-spacing settings, raising or lowering a word does not move the lines above or below it. Consequently, the text you are positioning begins to disappear as it moves into an adjacent line.

- **Kerning for fonts**. Kerning is a form of spacing that reduces the size of spaces between certain pairs of characters when you use a proportional font. For more on kerning, see the next section.

5. Click **OK** to save your changes and return to the active document.

Kerning

Avoiding spacing errors

Speaking of spaces, here's a tip you can use to ensure that when you cut and paste you don't end up with an extra space before a period or a missing space between two words. Open the **Tools** menu, choose **Options**, and click the **Edit** tab. Select the **Use smart cut and paste** check box. The next time you cut and paste, Word will watch out for the extra or missing spaces.

Although kerning is a technical printing term, the concept is actually pretty simple when you can visualize it. Some pairs of letters are shaped in such a way as to be able to fit closer together than others. For instance, the capital A and the capital W, when appearing together (WA or AW), are perfect for "snuggling." The same goes for a capital T and a lowercase y (Ty). Kerning takes such letter combinations and squeezes them together. Therefore, when you want to save room without distorting your text, use a proportional font and apply kerning.

However, if you are using a monospaced font (Courier is monospaced, for example), kerning has no effect. Monospaced fonts use the same amount of space for every character. In other words, the letter *w* is assigned the same amount of space as the letter *i*, even though the two are clearly not the same width. Proportional fonts, which do allow kerning, assign space on the basis of actual character size. Check out the following example to see the difference. Look closely and you'll see that the monospaced font characters don't always use all the space allotted them, whereas proportional font characters do.

M o n o s p a c e

P r o p o r t i o n a l

Animating Text

In addition to being able to dress up your fonts with styles and colors, you can also add animation to your text to really bring it to life. You can add blinking lights, marching ants, falling confetti, and more. Of course, this won't do much for your printed documents because the animations don't show up on hard copy, but it will add some pizzazz to the electronic versions.

Animating text

1. Highlight the text to animate.

2. Open the **Format** menu and choose **Font** to open the Font dialog box.

3. Click the **Animation** tab to view the animation options as shown in Figure 5.11.

FIGURE 5.11

Text animation is a good way to draw attention to important information.

4. Choose an animation from the **Animations** list. Check out the **Preview** window to see what the animation will look like.

5. Click **OK** to apply the animation and return to the active document.

Like other text formatting, animation should be used sparingly to ensure that it produces the maximum impact when you need it.

Viewing and Correcting Documents

Using Word document views

Working with multiple windows

Spell-checking your document

Grammar ~~ain't~~ isn't just for English majors

Using the Word thesaurus

Introducing Document Viewing and Correction

Word offers plenty of options for working with your documents, including the way you look at them and the way you keep them error free. Depending on the type of document you're creating and the work you're doing, you may find it helpful to use one of several Word views. However, no matter how many times you change your perspective, it won't eliminate your spelling or grammar errors. That's where Word's proofing tools come into play. You can use these handy tools to keep an eye on things while you type (alerting you to potential errors right away), or you can turn them off until you're ready to check the whole document at a later time.

Switching Document Views

Being able to view your document in more than a single way can be very helpful. For normal, everyday work, you'll probably do most of your work in the Normal view, which provides the most workspace and all the editing tools you need. If you want to keep a constant eye on how the document will look when printed, you'll want to use the Page Layout view to display your document precisely as the hard-copy version will appear. Those of you who are preparing documents to put on your Web site or on your intranet will want to use the Online Layout view.

Whatever you're doing, Word has a view for you. As with most Word features, switching between views can be accomplished in several ways. The quickest method is to use the document View buttons on the left side of the horizontal scrollbar as shown in Figure 6.1.

Even though they don't appear next to the menu items on the **View** menu, there are shortcut keys you can use to switch document views (except Online Layout):

Normal view	Alt+Ctrl+N
Page Layout view	Alt+Ctrl+P
Outline view	Alt+Ctrl+O
Print Preview	Alt+Ctrl+I

FIGURE 6.1

The document View buttons provide quick access to Word views.

1 Normal view

2 Online Layout view

3 Page Layout view

4 Outline view

You can also change document views by selecting **View** from the menu bar and choosing the view you want to switch to. If you are so inclined, you can even add View buttons to the toolbar of your choice.

SEE ALSO

➤ *To customize toolbars, see page 226*

Normal View

The Normal view is the default Word view and the one in which you will probably do the majority of your everyday word processing. It's the general-purpose view for typing, editing, and formatting your text. The document you're working on fills the entire document window so you can clearly see everything you're doing (see Figure 6.2).

One advantage of Normal view is speed. Unlike Page Layout, text layouts are not displayed, which means that editing and cursor movements are both quicker in Normal view. Another

FIGURE 6.2

The Normal view is great for most of your everyday word processing needs.

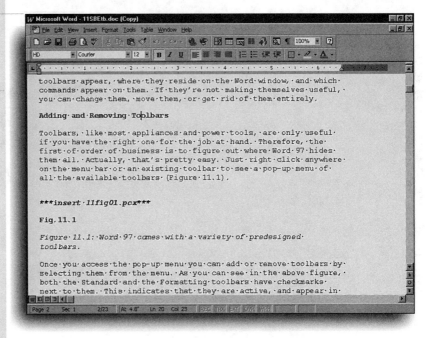

advantage is the capability to view the Styles area that shows the paragraph styles used in your document. The down side is that you cannot see headers, footers, page numbers, graphics, and other items that appear outside the body text.

Page Layout View

When you are extremely conscious of how your finished document will appear, you'll want to use the Page Layout view. Page Layout displays your document as the printed version will appear. Headers, columns, pictures, footnotes, and framed objects all appear in their proper locations (see Figure 6.3).

As soon as you insert a graphic into a document in any other view, Word automatically switches you to Page Layout so you can see the graphic where and how it will look in the printed document (color depends on your printer). As a matter of fact, Word automatically opens a document that contains graphics in the Page Layout view, regardless of which view you save it in.

One handy feature of the Page Layout view is the extra Zoom options that are available. In addition to the normal zoom

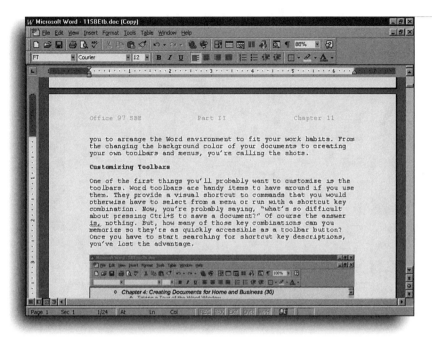

FIGURE 6.3

Page Layout view is a true
WYSIWYG (What You See Is
What You Get) view.

percentages and page width zoom available in other views, Page Layout offers both Whole Page and Many Page options. The Many Page option is great for checking the flow of text and graphics in a large document.

Using the Many Pages view feature

1. Open the **View** menu and choose **Zoom** to open the Zoom dialog box.

2. Click the button (looks like a computer monitor) just below the **Many Pages** option in the **Zoom to** section to open the **Many Pages** grid box as shown in Figure 6.4. Although, logically, you would think you'd have to click the **Many Pages** option first, you don't.

3. Hold down your left mouse button and drag the pointer across the grid to select the number of pages to display. An example of the number of pages chosen appears in the **Preview** area. The box below the Preview area shows how 12pt Times New Roman text will appear at the magnification resulting from your choice.

FIGURE 6.4

You can select from 1 to 24 pages per screen, using the **Many Pages** option.

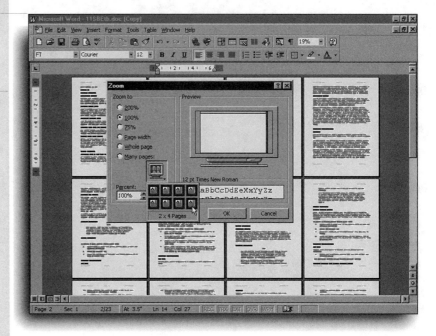

FIGURE 6.4

You can select from 1 to 24 pages per screen, using the **Many Pages** option.

4. Click **OK** to return to the active document and view it with the zoom selection in effect (see Figure 6.5).

You can also view multiple pages by dropping the zoom percentage to less than 30%. When you get down to 10%, you can see as many as 24 full pages onscreen.

One thing to note is that selecting a width that requires smaller pages may result in the actual grid being greater than the one originally selected. For example, selecting a 1×4 grid returns a 2×4 view, and a 2×6 grid becomes a 3×6 view. The reason for this is simple. No matter how many rows are displayed, the individual pages stay the same size, because to remain proportional the width automatically dictates the height.

Also, in case you haven't noticed, there's a zoom control drop-down list `100%` on the Standard toolbar that enables you to change zoom percentages no matter what view you're in. You can type in your own percentage or activate the drop-down list and select one of the preset percentages.

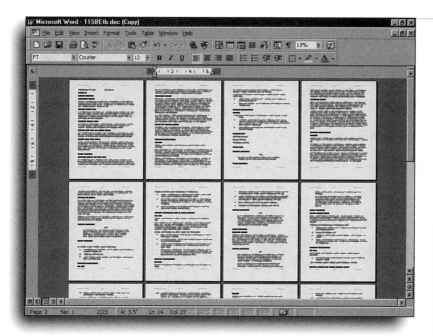

FIGURE 6.5
Although you can't read much in the Many Page view, you can get a good overview of how the whole document looks.

SEE ALSO
➤ *To learn more about zoom controls, see page 211*

Outline View

As you've probably already guessed, the Outline view is your best bet if you're going to create an outline. Although it leaves much to be desired as a full-fledged outliner, it will do the job. The Outline view enables you to see the structure of a document (see Figure 6.6).

The Outline view also enables you to reorganize topics by dragging them from one location to another. In addition, you can expand and collapse headings to show and hide subheadings.

In addition to dragging topics around in the Outline view, you can use the toolbar commands or the Tab and Shift+Tab keys to promote and demote headings.

Selective Copying of Outline Headings

I occasionally want to insert a copy of my outline, with only the level 1 or level 2 headings, into another document or an email

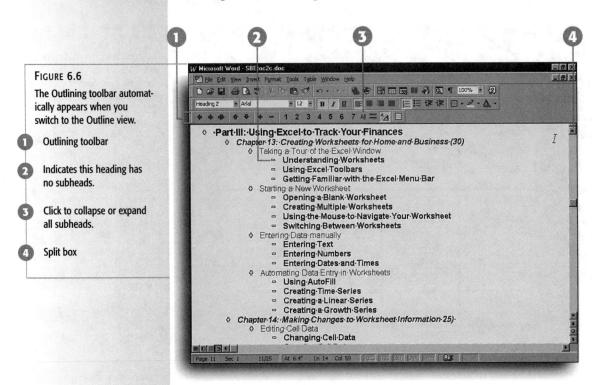

FIGURE 6.6

The Outlining toolbar automatically appears when you switch to the Outline view.

1. Outlining toolbar

2. Indicates this heading has no subheads.

3. Click to collapse or expand all subheads.

4. Split box

message. The problem is, there's no way to copy only certain headings—it's an all or nothing deal (unless I want to copy the particular headings one at a time—which I don't). A fairly simple solution is to create a table of contents from the outline, selecting only the heading(s) I want to copy, convert it to text, and then copy it wherever I want.

In the Outline view, place the insertion point where you want the table of contents created, and then open the **Insert** menu and choose **In**d**ex and Tables** to open the Index and Tables dialog box. Click the **Table of** **C**ontents tab. In the **Show lev-els** spin box, indicate the last heading you want to copy. If you only want level 1 headings, **Show levels** should be 1. If you want to include *only* level 4 headings, select 4 in **Show levels** and then click the **Options** button and delete the TOC level for headings 1, 2, and 3. Click **OK** until you return to the active document.

Select the new table of contents and press Ctrl+Shift+F9 to convert it to text. You can now copy it anywhere you want and treat it like normal text.

Online Layout View

New with Word 97, the Online view is designed to enable you to view documents as they will appear online. Text appears larger and wraps to fit the window. One thing to keep in mind is that this is not the way it will appear in the printed document. By default, the Document Map is automatically displayed, enabling you to navigate the document by any heading that the document contains. If your document does not contain headings in the built-in heading styles, it AutoFormats the document and uses any short paragraph that appears to be a heading (such as larger font, bold) in place of actual headings. Such is the case with my document, shown in Figure 6.7, that uses custom heading styles.

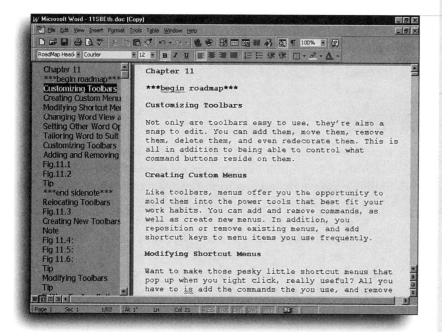

FIGURE 6.7

The Online view includes the Document Map for easy navigation.

Because the text in the Online view automatically wraps to fit the window regardless of how much you enlarge it, the Microsoft programmers decided to give us a little extra real estate by eliminating the horizontal scrollbar. That was very thoughtful of them; however, it drives me crazy every time I try to switch to another view and realize that the document view buttons are also gone! Yes, I know, I can go to View on the menu bar and select whatever view I want, but I like the buttons on the scrollbar.

To get them back all you have to do is open the **Tools** menu and choose **Options** to open the Options dialog box. Then click the **View** tab and place a check mark next to **Horizontal** scrollbar. Click **OK** to return to the active document and—voilà—the scrollbar and its document view buttons are back.

Print Preview

Before you print your document, take a quick trip to Print Preview and make sure everything looks the way you expected. You'll be very cranky if you print out a 50-page document only to find that you forgot to include the header or footer information you thought was there.

SEE ALSO

➤ For more information on Print Preview, see page 211

Full Screen

In addition to the "normal" views, you can choose the **View** menu and select **Full Screen** to explode the current document until it is the only thing onscreen. Everything, including the menu bar, toolbars (the one exception—Outline view), status bar, and scrollbars, disappears, except the document, and a one button toolbar that let's you close the Full Screen view. You can use Full Screen in any of the Word document views with the same results. The only variation is in the Outline view, which retains the Outlining toolbar even in Full Screen mode.

Working in Full Screen view is easy enough because you can still access the menu bar by moving your mouse pointer to the top of the screen. As soon as your pointer touches the top border of the document, the menu bar appears. Then move to the Menu title and click to open the menu. You can also add any toolbars you want by right-clicking on the menu bar and selecting the toolbar to display.

Navigating the Full Screen Document

Navigating through a Full Screen document can be a bit of a drag without the scrollbars available. Although you can't add scrollbars to the Full Screen view, you can do a couple of things to make navigation easier. Because the Standard toolbar has a number of commands you probably use quite frequently, you might as well have it available, so you can start by docking the Standard toolbar at the top of the window. Then add the Browse buttons and an AutoScroll button for easy navigating.

Access the menu bar at the top of the screen. Then right-click and select Standard. The Standard toolbar immediately appears at the top of the screen (the menu bar still slides down when you touch the border with your pointer). If you don't want to use the Standard toolbar, you can double-click the title bar of the Full Screen toolbar which will dock it at the top of the window. You can then perform the following operations by using the Full Screen toolbar instead of the Standard toolbar.

Now, double-click the blank area to the right of the last Standard toolbar button to open the Customize dialog box. Click the **Commands** tab and select **All Commands** from the **Categories** list box. In the **Commands** list, scroll down and find **AutoScroll**. Drag it to the end of the Standard toolbar, and drop it when you see the vertical I-beam indicating the insertion point for the new button. Do the same thing for the BrowsePrev, BrowseSet, and BrowseNext buttons. Click **Close** to return to the active document.

SEE ALSO

➤ *For tips on using the browse buttons, see page 45*

Mastering Document View

As your task increases in size, you may find that what you really need is a series of smaller documents that comprise a larger document. This is where the Master Document view comes into play. It's great for books, large catalogs, extensive reports that cover multiple subjects, and other documents that become unwieldy as they grow.

You can build an outline and create subdocuments from any of the headings or subheadings you choose. When you turn off the Master Document view, the document returns to its previous state, with subdocuments divided by continuous section breaks.

Using the Window Menu Views

Sometimes it's not a new view you need but multiple views of either the same document or different documents. Transferring information from one document to another is so much easier if you open both documents and arrange them onscreen together. Or, how about comparing different parts of the same document to ensure you're not repeating the same information? By taking advantage of the window views, you can arrange multiple documents on the screen at once, split the existing document in two, or create a new window that contains a clone of the active document.

Split Window

The **Split** command does just that—it splits the current window in two. It's great for copying or moving text from one section of a long document to another section or for comparing different parts of the same document.

Splitting the active document

1. Open or switch to the document you want to split.

2. Open the **Window** menu and choose **Split** from the menu bar to activate the split bar. As you move your mouse pointer up and down, the split bar moves with it.

3. Position the split bar where you want the document to split, and click to create two separate views of the document as shown in Figure 6.8.

Even though it appears that you have two separate documents, keep in mind that it is really two views of one document. Therefore, any changes you make to either view affect the document, and will be reflected in the other window.

To increase or decrease the size of the windows, place your pointer on the top border of the bottom window. When the pointer turns into a pair of vertical lines with an up-and-down

Quickly splitting a Window

You can also split a window by double-clicking the Split box (the small horizontal bar that looks like a thick hyphen) that appears directly above the up arrow on the vertical scrollbar.

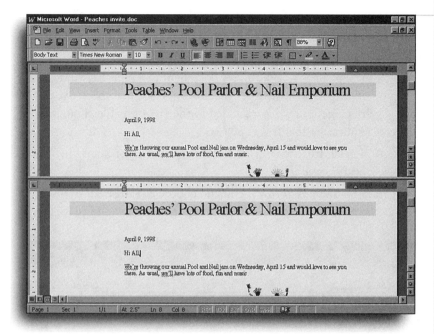

FIGURE 6.8
Splitting a document
provides two views of the
same document.

arrow, drag the split bar in either direction to resize the windows. To close the split, double-click the top border of the bottom window.

New Window

If you have an extremely long document, you may find that you want to cut and paste information from a number of different locations. Or perhaps you have a document that's been worked on by several people and you want to view each person's contribution simultaneously to see how well the writing styles are going to match. In either case, the Split feature discussed in the previous section won't work. You need to see more than two views, which is the limit of the split window.

With the New Window feature it's pretty easy to open as many copies of the current document as you need.

Using the New Window feature

1. Open or switch to the document you want to view.

2. Minimize all other open documents. This step is not necessary to create multiple copies of the active document;

however, it will keep the other documents from displaying onscreen.

3. Open the **Window** menu and choose **New Window** to create a copy of the active document in a separate window. Take a look at the title bar, and you'll see that the active document now has :2 added to the end of its filename, indicating that it is copy two.

4. Repeat this step for the number of copies you want opened at the same time.

5. Open the **Window** menu and choose **Arrange All** to display all the new windows simultaneously, as shown in Figure 6.9.

FIGURE 6.9

With the New Window feature, you can create multiple copies of the document. **Arrange All** puts them on the screen simultaneously.

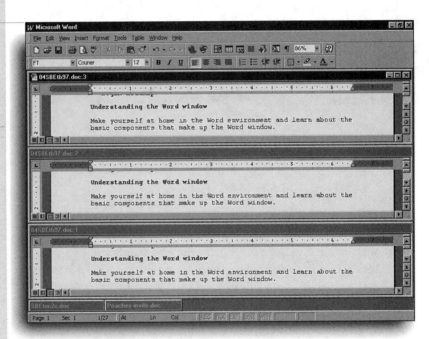

Arrange All

As you saw in the previous section, the **Arrange All** command resizes all open, non-minimized windows and displays them onscreen at the same time. This is handy, not only for working with new windows of the same document but also for comparing or transferring information between entirely different documents.

Any time you use the **Arrange All** command, you can switch between the visible documents by clicking one of them to make it the active document. You can also use some shortcut keys to work with open windows, as shown in Table 6.1.

TABLE 6.1   Shortcut keys for working with Word windows

Function	Shortcut Key
Switch to next window	Ctrl+F6
Switch to previous window	Ctrl+Shift+F6
Restore (after maximizing) active window	Ctrl+F5
Close active window	Ctrl+W
Maximize active window	Ctrl+F10

I'm so used to pressing Alt+Tab to switch between open applications in Windows 95 that I find myself automatically hitting Alt+Tab to switch between open documents in Word 97. Of course, it doesn't work; however, I found a great way to switch between documents and take advantage of my tendency to reach for Alt+Tab. I added a shortcut key to the **Next Window** command that utilizes the apostrophe/tilde key above the Tab key. Now when I reach for Alt+Tab and realize my mistake, all I have to do is move my middle finger from the Tab key and press the key to cycle through open Word docs.

Using the shortcut keys to cycle through the open documents takes you through those that are minimized as well as the ones that are displayed onscreen. It won't open the minimized documents, but it will make them active until you move to the next one. You should also be aware that although the Word Help file claims Ctrl+F9 will minimize the open window, the only thing it does for me is insert a field in the active document.

SEE ALSO

➤ *To learn more about creating shortcut keys, see page 232*

Using the Word Proofing Tools

Now that you can see your document any which way you choose, how does it look? Oops, got a few misspellings, I'll bet, and maybe a grammatical error or two. Unless you had your automatic proofing tools turned on, that is—in which case, Word alerted you immediately to the fact that it found something it didn't like, giving you the opportunity to make the corrections as you went.

The beauty of the Word proofing tools is how they make us look as though we actually stayed awake during our 9th grade English classes. From providing spell checking on-the-fly to reminding you that run-on sentences are poor writing, the proofing tools enable you to create professional-looking and -sounding documents without getting a degree in English.

The way Word alerts you to the fact that you have spelling errors in your document is by underlining them with a red wavy underline. However, to see the red wavy underline, you must have a couple of options set in the **Spelling & Grammar** tab of the Options dialog box. Open the Options dialog box by choosing the **Tools** menu and selecting **Options**. The **Check spelling as you type** option must be enabled (checked) and the **Hide spelling errors in this document** option must be disabled (unchecked).

Grammar-checking errors are handled in a similar fashion, except they appear with a wavy green underline. They also require options to be set in the Options dialog box. You'll find them in the **Grammar** section of the **Spelling & Grammar** tab.

Automate Spell Checking with AutoCorrect

I hate to admit it, but I love AutoCorrect. I tend to type fast and mangle simple words like *teh*, *yuo*, and *adn*. Fortunately Word knows I really mean to type *the*, *you*, and *and*, so it automatically corrects them without any prompting from me. That is Auto-Correct in action. AutoCorrect starts out with a sizable list of commonly misspelled words, to which you can add more of your own.

Creating AutoCorrect entries

1. Open the **Tools** menu and choose **AutoCorrect** to open the AutoCorrect dialog box as shown in Figure 6.10.

FIGURE 6.10

You can create AutoCorrect entries and set customization options on the **AutoCorrect** tab.

2. Enter the misspelling or common typing error in the **Replace** text box.

3. Tab to the **With** text box and enter the correct word or phrase with which to replace the misspelling. If, before you open the AutoCorrect dialog box, you select the text (correct version) you want to use for an AutoCorrect entry, Word will insert it in the **With** text box automatically.

4. Click **Add** to save the new entry.

5. Click **OK** to return to the active document.

The next time you misspell or mistype the new entry, Auto-Correct will automatically make the correction for you. As much as I love AutoCorrect, one thing about it drives me nuts—the fact that I have to fight to convince it that something I've typed is not a mistake. For example, as soon as I typed *teh* in the opening paragraph as an example of a common typing error, AutoCorrect immediately corrected it. However, this is one time I didn't want it corrected. Well, you can't just backspace and "correct" it because AutoCorrect will keep re-correcting it. What you *can* do is move your cursor back to the word, make the correction, and

AutoCorrect the easy way

The quickest way to add an AutoCorrect entry is to right-click on a misspelled word, select AutoCorrect from the shortcut menu that appears, and then select the correct spelling from the list of suggestions. A new AutoCorrect entry is automatically created.

then return the cursor to the place in your document where you left off, but that's a pain!

So what's the solution? Thankfully, it's pretty simple—just use **Undo**. As soon as AutoCorrect makes the automatic correction, press Ctrl+Z. **Undo** returns it to its pre-AutoCorrect state, and you can continue typing.

You can even use the AutoCorrect feature to create your own typing "shorthand." Long words or phrases that you type frequently can be replaced by an abbreviated version that you add as an AutoCorrect entry. Suppose you're writing a report on the plant life in the Arizona desert, and you have a lot to say about the night-blooming *cereus cacti* that grow there. Rather than type "night-blooming cereus" each time you refer to the plants, you might create an AutoCorrect entry that replaces *nb* with night-blooming cereus.

Adding AutoCorrect entries while correcting misspellings

1. Right-click the misspelled word to open the spelling shortcut menu as shown in Figure 6.11.

FIGURE 6.11

In addition to correcting, ignoring, and adding the word, you can also create an AutoCorrect entry from the spelling shortcut menu.

2. Click **AutoCorrect** to see the list of suggested spellings.

3. Select the correct spelling to create an AutoCorrect entry that replaces the misspelled word with the selected suggested spelling.

This operation not only creates the AutoCorrect entry but also corrects the currently misspelled word in your document. The only limitation to this method of creating an AutoCorrect entry is that you cannot type in a replacement word. If the word you need doesn't appear on the suggested list, you're out of luck and will have to use the first procedure I outlined.

Another handy use of AutoCorrect is to take care of words that require unusual capitalization, such as AutoCorrect. I got tired of going back and capitalizing it each time I forgot, so I created an AutoCorrect entry that replaces the lowercase version with the correctly capitalized version.

Setting AutoCorrect Options

AutoCorrect will also take care of a number of common capital-ization errors if you set the correct options. From automatically capitalizing the first letter of a sentence to converting the case when you accidentally hit the Caps Lock key and begin typing, you'll find these options quite helpful.

The AutoCorrect options include

- **Correct TWo INitial CApitals**. If you're a fast typist, you've undoubtedly experienced the situation where you've typed the second letter of a capitalized word before letting go of the Shift key. The result is two capitalized letters. Selecting the **Correct TWo INitial CApitals** option auto-matically converts a second capital to lowercase.

- **Capitalize first letter of sentences**. If you're a little sloppy about capitalizing the first word of a new sentence, don't worry. This option will take care of it for you. The first word it sees following a period is automatically capitalized.

- **Capitalize names of days**. That's right, the names of days are supposed to be capitalized. I forget all the time, but AutoCorrect never does, as long as I have this option turned on.

- **Correct accidental usage of cAPS LOCK key**. How many times are you zipping along when you reach for the Tab key or Shift key and hit the Caps Lock instead? The result, while being mildly entertaining, is not generally considered acceptable capitalization. This option corrects the case and turns off the Caps Lock.

- **Replace text as you type**. If you don't want AutoCorrect to automatically make corrections (based on the list of AutoCorrect entries) as you type, turn this one off.

All these options are turned on by default; therefore, you won't have to change them unless you want to turn them off.

Don't replace one mistake with another

When you create AutoCorrect entries, be sure your common misspelling or abbreviated ver-sion is not a word in its own right. I have a tendency to type `tow` when I really mean `two`, but I can't create an AutoCorrect entry, or else when I type `"I had to tow my car to the garage"` it will become `"I had to two my car to the garage."` Exchanging one mistake for another is not a great way to polish up your work.

Turning AutoCorrect options on and off

1. Open the **T**ools menu and choose **AutoCorrect** to open the AutoCorrect dialog box.

2. Click the **AutoCorrect** tab.

3. Add (on) or remove (off) the check mark next to the option you want to change.

4. Click **OK** to save the changes and return to the active document.

The options take effect as soon as you return to the current document.

Exceptions to the AutoCorrect Rule

Sometimes the capitalization rules that work most of the time just don't fit the situation at hand. When you run into one of these cases, AutoCorrect can be more of an annoyance than a help. You can bet that CDnow and CDworld go crazy if they use Word to create any of their marketing literature. Every time they type the business name, the AutoCorrect INitial CAps feature will change their respective names to Cdnow and Cdworld. Not quite the same, is it?

Another problem you may encounter is typing a word or abbreviation that requires a period before you get to the end of a sentence. Inc., co., etc., are a few examples for which Microsoft has already created AutoCorrect exceptions. Suppose you have esquire attached to your name and you want to use esq. Instead. Well, what happens is what you see in the preceding sentence. Instead was automatically capitalized because Word spotted the period at the end of esq and assumed the next word was the beginning of a new sentence.

If you run into any problems like this, you can eliminate them by creating your own AutoCorrect exceptions.

Creating AutoCorrect exceptions

1. Open the **T**ools menu and choose **AutoCorrect** to open the AutoCorrect dialog box.

2. Click the **Exceptions** button to open the AutoCorrect Exceptions dialog box shown in Figure 6.12

FIGURE 6.12
Creating AutoCorrect exceptions.

3. Select the tab appropriate to the exception you want to record.

4. In the text box, enter the text that you want AutoCorrect to ignore. For **First Letter**, the text box is **D<u>o</u>n't capitalize after** (by the way, you don't have to enter the period). For **INitial CAps**, it's **D<u>o</u>n't correct**.

5. Click **<u>A</u>dd** to attach the new abbreviation or word to the list.

6. Click **OK** to return to the AutoCorrect dialog box, and click **OK** again to return to the active document.

All in all, AutoCorrect is a very nice feature that, used properly, can save you a lot of time, effort, and embarrassing mistakes.

Spell Checking in Word

It's hard to recall life before automatic spell checking. Maybe I just don't want to recall those hours of poring over a large document, word for word, catching every minor typo and spelling error. Whatever the reason, I'm sure glad that I've got a word processor that looks over my shoulder and catches the majority of those pesky little mistakes my fingers make.

The Word spell checking tool is pretty smart, always available, and flexible enough to do things your way. It will check your spelling as you go or wait until you give the command. It enables you to add new spellings, proper names, and anything else you want in a custom dictionary. You can even create as many different custom dictionaries as you want.

How **A<u>u</u>tomatically add words to list** really works

The Word Help file informs you that the **A<u>u</u>tomatically add words to list** option in the AutoCorrect Exceptions dialog box works only if you back-space and change the capitalization after AutoCorrect "corrects" it. In reality, it only creates an exception if you use the **Undo** feature (Ctrl+Z) to change it back.

Using the Spell Checker

The default setting for the Word spell check feature is to check your document automatically as you type. Consequently, as you type, you'll probably see an occasional word with a red squiggly line under it, indicating that Word can't find it in its main dictionary and therefore considers it misspelled.

One way to make your spell checking a little easier is to tell Word not to proof selected text such as one-time lists of names, foreign words, or other items that will probably be seen as misspelled. Highlight the text you want Word to skip, open the **Tools** menu, point to **Language**, and choose the **Set Language** command to open the Language dialog box. Scroll to the top of the **Mark Selected text as** list until you find **(no proofing)**. Select it and click **OK**. The next time the spelling and grammar checker hits that block of text, it will completely ignore it.

Correcting a misspelled word

1. Place the insertion point anywhere on the word.
2. Right-click to open the spelling shortcut menu as shown in Figure 6.13.

FIGURE 6.13

The Word spell checker offers you suggestions for corrections, as well as other options.

3. Select the correct spelling from the list of suggestions, or use one of the other options:

   - **Ignore All**. If the word is spelled correctly and you don't want to change it, select **Ignore All**. In addition to this instance, Word will ignore all other occurrences of this spelling {in this document only), even if you close and re-open the document.

   - **Add**. If the spelling is correct and just missing from the Word dictionary, or if it's a proper name or other word you intend to use regularly, you'll probably want to add it to the custom dictionary. Click **Add** and Word will consider it correctly spelled the next time it encounters the word. By the way, be careful not to accidentally add truly misspelled words to the dictionary—Word will always think they are correct.

- **AutoCorrect**. Use this menu item to add the current word as an AutoCorrect entry. See the section on AutoCorrect earlier in this chapter.

- **Spelling**. If you want to do a full spell check, choose this item. The rest of the document from this word forward will be examined for spelling errors.

If none of the suggestions or options is suitable, click anywhere on the document to close the shortcut menu and return to the document. Move to the word in question and make the necessary change by hand.

To turn off automatic spell checking, from the **Tools** menu choose **Options**, open the **Spelling & Grammar** tab, and deselect the **Check spelling as you type** option.

Checking spelling for an entire document

1. Press Ctrl+Home to move to the beginning of the document.

2. Open the **Tools** menu and choose **Spelling and Grammar** to start the spelling and grammar check. You can also click the Spelling and Grammar button ![ABC check] on the Standard toolbar.

3. As soon as Word encounters its first error (of either kind), it opens the Spelling and Grammar dialog box as shown in Figure 6.14.

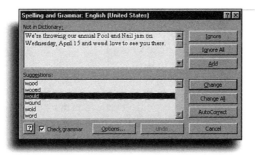

FIGURE **6.14**

The Spelling and Grammar dialog box highlights the error and places it in context so you can make an informed decision.

4. Select from the choices available in the dialog box.

Your spelling and grammar choices include

- **Ignore**. Click **Ignore** to leave the current instance as is but catch any additional occurrences of this spelling. When you make a manual change to the highlighted (red) word, this button becomes **Undo Edit**. Click it if you want to undo whatever change you made to the highlighted word. The button immediately reverts to **Ignore**.

- **Ignore All**. After you click this button, Word ignores all instances of this spelling it finds in this document.

- **Add**. Click this to add the word to the custom dictionary.

- **Change**. To change only this instance of the word, select a word from the **Suggestions** list box and click **Change**. You can also manually correct the highlighted word in the **Not in Dictionary** text box and click the **Change** button. If Word doesn't recognize the new manual spelling you enter, it warns you.

- **Change All**. This works the same as the **Change** option, except it changes every instance of the word it encounters in this document.

- **AutoCorrect**. Use this option to create an AutoCorrect entry for the highlighted word.

- **Check grammar**. If you don't want to conduct a grammar check along with the spell check, deselect this option.

- **Options**. To open the Spelling and Grammar options dialog box (identical to the Spelling & Grammar tab of the Options dialog box), click this button. Here you can change many of the basic spelling and grammar settings.

- **Undo**. Only available after you've taken at least one spelling or grammar action, this button enables you to reverse the previous actions one at a time, whether you made a correction or chose **Ignore**.

5. Repeat step 4 until you reach the end of the document.

6. When the spelling and grammar check is complete, Word informs you of the fact and requires you to acknowledge it by clicking **OK**.

If at any time during the spell check you want to stop the operation, click the **Close** button to return to the active document.

Creating Custom Dictionaries

Almost every profession has its own jargon and acronyms that are complete gibberish to the rest of the world. Consequently, the main Word spelling dictionary is only effective when used on general documents. If you do any kind of work that requires a specialized vocabulary—from plumbing to nuclear physics— you'll want to create your own custom dictionary to use when creating documents pertaining to your specialty.

Creating a custom dictionary

1. Open the **T**ools menu, choose **O**ptions to open the Options dialog box, and click the **Spelling & Grammar** tab.

2. Click the **Dictionaries** button to open the Custom Dictionaries dialog box as shown in Figure 6.15.

FIGURE 6.15

You can add, remove, and edit custom dictionaries in the Custom Dictionaries dialog box.

3. Click **New** to open the Create a custom dictionary dialog box.

4. Enter a name for the new dictionary and click **Save** to return to the Custom Dictionaries dialog box, where the new dictionary now appears in the **Custom dictionaries** list.

5. Click **OK** to return to the **Spelling & Grammar** tab, and click **OK** again to return to the active document.

You can add words to a custom dictionary by selecting it from the **Custom dictionary** drop-down list on the **Spelling & Grammar** tab before performing a spell check. Or, you can add words to it directly by opening it and typing them in. To do that, from the **Tools** menu, choose **Options**, and then select **Dictionaries** from the **Spelling & Grammar** tab. Highlight the desired dictionary and click **Edit** to open the dictionary. Type the new words in, one per line, and save the dictionary as you would any other Word document.

Setting Spell Checking Options

Everywhere you look, Word has options. Well, spell checking is no exception. To change the way Word handles some of the spell checking operations, open the **Tools** menu, choose **Options**, and click the **Spelling & Grammar** tab to access the spelling options as shown in Figure 6.16.

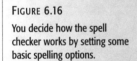

FIGURE 6.16

You decide how the spell checker works by setting some basic spelling options.

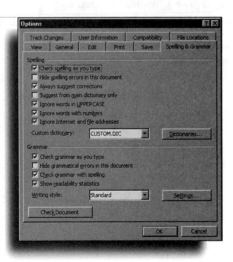

The spelling options you'll find on the Spelling & Grammar tab include

- **Check spelling as you type**. If you don't want Word looking over your shoulder as you type, deselect this one.

Otherwise it will nudge you each time it sees a typo, by putting a red squiggly line under it.

- **Hide spelling errors in this document**. Only available while the first option is enabled, this one allows you to hide the red squiggly line. If you enable it later, the red lines reappear.

- **Always suggest corrections**. If you don't want Word to offer suggestions when it encounters a word it doesn't recognize, deselect this option.

- **Suggest from main dictionary only**. Word automatically checks all dictionaries and offers suggestions for probable misspellings. If you enable this option, Word ignores the custom dictionaries and only make suggestions from the main dictionary.

- **Ignore words in UPPERCASE**. Type a word in uppercase letters, and Word accepts it as spelled correctly when you have this option enabled.

- **Ignore words with numbers**. Check this one, and the spell checker disregards any word that contains numbers.

- **Ignore Internet and file addresses**. Internet and file addresses are beyond the scope of any spell checker (unless you add them to a custom dictionary). Check this and Word ignores them all.

- **Custom dictionary**. From the drop-down list, select the custom dictionary to which you want to add words during a spell check.

- **Dictionaries**. Click to access the Custom Dictionaries dialog box where you can add, edit, and remove custom dictionaries.

- **Recheck Document** (or **Check Document** if you haven't yet run a spell check). This one's way down at the bottom, under the **Grammar** options. Use it to recheck the document with the new settings you've established.

After you set your options, click **OK** to return to the active document.

Getting Good Grammar

Grammar is one of those things that seems to confuse most people. I know it's got me stymied half the time. (Hmmm, I suppose that's not the kind of thing a writer should be putting into print, but it's true.) Sure, I know the basics—it is I, not it is me; ain't may be in the dictionary, but it still ain't good form to use it; sentence fragments and run-on sentences are not signs of good grammar. But who can remember where every comma is supposed to go? And what *is* a relative clause anyway? Oops, I guess you're really not supposed to start a sentence with AND, are you?

Running the grammar checker

1. Open the **Tools** menu and choose **Spelling and Grammar** to start the Spelling and Grammar check. Word insists on checking spelling during the grammar check, so you will be doing both, but we'll discuss only the grammar errors here. As soon as a possible grammar error is encountered, the Grammar dialog box appears with the "error" highlighted in green.

2. Click the button on the dialog box that corresponds to the action you want to take.

    Your choices are

    -   **Ignore**. Click this button to ignore the current instance of the "error." If you leave the dialog box open, clicking anywhere in the active document changes this button to Resume. Click it to start the grammar check again.

    -   **Ignore All**. Clicking this option ignores the current error and all other errors of the same type in the document.

    -   **Next Sentence**. Immediately moves to the next grammar error. Unlike the **Change** button, the **Next Sentence** button ignores any additional grammatical errors introduced by a manual change you make.

    -   **Change**. Either accept the suggested correction, or make the change manually and click **Change** to continue. If your manual change contains any questionable grammar, the grammar checker stops and points it out.

Perform a grammar check only

If you want to be able to run a grammar check without doing a spell check at the same time, add the Grammar command to one of your favorite toolbars or menus. Double-click a blank spot on the toolbar area to open the Customize dialog box and click the **Commands** tab. In the **Categories** list, select **Tools**. Then drag the **Grammar** command to the toolbar or menu of your choice, and drop it where you want it (wait till you see the bold I-beam).

- **Options**. Click to open the Spelling & Grammar options dialog box.

- **Undo**. Reverses previous actions, one at a time.

3. Repeat the process until the check is complete. Then click **OK** to return to the active document.

To stop the spelling and grammar check before it finishes and return to the active document, click **Close**.

Setting the Grammar Rules

One of the nice things about the Word grammar checker is that it offers you quite a bit of flexibility in determining how you define good grammar, as well as in how the checking is done. By setting the grammar options, you can control which style is used when the proofing is done, and even create your own custom style. To set the grammar options, open the **Tools** menu, choose **Options** to open the Options dialog box, and click the **Spelling & Grammar** tab.

The following grammar options are available:

- **Check grammar as you type**. Just like the spelling option of the same name, this one looks over your shoulder as you type.

- **Hide grammatical errors in this document**. If you don't want to see those squiggly green lines under your grammatical "errors," click this option. It's available only if the first option is enabled.

- **Check grammar with spelling**. Deselect this option to disable the automatic grammar check when you select the **Tools** menu and choose **Spelling and Grammar.**

- **Show readability statistics**. If you want to see how many words, sentences, or paragraphs your document contains, click this one. It will also give you a readability score based on the Flesch Reading Ease Standard and the Flesch-Kincaid Grade Level Standard.

- **Writing style**. Select from casual to technical to determine the level of grammar checking done. The available styles include Casual, Standard, Formal, Technical, and Custom.

■ **Se_t_tings**. To customize the preset styles or create your own custom style, click this button.

After setting your options, click **OK** to return to the document or **Reche_c_k Document** to run the grammar check with the new settings in place.

Customizing the grammar styles

1. Open the **_T_ools** menu, choose **_O_ptions** to open the Options dialog box, and click the **Spelling & Grammar** tab.

2. Click the **Se_t_tings** button to open the Grammar Settings dialog box as shown in Figure 6.17.

FIGURE 6.17

With Grammar Settings, you make up the grammar rules Word lives by.

3. Select the style to customize from the **_W_riting style** drop-down list.

4. Enable the **Grammar and style _o_ptions** you want to use during checking, by placing a check mark next to them. To disable an option, deselect it.

   For a description of each of the grammar style options, open the **_H_elp** menu and choose **_C_ontents and Index** to open the Help Topics dialog box. Click the **Index** tab and type gr in the first text box. This brings up **grammar checking** in the index entry window. Double-click on **options**. In the Topics Found dialog box, double-click **Grammar and writing style options**.

5. Move to the **Require** section and choose the desired setting for each option from its drop-down list.

6. Click **OK** to save the new settings and return to the **Spelling & Grammar** tab.

7. Click **OK** to return to the active document.

If, after making changes to the existing styles, you decide you want to return them to their original state, you can use the **Reset All** button in the Grammar Settings dialog box.

Using the Word Thesaurus

The success of a piece of writing is not determined by the number or size of the words you use but by the quality of the words. It doesn't matter whether it's a budget report or a fantasy (there is a difference, right?)—if you want to get your writing read, make it understandable and interesting. One of the best ways to do this is by choosing your words carefully.

This is where Word's *thesaurus* comes in handy. It contains a slew of synonyms for thousands of words. Whenever you type a word that doesn't feel or sound right, fire up the thesaurus and see what Word has to offer for a replacement (stand in, surrogate, substitute, proxy, alternate . . .).

Using the thesaurus

1. Place the cursor on the word for which you want to find a synonym.

2. Press Shift+F7 to open the Thesaurus dialog box as shown in Figure 6.18. From the **Tools** menu you can also choose **Language** and then select **Thesaurus** from the **Language** submenu.

FIGURE 6.18

Select a suitable synonym from the Word thesaurus.

3. Select the definition from the **Meanings** list box that most closely matches the intended use of the word.

4. Choose a synonym from the **Replace with Synonym** list box.

5. Click **Look Up** to see synonyms for the selected synonym. You can keep this up indefinitely. When you finally discover an acceptable synonym, move to step 6.

   You can also type a word in the **Replace with Synonym** text box and click **Look Up** to search for a synonym.

6. Click **Replace** to substitute the selected synonym for the original word and return to the active document.

7. If you don't find a suitable synonym, you can close the thesaurus and return to your document by clicking **Cancel**.

At any point in your search for synonyms, clicking the **Previous** button returns you to the last set of synonyms you viewed.

If you use all three of the Word 97 proofing tools, you'll end up with documents that even your 9th grade English teacher would approve of.

Organizing Information in Tables and Lists

Working with tables

Editing a table

Formatting tables

Using AutoFormat

Sorting and calculating in tables

Using numbered and bulleted lists

Introducing Tables and Lists

The way you present information has a significant impact on how useful it becomes to the reader of your documents. Some information needs to be presented in full detail so it can be scrutinized, analyzed, and given the third degree. Other information just needs to be thrown in a lineup so your reader can make a quick identification. When presenting the latter type, you can take advantage of a couple of Word features that will make the information step forward and let the reader have a good look at it. You can use tables, numbered lists, and bulleted lists to present information in a straightforward, easy-to-follow manner. Even complex information can be made easier to understand when you utilize one of these features.

Working with Tables

Tables are those handy word processing gadgets that look, feel, and—to a limited extent—act like spreadsheets. They have rows and columns like a spreadsheet, contain cells just like a spreadsheet, and even do simple mathematical calculations for you. All that having been said, let's be clear: although tables have certain attributes in common with spreadsheets, they are not spreadsheets. Their main purpose in life is not to crunch numbers but rather to present information in a structured manner for easy identification, as you can see in Table 7.1.

TABLE 7.1   A table and spreadsheet comparison

Feature	Word 97 Table	Excel 97 Spreadsheet
Columns	63 maximum	256 maximum
Rows	32,767 maximum	65,536 maximum
Cells	2,064,321 maximum	16,777,216 maximum
PivotTables	No	Yes
Calculation	Yes	Yes
Charts	No	Yes

SEE ALSO

➤ *To learn more about spreadsheets, see page 256*

Creating a Table

If you like the idea of a table and you're dying to jump in and
create your own, I've got good news for you—it's as easy as
falling off your diet. To make it even more useful, you can use
several different methods to build your tables. For a quick down-
and-dirty table, you can use the Insert Table button on the
Standard toolbar. For the graphically inclined, there is the Draw
Table command. Finally, for those large tables for which you
have the exact dimensions, the **Insert Table** menu command is
just the ticket.

Inserting a Table

Creating a table with the Insert Table button

1. Open your Word document and place the cursor at the
   point in your document where you want to insert the table.

2. Click the Insert Table button 🔳 to open the row and column grid shown in Figure 7.1.

FIGURE 7.1
Highlight the desired number
of columns and rows to create
your table.

3. Hold the left mouse button down and drag the pointer over
   the grid to highlight the exact number of columns and rows
   to include in the table.

4. Release the left mouse button when your selection matches
   the dimensions of the table you want to create. The table is
   immediately inserted in your document at the cursor.

But what do you do if you need a table that's larger than the
4×5 grid that appears when you click the Insert Table button?
Well, you've got two choices—either keep dragging your mouse
pointer to extend the size of the grid or use the **Insert Table**
command from the **Table** menu. Extending the size of the grid
is best used for relatively small tables because the grid will not

extend beyond the borders of the document window. The **T_able** menu's **Insert Table** command, on the other hand, provides a dialog box into which you can enter the number of rows and columns to include in your table.

Using the T_able menu's _Insert Table command to construct your table

1. Open your Word document and place the cursor at the point where you want the table inserted.

2. Open the **T_able** menu and select **_Insert Table** to open the Insert Table dialog box shown in Figure 7.2.

FIGURE 7.2
You can enter the precise dimensions of your table in the Insert Table dialog box.

3. Enter in the spin boxes the number of columns and rows you want to include in the new table. You can either type in the numbers or use the arrow buttons to increase (up) or decrease (down) the numbers.

4. Tab to the **Column _width** spin box and enter the desired width of each column. If you accept the default width of **Auto**, the columns will be the size necessary to fit the table within the margins set for the page. In other words, if you have three columns and six inches of usable document space within the page margins, each column will be two inches wide.

5. Click the **_AutoFormat** button if you want to use one of the predesigned table formats. When you're finished making your choices, click **OK** to return to the Insert Table dialog box. For more information on **_AutoFormat**, see the "Using AutoFormat" section later in this chapter.

6. Click **OK** to create the new table.

The finished product is a table of the dimensions you specified, at the location you indicated.

What _Insert Table commands don't do

Although both **Insert Table** commands produce quick tables, there is one thing they don't allow you to do–vary the width of different columns or the height of different rows. To do that you have to format them after you create the table.

Drawing a Table

A better alternative is to use the **D̲raw Table** command, which enables you to literally draw a table of the dimensions you desire. It really comes in handy for designing forms with unique column and row requirements, such as an invoice form or purchase order form.

Using D̲raw Table to create a table

1. Open the Word document in which you want to insert the new table.

2. Position the insertion point at the location for the new table.

3. Open the **Ta̲ble** menu and choose **D̲raw Table** to activate the Draw Table tool and display the Tables and Borders toolbar (see Figure 7.3).

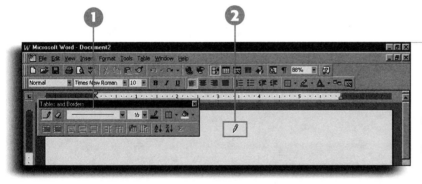

FIGURE 7.3

Your mouse pointer changes to a pencil when you choose **Draw Table**.

1. Tables and Borders toolbar

2. Mouse pointer/Table Drawing tool

4. Position the mouse pointer/Table Drawing tool where you want the top-left corner of the new table to appear.

5. Click and hold the left mouse button while dragging the pointer to create the outside border of the new table. The line style for the border, which appears as soon as you start dragging, is a dotted or broken line (see Figure 7.4).

6. Position the mouse pointer/Table Drawing tool on any of the four sides of the table, at the point where you want to create a row or column. Press the left button and drag to the opposite side. A straight line appears, creating the new row or column border.

Creating a full-page table

When I'm building a table or a form that will take up the entire page, I find it easier to work on if I switch to Page Layout view and select **Whole Page** from the Zoom drop-down list on the Standard toolbar. I then dock the Tables and Borders toolbar off to one side (just drag it all the way to the side of the document window and let it go) to get it out of the way. Now I can see exactly what I'm doing.

FIGURE 7.4

Make the outside border of
the table as large or small as
you need.

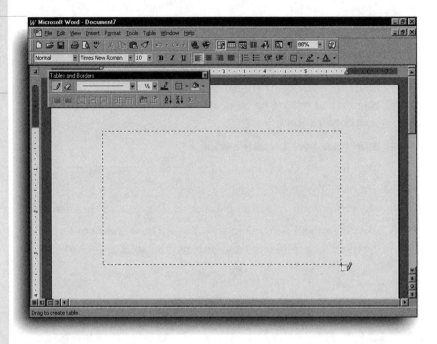

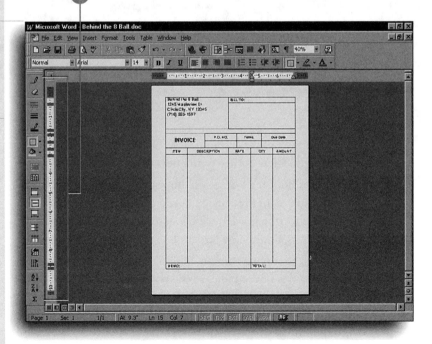

FIGURE 7.5

Creating forms is a snap with
the Draw Table feature.

1 Tables and Borders toolbar
docked to left side

7. Draw your columns and rows exactly where you need them until you finish building your table or form (see Figure 7.5).

SEE ALSO

➤ *To learn more about Page Layout view, see page 114*

➤ *To learn more about docking toolbars, see page 222*

As you can see in Table 7.2 the Tables and Borders toolbar contains all the tools you need to create sophisticated tables.

TABLE 7.2   Tables and Borders toolbar commands

Icon	Command	Description
	Draw Table	Turns the mouse pointer into a Table Drawing tool.
	Eraser	Turns the mouse pointer into a Line Eraser. Use it to "undraw" lines.
	Line Style	Displays drop-down list with choices for inside and outside border line styles.
	Line Weight	Displays drop-down list of line weights (thickness).
	Border Color	Displays a pop-up palette of colors to use for line drawing.
	Border	Adds or removes cell borders. A pop-up menu provides border choices.
	Shading Color	Adds shading to rows, columns, or cells for emphasis.
	Merge Cells	Removes borders between adjacent cells and combines the contents of both into one.
	Split Cells	Creates a mini-table in a cell by splitting the cell into as many rows and columns as you like.
	Align Top	Aligns all text in the cell toward the top of the cell.
	Center Vertically	Centers all text in the cell vertically.

continues…

Using the Tables and Borders tear-off palettes

If you find yourself frequently clicking the Borders and the Shading Color buttons on the toolbar to access their drop-down palettes, you might rather just "tear off" the palettes and float or dock them as toolbars. Open the palette you want (click the arrow to the right of the button), grab it by the thin gray bar at the top, and drag it anywhere in the document window. Let go and it immediately becomes a toolbar. To close the toolbar, click the X in the top-right corner.

The Border button changes for your convenience

The Border button changes its appearance and ScreenTip name based on what's selected in its drop-down palette. If outside borders have been selected, it's the Outside Border button; if all borders are selected for the table, it's the All Borders button. If the icon for the border you want is already displayed on the button, simply click the button instead of selecting from the drop-down palette.

Use the shortcut menu for quick access to table commands

You can also find many of the Tables and Borders toolbar commands on the shortcut menu that appears when you right-click with the mouse pointer/Table Drawing tool. It is often much quicker to right-click and select from the shortcut menu than to hunt for the toolbar command because the menu item includes text as well as an icon.

TABLE 7.2   Continued

Icon	Command	Description
	Align Bottom	Aligns all text in the cell toward the bottom of the cell.
	Distribute Rows Evenly	Makes selected rows the same height. Distributes total height of all selected rows evenly.
	Distribute Columns Evenly	Makes selected columns the same width by distributing total width of all selected columns evenly.
	Table AutoFormat	Opens a dialog box with choices of pre-designed table formats.
	Change Text Direction	Rotates text so that it is vertical or horizontal.
	Sort Ascending	Sorts the selected items in ascending order (A to Z).
	Sort Descending	Sorts the selected items in descending order (Z to A).
	AutoSum	Automatically creates a formula that adds the values of cells above or to the left of the cell in which the cursor rests.

Converting Existing Text to a Table

Sometimes I'm just too lazy to bother creating a table, so I decide to make a short list of items and separate them with tabs instead. When the list continues to grow and it becomes clear that I really need a table, I've got two choices—I can either start all over and build a table from scratch, or I can convert the text into a table. I'll bet you can guess what my choice is. That's right, I convert the text to a table.

Converting existing text into a table

1. Open the Word document with the text you want to convert.

2. Select the text to convert.

3. Open the **Ta̲ble** menu and choose **Con̲vert Text to Table** to open the Convert Text to Table dialog box (see Figure 7.6).

FIGURE 7.6
Word analyzes the selected text and pre-sets the Convert Text to Table options.

4. Set the Convert Text to Table options to suit your needs if the suggested settings aren't adequate.

The available Convert Text to Table options include

- **Number of columns**. Enter the number of columns you want in the new table. If you enter more columns than there are separators (see **Separate text at**), you will end up with blank columns. This is handy if you have additional information you'd like to include.

- **Number of rows**. This number is predetermined by the number of paragraph marks (hard returns) present in your text. Each paragraph mark starts a new row.

- **Column width**. Indicate how wide you want each of the columns to be. Selecting the **Auto** setting produces equal-size columns that stretch the entire width between margins.

- **Table format**. If you use the **AutoFormat** feature, the selected format appears here.

- **Separate text at**. Your choice here becomes the determining factor for building the table. Select **Paragraphs** if you want each paragraph to appear in its own row. Selecting **Tabs** results in a new column being created each time a tab is encountered and a new row for each paragraph mark. If you have used **Commas** to separate list items, a new column appears for each comma and a new row for each paragraph mark. Select **Other** and enter the character you've used to delimit (separate) the items.

- **AutoFormat**. This handy feature provides a selection of predesigned table layouts from which you can choose. For more information on AutoFormat, check out the section on "Using AutoFormat" later in this chapter.

5. Click **OK** to create the new table.

If you find that the selections you made don't suit your needs, you can press Ctrl+Z to undo the newly created table and try again.

Editing a Table

There will, no doubt, be times when the information or your needs change after the table has been created. Fortunately, it's fairly simple to go back and edit the table to update or modify it.

You may find that you need to add additional information, which will require more columns or rows. On the flip side, you might decide to remove some information, which means getting rid of the row or column in which it resides. You can even make changes to individual cells or groups of cells, if you're so inclined.

Inserting Columns and Rows

I frequently design a table and then think of a column or row I should have included. When this happens, I don't panic. I just squeeze another column or row at one end or the other, or between two existing columns or rows.

Inserting columns in a table

1. Place your cursor in a cell in the column just right of the point at which you want to insert the new column. If you want to insert a column after the last column on the right, place your cursor to the right (outside) of the column.

2. From the **T**a**ble** menu, choose **Select** **C**olumn to highlight the desired column (see Figure 7.7).

3. Right-click and select **I**nsert **Columns** from the shortcut menu to add a new column to the left of the selected column. You can also open the **T**a**ble** menu and choose **I**nsert **Columns**.

Another way to highlight a column

You can also highlight a column by moving your mouse pointer just above the column until the pointer turns into a thick black down arrow, and then clicking.

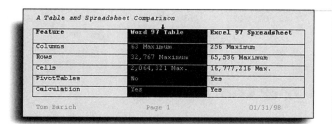

FIGURE 7.7

The **Insert Columns** command places a new column to the left of the highlighted column.

The operation for inserting rows is similar to inserting columns.

Inserting rows in a table

1. Place your cursor in the row below which you want to insert a new row. To add a new row to the bottom of the table, place your cursor below the last row.

2. From the **Table,** choose **Select Row** menu to highlight the row with the cursor (see Figure 7.8).

3. Right-click and select **Insert Rows** from the shortcut menu to add a new row above the highlighted row. You can also choose the **Table** menu and select **Insert Rows**.

You can also highlight a row by moving the cursor into the page margin directly to the left of the desired row and clicking as soon as the pointer turns into a right-leaning arrow.

Keep an eye on the Tables and Borders button on the Standard toolbar

The Tables and Borders button on the Standard toolbar is a tricky little devil that changes as you perform different table operations. For example, when you highlight a column, it turns into an Insert Columns button. When you highlight a row, it becomes an Insert Rows button, and so on. Learn to check it out while working with tables. It can save you unnecessary mouse clicks.

FIGURE 7.8

The new row will appear above the selected row.

Deleting Rows and Columns

The procedure for deleting columns and rows is almost identical to that for inserting them, except that in the final step from the **Table** menu, select **Delete Columns** or **Delete Rows**. To delete multiple rows or columns, highlight as many adjacent rows or columns as you want and delete them. To highlight multiple columns or rows, use the mouse method of highlighting, and drag the pointer over each column you want to delete.

If you want to delete the contents of the rows and columns but not the rows or columns themselves, you can press the **Delete** key.

Merging Cells

After creating a table, I usually want to give it a title, but I hate sticking the title in a text box above the table. An easier way is to create one more row than you really need and merge the cells in the top row, which creates one big cell. You can merge adjacent cells, columns, or rows.

Creating a title bar or multi-column header by merging cells

1. Open a Word document containing the table for which you want to add a title bar.

2. Follow the steps in the previous exercise and insert an extra row at the top of your table.

3. Highlight all the cells in the top row.

4. Right-click and select **Merge Cells** from the shortcut menu to remove all inside vertical cell borders, making the top row a large single cell.

   You can also choose the **Table** menu and select **Merge Cells** or choose the Merge Cells button 🔲 on the Tables and Borders toolbar.

5. Enter your title and format the text as necessary. You'll probably want to center it horizontally, and perhaps vertically as well. See the section later in this chapter on "Text Formatting."

Keep in mind that you can use this process to merge adjacent columns and rows as well.

Splitting Cells

You may have already noticed that when you place your cursor in any cell of an existing table, the **Insert Table** command disappears from the **Table** menu. What Word is trying to tell you is that you can't build a table within a table. However, the **Split Cells** command lets you do precisely that.

It allows you to add columns and rows to any cell, effectively creating a mini-table within your table. It comes in handy when you have an occasional row item that has two values for the same column. For example, in a table of parts and part numbers, some items might have both name-brand and generic part numbers. Rather than create a new row, you can split that row's part-number cell in two.

Splitting cells in a Word table

1. Highlight the cell you want to split.

2. Right-click and select **Split Cells** from the shortcut menu to open the Split Cells dialog box shown in Figure 7.9.

FIGURE 7.9
The Split Cells dialog box enables you to subdivide any cell by adding columns and rows.

3. Enter the number of columns and rows you want to add. If you only want to add either columns or rows, enter the number for that element and leave the other element set at one. For example, to add three columns and no rows, enter 3 in the **Number of columns** spin box and 1 in the **Number of rows** spin box.

4. Click **OK** to add the new columns and rows and return to the active document.

If you're wondering about the disabled **Merge cells before split** check box in Figure 7.9, this option is available only if you highlight multiple cells before choosing **Split Cells**. It then allows you to merge cells first and create new columns and/or rows that will span the newly created merged cell.

Formatting a Table

As with most Word features, you can spruce up your tables and make them presentable in a number of ways, no matter what the occasion. You can change the width of your columns and the height of your rows, add shading to emphasize cells, change the line types, color, and thickness of cell borders, and more.

Changing Column Width and Row Height

Changing the size of columns and rows is a common task, necessitated by having to add or remove columns and rows or to adjust for different sizes of text used in the cell contents. Resizing columns and rows can be accomplished in a couple of ways. You can grab a column or row border and drag it to change the size, you can drag the column or row markers on the horizontal or vertical rulers, or you can use the **Table** menu's **Cell Height and Width** command.

Try dragging the cell borders to change the size of your columns and rows.

- *Dragging cell borders.* To resize either a column or a row, move the mouse pointer over the appropriate border until it becomes a double-headed horizontal arrow (see Figure 7.10). Then grab the border and drag it in the direction that will change its size to suit you.

- *Dragging column or row markers.* As you can see in Figure 7.10, column markers appear on the horizontal ruler, and row markers appear on the vertical ruler (Page Layout and Print Preview only). As with dragging cell borders, place your mouse pointer over the appropriate marker and drag to resize the column or row.

One more method you can use to change the size of columns and rows is the **Cell Height and Width** command.

Resizing columns and rows with the Cell Height and **W**idth command

1. Highlight the row or column you want to modify.

2. Open the **Table** menu and choose **Cell Height and Width** to open the Cell Height and Width dialog box shown in Figure 7.11.

Be careful what you grab

If you attempt to resize an entire column by grabbing the vertical border of a highlighted cell, you will move the border only for the highlighted cell, not the entire column. Therefore, before resizing a column, it's always a good idea to make sure nothing within the table is highlighted.

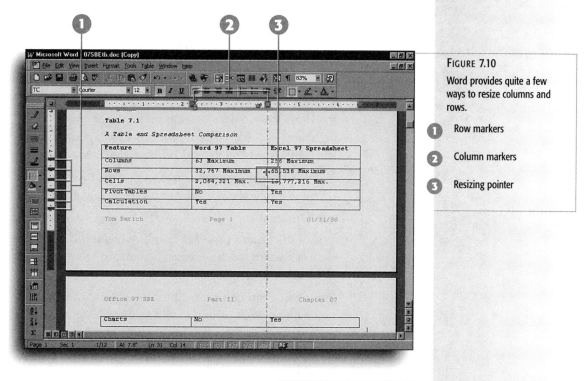

FIGURE 7.10

Word provides quite a few ways to resize columns and rows.

1 Row markers

2 Column markers

3 Resizing pointer

FIGURE 7.11

The appropriate tab is displayed, depending on whether you highlight a row or a column.

3. Set the options to suit your needs.

The following cell height and width options are included

Row Options:

- **Height of row 1**. Select **Auto** to let Word automatically adjust the height, **At Least** to specify (in the At box) a minimum height, or **Exactly** to specify (in the At box) an exact height.

- **At**. Enter the size to be used for the previous option.

- **Indent from left**. Enter the distance from the left table margin that you want the selected row(s) indented.
- **Alignment**. Align the row(s) at the left page margin, centered between left and right, or at the right page margin.
- **Previous Row**. Select the row before the one you highlighted so that you can change its settings without leaving the Cell Height and Width dialog box.
- **Next Row**. This one's the same as **Previous Row** except it selects the row *after* the one you highlighted.

Column Options:

- **Width of column [*number of selected columns*]**. Enter the exact width for the selected column, or select **Auto** to let Word determine the size.
- **Space between columns**. Enter the amount of space you want between columns. This option creates a buffer (of the size you indicate) between the left and right cell borders and the cell contents.
- **Previous Column**. Highlights the previous column so that you can adjust the settings without leaving the Cell Height and Width dialog box.
- **Next Column**. The same as **Previous Column**, except it highlights the *next* column.
- **AutoFit**. Resizes the column to the exact size needed to fit the contents.

4. Click **OK** to save the settings and return to the active document.

Remember, these settings can be applied to single cells as well as to rows and columns.

Borders and Shading

The border and shading options are not just for tables. They can be applied to text, paragraphs, sections, and pages as well, which is why you won't find the **Borders and Shading** command on the **Table** menu (it's on the **Format** menu). When applied to tables, borders and shading can be used for emphasis and clarity. It's much easier to follow the contents of a row, especially one with a lot of data, if every other row is shaded (see Figure 7.12).

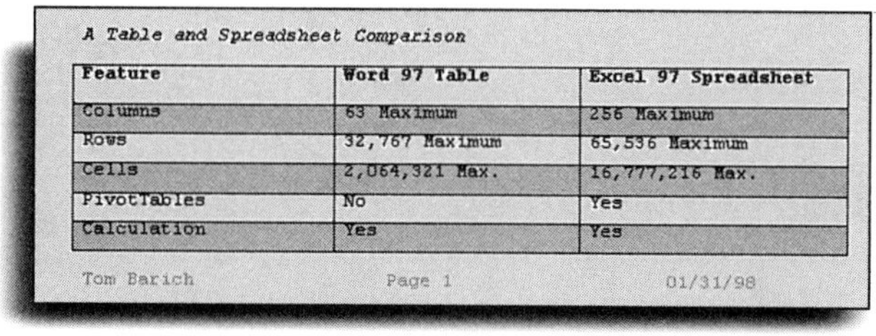
A Table and Spreadsheet Comparison

Feature	Word 97 Table	Excel 97 Spreadsheet
Columns	63 Maximum	256 Maximum
Rows	32,767 Maximum	65,536 Maximum
Cells	2,064,321 Max.	16,777,216 Max.
PivotTables	No	Yes
Calculation	Yes	Yes

Tom Barich Page 1 01/31/98

FIGURE 7.12
Row shading helps your eye follow the path of information.

You can apply borders and shading to a single cell, a group of cells (row or column included), or an entire table. Simply highlight the cell(s) to which you want to apply the Borders or Shading options. Then right-click and select **Borders and Shading** from the shortcut menu to open the Borders and Shading dialog box shown in Figure 7.13.

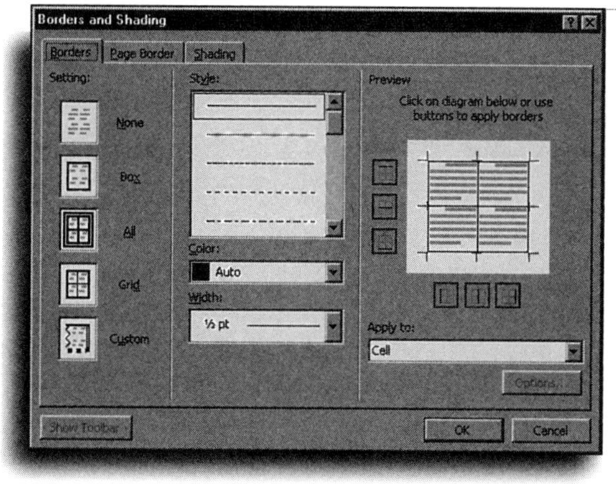

FIGURE 7.13
The border and shading options you can apply to tables are quite extensive.

To see the available Borders and Shading options, check out Table 7.3. The commands listed in the table appear on the **Borders** and **Shading** tabs of the Borders and Shading dialog box, as well as on the Tables and Borders toolbar.

TABLE 7.3 **Border and shading options available on the Tables and Borders toolbar and in the Borders and Shading dialog box**

Icon	Toolbar Command	Dialog Box Option	Description
	No Border	Borders, None	Eliminates all borders from the highlighted cell(s) or the selection in the **Apply to** box, if different.
	Outside Border	Borders, Box	Places a border around the entire selection (either highlighted cells or **Apply to** box choice).
	All Borders	Borders, All	Applies inside and outside borders to selected cell(s) or **Apply to** selection.
		Borders, Grid	Inserts a 3-D box border around the highlighted cell(s) or **Apply to** selection.
	Individual borders	Borders, Custom	Enables the border buttons in the Preview diagram so you can create your own customized borders.
	Line Style	Borders, Style	Select a line style from the list for the border type chosen in the **Setting** option.
	Border Color	Borders, Color	Choose a color from the **Color** drop-down list to apply to the selected border.
	Line Weight	Borders, Width	Adjust the thickness of the border lines by selecting a width from the **Width** drop-down list.
		Borders, Preview	Shows you the effect your option setting choices will have on the selected cell(s).

Icon	Toolbar Command	Dialog Box Option	Description
		Borders, Apply to	Select, from the **Apply to** drop-down list, the element you want your settings applied to. **Apply to** settings take precedence over highlighted cells.
		Borders, Options	This button is disabled unless the **Apply to** selection is **Paragraph**. When enabled, you can set the distance between the border and the text.
		Borders, Show Toolbar	Displays the Tables and Borders toolbar. This button is disabled if the toolbar is already displayed.
		Page Border	The options on this tab apply to the entire document page only, not to tables.
	Shading Color	Shading, Fill	From the color palette select the shading color.
		Shading, Style	Select a shading percentage or pattern from the **Style** drop-down list.
		Shading, Color	Select a color for the pattern style selected. This works only if a color other than gray is selected on the **Fill** palette.
		Shading, Preview	Displays a sample table with selected shading options applied.
		Shading, Apply to	Select the portion of the document to which you want the shading options applied.

continues...

TABLE 7.3   Continued

Icon	Toolbar Command	Dialog Box Option	Description
		Shading, Show Toolbar	Displays the Tables and Borders toolbar. This button is disabled if the toolbar is already displayed.

When you're finished changing the Borders and Shading settings, click **OK** to save the new settings and return to the active document. If you intend to print a document that includes shaded tables or text, you might want to test-print the shaded selection to ensure that the hard copy matches what you're seeing on the screen. Depending on your printer, the results may vary.

Using AutoFormat

For those times when you want to give your table a little flair, but don't have the time to go through the process of customizing the borders, shading, fonts, and so on, you can let the AutoFormat feature do all the work for you.

AutoFormat is really a set of predesigned table layouts with formatting applied. You choose the overall table format first, and then select the specific formatting options you want applied to your table.

Formatting an existing table with AutoFormat

1. Place your cursor anywhere in the table you want to format.

2. Right-click the table and select 🖾 **Table AutoFormat** from the shortcut menu to open the Table AutoFormat dialog box (see Figure 7.14). From the **Table** menu you can also select **Table AutoFormat** or click the Table AutoFormat button on the **Borders and Shading** toolbar.

3. Choose the table format from the **Formats** list. The sample table in the **Preview** area gives you an idea of what your table will look like with the selected format.

4. Select the **Formats to apply** options by placing a check mark next to the options you want applied. Enable or disable (remove the check mark) each one to see the effect it has on the **Preview** table.

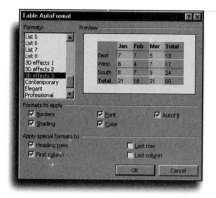

5. Choose the **Apply special formats to** options you want applied to your table. To see the effect each one has, enable or disable it and check out the **Preview** table.

6. Click **OK** to apply the formatting and return to the active document.

Even after using the AutoFormat feature, you can still manually apply any formatting you want to the cells, rows, or columns of the AutoFormatted table. If you later decide you don't like the AutoFormat selection, you can return to the Table AutoFormat dialog box and change the style or select **(none)** to remove the style.

Text Formatting

In addition to formatting the table, you can also format the contents of the cells. You can apply styles, character formatting, and even paragraph formatting to the contents of cells, rows, and columns.

SEE ALSO

➤ *To format text in a table, see page 103*

Sorting and Calculating in Tables

Because the purpose of tables is to organize information, it only makes sense that on occasion you may want to rearrange the contents of a given table. Therefore, it's not surprising that one of the features available for working with tables is sorting.

Another feature that comes in handy is the capability to perform simple calculations in a table. Rather than create a spreadsheet for information that requires simple addition of a column of numbers, it's a lot easier to create a table and enter a formula in the last cell.

Sorting Word Tables

Sorting allows you to reorganize the contents of a table alphabetically, numerically, or by date (only if you have dates in the table). You can even perform a sort by using multiple sort criteria (for example, sort first by column 1 and then by column 2).

Sorting the contents of your table

1. Place the cursor in the column you want to use for the primary sort.

2. Open the **Table** menu and choose **Sort** to open the Sort dialog box shown in Figure 7.15.

FIGURE 7.15

Reorganizing your table contents is a breeze when you use the Sort dialog box.

3. Select the sort option you want to apply to the contents of your table.

The available sort options include

- **Sort by**. Select the column to use for the primary sort. If the first row of your table is a header row and contains column headers, the selections available in this drop-down list will be the column headers (make sure the **My list has Header row** option is selected).

- **Type**. From the **Type** drop-down list, indicate whether the contents of the **Sort by** selection are text, numbers, or dates.

- **Ascending/Descending**. Click **Ascending** to sort from A to Z or **Descending** to sort from Z to A.

- **Then by/Type/Ascending/Descending**. These are duplicates of the first set of options and are used to set a second and third sort order.

- **My list has**. Check **Header row** if your first row contains column headers that should not be included in the sort. Click **No header row** if you want the contents of all rows included in the sort.

- **Options**. Advanced options for sorting a single column, using capitalization as part of the sort, and more.

4. Click **OK** to perform the sort and return to the active document.

You can also use the Sort Ascending ⬇ and Sort Descending ⬇ buttons on the Tables and Borders toolbar to sort your table.

Performing Calculations in Tables

When you create a table that contains numbers, it's not unusual to want to include a mathematical calculation. A table that illustrates sales numbers for a given region will have more impact if you can also provide a total sales figure or an average sales figure.

Adding mathematical calculations to a table

1. Place your cursor in the cell where you want the results of the calculation to appear.

2. From the **Table** menu, choose **Formula** to open the Formula dialog box (see Figure 7.16).

3. Change the formula in the **Formula** text box if you want a calculation other than the sum of all cells above the cell with the formula. You can select a function from the **Paste function** drop-down list to change the formula.

4. Select the format for the results of the calculation from the **Number format** drop-down list.

5. Click **OK** to perform the calculation and return to the active document.

What's the formula for a formula?

To create a table formula, you need three things—an equals sign (=) to let Word know this is a formula, a function (such as Sum, Average, Count) to perform the calculation, and the range of cells to which to apply the function. The range appears after the function and is enclosed in parentheses.

FIGURE 7.16

Word assumes you want to perform a summary operation and enters the formula for totaling all cells above the cell containing the formula.

To add a quick summary calculation to a table, use the AutoSum button **Σ** on the Tables and Borders toolbar.

Using Numbered and Bulleted Lists

As useful as tables are, they don't always fit the bill. Sometimes you need to organize your information in a way that makes it stand out, but you can't manage to squeeze it into a table. Some information is just better suited to a list format.

- Instructions for performing tasks
- Terms that require definitions or explanations
- Information that contains steps
- Important pieces of information that would be lost in the body text

For example, imagine trying to fit the steps from the previous section (on creating a formula) into a table. I tried, and there was no way; consequently, I opted for a numbered list. If the information presented had not been of a sequential nature, I might have chosen a bulleted list instead.

Creating Numbered or Bulleted Lists

Creating numbered and bulleted lists is a snap in Word. All you have to do is place your cursor at the beginning of a new line, from the **Format** menu, choose **Bullets and Numbering** and select your list format from the Bullets and Numbering dialog box (see Figure 7.17).

FIGURE 7.17

You've got a lot of choices for both bullets and numbers that will make your lists stand out.

As soon as you make your selection and click **OK** to return to the document, you're ready to begin your list. The symbol or number format that you selected appears at the beginning of the line your cursor is sitting on. Type in the information for the first line. Then press Enter to create a new line, which will start with another symbol or with the next number in the sequence.

If you want a simple (no format choices) bulleted list or numbered list, you can use the Numbering [icon] or Bullets [icon] buttons on the Formatting toolbar instead.

Adding Numbers or Bullets to an Existing List

If you run into a situation where you've created a list or pasted it into your document from somewhere else and later decide that you want to add some emphasis, you can turn it into a numbered or bulleted list whenever the mood strikes you.

All you have to is select the list, open the Bullets and Numbering dialog box by choosing the **Format** menu and selecting **Bullets and Numbering**, and then select the list format you want to use. When you return to the active document, the new format is already applied to the selected list items. Here again, you can use the toolbar buttons to add a simple number or bullet format.

Customizing Numbered and Bulleted Lists

Although Word supplies quite a few list styles, your needs may require something just a little different. When that happens, the solution is simple—just take one of the default lists and customize it to suit your needs. You can change the bullet characters, as well as the bullet and text positions in bulleted lists.

Customizing a bulleted list

1. Open the **Format** menu and choose **Bullets and Numbering** to open the Bullets and Numbering dialog box (refer to Figure 7.17).

2. Click the **Bulleted** tab and select the style you want to customize.

3. Click the **Customize** button to open the Customize Bulleted List dialog box shown in Figure 7.18.

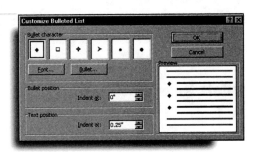

FIGURE 7.18
Create the bulleted list style that meets your needs.

4. Make the appropriate changes to the existing list. The **Preview** area reflects the changes made to the various options.

   Bulleted list customization options include

   - **Bullet character**. Choose one of the preset bullet characters by clicking the character of your choice.

   - **Font**. Bullets are actually characters of a particular font. Select the font to use. The default fonts are Wingdings and Symbol.

- **Bullet**. The bullet is actually any character from the font selected. Click here to see a palette of characters available for the particular font.

- **Bullet position**. Indicate how far from the left margin you want the bullet placed.

- **Text position**. Indicate how far to the right of the bullet the text should begin.

5. Click **OK** to save the new settings and return to the active document. The changes will be made to existing lists immediately.

If you're working with numbered lists, you'll find you can do a little more to modify the existing lists. The numbered list customize options include number format, style, position, and more.

Customizing a numbered list

1. Open the **Format** menu and choose **Bullets and Numbering** to open the Bullets and Numbering dialog box (see Figure 7.17).

2. Click the **Numbered** tab and select the style you want to customize.

3. Click the **Customize** button to open the Customize Numbered List dialog box shown in Figure 7.19.

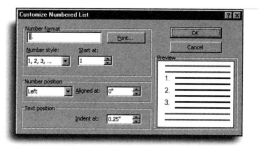

FIGURE 7.19
Create the numbered list style that meets your needs.

4. Make the appropriate changes to the existing list. Watch the **Preview** area to see the effect your changes will have on your list.

Numbered list customization options include

- **Number format**. Enter text to accompany the numbers (or letters), such as brackets or punctuation. This text becomes a noneditable part of a numbered list.

- **Font**. Select the font to use for the numbering characters.

- **Number style**. Select a style from this drop-down list, which includes numbers, letters, Roman numerals, and more.

- **Start at**. Choose the character to start the numbering scheme. The selection changes, depending on which style you select in the **Number style** option. However, regardless of which style you choose, the **Start at** choice presented is always the logical beginning point for that style. For example, if it's a numbering style, **Start at** begins with 1, or if it's a lettering style it begins with A, and so on.

- **Number position**. This is the alignment of the numbering characters relative to the **Aligned at** setting; however, someone at Microsoft seems to have redefined the terms *left* and *right*. When you select **Left** from this drop-down list, the characters are moved to the right of the **Aligned at** point, and when you select **Right**, they are moved to the left.

- **Aligned at**. This is the distance you want the numbering characters to start from the left margin.

- **Indent at**. This indicates the distance between the numbering characters and the list text.

5. Click **OK** to save the new settings and return to the active document. The changes will be made to existing lists immediately.

Dressing Up Documents with Graphics

Adding graphics

Using AutoShapes

Copying and pasting graphics

Wrapping text around your graphics

Adding a watermark

Using Graphics in Your Documents

I'm going to say it and I don't want to hear any groaning—a picture really is worth a thousand words. Why do you think there are so many pictures in this book? That's right, because it would take forever to describe what I can show you with a single screen shot (picture). Just to prove it, take a look at Figure 8.1.

FIGURE 8.1
How many words will it take to describe what's in this picture?

Let's see . . . Figure 8.1 contains a shot of the Microsoft Clip Gallery 3.0, which has four tabs—Clip Art, Pictures, Sounds, and Videos. The first tab is divided into a small pane on the left and a display area in the center. The display area contains a picture of a blank scroll with a small medallion in the bottom right hand corner. There's a ribbon hanging off the medallion. To the right of the scroll is a picture of a magnifying glass with a handle. Next to the magnifying glass is a graphic showing six people sitting around a conference table watching a seventh person give a presentation . . . Had enough yet?

In addition to economizing on words, graphics can spruce up your document, catch your reader's attention, and clarify and add impact to your text by illustrating your point. So, if we all agree that graphics are more than just window dressing, let's get on with it and learn how to use them in Word documents.

Adding Graphics

Before you actually plunk a graphic down in the middle of your document, you'll want to give it a little thought. Decide what type of graphic you want, how big it should be, whether or not color is important, and so on. A black-and-white pie chart may be ideal for a budget report, but it probably won't do much for a children's story (unless you use a real pie and add lots of color). As soon as you've determined the particulars, you're ready to get the show on the road. You've got several choices for adding pictures to a Word document—you can use the **Insert Picture** command, you can copy a graphic from another document or Windows program and paste it into your document, or you can import a graphic from a file.

Inserting Graphics

Word 97 comes with a number of graphics that can be inserted directly into a document without the need for special graphics converters. They include the pictures contained in the Microsoft Clip Gallery, AutoShapes, and WordArt.

Because Normal view and Outline view do not support the displaying of graphics, Word automatically switches to Page Layout view if you insert a picture while in either of those two views.

SEE ALSO

➤ *For details about using WordArt (in MS Publisher), see page 539*

Cruising the Microsoft Clip Gallery

The Microsoft Clip Gallery is an extensive collection of images, photos, sounds, and video clips that you can drop into any Word 97 document and use, royalty-free, in your publications. As a matter of fact, there are so many files in the Clip Gallery that during a typical install quite a few are left on the CD. Consequently, the first time you attempt to use the Clip Gallery you receive a message informing you that more clips are on the CD-ROM.

Finding clip art on the Web

A tremendous amount of clip art can be found on the Internet. Some is public domain, some royalty-free for personal use, and some is for sale. A great place to start searching for clip art is at 4clipart.com (`http://www.4clipart.com/`), which has links to other clip art sites.

Inserting a picture from the Clip Gallery

1. Place the insertion point in the document at the location where you want the picture to appear.

2. Open the **Insert** menu, point to **Picture**, and then select **Clip Art**. The first time you open the Clip Gallery, a dialog box appears telling you that more clips are available on the CD-ROM (see Figure 8.2). If you've already inserted the CD-ROM, you bypass this message and go directly to the Clip Gallery (refer to Figure 8.1).

FIGURE 8.2

The Office 97 Small Business Edition CD-ROM contains a lot more of everything.

3. Click **OK** to open the Gallery. If you don't want to see this reminder each time you open the Clip Gallery, click the **Don't remind me again** check box.

4. Select a tab to choose the type of clip you want to insert in your document.

Your choices for clip types include

- **Clip Art**. Drawings, cartoons, and other vector (draw type) images.

- **Pictures**. Photos and bitmap graphics are included in this category. Depending on your choices during installation, sound clips may or may not be available without the CD-ROM inserted.

- **Sounds**. Here you'll find wave and midi sound files. Depending on your choices during installation, sound clips may or may not be available without the CD-ROM inserted.

- **Videos**. The Clip Gallery includes short video clips supported by the Windows 95 Media Player. Depending on your choices during installation, sound clips may or may not be available without the CD-ROM inserted.

5. Select a category from the pane on the left to display the available images or sounds in the clip preview list.

6. Double-click the desired image or sound clip to insert it in your document. The first time you select a clip, the Picture toolbar appears as well. See the next section for more information on the Picture toolbar.

7. The picture appears immediately following the last paragraph mark before the insertion point.

SEE ALSO

➤ *To learn more about the Clip Gallery, see page 538*

As soon as you insert the clip in your document, the Clip Gallery closes. To insert another picture by using the Clip Gallery, repeat the preceding steps.

The graphic is inserted as a floating picture, which means that you can pick it up and drag it to any location in your document. However, as a floating picture you cannot position it precisely in the text.

Turning a floating picture into a docked picture

1. Right-click the graphic and select **Format Picture** from the shortcut menu that appears to open the Format Picture dialog box shown in Figure 8.3. You can also open the **Format** menu and select **Picture**.

Adding clip art from the Microsoft Web site

If you have an Internet connection and a Web browser, you can access the Microsoft Clip Gallery Live Web site by clicking the **Connect to Web** button in the bottom-right corner of the Clip Gallery. There you can select clip art to add to your Clip Gallery.

Resizing a picture

To resize a picture, select it and drag any of its selection handles. To maintain the picture's proportions, hold down the Shift key while dragging a corner selection handle. Dragging a handle on the sides of the selection rectangle distorts the picture, an effect you may occasionally want.

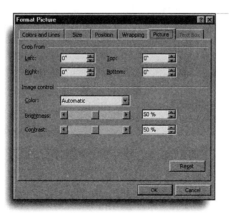

FIGURE 8.3

The Format Picture dialog box offers lots of options for modifying the graphic and its behavior.

2. Click the **Position** tab to see the position options.

3. Deselect (remove the check mark) from the **Float over text** check box.

4. Click **OK** to return to the active document.

5. Place your mouse pointer anywhere on the picture (don't use the resizing handles), and drag it to the precise location in which you want it to appear.

6. Release the left mouse button. The picture parks itself where you indicated.

Using the Picture Toolbar

The first time you insert a clip from the Clip Gallery, the Picture toolbar appears (see Figure 8.4).

FIGURE 8.4

You can adjust the picture's appearance as well as modify settings and formatting options from the Picture toolbar.

Because the Picture toolbar is of little use unless you're working with an image, it remains visible only when an image is selected. As soon as you return to working on the document (and therefore deselect the clip), the Picture toolbar disappears. If for any reason you close the Picture toolbar while it is active, it will not reappear again until you right-click an image and select **Show Picture Toolbar** from the shortcut menu that appears. Until you manually close the toolbar again, it automatically appears and disappears each time you select and deselect an image.

The following commands, available on the Picture toolbar, enable you to manipulate images:

- *Insert Picture* . Click this button to insert an image from a file. From the Insert Picture dialog box that appears, you can locate and insert the graphics file you want.

- *Image Control* . Change the image from color to grayscale or black and white, or even create a watermark from it.

Click the Image Control button and make a selection from
the drop-down menu that appears.

- *More Contrast* ⬛. Click this button to increase the contrast
  of the image.

- *Less Contrast* ⬛. Click this button to reduce the contrast.

- *More Brightness* ⬛. Click this button to increase the brightness.

- *Less Brightness* ⬛. Click this button to decrease the brightness of the image.

- *Crop* ⬛. Trims the image so you can cut or copy only a
  portion of the image. Click the Crop button and use the
  resize
  handles on the image to crop it.

- *Line Style* ⬛. Change the line style of the image border (by
  default, there is no border). Click the button and select a
  line style from the drop-down menu.

- *Text Wrapping* ⬛. Click this button and choose a style for
  wrapping text around the image.

- *Format Picture* ⬛. Click this button to display the Format
  Picture dialog box, which contains colors, size, position,
  wrapping options, and more (see Figure 8.3).

- *Set Transparent Color* ⬛. This command, which works only
  with drawing objects, enables you to choose one of the
  image colors as transparent.

- *Reset Picture* ⬛. Use this command to restore the image to
  its original condition and remove any contrast, brightness,
  color, or cropping changes that you've made.

You can also display the Picture toolbar by right-clicking a blank
spot on the Word 97 toolbar area and selecting **Picture** from the
pop-up menu that appears.

Using AutoShapes

AutoShapes are part of the vast array of drawing features available in Word 97. As you can probably guess from their name,
AutoShapes are an extensive collection of pre-drawn shapes
available for insertion in your document with the click of your

mouse. They range from simple circles and squares to arrows, stars, text balloons, and more.

Inserting AutoShapes

1. Open the **Insert** menu, point to **Picture**, and select **AutoShapes**. This displays the Drawing and AutoShapes toolbars shown in Figure 8.5.

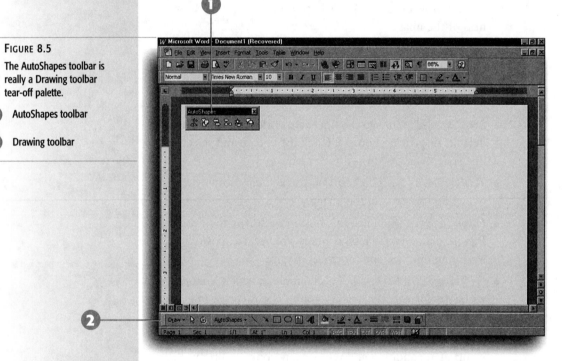

FIGURE **8.5**

The AutoShapes toolbar is really a Drawing toolbar tear-off palette.

1 AutoShapes toolbar

2 Drawing toolbar

2. Click one of the buttons on the AutoShapes toolbar to see a menu of shapes you can choose (see Figure 8.6). Let your mouse pointer hover over each button for a description of the type of shapes available.

FIGURE 8.6

Select a shape from the menu and draw it in your document.

1 Tear-off bar

3. Click the shape you want to draw. Then position your pointer, which turns into a crosshairs pointer, at the location where you want the shape inserted.

4. Click and hold the left mouse button while you drag down and to the right to create the AutoShape.

5. When the shape reaches the desired size, release the left mouse button to insert the new image.

SEE ALSO

➤ *To learn more about AutoShapes, see page 542*

➤ *To learn more about tear-off palettes, see page 147*

If you select one of the Callouts shapes, you also activate the Text Box toolbar because the Callouts shapes are really just text boxes with unique shapes. Like the Picture toolbar, the Text Box toolbar is active only while a text box is selected. Also like the Picture toolbar, closing the Text Box toolbar manually causes it to remain hidden until you manually display it again. The only way to activate the toolbar again is to select a text box, right-click a blank spot in the toolbar area of the document window, and select **Text Box** from the pop-up menu. To close the Text Box toolbar, click the Close button (x) in the top-right corner.

Importing Graphics

Such a wide variety of graphics are available today that you will probably find yourself wanting to use an image that you've found on the Web or located in a third-party clip art collection. When that happens, all you have to do is insert the graphic from a file (import it).

Tearing off commonly used palettes

Each of the AutoShapes palettes is a tear-off palette. This means that you can "tear" it from the AutoShapes menu and plant it anywhere in the document window as an independent toolbar (floating or docked). Grab the desired palette by the thin gray bar at the top, drag it to a new location, and drop it.

Resizing, moving, and copying the AutoShape

After you've drawn an AutoShape, you can resize it by using its selection handles. You also can move the AutoShape by dragging, or copy the AutoShape by holding down the Ctrl key while dragging it.

Importing pictures from files

1. Position your cursor at the point in your document where you want the picture inserted.

2. Open the **Insert** menu, point to **Picture**, and select **From File**. This opens the Insert Picture dialog box shown in Figure 8.7.

FIGURE 8.7

By default, the Insert Picture command looks in the Office clip art directory first.

Adding clip art to the Clip Gallery

If you've got a favorite piece of clip art (or a whole collection), you can add it to the Clip Gallery by clicking the **Import Clips** button on the Clip Gallery. Then locate the graphics file to import, and click **Open**. Enter a keyword and select a category for the new entry, and click **OK** to add the new clip art. Depending on the file type, it appears on either the **Clip Art** tab or the **Pictures** tab.

3. Use the **Look in** drop-down list to locate the folder that contains the picture file you want to import.

4. Enter the name of the picture file you want to open, and click the **Insert** button. You can also double-click the file name in the **Look in** display window. Either way, the picture is immediately placed in your document at the insertion point and the Insert Picture dialog box closes.

Copying and Pasting Graphics

Sometimes while working with another document, you may find a picture that you just have to have in yours. Or perhaps you want to move a picture from one location to another within a document. With Word 97, all you have to do is clip the picture out of the original document or location and paste it in the new one.

Using Copy and Paste to insert pictures in documents

1. Locate the picture you want to copy or move, and click to select it.

2. Press Ctrl+C to copy the picture or Ctrl+X to cut (move) it. You can also open the **Edit** menu and choose **Copy** or **Cut**, or click the Copy 🖻 or Cut ✂ buttons on the Standard toolbar.

3. Move the insertion point to the spot in your document where you want it to appear, and press Ctrl+V to paste the picture. You can also open the **Edit** menu and select **Paste**, or click the Paste button 🖻 on the Standard toolbar.

SEE ALSO

➤ *To learn more about AutoCorrect, see page 126*

Wrapping Text Around Your Graphics

As soon as you insert a picture in a document that already contains text, you can see the impact the graphic has on the surrounding text. The graphic immediately makes room for itself by pushing everything else out of the way. Although you have to accept the fact that it's going to push the text around, you can at least control the way the text moves in relation to the graphic. In other words, you can set the manner in which the text wraps around or through the picture.

Wrapping text around graphics

1. Right-click the graphic for which you want to set the text-wrapping.

2. Select **Format Picture** from the shortcut menu to open the Format Picture dialog box. You can also click the Format Picture button 🖋 on the Picture toolbar or open the **Format** menu and choose **Picture**.

3. Click the **Wrapping** tab to access the text-wrapping options (see Figure 8.8).

Assigning frequently used pictures to AutoCorrect

If you find yourself using a particular graphic–such as a logo– quite a bit, you might consider adding an AutoCorrect entry that inserts the picture each time you type a short abbreviation. First, highlight the graphic. Then open the **Tools** menu and select **AutoCorrect** to open the AutoCorrect dialog box. Click the **AutoCorrect** tab and enter the abbreviation in the **Replace** text box. Be sure to check the **Formatted text** option when you add the entry. The next time you type the abbreviation, the graphic will be inserted in the document.

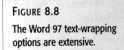

FIGURE 8.8
The Word 97 text-wrapping options are extensive.

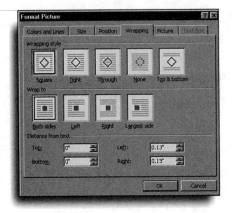

4. Select a **Wrapping style** by clicking the appropriate icon.

   The available Wrapping styles include

   - **Square**. Use this selection to wrap text around the square frame (invisible by default) that surrounds each picture.

   - **Tight**. This one wraps the text around the edges of the picture.

   - **Through**. In addition to wrapping text around the edges of the graphic, this option also wraps inside any open spots on the graphic.

   - **None**. It's just that simple. When you select **None**, there is no wrapping. The text appears directly over or under the graphic, depending on the **Order** options you've set. Order options determine the drawing layer in which the picture appears and can be set by right-clicking the picture and selecting **Order** from the shortcut menu.

   - **Top & bottom**. This option, which forces the text to appear above and below the graphic but not on either side, is the default.

5. Select an appropriate **Wrap to** option.

   The Wrap to options include

   - **Both sides**. When room permits, selecting this object causes text to wrap around both sides of the picture as well as the top and bottom.

- **Left**. Select this option to limit the text-wrapping to the top, bottom, and left sides of the picture.

- **Right**. This option limits the text-wrapping to the top, bottom, and right sides of the graphic.

- **Largest side**. This option picks either the left or right side to wrap to, depending on which has the most room.

6. Set the **Distance from text** options if they are available. Because these settings apply to specific sides, they may or may not be available, depending on the other options selected. When they are available, you can indicate the distance you want the text to be separated from the graphic.

7. Click **OK** to return to the active document and apply the text-wrapping settings (see Figure 8.9).

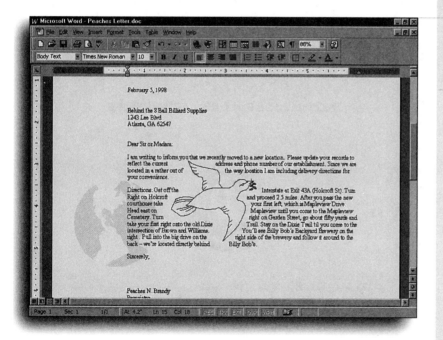

FIGURE 8.9

After you set the text-wrapping options, the text flows according to your directions.

You can adjust the text-wrapping at any time by reopening the Picture Format dialog box and changing the settings on the **Wrapping** tab. You can also change a few basic wrapping options by clicking the Text Wrapping button 🔲 on the Picture toolbar.

Adding a Watermark

If you want to give your letterhead or other important document a professional look, consider adding a *watermark*. Watermarks are those faint images that appear on the background of a document. It could be a company logo, a word or phrase, or just a decorative graphic.

Creating a watermark

1. Open the document in which you want to create the watermark.

2. Use one of the previously discussed picture insertion methods to add a graphic to the document (see Figure 8.10).

FIGURE 8.10
Don't worry about the picture's exact location yet.

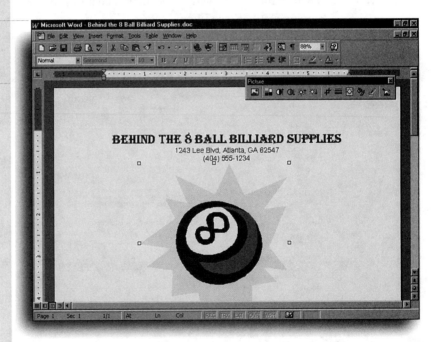

3. Resize the graphic if it's too large or small by placing your pointer over one of the handles until the pointer turns into a double-headed arrow, and then drag it in the appropriate direction (Figure 8.11).

FIGURE 8.11
Make the graphic any size you want by dragging its borders.

4. If the Picture toolbar does not appear, right-click the graphic and select **Show Picture Toolbar** to display the Picture toolbar.

5. Select the picture, click the Image Control button 🔳 on the Picture toolbar, and select **Watermark** from the drop-down menu. This reduces the image to a faint rendition over which text can be placed and easily read. If you're using a color picture, you might want to convert it to grayscale by clicking the Image Control button and selecting **Grayscale**.

6. Click the Text Wrapping button 🔳 and select **None** from the drop-down menu that appears. Turning off text-wrapping ensures that text will appear directly on top of the image.

7. Drag the graphic to the exact location in which you want it to appear. Don't worry if it hides some of the text (see Figure 8.12).

FIGURE 8.12
Place the graphic right on top of the existing text for now.

8. Right-click the picture and select **Order** from the shortcut menu. Then select **Send behind text** to position the picture behind the text (see Figure 8.13).

SEE ALSO
➤ *To learn more about watermarks, see page 596*

FIGURE 8.13

The new watermark appears in the background.

In some cases you may want the watermark to appear over your text (a SOLD banner on an ad, for example). In that case right-click the graphic, select **Or̲der** from the shortcut menu, and then select **Bring in F̲ront of Text**.

There are a number of other tasks you can accomplish by using graphics in your documents, such as creating letterheads, business cards, text with special effects, and more. However, because Publisher 97 is designed just for that purpose, you might want to check it out for many of these graphics tasks.

Creating Form Letters and More with Mail Merge

Introducing Mail Merge

Regardless of whether you've ever created mail merge documents, I'm willing to bet that you are nevertheless quite familiar with them. Unless you've been stranded on a desert island for the last couple of decades, you couldn't possibly have avoided mail merge documents, no matter how hard you tried. You know what I'm talking about—those letters that start off "Dear Ms. [insert your name here]; you're among the select few (that's direct marketing jargon for eight gazillion) who have been chosen to participate in this once-in-a-lifetime [insert 'sweepstakes,' 'offer,' 'preferred customer sale,' 'opportunity']."

Mail merge is that miracle of modern word processing technology that enables you to create a single document and customize it for any number of individuals by using an existing database of names and addresses. With Word's mail merge feature, you can create form letters, labels, envelopes, and more. It's easy—create a mail merge document, throw in a couple of merge fields, add an address book, and you're ready to start your own sweepstakes promotion.

Creating the Mail Merge Structure

Although that last sentence is rather simplistic, it is, in a nutshell, what mail merge is about. Three elements are required for structuring a mail merge:

- *A document*. Whether it's a form letter, envelopes, or labels, you have to create a Word document of some type as the basis of your mail merge operation.
- *A data source*. This can be an address book, the contents of a database, or the contents of a spreadsheet. You can even create your own original data source for your mail merge (and then you can reuse it).
- *Merge fields*. Merge fields are placeholders that tell Word where, in the document, to insert the data (usually name, address, city, and so on) from the data source.

Establishing the Mail Merge Elements

Word has a mail merge feature that walks you through the steps you'll need to put together the elements required for your merged document. The steps follow a logical order, beginning with a document, moving on to identify the location of the data and insert the fields from the data source into your document, and—finally—merging everything.

Using the Mail Merge Helper to create the main document

1. Open a blank or existing Word document that will form the basis of the new main document. For example, perhaps you sent a letter to one individual and then realized it would be a good idea to send it to some or all your contacts.

2. Open the **Tools** menu and choose **Mail Merge** to open the Mail Merge Helper shown in Figure 9.1.

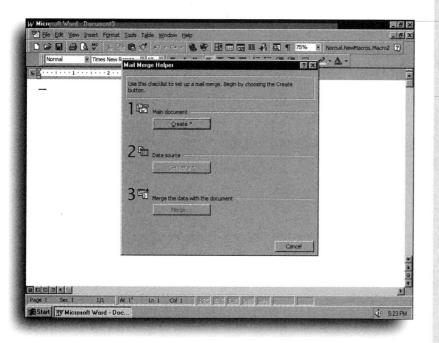

FIGURE 9.1

The Mail Merge Helper makes creating form letters and other mail merge documents a snap.

3. Click **Create** and use the drop-down list to select the type of mail merge document you want to create (see Figure 9.2). The most common document type for mail merge is a form letter.

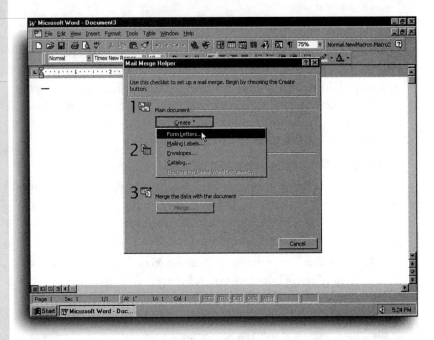

FIGURE 9.2

Word is prepared to handle any form of document.

Mail merge document types

Form Letters, **Mailing Labels**, and **Envelopes** are self-explanatory. The **Catalog** is really nothing more than a way to create a continuous listing (catalog) of information from your data source. This is a time-saver if you send frequent mailings to the same list because when you save the file, the Mail Merge toolbar and the data fields you created are saved with it.

4. A dialog box appears, asking if you want to use the **Active Window** (the document currently in the Word window) or create a **New Main Document**. Most of the time, your current document is the one you'll want to use, but if not, choose **New Main Document** to open a new blank document window.

5. Choose **Get Data** to specify the source of your data. Choose the appropriate source from the list that displays (see Figure 9.3), using the following guidelines:

- **Create Data Source**. Use this choice to build your own database structure and insert the data you need. See "Creating Your Own Data Source" later in this chapter for more information.

- **Open Data Source**. This option opens an existing data file (usually from a software program such as Access or Excel).

- **Use Address Book**. Choose this option if you have an email program or Personal Information Manager that maintains an address book. If you're using Outlook,

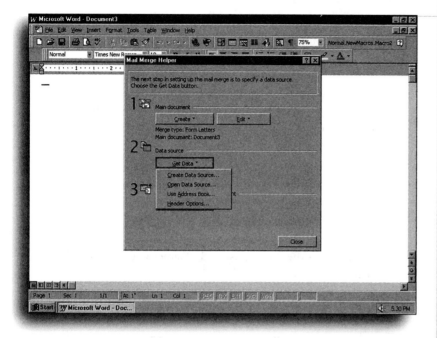

FIGURE 9.3

Choose the type of file to open to access the names you need.

you can use one of the address books you keep for mail or contacts.

- **Header Options**. This option is a bit more complicated, but if you're comfortable working with database structures, it provides some robust configuration choices. You can use this feature to access header information from one source and data from another source. The header information can be created during the mail merge process or obtained from an existing source. (If you're not familiar with database structures, a header is essentially a field name.)

Now all the elements are identified and your basic structure is complete. If you haven't preconfigured your document (form) with fields from your data source, a dialog box appears, inviting you to do so now. Choose **Edit** **Main Document** to begin configuring the fields for your document.

Creating the Mail Merge Document

Your main document is in the window, and it requires two essential elements:

- Text (usually the form document is a letter)
- Fields (the ones you want to use from your data source)

You can begin by entering fields and text.

For this example, we'll create a letter and send it to a list of people. This letter isn't very different from any other letter in its form and execution. For example, most letters start with a date, followed by the name and address of the recipient. Then there's a salutation, an empty line, and the contents of the note. Finally, there's a closing and a signature.

The letter you create for a mail merge follows exactly the same format. The difference is you won't be entering any names or addresses, you'll just indicate them with field names. They'll be filled in during the merge, using the names and addresses in your list.

Editing the mail merge document

1. Enter the text that appears above the name and address of the recipient. This could be your return name and address (or a company name and address) and the date, or just the date if you're printing on letterhead.

2. Position your insertion point where the first line of the address block should be located, and click Insert Merge Field on the Mail Merge toolbar.

3. When the list of fields from your data source appears (see Figure 9.4), choose the field you want to use as the first field in the address block.

   The field appears in the document, surrounded by brackets to indicate a field instead of text.

4. Repeat the process to add all the fields for the address block. Remember to press Enter, add spaces, and insert punctuation as necessary.

5. Press Enter twice after the address block. Then enter the salutation, followed by the field you want to use for the salutation line.

6. Enter the text of the message and the closing.

Set margins to accommodate the letterhead

If you are printing your document on letterhead or any other preprinted form, be sure to set the top page margin deep enough to clear the printing.

Imagine a real address

The most common mistake is erroneous spacing and punctuation. People forget commas and spaces (especially between the first and last name) and even forget to press the Enter key as they build address blocks. These are errors you don't notice until you've completed your merge, and then you have to start all over. When I train people to use mail merge, I find it useful to urge them to imagine that their own information is being entered for each field. That way it's easier to remember that you have to press Enter after the name and the street address and then put the city, state, and zip code on the same line (with the correct spaces and punctuation, of course).

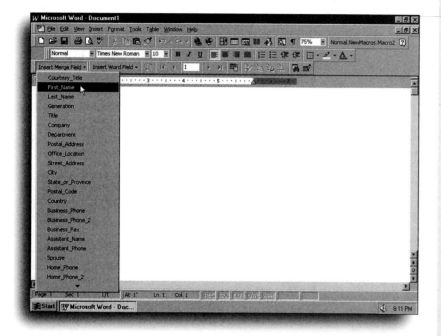

FIGURE 9.4

Choose the first element in the address block, which could be a title (if the database has such a field) or the first name.

Your form is complete, and you should save it with a filename that's connected with this mail merge activity. Figure 9.5 shows a typical filled-out document—notice the personal touch in the third paragraph.

Creating Your Own Data Source

A great many mail merge procedures are for a specific purpose and have a specific list of recipients. It's unusual to find a pre-configured address book that has exactly the list you need. If your mass mailing isn't very large, you can create the database of recipients specifically for the mail merge.

A database has two parts:

- *Fields.* These are the headers, or categories, in the database.

- *Records.* A collection of field data forms a *record.* For example, if the fields are "Last_Name," "First_Name," and "Grad Year," the record for Betty Booper consists of data "Booper," "Betty," and "1975."

FIGURE 9.5

The database of old grads will
provide the data for the fields
when the mail merge is run.

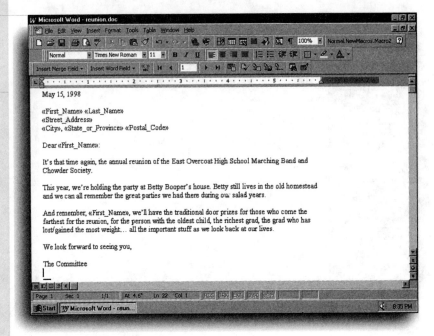

Creating Fields

After you choose **Create Data Source**, Word opens the Create
Data Source dialog box (see Figure 9.6) and even provides some
common fields so that you don't have to reinvent the wheel.

Creating database fields

1. Create any fields you need and choose **Add Field Name** to
   place them in the header row.

2. Select any field you don't need and choose **Remove Field
   Name**.

3. Change the order of the fields by selecting a field and clicking the appropriate Move arrow.

4. Choose **OK** when you have the fields you need. A Save As
   dialog box opens so that you can save your database.

5. Enter a name for the data source and click **Save**.

Entering Data

Your database exists, but there aren't any records in it. Word displays a dialog box that offers a choice between adding data now

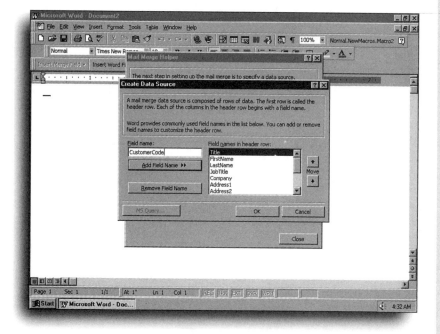

FIGURE 9.6
Most of the work is done.

or working on your main document. This is a good time to add records, so choose **Edit Data Source**.

Adding records to your database

1. In the Data Form dialog box, enter data for the first record (see Figure 9.7).

2. Choose **Add New** to open the next blank record and enter data. Repeat the process to enter all your data.

3. Choose **OK** when everything is entered.

There is another data entry method, and you might find it easier and quicker (most people do). The database structure is displayed as a table, and you use the normal table entry procedures to fill out the records. Try it by choosing **View Source** from the Data Form dialog box.

Using a table for data entry

1. Enter the information for each field in the appropriate cell (see Figure 9.8).

2. Press the Tab key to keep moving through the fields. When the Tab key moves you to the next row, you've started a new record.

FIGURE 9.7

Enter the information for each record in your database.

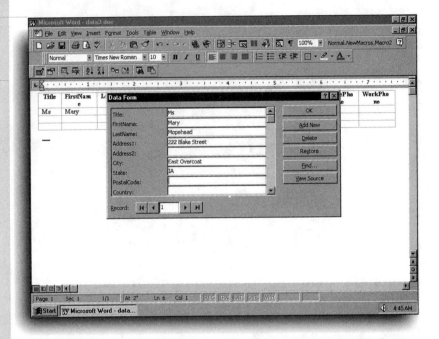

FIGURE 9.8

Some people find working in a table format easier.

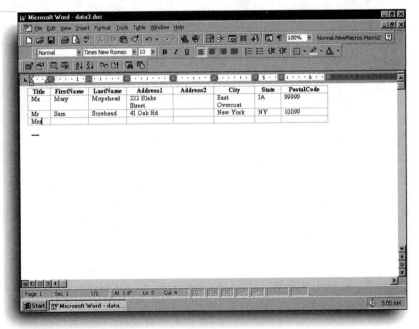

3. Use the commands on the **Table** menu to delete unneeded fields from the database (selecting and deleting columns) or to delete records (selecting and deleting rows).

4. Click the Data Form button ▦ on the Database toolbar to return to the original form.

SEE ALSO

➤ *To learn more about working with tables, see page 152*

After you've created the database and saved it, use the **Open Data Source** command on the **Get Data** menu of the Mail Merge Helper when you want to use this database for future mail merge processes.

Running the Mail Merge Procedure

Your data is ready and your document is prepared, so now you can begin your mail merge procedures. You can take several steps to make sure everything is working properly before you send the mail merge documents to the printer.

Checking for Errors

You can have Word perform an error check of your merge procedure, and you can perform your own spot-check to see if there are any errors.

Having Word Perform an Error Check

Click the Check for Errors button ▦ on the Mail Merge toolbar to open the Checking and Reporting Errors dialog box shown in Figure 9.9.

The choices are self-explanatory, and you should pick the one with which you're most comfortable.

Performing Your Own Check

You can take a quick look at a sample merged document by clicking the View Merged Data button ▦ on the Mail Merge toolbar. The field names are replaced with the field data of the first record. To be sure, use the Next Record arrow to view additional merged records (see Figure 9.10).

FIGURE 9.9

Choose the error-checking method you want Word to use.

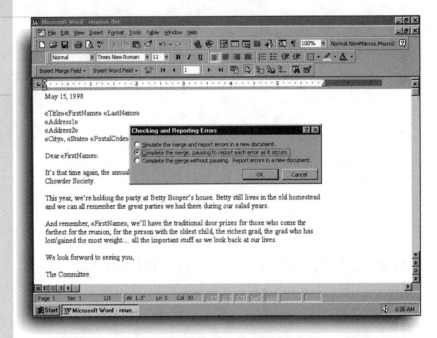

FIGURE 9.10

It's easy to see a space is needed between the Title and FirstName fields.

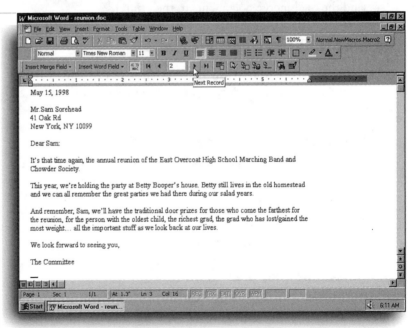

Click the View Merged Data button again to toggle the view back to the fields and make any corrections.

Running the Merge

You can plunge ahead and perform the merge by using the buttons on the toolbar:

- *Merge to New Document.* Click this button to perform the entire mail merge to a document. The document will have a page for each record. After you check the document, you can print it and can even save it.
- *Merge to Printer.* Click this button to perform the final process, printing the mail merge documents. This requires some courage.
- *Mail Merge.* Click this button to configure the mail merge process with the Merge dialog box shown in Figure 9.11. Then choose **Merge** to perform the merge as specified.

In the **Records to be merged** area of the Merge dialog box, you can select **All** to merge all the records, or you can set a range by selecting the **From** option button and entering the range in the **From** and **To** text boxes. In the **When merging records** area, you can select whether to print or omit printing blank lines when data fields are empty.

After you confirm that your mail merge document is correct, you can print it by opening the **File** menu and selecting **Print** or by clicking the Print button 🖨 on the Standard toolbar.

Filtering Records

The Merge dialog box provides a way to select specific records instead of sending your letter to everyone in your database.

Including and excluding records

1. Choose **Query Options** in the Merge dialog box to bring up the Query Options dialog box shown in Figure 9.12.
2. Select a field from the **Field** drop-down list—**State** in this example. Then enter the criteria for comparison to that field. For example, if you want to exclude records where the

FIGURE 9.11

Configure all the details and select records with the Merge dialog box.

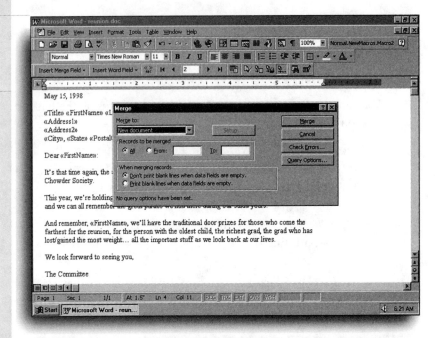

FIGURE 9.12

The reunion committee decided to exclude everyone who lives in Florida.

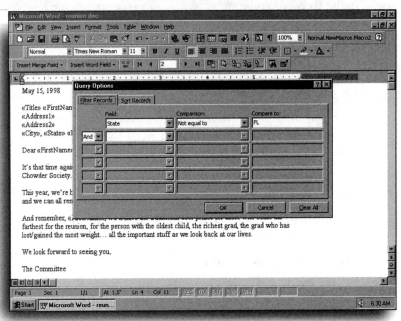

state is Florida (FL), select **Not equal to** in the **Comparison** drop-down list and type FL in the **Compare to** text box.

To focus your choices further, you can include secondary criteria by choosing a comparison operator and entering fields and criteria on additional rows of the **Filter Records** tab.

3. On the **Sort Records** tab, you might want to sort the database records. This is usually done if you're mailing with a bulk permit and your bundles need to be sorted by zip code.

4. Choose **OK** to return to the Merge dialog box.

When everything is set, perform your merge. If you merge to a document, your window displays the new document with a Section Break (Next Page) between individual forms.

5. Print the document (and save it if you think you'll need it again—a common procedure for fund-raising letters).

If you need envelopes or labels to complete your mailing, run another mail merge procedure and choose the appropriate form (using the same database and filters, of course).

Printing Documents

Setting Up Your Printer

You've probably noticed that no one seems to be talking about the paperless office anymore. It wasn't that long ago that everyone was convinced that the advent of computers would do away with the need for paper. How wrong they were! As a matter of fact, if anything, computers have resulted in the generation of more printed matter than ever before. The truth is, computers have made it so easy to produce *hard copy* (printouts of electronic documents) that everyone's doing it.

If you plan to join the crowd and create your hard copy, you must take care of a few things first. All software applications, including Word 97, need to get some basic information about your printer, as well as specific instructions on how and what to print.

Before going any further, let's make sure we're all working from the same page. I'm assuming you've already installed at least one printer in Windows 95. As long as you have one or more printers attached to your computer and installed in Windows 95, you're ready to proceed. If you don't have at least one printer installed, you need to do it now or you won't be able to print hard copy from Word.

The first thing you have to do is tell Word which printer you want to use. Depending on how much of the Small Business Edition suite you've installed, you may have a number of choices in addition to your installed printer.

Getting help with installing printers

If you need help installing a printer in Windows 95, you might want to pick up a copy of *Using Windows 95* by Kathy Ivens.

Viewing printer options

1. Open the **File** menu and choose the **Print** command to open the Print dialog box shown in Figure 10.1.

2. Click the down arrow to access the Printer **Name** drop-down list and display all the available printers. What you see in this list depends on the printers and software you have installed.

3. Select the printer you want to use for the current print job. Because Word assumes you want to use your default Windows 95 printer you'll only have to change this setting when you want to use a different printer.

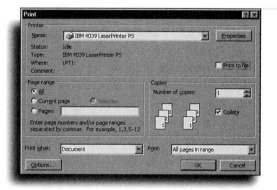

FIGURE 10.1
Word 97 offers a variety of
print options.

If you have Microsoft Publisher installed, you will notice, in addition to your printer, you also have a listing for two MS Publisher printers that are used to create Publisher files to send to professional printers.

4. Click the **Properties** button to set the printer-specific options. The options available here depend entirely on the printer you have.

SEE ALSO

➤ *To learn more about some of the printer settings, see page 68*

Deciding What to Print

After you select the printer to use, your next decision must be about what part of the document to print. Starting with the **Print range** section of the Print dialog box, your options are fairly extensive:

- **All**. Print the entire document from first page to last.

- **Current page**. Print only the page on which the cursor resides. Don't make the mistake of thinking that means the page you can see. When you page up or down or scroll through the document, the cursor remains where you last performed an action. Before you use this option, click to place the insertion point anywhere in the page you want to print.

- **Selection**. You can print just a portion of the text in your document by highlighting it first and then choosing this option.

- **Pages**. You can print a single page, a series of consecutive pages, or as many nonconsecutive pages as you want with this option. After you click the option, enter the page numbers to print in the text box. Separate nonconsecutive pages with a comma and consecutive pages with a hyphen. For example, entering 1,3,5 will result in pages 1, 3, and 5 being printed. Entering 1-5 will cause pages 1, 2, 3, 4, and 5 to print.

- **Print what**. This drop-down list contains a number of items you can choose to print (see Figure 10.2). The default is Document, which means just that—print the document. Other selections include various document elements, such as comments, styles, and AutoText entries.

FIGURE 10.2

Word gives you a number of choices when it comes to deciding what to print.

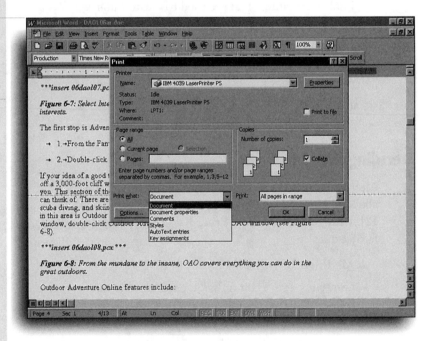

- **Print**. This drop-down list gives you the choice of printing all the pages in the range selected or just the odd pages or just the even pages.

- **Print to file**. This option comes in handy if you want to print your document on a high-resolution or color printer owned by a friend or in a commercial printing shop. Set up the desired printer in Windows 95, select it as the printer, and then use **Print to file** to save the document to disk in a format compatible with the selected printer. If you've installed Publisher, you'll see that two printers have been installed for precisely that purpose—MS Publisher Color Printer and MS Publisher Imagesetter.

- **Number of copies**. This one is just what it appears to be. Enter the number of copies of the document you want to print.

- **Collate**. If you are printing more than one copy of a multipage document, Word will print one page at a time unless you check the **Collate** option. In other words, if you print three copies of a five-page document without checking **Collate**, you'll get three copies of page 1, then three copies of page 2, and so on. When you check **Collate**, you get one copy of pages 1 through 5, then a second copy of pages 1 through 5, and finally a third set.

Printing on Both Sides of the Page

If you're printing a long document and want to save paper, or if you just want to keep the thickness of the printed document to a minimum, you can use both sides of the paper if you have a laser printer.

The first thing you need to do is determine how the paper feeds into your printer. First, open the printer tray and mark the top of the first sheet of paper with a *T* and the bottom with a *B*. Then print a test page. This way you'll be able to tell which side of the page is printed on and which end enters the printer first.

Testing two-sided printing

1. Open the **File** menu and choose the **Print** command.

2. Select your printer and choose **All** in the **Print range** section.

3. In the **Print what** drop-down list, select **Document**.

4. In the **Print** drop-down list, select **Odd pages** and then click **OK** to print.

Use collate sparingly

Don't use **Collate** unless you have a fast printer with lots of memory, or unless you don't care how long the print job takes. When you print multiple copies of an uncollated document, the data for each page is sent to the printer once, and the selected number of copies is printed. However, when you use **Collate**, the data is sent for each page as it is printed, which can result in an extremely time-consuming print job.

5. After all the odd pages print, place them back in the paper tray. Make sure to put them in so the blank side will be printed on this time and they feed in the right direction.

6. Return to the Print dialog box and set **Print** to **Even pages**. Click **OK** to print.

Depending on how your printer outputs the printed document, you might find you have to reverse the print order for this trick to work properly. To do that, open the Print dialog box and click the **Options** button located in the bottom-left corner. From the printing options, select the **Reverse print order** check box and click **OK**.

Setting Print Options

The basic options found in the Print dialog box provide a great deal of flexibility when it comes to deciding what to print and how to print it. Although these options will probably suffice for most of your everyday printing jobs, there may be times when special circumstances require more advanced printing options.

To set the additional options, click the **Options** button in the Print dialog box to open another Print dialog box, as shown in Figure 10.3. You can also access these options anywhere in Word by opening the **Tools** menu, selecting **Options,** and clicking the **Print** tab.

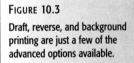

FIGURE 10.3
Draft, reverse, and background printing are just a few of the advanced options available.

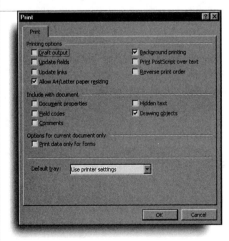

The majority of the additional print options fall into one of two categories—**Printing options** or **Include with document**.

What you'll find in **Printing options**:

- **Draft output**. Select this check box to speed up printing. The downside to using this option is that formatting and graphics will not be printed. In addition, some printers do not support draft output.

- **Update fields**. If your document contains *fields*, they will automatically be updated prior to printing if you select this check box.

  Further description of fields is beyond the scope of this book. You can read more about fields in Word's Help topics.

- **Update links**. If you have linked information from another document, such as a spreadsheet, selecting this check box will cause all links to be automatically updated before the current document prints. This is a good option to choose if your links are all set for manual updates.

- **Allow A4/Letter paper resizing**. If you receive documents prepared for a different paper size, selecting this check box causes Word to automatically adjust the document to fit the paper size you use.

- **Background printing**. Selecting this check box enables the printing to proceed in the background while you continue to work in Word. If your system resources allow, this is a handy option to enable. If you find that your printing is unbearably slow, disable this option and see if it helps.

- **Print PostScript over text**. If you're printing a document that's been converted from Word for the Macintosh, enabling this check box allows you to print postscript code *over* the document text rather than under it. This will work only if you have a postscript printer.

- **Reverse print order**. The normal print order is from front to back, starting with page 1. Select this check box to start printing from the last page of the document, forward. This is handy if your printer has an optional straight-through output path, which generally results in the normal print order being reversed because the pages are dropped in the tray face up.

The available options in the **Include with document** section:

- **Document properties**. If you want a copy of the document Properties Summary sheet (shown in Figure 10.4) to print with the document, select this check box. The Properties Summary sheet, which can be accessed by opening the **File** menu and selecting **Properties** and then **Summary**, includes basic information about the document, such as title and author.

- **Field codes**. If your document contains fields, selecting this

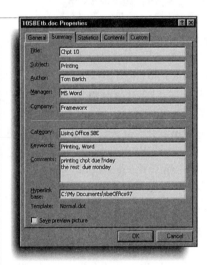

FIGURE 10.4

The document Properties Summary sheet provides basic information about the document and the author.

check box will cause the field codes (rather than the field results) to be printed in the document. This is a great way to check a document with a lot of fields to ensure that all the field instructions are accurate.

- **Comments**. If your document contains comments, you can print them all out with the document if you select this option.

- **Hidden Text**. Hidden text that's present in your document does not print unless you select this check box.

- **Drawing objects**. With this option selected, drawing

objects are included when the document is printed. However, if you are printing a draft version and not the finished document, you may want to deselect this option to speed up the printing process.

The final two options are only for the current document. **Print data only for forms** is handy if you use online forms to collect information. By enabling this check box, you print only the information entered into the form and not the entire form.

The second option, **Default tray**, enables you to direct Word to use a specific paper tray if your printer has more than one. This is useful if you keep different types of paper in different trays. For example, you might have letterhead in one and plain laser paper in another.

SEE ALSO

➤ *To learn more about linking, see page 12*

Previewing and Printing Your Document

Look before you leap . . . Sound familiar? Perhaps even corny? Well, as timeworn and weary as the phrase might be, it applies to printing. I hate it when I print a 30-page document only to find I forgot to add the header, and then have to go back and reprint the whole document. That's the point at which I bang my head on the desk (repeatedly) and wonder why I didn't do a Print Preview. It's so easy and simple that there's no reason not to do it.

You can preview your document at any time by opening the **File** menu and choosing **Print Preview** or by clicking the Print Preview button on the Standard toolbar. The first time you open the Print Preview window, Word presents a true representation of what the current page will look like when you print it (see Figure 10.5).

Zooming In

The default Print Preview view shows the entire page, which is great for examining the basic page layout but doesn't show you much detail. If you want to scrutinize the document a little more closely, you have two options: You can either use the Magnifier or the Zoom control.

FIGURE 10.5

With Print Preview, what you
see is what you will print.

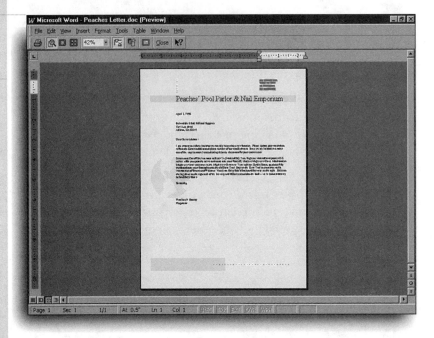

As soon as you open the Print Preview window, the Magnifier is
activated. As you move the mouse pointer over the document
page, you can see that it changes from an arrow to a magnifying
glass. To use the Magnifier, position it over the area of the page
you want to enlarge and click. Word immediately zooms in and
increases the selected area to the actual size (100%) it will appear
in the printed document (see Figure 10.6).

Click the Magnifier a second time, and the page reverts to its
original size.

To use the Zoom control, click the Zoom drop-down list on the
Print Preview toolbar and enter a percentage from 10 to 500, or
click the arrow and make a selection from the Zoom drop-down
list as shown in Figure 10.7.

Viewing Multiple Pages

Another handy Print Preview feature is the capability to preview
more than a single page at a time. It's nice to see how text is
going to flow from page to page. I don't know about you, but I

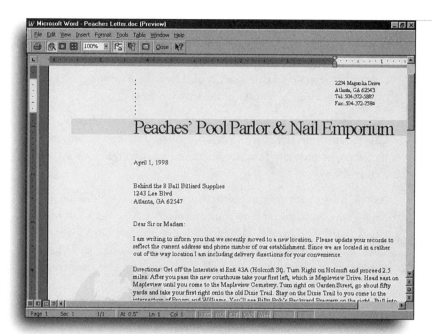

FIGURE 10.6

The Magnifier lets you see the document at the size it will print.

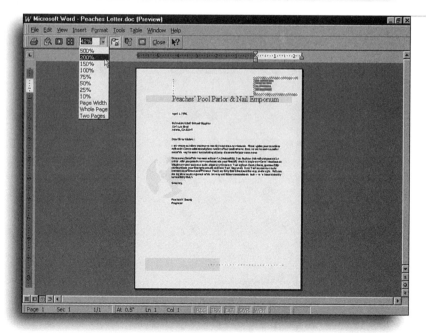

FIGURE 10.7

The Zoom control give you a number of choices for enlarging or reducing the Print Preview.

Using the Shrink to Fit feature

You can use the Shrink to Fit button on the Print Preview toolbar to automatically lop off the last page and force everything onto the remaining pages. Word does this by reducing the size of all the fonts, but be careful–the change becomes permanent when you save the document. Before you save, you can reverse the change by using Undo.

hate having the last page of my document end with one line of text on it. Therefore, if I do a preview and notice a lonely line or two dangling at the end of my document, I'll find some way to remedy it. If I can't easily rewrite it, I'll make a minor change in my margins to accommodate the orphan lines.

To preview more than one page at a time, click the Multiple Pages button on the Print Preview toolbar and select the number of pages to view from the selection box that opens (shown in Figure 10.8).

As you move your mouse pointer over the box, the individual page icons are highlighted. You can select two, three, four, or six pages to view at a time. The status line at the bottom of the selection box indicates how many pages you've selected. When you've made your choice, click and the Print Preview displays the number of pages you selected (see Figure 10.9).

Just as in the single Print Preview, you can zoom and edit individual pages by using the Magnifier and Zoom control.

FIGURE 10.8

You can Print Preview as many as six pages at a time with the Multiple Pages option.

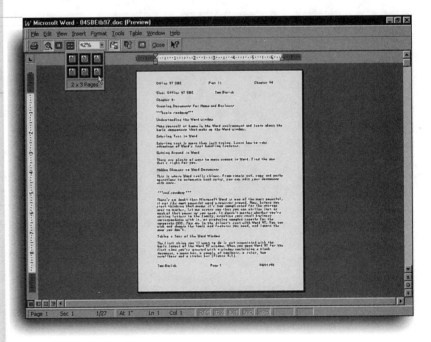

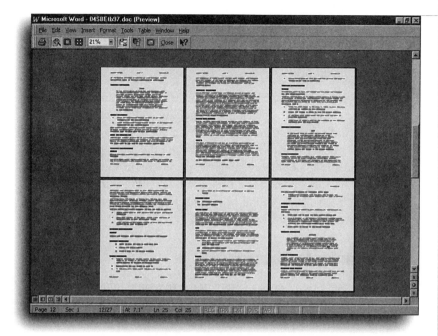

FIGURE 10.9
With the Multiple Page preview you get to see the big print picture.

Editing in Preview Mode

If, while previewing a page, you encounter something that needs to be changed, you can edit the document from within Print Preview instead of returning to the previous view. Simply click the Magnifier button on the toolbar. The mouse pointer turns into an I-beam cursor, indicating that you can now work with text. In addition, you'll find that most of the menu bar commands are available to you while you're in Print Preview. You can make whatever changes are necessary, save the document, and proceed with your preview, without ever leaving the Print Preview screen.

Using the ruler to format in Print Preview

You can adjust margins, tabs, and indents in Print Preview by clicking and dragging on the ruler. If the ruler is not displayed, open the **View** menu and choose **Ruler**.

Printing the Document

Actually, this is the easy part after you've done everything else. After you choose your printer and set all your options in the Print dialog box, all you have to do is click **OK** and you're off and printing.

Your other option is to use the Print button found on both the Standard and Print Preview toolbars. As soon as you click the

Print button, the document prints with all the default settings contained in the Print dialog box. In other words, unlike using the **File** menu's **Print** command, you don't have any say in how the document prints.

While your job is printing, a small print icon appears in the status bar, temporarily replacing the Spelling and Grammar status icon. It indicates that the job is printing and shows which page is currently being sent to the printer. While the job is printing, you can cancel it by double-clicking the print icon in the status bar. This only works if you have background printing turned on. If you don't have background printing turned on, you can press Escape to stop a print job.

Printing Multiple Documents

If you have a number of documents in the same folder that are complete and ready to be printed, you can send them all to the printer at once without having to open them individually and print them one at a time.

Printing multiple documents

1. Click the Open button, or open the **File** menu and choose the **Open** command to display the Open dialog box shown in Figure 10.10.

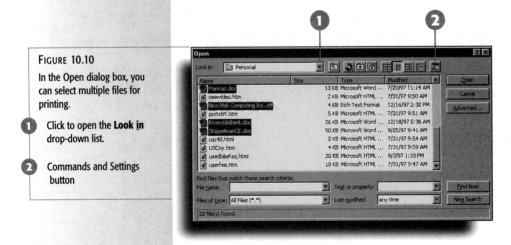

> **Canceling a print job sent to a laser printer**
>
> If you have a laser printer that contains its own memory, all or part of any print job will be sent to the printer before you get the chance to cancel it in Word. You will have to pause the printer and cancel the print job from the Printers dialog box in Windows 95.

FIGURE 10.10

In the Open dialog box, you can select multiple files for printing.

❶ Click to open the **Look in** drop-down list.

❷ Commands and Settings button

2. Use the **Look in** drop-down list to open the folder that holds the documents to print.

3. Click the first document to print. Then hold down the Ctrl key and select the remaining documents. By using this selection method, you can select nonadjacent as well as adjacent documents.

4. Click the Commands and Settings button to activate the drop-down menu shown in Figure 10.11.

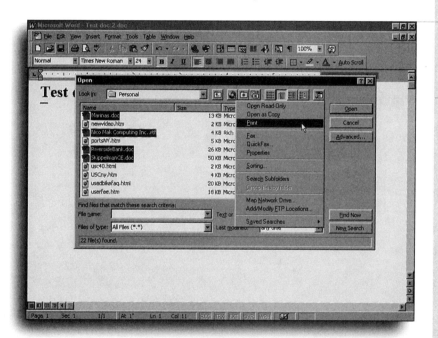

FIGURE 10.11
You can perform quite a few operations from the Open dialog box.

5. Select **Print** from the menu to start the selected documents printing.

There is another method for printing multiple documents from the Open dialog box. After you select all the documents you want to print, right-click any of the selected items to open the shortcut menu, and then choose **Print**.

Tailoring Word to Suit Your Needs

Customizing toolbars

Relocating toolbars

Creating new toolbars

Modifying toolbars

Editing toolbar buttons

Adding and removing menu items

Creating new menus

Creating shortcut keys—customize, keyboard

Customizing shortcut menus

Setting Word options

Customizing Toolbars

In addition to more features, every new version of Word offers more opportunities to make it work the way you want it to. While no software application can be everything to everyone, Word comes pretty darn close.

One of the first things you'll probably want to customize is the toolbars. Word toolbars are handy items to have around if you use them. They provide a visual shortcut to commands you would otherwise have to select from a menu or run with a short-cut key combination. Now, you're probably saying, "What's so difficult about pressing Ctrl+S to save a document?" Of course, the answer is, "Nothing." But, how many of those key combinations can you memorize so they're as quickly accessible as a toolbar button? When you have to start searching for shortcut key descriptions, you've lost the advantage.

The most important thing to remember about Word 97 toolbars is that they are there for your convenience. You control which toolbars appear, where they reside on the Word window, and which commands appear on them. If they're not making themselves useful, you can change them, move them, or get rid of them entirely.

Showing and Hiding Toolbars

Toolbars, like most appliances and power tools, are only useful if you have the right one for the job at hand, so the first order of business is to figure out where Word 97 hides them all. Actually, that's pretty easy. Just right-click anywhere on the menu bar or an existing toolbar to see a pop-up menu of all the available toolbars (see Figure 11.1).

After you access the *pop-up menu*, you can show or hide toolbars by selecting them from the menu. As you can see in the above figure, both the Standard and Formatting toolbars have check marks next to them, indicating that they are active and appear in the current Word 97 window.

Suppose you decide you want to add the AutoText toolbar to the window. All you have to do is select it by clicking the toolbar name, **AutoText**. The toolbar is immediately displayed in the

FIGURE 11.1

Word 97 comes with a variety of predesigned toolbars.

window. If you right-click in the toolbar area to open the pop-up menu, you will see that AutoText now has a check mark. To remove the check mark, click AutoText again, and the AutoText toolbar disappears from the window.

Showing or hiding several toolbars at once

1. Open the **Tools** menu and choose **Customize** to open the Customize dialog box.

2. Click the **Toolbars** tab to view the available toolbars (see Figure 11.2).

FIGURE 11.2

You can hide or activate as many toolbars as you want.

3. Make your selection by placing a check mark next to the toolbars you want to display and removing the check mark from those you want to hide. Click the toolbar check box to add or remove a check mark.

4. Click **Close** to finalize your choices and return to the current document.

Quick ways to open the Customize dialog box

You can open the Customize dialog box by double-clicking the blank area next to a toolbar. You also can right-click a toolbar and select **Customize** from the bottom of the shortcut menu.

The toolbar actually appears as soon as you place a check mark in the appropriate box. Therefore you can decide, before closing the Customize dialog box, whether or not you want to keep the newly displayed toolbar. If you select the wrong toolbar, just click the name again to remove the check mark, and the toolbar disappears.

Relocating Toolbars

One of the nice things about the Word toolbars is that you can move them around the window and place them pretty much where you want them. You can even let them "*float*" on your document if you're so inclined. Toolbars that are attached to one of the edges of the Word window are considered "*docked*."

Docked toolbars have a *move handle* that is located on the toolbar's left edge. It appears as a pair of raised vertical lines. To move a *docked toolbar*, you simply grab the move handle with your mouse, drag the toolbar to a new location, and drop it. If you move it to one of the four edges of the window and drop it, it becomes docked along that edge. Or you can reposition it within the toolbar area at the top of the window by moving it to the left, right, up, or down. If, however, you drop it somewhere on the document itself, it changes shape and floats there. Well, it doesn't really float; it stays anchored until you move it again—it just appears to be floating because it hides whatever text is under it (see Figure 11.3).

In addition to the change in position, a *floating toolbar* differs from a docked toolbar in other ways. As soon as a toolbar changes from docked to floating, it sheds its move handle. Not to worry, though. You can still move it, but now you have to grab it by its title bar—the blue bar that contains the toolbar title.

Another difference is the shape of the toolbar. When docked along the edge of the window, the toolbar stretches itself out to be as unobtrusive as possible. When it becomes a floating toolbar, figuring out the least obtrusive position is not so easy, so it assumes a rectangular shape. To make the toolbar even more manageable, you can change its dimensions by dragging any of its four edges.

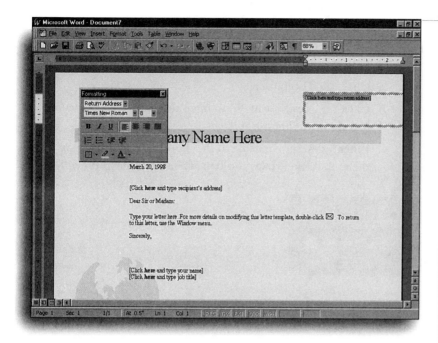

FIGURE 11.3

You can drop a floating toolbar anywhere on the document and it will stay there until you move it again or close it.

The other difference is that you can close a floating toolbar by clicking the Close button (the small button with the X) in the upper-right corner.

Creating New Toolbars

Now to the fun part—creating your own toolbars. No matter how hard they tried, there's no way the Microsoft programmers could have anticipated the needs of every user. Realizing that, they designed the toolbars so that any command from any toolbar can be added to any other toolbar, including an entirely new toolbar. So, no matter what your needs, you can pick and choose among the Word commands and build your own toolbar. It's a little like the old ice cream parlors where you could make your own sundae. No matter how strange your choice of flavors might seem to everyone else, it was just right for you.

Creating a new toolbar is a two-phase operation. The first phase entails creating a blank toolbar. The next phase is adding commands to the new toolbar.

A command is a command, no matter where you put it

The commands that you add to toolbars as buttons are the same commands that can be placed on menus as menu items. As a matter of fact, you can pull a command right off a toolbar and add it to a menu, or vice versa (when the Customize dialog box is open).

Creating a blank toolbar

1. Double-click a blank spot in the toolbar area to open the Customize dialog box.

2. Click the **Toolbars** tab.

3. Click the **New** button  to open the New Toolbar dialog box shown in Figure 11.4.

4. Enter a descriptive name in the **Toolbar name** text box, and then tab to the **Make toolbar available to** drop-down list.

FIGURE 11.4
Give your new toolbar a unique name.

5. From the drop-down list, choose the template or document where you want to store the new toolbar. If you want the new toolbar to be available to most of your documents, select **Normal.dot**.

6. Click **OK** to return to the Customize dialog box and the new, blank toolbar (see Figure 11.5).

FIGURE 11.5
The new toolbar is ready for your custom command set.

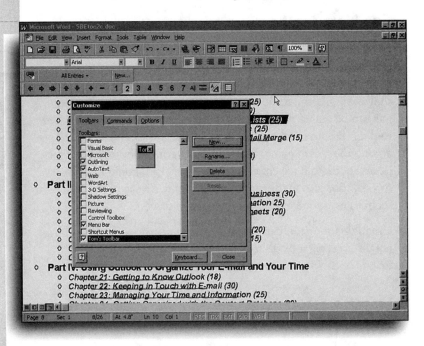

Now that you've got the blank toolbar, it's time to add the commands. Let's say for the first command you want to add the What's This? Help pointer. If you use it a lot and hate to have to open the **Help** menu and choose the **What's This?** command, it will be a lot easier if it's available on the toolbar.

Adding the commands to a toolbar

1. Move the blank toolbar off the Customize dialog box so it won't be in your way.

2. Click the **Commands** tab on the Customize dialog box to view the available commands.

3. Scroll down the **Categories** list box and select the **Window and Help** category to display the available commands in the right pane.

4. Scroll down the **Commands** list box to **What's This?**, and drag it to the blank toolbar. As soon as you click the command and hold down the left mouse button, a small button and a plus sign appear at the pointer (see Figure 11.6)

FIGURE 11.6

Adding a command to a toolbar is easy with drag and drop.

5. Drop the command on the blank toolbar. An I-beam appears, indicating where on the toolbar the command will be placed.

6. Repeat this process to choose commands from any category you wish until your new toolbar is complete. Remember, you can add or remove commands whenever you want.

7. Click **Close** to return to the active document.

8. Position your new toolbar wherever you want it.

Modifying Toolbars

If, while building your custom toolbar, you decide to remove a command, simply drag the command off the toolbar and drop it anywhere on the document. It will disappear from the toolbar. Removing it from the toolbar does not remove it from the list of available commands. To move a command button from one spot to another while creating a toolbar, just drag it to a new location on the toolbar and drop it.

Editing Toolbar Buttons

While in the Customize dialog box, you can modify a number of toolbar button attributes. You can change the appearance of the buttons, as well as copy, paste, and rename buttons. You can even create button groups, so you can separate them into clusters on a toolbar.

Modifying a toolbar button

1. Double-click a blank spot in the toolbar area to open the Customize dialog box.
2. Select the **Commands** tab.
3. On an existing toolbar, click the button you want to modify.
4. Then click the **Modify Selection** button on the Commands tab of the Customize dialog box to open the editing menu shown in Figure 11.7.
5. Finally, choose the appropriate command from the menu to edit the selected button.

The available toolbar button editing commands include

- **Reset**. Restores the button to the state it was in at the beginning of this editing session.
- **Delete**. Removes the selected button from the toolbar.
- **Name**. The current name of the button appears in the text box. To change it, place your cursor in the text box and edit the name. You'll notice an ampersand (&) in some names. When used as part of a word, the ampersand converts the next letter to a shortcut for running the command. In other words, the command associated

---

Converting toolbars from floating to docked and back again

Double-clicking a floating toolbar's title bar repositions the toolbar, either beneath the last toolbar at the top of the document or in the last position it held in the toolbar area at the top of the document. Conversely, double-clicking a docked toolbar's move handle returns it to its last position as a floating toolbar.

An easy way to modify your toolbar

You can move or remove command buttons from a toolbar during normal Word operations without opening the Customize dialog box. Hold down the Alt key, and drag the button to a new location, or onto the active document to remove it altogether.

To copy a command button during normal operations, hold down Alt+Ctrl and drag the button to a new toolbar or location and drop it. The original button remains where it was, and a copy is placed in the new location.

Both of these tricks also work for moving or copying a command from a toolbar to a menu (but not the other way). Hold down the Alt key (or Alt+Ctrl) and drag the command from the toolbar to the menu title. When the menu opens, move the mouse pointer to the place on the menu where you want to insert the command, and drop it.

FIGURE 11.7
Word offers a variety of toolbar-button editing functions.

with a toolbar button named &Print can be run by pressing Alt+P.

- **Copy Button Image**. Select a button and use this command to copy the image (not the button or the command).

- **Paste Button Image**. Used in conjunction with the Copy Button Image command, this one pastes the copied image to another button that you select.

- **Reset Button Image**. If you decide, after changing the image on a button, that you like it better the way it was, you can return to the original image by selecting this command.

- **Edit Button Image**. Choose a button with an image that you want to modify, and click this menu command to open the Button Editor shown in Figure 11.8. Select a color from the palette and click a pixel (one square) to change its color. A second click removes the color. Edit

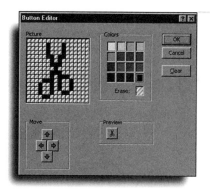

FIGURE 11.8
You can even redesign existing button graphics.

the image and click **OK** to return to the Customize dialog box.

- **Change Button Image**. If you don't like the existing image, or if the button doesn't have one, you can use this command to add a new graphic to the button. As soon as you select this command, a submenu of alternative images appears. Click one to add it to the selected button.

- **Default Style**. The Word default style for a toolbar button is graphics only, no text. Choosing this command returns the selected button to the graphics-only style. If the button has only a text title, the text disappears and the button appears blank.

- **Text Only (Always)**. Because the toolbar buttons are really commands that assume the form of buttons when placed on a toolbar, they can also be used on menus. This command ensures that the button always appears with a text title only, and no graphics, regardless of where the command is placed.

- **Text Only (in Menus)**. This command allows the selected command button to appear with a graphic in a toolbar but only with text if used in a menu.

- **Image and Text**. With this command chosen, the button always shows both the graphic and the text title.

- **Begin a Group**. Use this command to add a vertical bar to a toolbar to separate groups of buttons.

While you have the Customize dialog box open, you can also copy a command button from one toolbar to another by pressing Ctrl and dragging a clone of the button to a new location.

Made-to-Order Menus

Practically everywhere you go in Word, you can find menus that make your job a little easier. The major source of menus—the menu bar—is always with you, wherever you are. Shortcut menus that appear when you right-click are available for the majority of operations that you perform. Even some toolbar buttons have menus. Because they fold up or disappear when not in use, menus enable you to keep a large number of features at your fingertips without cluttering your screen.

Getting Familiar with the Word Menu Bar

The menu bar, which Word actually considers a toolbar (you can find it in the Customize dialog box under the **Toolbars** tab) is your command center. This is where the bulk of the Word 97 commands reside. Because the menu bar is a toolbar, it has many of the toolbar properties. You can dock it, float it, change its shape, or customize it just like any other toolbar.

You can move the menu bar the same way you move a toolbar, by grabbing its move handle and dropping it where you want it to go. If you place it at the edge of the screen, it docks itself and rearranges its buttons to accommodate its new position (see Figure 11.9).

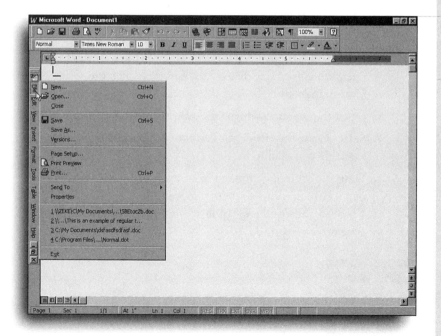

FIGURE 11.9
The menu bar is just as flexible as the other toolbars.

Drop the menu bar on the document and, like a toolbar, it alters its shape and floats over the document. You can change its dimensions by dragging any of the four edges; however, unlike the other toolbars, you cannot close the menu bar. It must remain visible at all times. Even if you open the Customize dialog box, you cannot remove the check mark next to **Menu Bar**.

Another thing to take note of is the shortcut key combinations that appear next to some of the commands. These are generally the more common commands, such as Open, Save, Print.

Adding and Removing Menu Items

Although the menu bar contains a large selection of frequently used commands, there's no way it can satisfy everyone's needs. You're bound to find yourself wishing you could add some commands that are missing or remove others that you never use. Well, there's no need to wish. With a minimal amount of effort, you can customize the Word menus to suit your needs.

The procedure for adding and removing menu items is very similar to the process you used to add and remove toolbar command buttons earlier in this chapter.

Adding and removing menu items

1. Double-click a blank spot to the right of the toolbars to open the Customize dialog box, and then click the **Commands** tab.

2. Open the menu to which you want to add a new command.

3. Select a category from the **Categories** list to display the available commands.

4. Drag the desired command from the **Commands** list to the menu bar and drop it where you want it. A horizontal I-beam indicates the location at which the new item will appear (see Figure 11.10).

FIGURE **11.10**

Add your favorite commands to the menu bar.

5. Repeat the process until you've added all the desired commands.

6. Click **Close** to shut down the Customize dialog box and return to the active document.

While you have the Customize dialog box open, you can move, copy, and delete commands from the menus. To move a menu item from one location to another or from one menu to another, just drag it to the new location and drop it. You can remove a menu item by dragging it off the menu and dropping it onto the active document. To copy a menu item from one menu to another, hold down the Ctrl key while dragging the item.

Creating New Menus

As with toolbars, sometimes modifying the existing menus just isn't enough. You may have a specialized need that requires a series of commands (from different categories) all grouped on one menu. In that case, you can create your own menu and fill it with exactly the commands that you need (or want).

Creating a new menu

1. Double-click a blank spot on the toolbar area to open the Customize dialog box, and then click the **Commands** tab.

2. Scroll down the **Categories** list and select **New Menu**.

3. Drag the **New Menu** command from the **Commands** list box to the menu bar and drop it where you want the new menu to appear.

4. Right-click the New Menu button 🔲 that appears on the menu bar to open the shortcut menu.

5. In the **Name** text box, enter a title for the new menu.

6. Return to the Customize dialog box and add menu commands, using the procedure outlined in the previous section on adding and removing menu items.

This not only works for adding new menus to the menu bar, but also for adding new submenus to existing menus. Suppose, for example, you want to have a submenu on the **Tools** menu that includes all the available spelling and grammar commands. Drag

Removing menu items in a flash

Try this trick to remove a menu item during normal Word operations, without having to open the Customize dialog box. Press Alt+Ctrl+Hyphen to turn the mouse pointer into a thick horizontal bar. Then open the menu, move to the menu item you wish to remove, and click the item or press Enter. The item is removed and the mouse pointer returns to normal. By the way, you must use the hyphen located on the same key as the underscore. The minus sign on the number pad won't work.

the **New Menu** command, drop it on the menu of your choice, and then add all the spelling and grammar commands to it. The result is a new submenu like the one in Figure 11.11.

FIGURE 11.11
You can add submenus of related commands to any existing menu.

Creating Shortcut Keys—Customize Keyboard

If you find menus and toolbars annoying and prefer using short-cut keys, Word has plenty to choose from. If you find that your favorite commands don't have their own shortcut keys, the solution is simple—add your own.

Creating shortcut keys for frequently used commands

1. Open the Customize dialog box by double-clicking a blank spot on the toolbar area.

2. Open the Customize Keyboard dialog box (shown in Figure 11.12) by clicking the **Keyboard** button that appears on the bottom of any of the three tabs.

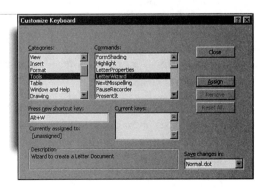

FIGURE 11.12
Select the **Word** command and press the key combination to use as the shortcut key.

3. Select the category from the **Categories** list to display the available commands.

4. Highlight the desired command in the **Commands** list.

5. Move to the **Press new shortcut key** text box and press the key combination you wish to use. Don't type in the key combination; press the actual keys on your own keyboard.

   If the key combination has already been assigned to another command, it will appear beneath the box where it says **Currently assigned to**. If the command already has a short-cut key, it will appear in the **Current keys** list box.

6. Click **Assign** to save the new shortcut key.

7. Repeat the process until you're finished, and then click **Close** to return to the Customize dialog box.

8. Click **Close** again to return to the active document.

Any time you want to eliminate all the custom shortcut keys you've created, return to the Customize Keyboard dialog box and click the **Reset All** button. A confirmation dialog box appears, asking if you're sure you want to reset the key assign-ments. Click **Yes** to reset or **No** to cancel the reset operation.

Customizing Shortcut Menus

Shortcut menus are those handy little menus that pop up when you right-click your mouse. They can be extremely convenient and useful, but only if they contain the commands you need when you summon them. If they don't, they end up being more annoying than helpful. You can't create new shortcut menus or delete existing ones, but you can add commands and submenus of commands to the ones that come with Word.

Editing existing shortcut menus

1. Double-click a blank spot on the toolbar area to open the Customize dialog box.

2. Click the **Toolbars** tab and scroll down to **Shortcut Menus**.

3. Place a check mark in the box next to **Shortcut Menus** to access the Shortcut Menus toolbar shown in Figure 11.13. If you don't see the Shortcut Menus toolbar, it might be hiding

behind the Customize dialog box. To check it out, just grab the Customize dialog box by its title bar and drag it out of the way.

FIGURE 11.13

Shortcut menus come in three flavors—Text, Table, and Draw.

4. From the Shortcut Menus toolbar, click the shortcut menu type, and then click the menu name to open the desired shortcut menu (see Figure 11.14).

FIGURE 11.14

After you open the shortcut menu, you can add and remove commands.

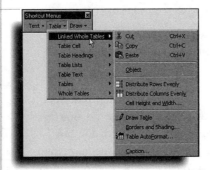

5. Click the **Commands** tab on the Customize dialog box.

6. Drag new commands to the selected shortcut menu to add them.

7. To remove a command from the shortcut menu, drag it onto the active document and drop it.

8. When you finish modifying the shortcut menus, click the **Close** button on the Customize dialog box to close the Shortcut Menu toolbar and the Customize dialog box.

The next time you access the modified shortcut menu(s) by right-clicking, the changes will be in effect.

Changing the Way Word Looks

Not all Word customization options are about function. Some are about form, and then there are others that are about both. It's not only important to have the right tools while working but also the right environment. That's where Word's View and General options come into play, and—to a lesser extent—the Customize options.

View Options

The View options that, not surprisingly, can be found on the **View** tab of the Options dialog box, are there so you can change the way certain things display in the various Word views. In other words, the options you see when working in Normal view will not always be the same options you see when you're working in the Page Layout or Outline views. To set the options for the view you're currently in, open the **Options** menu, select **Tools**, and then click the **View** tab as shown in Figure 11.15.

Table 11.1 shows you the options available, depending on the view you're in.

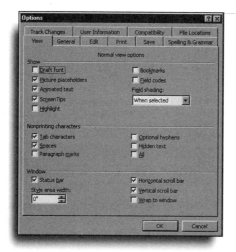

FIGURE 11.15
With View options, you can make Word see things your way.

TABLE 11.1 View options in Word 97

Option	View(s)	Function
Drawings	Online Layout, Page Layout	When selected, drawing objects are shown in the document. Deselect this option to speed up document scrolling by concealing drawing objects.

continues...

TABLE 11.1   **Continued**

Option	View(s)	Function
Object anchors	Online Layout, Page Layout	When you show all nonprinting characters, any object anchors will also display if this option is selected. Object anchors indicate that an object is exclusively assigned to one paragraph, which means you can't move one without the other.
Text boundaries	Online Layout, Page Layout	To show the areas within which text is confined, turn this option on so Word displays dotted lines to mark the boundaries.
Draft font	Normal, Outline	To speed up the screen display, select this option to show the formatting in your document as bold and underlined. This only affects the display and does not change the formatting of the actual document. Graphics are shown as empty boxes.
Picture placeholders	Normal, Online Layout, Page Layout, Outline	Like draft font, this option speeds up scrolling by displaying graphics as empty boxes.
Animated text	Normal, Online Layout, Page Layout, Outline	If you're creating a document to use online, this option enables you to show or hide your animated text. To see how your document will print, turn off Animated text.
ScreenTips	Normal, Online Layout, Page Layout, Outline	If you add comments to your document, this option shows them in pop-up text boxes when the reader pauses over a comment reference mark.
Highlight	Normal, Online Layout, Page Layout, Outline	Use this option to show or hide highlighting you've applied to text.
Bookmarks	Normal, Online Layout, Page Layout, Outline	To see bookmarks onscreen, turn this option on to display them in square brackets. With this option selected, bookmarks appear in the onscreen document (but not in the printed version).

Option	View(s)	Function
Field codes	Normal, Online Layout, Page Layout, Outline	If you insert fields into your document, selecting this option displays the field codes instead of the actual results. For example, if you turn this option on and move to a date field, you see { DATE \@"M/d/yy" \} rather than 4/7/98.
Field shading	Normal, Online Layout, Page Layout, Outline	To make fields easy to spot onscreen, add shading with this option. Shading does not appear in the printed document.
Tab characters	Normal, Online Layout, Page Layout, Outline	Show tab characters in your document, even if you have all other hidden characters turned off.
Spaces	Normal, Online Layout, Page Layout, Outline	To display all spaces in your document as dots, turn this option on. It can be used in conjunction with any other hidden-character option.
Paragraph marks	Normal, Online Layout, Page Layout, Outline	Paragraph marks indicate hard returns. To make them visible in your document, select this option.
Optional **hyphens**	Normal, Online Layout, Page Layout, Outline	To ensure that a word breaks in a certain way if hyphenation becomes necessary, you can insert an *optional hyphen*. Selecting this option displays optional hyphens onscreen.
Hi**dden text**	Normal, Online Layout, Page Layout, Outline	When you want to see hidden text, turn this option on. The hidden text appears with a dotted underline, which shows onscreen but does not print.
All	Normal, Online Layout, Page Layout, Outline	If you don't want to fool around with individual nonprinting characters, this options handles them all in one shot. Either turn them all off, or turn them all on.
Status bar	Normal, Online Layout, Page Layout, Outline	If you want to eliminate the status bar from the bottom of the Word window, deselect this option.

continues…

TABLE 11.1   **Continued**

Option	View(s)	Function
Style area width	Normal, Outline	To see the styles used in your document, set the Style area width to a number greater than zero. This opens the Style area pane in which you will see the names of the styles applied to each paragraph.
Enlarge fonts less than	Online Layout	For better online viewing, you can force Word to automatically enlarge all fonts smaller than the indicated size.
Vertical ruler	Page Layout	If you find a vertical ruler helpful, turn this option on.
Horizontal scrollbar	Normal, Online Layout, Page Layout, Outline	Some people hate the scrollbars. If you're among that number, here's your chance to get rid of the horizontal scrollbar—deselect this option.
Vertical scrollbar	Normal, Online Layout, Page Layout, Outline	If you didn't like the horizontal scrollbar, chances are you're not going to like the vertical one, either. To turn it off, deselect this option.
Wrap to window	Normal, Online Layout, Outline	You'll like this one if you work in reduced-size document windows. Select this option and Word will wrap the text, no matter how narrow you make your document window.

General Options

Are you a recent convert from WordPerfect or one of the other word processors that offers a blue document background with white text? Do you like an audio confirmation when certain events take place in Word? Would you like to oversee the conversion process before Word opens a non-Word document? If you answered yes to any of these questions, you might want to stop by the General tab of the Options dialog box and check the settings available there. Open the **Tools** menu and choose the **Options** command, and then click the **General** tab to see the General options (see Figure 11.16).

FIGURE 11.16
General options cover things that don't fit neatly into other option categories.

Here's what you'll find in the **General** tab:

- **Background repagination**. As you insert text into a document, the page numbers change. To have Word automatically repaginate as you type, select this option. Because automatic repagination is required in the Page Layout view (and can't be turned off), this option is not available there.

- **Help for WordPerfect users**. If you're just switching over from WordPerfect, you might want to keep this option selected until you become familiar with Word.

- **Navigation keys for WordPerfect users**. Old habits are hard to break, so WordPerfect users might prefer to reassign some keyboard keys to their WordPerfect equivalents. The keys in question are Page Up, Page Down, Home, End, and Esc.

- **Blue background, white text**. There's not much more to say. If you want your document background blue and your text white, check this option.

- **Provide feedback with sound**. Some Word events have an accompanying sound to identify them. If you want to hear the sound when the event occurs, select this option.

- **Provide feedback with animation**. Rather than wonder if anything is really happening while Word performs a function such as saving or printing, turn this option on to see special, animated cursors.

- **Confirm conversion at Open**. Without this option selected, Word 97 makes its own decision about which converter to use when it encounters an alien (non-Word 97) document. If you want the opportunity to oversee the conversion process, turn this option on.

- **Update automatic links at Open**. It's not uncommon to link information from another source to a Word document and then make changes to the original file. If you want those changes reflected in the Word document, you must update the link manually or have Word do it automatically. This is where you can turn on the automatic update option.

- **Mail as attachment**. In the event that you want to include the current document with an email message, you can choose how the document accompanies the message. With this option selected, the document is sent as an attachment (a separate file attached to the message). Otherwise, the contents of the document will be inserted into the body of the email message.

- **Recently used file list**. This handy option enables you to indicate how many recently opened documents Word "remembers." Each time you close a document, its path and name are placed at the top of the MRU (Most Recently Used) list that appears at the bottom of the File menu. You can then reopen the document by clicking the MRU listing rather than going to the Open dialog box and hunting for it. You can store up to nine entries on the MRU list.

- **Macro virus protection**. Because Word has been the target of a number of viruses transmitted by macros, Microsoft has implemented an automatic (if you select this option) macro warning to alert you to potential carriers of macro viruses. This does not mean that a virus is present, just a potential carrier, which includes *all* macros as well as all customized toolbars, menus, and shortcuts.

- **Measurement units**. When Word dialog boxes ask for a measurement, this option determines what measurement unit is used. Your choices include inches, centimeters, points, and picas. This unit is also used in the horizontal and vertical rulers (Page Layout view only).

Customize Options

Four additional display options can be found on the Options tab of the Customize dialog box. To access these options, open the **Tools** menu, choose the **Customize** command, and click the **Options** tab (see Figure 11.17).

FIGURE 11.17

Change the way ScreenTips and icons appear in Word with the Customize options.

The Customize options include

- **Large icons**. If you're having difficulty making out the toolbar *icons*, you can select this option to enlarge them. This makes the toolbar buttons easier to decipher, but you will lose access to buttons that disappear off the right side of the screen unless you make the toolbar a floating toolbar.

- **Show ScreenTips on toolbars**. As you pass your mouse over each button on a toolbar, small text boxes called *ScreenTips* appear with descriptions of button features. To turn them off, deselect this option.

- **Show shortcut keys in ScreenTips**. If a toolbar button command has a shortcut key assigned to it, selecting this option will add the shortcut key to the ScreenTip.

- **Menu animations**. Word menus usually just appear when you click a menu title; however, with this option you can add a special effect to the menu opening. Your choices are None (the default), Random, Unfold, and Slide. Random allows Word to randomly switch between Unfold and Slide.

When you finish setting these options, click **Close** to return to the active document.

Changing the Way Word Works

Many of the options in the previous section dealt with display matters. There's no doubt that they're important and play a significant role in the way you get work done; however, you can't afford to ignore some of the other settings that affect the way Word features actually function. From turning drag-and-drop text-editing off to telling Word where to look for clip art, you can modify many of its basic operating modes.

Editing Options

The editing features in Word are probably the most used of all its features; therefore, being able to make sure they work the way you work is important. Would you like to fine-tune the text selection feature? Do you want to automatically insert text as you type, or do you want to replace existing text? You can even make allowance for French language formatting.

Start by opening the **Tools** menu and choosing **Options.** Then click the **Edit** tab to access the Editing options shown in Figure 11.18.

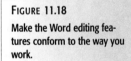

FIGURE 11.18

Make the Word editing features conform to the way you work.

What you'll find are the following options:

- **Typing replaces selection**. Whenever you tab to a text box in Word, the existing text is automatically highlighted. With this option selected, typing automatically clears the text box and replaces the existing text with the new text. If you turn this option off, the new text is inserted into the text box beside the old text.

- **Drag-and-drop text editing**. If you want to be able to move or copy selected text by dragging and dropping it, choose this option. If you disable this option, dragging selected text results in extending the selection area.

- **When selecting, automatically select entire word**. This one's a little misleading—it only works when you select more than one word. If you select at least one entire word and then extend the selection to the next word, the second word is immediately highlighted as soon as you touch the first letter.

- **Use the INS key for paste**. To use the Insert key as a shortcut key for pasting the Clipboard contents into a document, turn this option on.

- **Overtype mode**. With Overtype mode selected, any text you type in your document replaces existing text at the cursor, one character at a time. To insert the new text rather than replace the old, turn this option off.

- **Use smart cut and paste**. Do you have a habit of cutting exactly the text you want, without leading or trailing spaces? If so, you know how annoying it is when you paste it in the middle of existing text and it plasters itself directly against an adjacent word. With smart cut and paste, Word ensures that a space appears between existing and inserted text, regardless of whether you included it or not.

- **Tabs and backspaces set left indent**. To increase or decrease left indents when you use Tab or Backspace, select this option.

- **Allow accented uppercase in French**. Parlez-vous Francais? If you do, you might want to enable this option so you can include accent marks for uppercase letters in text that has been formatted as French.

- **Picture editor**. If you have other picture-editing programs, such as Microsoft Photo Editor, you can select the program to use as the default picture editor.

File Locations

If you want to make your word processing life a little easier, let Word know where you keep the files that you'll be accessing frequently. This includes everything from documents to clip art. To inform Word of your file locations, open the **Tools** menu, choose **Options**, and click the **File Locations** tab (see Figure 11.19).

FIGURE 11.19

Word checks the location you enter here when it needs to find a certain type of file.

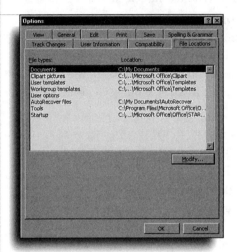

Adding or changing a file location is a simple matter of selecting from the **File types,** clicking the **Modify** button, and entering the correct path for that type. By default, Word does not include a path for AutoRecover files but instead drops them in the DOS directory (if you have one) or the Windows system directory. Suppose you want to keep an eye on them and be able to find them in case of a system crash. You would have to go searching for them. Why not create an AutoRecover folder and tell Word to store the AutoRecover files in it?

Adding a file location for AutoRecover files

1. Highlight your selection in the **File types** list of the **File Locations** tab.

2. Click the **Modify** button to open the Modify Location dialog box shown in Figure 11.20.

FIGURE 11.20
Use the Modify Location dialog box to locate an existing folder or create a new one.

3. Use the **Look in** drop-down list to locate (and open) the folder in which to create the AutoRecover subfolder. In this case, I'm going to put it in the My Documents folder.

4. Click the **Create New Folder** button to open the New Folder dialog box.

5. Type AutoRecover in the **Name** text box and click **OK**. The New Folder dialog box closes and the AutoRecover folder appears in the folder list.

6. Click the new AutoRecover folder so it is included in the path in the **Folder name** drop-down list. Then click **OK** to return to the **File Locations** tab.

The new path appears in the Location list for AutoRecover files. Check to make sure it is accurate. If it's wrong, click the **Modify** button and change it.

7. Repeat the process to add or modify other locations as necessary.

8. Click **OK** to save the new location(s) and return to the active document.

SEE ALSO

➤ *To configure AutoRecover, page* 47

Using Excel to Track Your Finances

Creating Worksheets for Home and Business

Identify and understand the parts of your Excel window

Begin a new, blank worksheet

Create multiple worksheets simultaneously

Enter text and data to fill out your worksheet

Use Excel's AutoFill feature

Taking a Tour of the Excel Window

Microsoft Excel is a spreadsheet program that enables you to store data in a large table of intersecting columns and rows, where each intersection is called a *cell*. Each cell can contain text or numbers, and the numbers can be manipulated in formulas, which are also entered into cells. An Excel spreadsheet can be described as the electronic version of a sheet in an accountant's analysis pad.

Also, like an accountant's analysis pad, your Excel spreadsheets can contain both numbers and text that relates to numbers, primarily for keeping track of quantities. Excel enables you to keep track of things such as money, items in inventory, sales figures, or services you provide and for which you bill your customers. Although you can store this same text and numeric data in a Word table, you'll find that Excel affords you greater powers for working with your data than you'll find in a simple table. You can create both simple and complex formulas, sort and filter your columns and rows in many ways, and create charts and graphs to illustrate your content.

A single Excel file is called a *workbook*. Each workbook is made up of separate sheets (called *worksheets*), containing 256 columns and 8,192 rows. If you've got your calculator turned on, that means 2,097,152 cells per sheet. Each workbook can contain up to 16 sheets, so that's 33,554,432 cells per book, potentially. Don't let these huge numbers scare you! The average worksheet typically only uses a fraction of those cells. They're there if you need them, but you probably won't. Figure 12.1 shows the Excel window with a blank workbook displayed.

The Excel window gives you access to all the tools you'll need to successfully create and develop your worksheets. The screen pictures in this chapter show how Excel looks on a 15", 800×600 resolution monitor—if you see slight variations between these pictures and your screen, they are likely caused by your screen's size and resolution.

To access Excel, click the **Start** button and then choose **New Office Document**. In the resulting New Office Document dialog box, click the **General** tab and then double-click the **Blank**

FIGURE 12.1

Although each worksheet contains over two million cells, you can see only approximately 200 of them at a time.

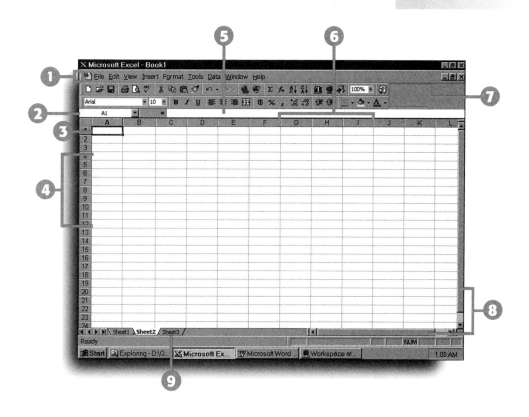

1 Menu bar	**6** Columns
2 Address of active cell	**7** Toolbars
3 Active cell	**8** Scrollbars
4 Rows	**9** Sheet tabs
5 Formula bar	

Workbook icon. This opens Excel with a blank worksheet, ready for you to make your entries.

You will notice that the Office Assistant, along with other Help, is available in Excel.

SEE ALSO

➤ *To learn more about opening Excel, see page 2*

➤ *To use the Help system in Excel, see page 26*

Getting Familiar with the Excel Menu Bar

Just below Excel's title bar, you'll see a series of menus. Each one, when displayed, contains commands for entering, editing, and manipulating your worksheet's content. Down the left side of some menus, next to the menu commands, you'll see icons corresponding to the icons on the toolbars for the same commands. On the right side of the menu commands, you'll see keyboard shortcuts, again for only some of the commands. Use these for faster access to your most commonly used menu commands. Figure 12.2 shows the **File** menu.

FIGURE 12.2

The menus not only give you access to Excel's commands, but provide reminders of the toolbar and keyboard equivalents for your most commonly used commands.

1 Keyboard shortcuts

2 Icons

3 Most recently used files

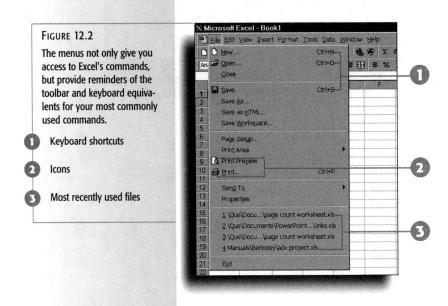

- **File**. This menu (shown in Figure 12.2) contains a list of commands that enable you to create, open, save, and print your files. You'll also see a numeric list of files at the bottom of the menu. As a convenience, Excel maintains a list of the last four files you used, making it faster and easier to re-open them.

- **Edit**. This menu gives you access to the Clipboard through the **Cut**, **Copy**, and **Paste** commands. You'll also find **Undo** on this menu, which reverses your last action. You'll find this very useful!

- **View**. Use the commands in this menu to select your onscreen tools and set your Zoom, bringing you visually closer to or farther away from your worksheet.

- **Insert**. The most commonly used commands on this menu enable you to add columns and rows to your worksheet. The **Insert** menu also contains a list of items that can be added to your worksheet, such as charts, maps, pictures, or hyperlinks.

- **Format**. Use this menu to change the appearance of your worksheet—to change the font and size of your text and numbers, the width of your columns, or the height of your rows. You can also format cells to set up the type of data they'll contain.

- **Tools**. This menu contains a list of utilities for such activities as checking your spelling, sharing your work, working with a team to develop a worksheet, or creating a macro to automate frequently performed tasks. You'll also find commands for customizing the way Excel looks and works.

- **Data/Chart**. This menu changes, depending on the content of your workbook. Normally appearing as **Data**, if you add a chart to your workbook and that chart is the active element, the **Data** menu changes to a **Chart** menu, offering tools for editing the selected chart. When the menu appears as the **Data** menu, you'll find tools for maintaining lists of items in a database. The **Data** menu gives you commands for sorting and filtering your data onscreen and in printed reports.

You may also have an Accounting menu

If your Excel menu bar contains an Accounting menu (due to your having installed the Small Business Financial Manager), you'll find commands that enable you to integrate Excel and the Financial Manager program.

- **<u>Window</u>**. Use this menu when you have more than one workbook open and want to switch between or among your open files. You can also choose ways to simultaneously display your open workbooks by clicking the **<u>Arrange</u>** command and choosing the way the separate files will appear onscreen.

- **<u>Help</u>**. As the name implies, this menu gives you access to Excel's Help files—informative articles that explain how Excel works and assists you with the use of its features.

Using the Excel Toolbars

When you open Excel for the first time, you'll see two toolbars across the top of your screen, just below the menu bar. The top row, called the Standard toolbar, contains all picture buttons, each one representing a command that can also be found on a menu. These commands perform immediate tasks or open dialog boxes that enable you to customize the way a given task will be performed.

The second row of tools is called the Formatting toolbar. These tools enable you to change the appearance of your worksheet content—everything from choosing a font for your text to reducing the number of decimal places in numeric content. Figure 12.3 shows the Currency Style ToolTip.

Use ToolTips and What's This? to get help with tools

To see the name of each tool (in either toolbar), point your mouse (without clicking) on a tool and wait for the ToolTip to appear in a small box. You can also use the "What's This?" command from the **Help** menu (or press Shift+F1) to identify tools. When your mouse pointer has a question mark on it, click any tool for a pop-up description of how the tool works. Press Esc to close the pop-up.

ToolTips versus ScreenTips

ToolTips are the boxes that come up when you point to a toolbar button, identifying the tool. ScreenTips are the boxes that appear when you point to a screen element such as the Formula bar or Name box.

FIGURE 12.3

Click the toolbar buttons to execute immediate commands, open a dialog box, or see a list of options.

1 Standard toolbar

2 Formatting toolbar

3 ToolTip

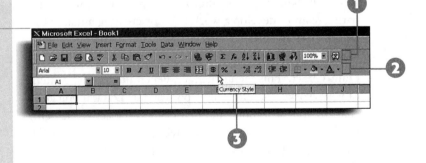

Understanding Worksheets

In older versions of Excel (prior to version 4.0), each file was a single sheet. As the product has been improved, the capability for a worksheet to have depth was added, necessitating the term "workbook" to differentiate an entire file from the sheets that it contains.

Each new Excel file is a workbook that contains three sheets, named Sheet1, Sheet2, and Sheet3 (see Figure 12.4). To activate a sheet ("turn" to that page in the book) and click its tab.

If you want to rename a sheet tab, you can double-click it, or open the **Fo**rmat menu, point to **S**heet, and choose **Rename**. In either case, the current name becomes highlighted, and you can replace it by typing the new name and pressing Enter. Your new name can have up to 31 characters, including spaces and punctuation.

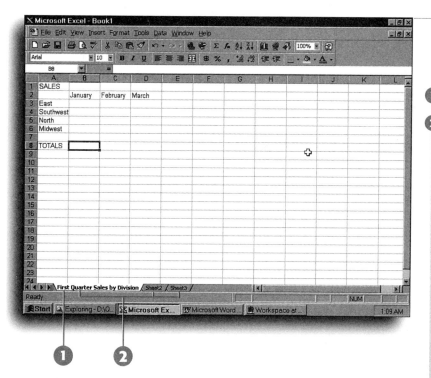

FIGURE 12.4

When you open a blank workbook, you have three blank sheets.

1 Active sheet (renamed)

2 Sheet tabs

Starting a New Worksheet

Starting a second blank workbook

If you already have a workbook open and need a new blank one in addition to it, click the New button. This toolbar button gives you a blank, new workbook without having to open the New Office Document dialog box.

How you open Excel determines what steps you must go through to get to a new, blank worksheet. If your **Start** menu contains the **New Office Document** command, you can select it and then choose **Blank Workbook** from the **General** tab in the New Office Document dialog box (see Figure 12.5). You can either double-click the Blank Workbook icon or click it once and click **OK**. If you have Microsoft Excel on your **Programs** menu, select it to take you directly to a new blank workbook, no questions asked.

FIGURE 12.5

Choose Blank Workbook from the **General** tab in the New Office Document dialog box.

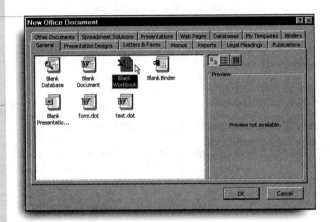

Opening a Blank Worksheet

Whether from the New Office Document dialog box or as the default starting sheet when you open Excel, the blank workbook contains no data and no formulas and adheres to the application's very "vanilla" defaults for fonts, column width, row heights, and alignment of text or numbers within your cells.

The blank worksheet opens with cell A1 active. You can tell the active cell by the dark border around it. You'll also notice that A1 appears on the left end of the Formula bar, in the Name box (see Figure 12.6). This box reminds you of the address of your active cell.

To begin using your sheet, you can begin typing in cell A1 (or whichever cell you want to start in) by clicking in that cell and

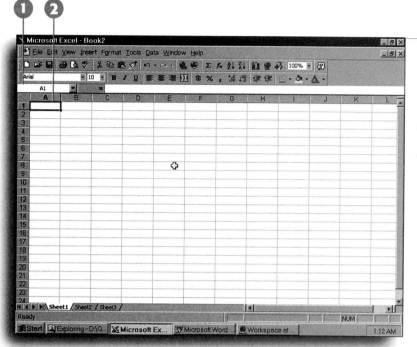

FIGURE 12.6

Cell A1 is active in a blank, new sheet. The Name box shows the address of the active cell.

1 Name box

2 Active cell (A1)

typing. No "rules" apply for entering data, although we'll discuss simple and efficient methods for doing so later in this chapter.

Using the Mouse to Navigate your Worksheet

Before you start entering your data, it's a good idea to get a feel for how to move around in your worksheet. You can navigate your sheet (all two million + cells of it) with your mouse, your keyboard, or your scrollbars.

- *Use your mouse.* You can click directly in any cell to make that the active cell (your mouse takes the shape of a white cross while hovering over the worksheet area). This, of course, applies only to cells that are currently onscreen.

- *Use the scrollbars.* Although this method won't change the active cell, you can bring your desired cell into view (by scrolling up, down, left, or right). After the cell is onscreen, click in the cell to activate it.

■ *Use the keyboard.* To move from cell to cell, use your arrow keys to move up, down, left, or right, one cell at a time. Use the Tab key to go to the cell to the right of your active cell. Other keyboard navigation commands are listed in Table 12.1.

TABLE 12.1   Keyboard navigation commands

To . . .	Press
Go back to cell A1 from anywhere in your worksheet	Ctrl+Home
Go back to the first cell in the row you're in	Home
Go to the end of the data in your current row	Ctrl+End
Go to any cell in the worksheet	Ctrl+G and type the cell address. Press Enter to go to the cell (see Figure 12.7).
Move to the end of similar data within your current row	Ctrl+Right arrow
Move to the beginning of similar data within your current row	Ctrl+Left arrow
Move down one screen	Page Down
Move up one screen	Page Up

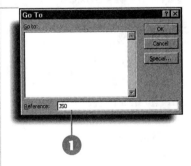

FIGURE 12.7

The Go To dialog box can be used to go to any cell address in your worksheet. Use it to save time getting to a cell that is far from your current location.

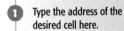 Type the address of the desired cell here.

Selecting Cells

Just as selecting text in Word enables you to format, edit, or delete that text, selecting cells in Excel enables you to enter your content, set up cells for certain types of data, or edit the cell's content, including deletions if necessary.

To select a single cell, click it once with your mouse. To select a range or block of contiguous cells, click in the first cell of the range and drag through the rest of the desired cells. The first cell in the range remains white while the rest turn black, and any content in the blackened cells appears white (see Figure 12.8).

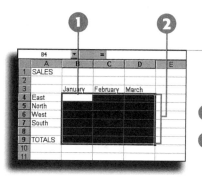

FIGURE 12.8

The first cell in a selected range remains white.

1 First cell in range

2 Selected range (B4 through D9)

After a cell or range of cells is selected, you can apply formats to the appearance and function of the cells. You can also move, copy, or delete their contents. To edit cell content, cells must be selected individually. When a range of cells is selected, only the content of the first cell in the range appears in the Formula bar, as seen in Figure 12.8.

To select an entire row (across all 256 columns), click the row number to the left of the row. To select an entire column (down all 8,192 rows), click the column letter at the top of the column. To select multiple columns or rows, drag through the desired column letters or row numbers with your mouse.

Entering Data Manually

The most important and essential step in creating a spreadsheet is to enter your data. Entering it efficiently and accurately (although it's easy to edit if you make mistakes) is very important to your successful and satisfying use of Excel.

"Manual" entry of content refers to your typing it in the cells. You'll find out later that you can use Excel's AutoFill feature to make the software do the entry for you!

Selecting noncontiguous sections

When you select a range of cells, all the cells in the range must have a common side or sides. You can, however, select multiple ranges that do not connect by selecting the first range and then pressing and holding the Ctrl key. Drag through your second range, and release the mouse button and then the Ctrl key. You can use this method to select as many noncontiguous ranges as you need to.

Entering Text

When you start a blank workbook, you start out in Sheet1 and in cell A1. Most people place the title of their worksheet in that cell, as shown in Figure 12.9. As shown in the figure, the text overflows the cell into the adjoining cells in row 1. This is okay because nothing but the title will be in this row, and therefore nothing will interfere with the overflow. If there were text in the adjoining cell, the content of A1 would be truncated (chopped off) at the point of overlap. You can widen columns as needed, to accommodate entries that exceed the default column width.

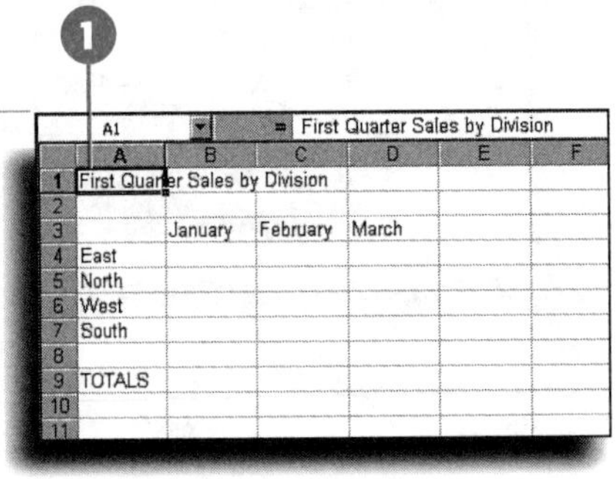

FIGURE 12.9

Title text is typically placed in cell A1 and can overflow into B1 and C1 if necessary.

1 A1 is active and contains all title text.

One or two rows below your title, you'll want to start entering your spreadsheet data in columns and rows. Notice that your text is automatically left-aligned in the cells. Excel applies a left alignment to any text content that contains text as opposed to numbers.

Typically in row 2 or 3 you will enter your categories for each column, such as months, years, or products, as shown in Figure 12.10. Also shown in this figure is the breakdown of these categories, labeled in the cells of column A.

When entering data across a row, you can press the Tab key to move to the next cell (moving left to right). You can also select the range of cells within that row into which you'll be entering data—you can then use the Enter key to move from cell to cell across the row. Press the Home key to move back to column A, and start your next row by pressing the down arrow.

SEE ALSO

➤ *For more information on changing column width, see page 279*

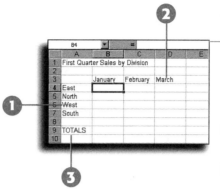

FIGURE 12.10

After your title, you'll begin entering your categories in row 2 or 3 for the data that will be entered into your columns.

1 Breakdown of row 3 categories in column A

2 Column headings in row 3

3 Text is left-aligned in the cells.

Entering Numbers

The process of entering numbers is the same as entering text—activate the cell that you want to fill, and type your content. The difference is in how Excel treats the numeric content. You'll notice immediately that numeric content is automatically right-aligned in the cells (see Figure 12.11).

FIGURE 12.11

Numeric data is automatically right-aligned in the cells.

Formatting Numbers as Currency

In addition to entering numbers into your cells, you can set up your cells to treat their numeric content as currency—just one of the many numeric formats available to you. This can be done before or after the content is entered.

Formatting selected cells as currency

1. Select the range of cells to be formatted. It doesn't matter if the cells have content or not.

2. Open the **Format** menu and choose **Cells**. You can also right-click the cell or range of cells and choose **Format Cells** from the shortcut menu.

My numbers appear as pound signs (#)

If the number you've entered is wider than the column's current width allows, the numbers appear as pound signs (#) rather than truncated. Find the divider between the column button at the top of the column containing the pound signs and the column to its right, and double-click it. The column on the left automatically widens to fit the widest entry.

3. In the Format Cells dialog box, click the **Number** tab.

4. From the **Category** list box, select **Currency** (see Figure 12.12) and choose the number of decimal places, currency symbol, and desired appearance of any negative numbers.

FIGURE 12.12

Choose the way your currency-formatted numbers will appear by exercising your options in the Format Cells dialog box.

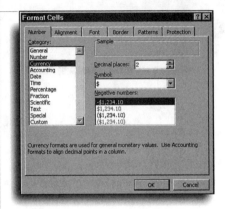

5. Click **OK** to confirm your settings and apply them to the selected range.

To quickly apply the currency format with two decimal places and have your negative numbers appear in parentheses, click the Currency Style button on the toolbar $.

Using Date and Time Formats

Many worksheets require dates and times to be entered—employee time sheets, invoices that bill for hourly work, or lists of tasks or projects are just a few examples.

Formatting cell content as dates or times

1. Select the range of cells to be formatted. It doesn't matter if the cells have content or not.

2. Open the **Format** menu and choose **Cells**. You can also right-click the cell or range of cells and choose **Format Cells** from the shortcut menu.

3. In the **Number** tab, select the **Date** or **Time Category**, and then select a **Type** (see Figure 12.13).

4. Check the **Sample** box to make sure you have chosen the correct format, and click **OK** to apply it to the selected cells.

Other numeric formats

You can apply formatting to your numeric content that will display the numbers as fractions, percentages, dates, or times, or as text for numbers that contain hyphens (such as social security numbers).

Excel's default date feature

If you enter the date 2/3 (for example), Excel converts it automatically to 3-Feb. If you enter 2/3/98, Excel leaves it as you've entered it—a mm/dd/yy-formatted date. If you enter the date with dashes (2-3-98), Excel replaces the dashes with slashes, and the cell contains 2/3/98 after you press Enter.

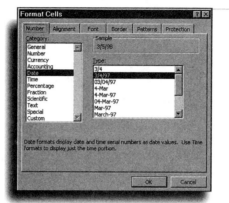

FIGURE 12.13
Choose the appropriate Date or Time format for your selected cells from the Format Cells dialog box.

Automatic Data Entry in Worksheets

Excel's AutoFill feature enables you to enter a single cell's content and use that content as a sample for a series of entries. For example, you can type the word January in cell B3 (see Figure 12.14) and have Excel automatically fill in February, March, and April in cells B4 and B5 for a first-quarter report.

You can also create a series of incrementing numbers by establishing a pattern of numbers in two cells and then using that pattern to establish a series.

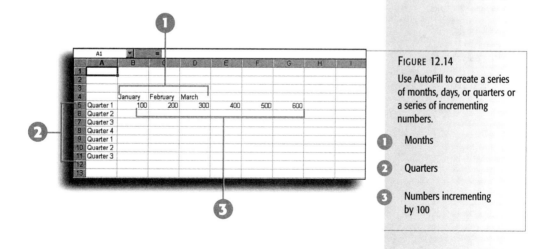

FIGURE 12.14

Use AutoFill to create a series of months, days, or quarters or a series of incrementing numbers.

❶ Months

❷ Quarters

❸ Numbers incrementing by 100

Creating a Time Series

AutoFill is a mouse-controlled feature. To apply a time-series AutoFill, you must enter a starting word or value, such as a month, day of the week, or quarter of the year.

Creating a time series

1. After entering the content, notice the small black square (called the AutoFill handle) in the lower-right corner of the cell containing your entry. Position your mouse over the handle and see your pointer turn into a black cross.

2. Drag your mouse across the row or down the column that should contain your series, and then release the mouse button.

The cells within the range through which you dragged will now be filled with a series based on your first value (see Figure 12.15).

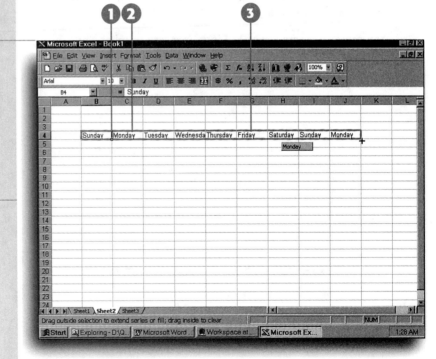

FIGURE 12.15

Drag the small black square across the cells into which you want to AutoFill a series.

1 AutoFill handle

2 Starting cell value

3 Completed series

Creating a Linear Series

A linear series is one that follows a pattern—incrementing numbers by 1, 100, or any number you establish in the pattern. Your pattern must be established in two consecutive cells, and then those cells are used as the example for the creation of the linear series. Figure 12.16 shows two sample cells containing the pattern (incrementing by 100) and then the resulting linear series.

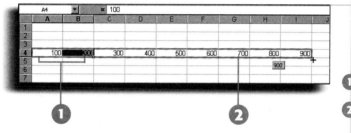

FIGURE 12.16

Enter the sample cells to show Excel the pattern you'd like to create.

1 Selected sample cells

2 Completed series

Creating a linear series

1. Enter content in your two consecutive cells.
2. Select the two cells and grab the AutoFill handle in the last of the two cells.
3. Drag down the column or across the row to select the cells into which the linear series should be entered.
4. Release the mouse button and observe your series.

Linear series can increase or decrease

If your first two cells contain the numbers 100 and 50, 50 being in the second cell, the numbers in the series created will decrease by 50 for each cell of the series.

Creating a Growth Series

A growth series is somewhat more complex than a linear series in that the numbers in the series will be multiplied by a number established in your sample cells. For example, if your sample cells contain the numbers 1 and 2, 2 being in the second cell, the growth series will contain the numbers 4, 8, 16, 32, 64, and so on. A pattern of doubling the number in the last cell is established.

Creating a growth series

1. Enter sample cell content in your first two cells.
2. Select the sample cells.

3. Open the **Edit** menu, choose **Fill**, and then choose **Series**. The Series dialog box opens (see Figure 12.17).

FIGURE 12.17

In the Series dialog box, you can choose how your series will grow and when it will stop.

4. Choose to have your **Series in Rows** or **Columns**.

5. Click the **Growth** option button.

6. Enter the **Step value**, or number by which the series should increase or decrease. If entering a number to decrease, be sure to make it negative by typing a minus sign in front of it.

7. Enter the **Stop value**, or value with which the series should end.

8. Click **OK** to create the series.

Working with Multiple Worksheets

Imagine that your company has two divisions or locations. You want to set up the same worksheet for both of them—identical listings in the columns and rows, the same formulas throughout—the only thing that will be different is the division-specific content. If your two locations both sell Widgets, for example, both sheets will contain a cell for the total number of Widgets sold, among other common cells.

Excel gives you the capability to simultaneously create identical sheets for just this purpose. You can link two or more sheets together and enter your common content once—it will appear automatically on all the linked sheets.

Creating Multiple Worksheets

To create two or more identical sheets simultaneously, you must link them by holding the Shift key as you click their tabs. All the tabs that you click while the Shift key is depressed turn white, and any remaining, unlinked sheets remain gray.

As soon as your sheets are linked, you can begin entering the common content on any one of them. All the linked sheets will be built at the same time, with the content you enter while they're linked appearing on all the linked sheets, in exactly the same cells. Figure 12.18 shows a group of linked tabs and some common data entered on the top sheet.

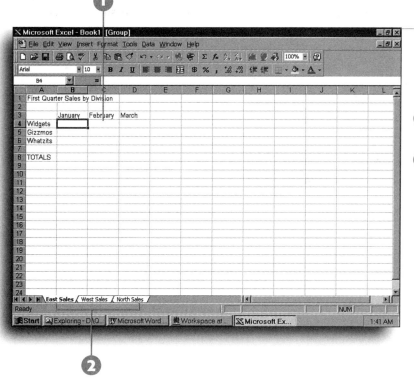

FIGURE 12.18

You can create multiple sheets simultaneously by linking them and then entering the content common to all of them.

❶ Content common to all linked sheets

❷ Linked tabs

To break the link and begin entering content on the sheets individually, click once on any of the unlinked sheet tabs. If you don't have any sheets that aren't part of the linked group, right-click any of the sheet tabs and choose **Ungroup Sheets** from the shortcut menu.

Switching Between Worksheets

Whether your sheets were linked (and therefore contain common content) or were all created individually, you will want to hop back and forth between them to compare content, copy content from one to another, or create formulas that refer to data in more than one sheet.

To switch between sheets, click the tab of the sheet you want to go to, and that sheet becomes the active (top) sheet. If you have so many sheets that not all their tabs can be seen simultaneously, use the Tab Scrolling buttons to the left of the sheet tabs (see Figure 12.19). You can use these buttons to move to the first, previous, next, or last tab.

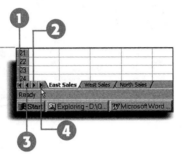

FIGURE 12.19

Use the Tab Scrolling buttons to switch to a sheet whose tab may be out of your current view.

1 First tab

2 Next tab

3 Previous tab

4 Last tab

Making Changes to Worksheet Information

Edit the content of your cells

Use the Clipboard to cut and copy worksheet data

Add rows and columns

Cut, copy, merge entire worksheets

Hide worksheets from view and then redisplay them

Editing Cell Data

You've entered data into your cells, and now you spot an error or find that some of your information is out of date. Excel makes it simple to edit the content of your cells, from making minor changes to the text or numbers in a cell to completely replacing a cell's contents.

Editing your cell content is done one cell at a time. Cell ranges (blocks of cells or entire columns or rows) can be copied or moved, and certainly any selected group of cells can be emptied. To correct spelling or change a number in a specific cell, however, you must select that one cell.

When a cell is active, its content appears not only in the cell but in the Formula bar (see Figure 13.1). The cell's content can be edited in the cell or on the Formula bar, which gives you a roomier place to work for editing—without other cells and their content on all four sides as there are when you're editing in the cell.

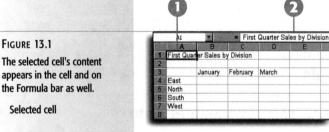

FIGURE 13.1

The selected cell's content appears in the cell and on the Formula bar as well.

1 Selected cell

2 Cell content on Formula bar

Editing with the Formula Bar

The Formula bar is like a small word processor—your mouse pointer turns to an I-beam (see Figure 13.2) whenever you point to the content in the bar.

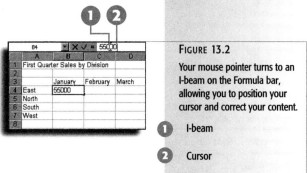

FIGURE 13.2

Your mouse pointer turns to an I-beam on the Formula bar, allowing you to position your cursor and correct your content.

1 I-beam

2 Cursor

Editing cell content in the Formula bar

1. With your cell selected, move your mouse pointer to the Formula bar. Click to position your cursor somewhere in the cell's content.

2. Using the Backspace or Delete keys, remove any erroneous text or numbers. Then type the correct content.

3. Confirm your entries by pressing Enter or clicking the green check mark to the left of the Formula bar ☑.

You can also simultaneously remove and replace your cell content by typing the replacement text while the erroneous content is selected. Figure 13.3 shows a word highlighted within the Formula bar.

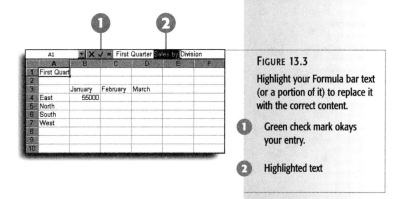

FIGURE 13.3

Highlight your Formula bar text (or a portion of it) to replace it with the correct content.

1 Green check mark okays your entry.

2 Highlighted text

Editing Directly in the Cell

Sometimes it's simpler to edit a cell's content right in the cell—you're already there from having selected the cell, and you don't have to go up to the Formula bar to place your cursor or select the content that needs to be changed.

To completely replace the cell's current content with new content (changing "1997" to "1998" or "Bob" to "Robert," for example), click once in the cell and simply type the replacement content. Press Enter or click into another cell to confirm your entry.

If you only need to change part of a cell's content and you want to do it in the cell, you must double-click the cell or press the F2 key while the cell is active. This places your cursor in the cell, and you can then edit the content with your Backspace and Delete keys or highlight the portion you need to fix and type the replacement content. Figure 13.4 shows a cell's content being edited in the cell.

Active cells are vulnerable cells

Whenever a cell is active, its content is vulnerable—the very next thing you type will replace the cell's current content. This can work *for* you in the case of quick replacements or *against* you if you bump a key by mistake. If you accidentally replace a cell's content, press Esc to revert the cell to its previous content. You can also press Ctrl+Z or click the Undo button .

FIGURE 13.4

Edit your content right in the cell by double-clicking the cell or pressing F2 to activate your cursor.

1 Active cell

2 Highlighted text in the cell

Using the Spell Checker

Some users are surprised to find that Excel has a spell checker in it, but of course it does as part of the Office suite. Spreadsheets can become rather complex, with text and numbers distributed throughout the sheets of a workbook, making manual proofreading virtually impossible.

Unlike Word, Excel does not spell check as you type—no red, wavy underline warns you that your cells contain a spelling error. For this reason, it is especially important that you run the Spelling program before you print or distribute your workbook to other users.

Running spell check

1. With your cursor in any cell that has content within your active sheet, open the **Tools** menu and choose **Spelling**.

2. The Spelling dialog box opens, displaying the first spelling error it finds on your active sheet (see Figure 13.5).

3. Choose from the following options for handling the misspelled word:

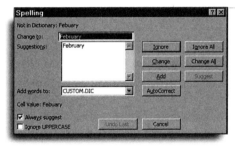

FIGURE 13.5

Ignore, change, or add the words that Excel thinks are misspelled as you run the spell check.

- **Ignore** or **Ignore All**. If you know the word is spelled correctly—perhaps it's a person's name or a city—you can choose to skip the word. If you know you've used the word again in your sheet, click **Ignore All** to save having to ignore each instance individually.

- **Change** or **Change All**. You can choose an alternative spelling from the list of **Suggestions** or type your own corrected version in the **Change to** box. In either case, after indicating the correct spelling, click **Change** to fix this one error or **Change All** if you think you've repeated the error elsewhere in the sheet.

- **Add**. If the word is spelled correctly and it's one that you'll be using in future sheets, add it to the dictionary. This will save you having to deal with the word as an error in future spell checks.

Ignore words in UPPERCASE

If you're tired of finding your product numbers or serial numbers (such as ABC123) marked as misspelled, check the **Ignore UPPERCASE** option box in the Spelling dialog box. Of course, this only works if your product or serial numbers are in uppercase (capital letters).

Add words to the dictionary with care

When adding a word to the dictionary, take a second before clicking the **Add** button to make sure the word is spelled correctly. You don't want to have to edit the dictionary to get rid of the misspelled word!

4. As soon as you resolve one spelling error by ignoring, changing, or adding it, Excel moves on to the next error (if any). When you've come to the end of the sheet and there are no more errors, a prompt appears to tell you that the spell check is complete (see Figure 13.6). Click **OK**.

FIGURE 13.6

You must spell check each sheet individually. When one sheet's spell check is complete, this prompt appears.

SEE ALSO

➤ *For more information on using the Office proofing tools, see page 126*

Using Find and Replace to Edit Cells

Find and Replace are especially useful if you're using an older worksheet and want to make global changes to names or dates. You can use **Find** all by itself to merely locate a cell by its content, or use **Replace** with **Find** to locate content and change it.

Using Find and Replace to edit cell content

1. On your active sheet, press Ctrl+Home to go to cell A1.

2. Open the **Edit** menu and choose **Replace**. The Replace dialog box opens (see Figure 13.7).

FIGURE 13.7

Use Find and Replace to catch out-of-date names or dates in your worksheet.

3. In the **Find what** box, type the cell content that you're looking for. Press the Tab key to move to the next field in the dialog box.

4. In the **Replace with** box, type the text or numbers that should replace the found content.

5. Choose to **Search By Rows** or **By Columns** (it doesn't really matter).

6. Turn on the **Match case** and/or **Find entire cells only** options to refine your search to words in uppercase or lowercase or to look for the **Find what** text only when it is the only text in the cell.

7. Click **Find Next** if you want to see each occurrence and decide whether to **Replace** it. Click **Replace All** if you want to have Excel make all the changes without prompting you on each one.

8. If you're using **Find Next** and **Replace**, when you run out of occurrences of the word or words you're looking for, Excel prompts you that there are no more matches. Click **OK** in the prompt box and then click **Close** to close the Replace dialog box.

9. If you choose **Replace All**, the changes are made instantly and the dialog box closes without any further interaction from you.

Copying Cells

Cell data in individual cells, ranges of cells, or in entire rows or columns can be used in more than one place in your worksheet or workbook without your having to retype it. Depending on the source (current location) and target (where you want to place it), you can choose from a variety of copying methods.

Using the Clipboard to Copy Cell Data

The Windows Clipboard is a space within your computer's memory that holds onto selected text for moving or copying it to another location. You can invoke the Clipboard to copy your selected cells in any one of the following ways:

Using Replace All can be a leap of faith

Replace All is a fast way to make global changes to a sheet—there's no denying that. It can, however, make changes you didn't want, especially if you don't use the **Match case** or **Find entire cells only** options. For example, if you're changing 1997 to 1998, **Replace All** will change a sales figure of $11,997 to $11,998 if you don't specify **Find entire cells only**.

■ *Use the* **Edit** *menu.* Select your cells, open the **Edit** menu, and choose **Copy**. A copy of the content of your cells is placed on the Clipboard, waiting for you to place it in another location. Click in the cell where you want to place the copied cell or cells (if it's a range, click in the first cell of the target range) and choose **Paste** from the **Edit** menu.

■ *Use the toolbar.* Select your cells and click the Copy button ▣. To place your selection in the new location, click in the target cell or in the first cell of the target range and click the Paste button ▣.

■ *Use the right mouse button.* Select the cell or cells to be copied and right-click the selection. Choose **Copy** from the shortcut menu. Move to your target, click the right mouse button again, and choose **Paste** from the shortcut menu.

The method you choose will depend on the way you mentally approach a task and your facility with the mouse. Don't worry about learning and memorizing all three methods—stick with the one that seems most natural to you.

Using Fill to Copy Cell Content

The Clipboard is best for copying from the source to the target when the source and target are not simultaneously visible onscreen or when the source needs to be copied only once. If, however, you need to copy a cell's content to several adjoining cells (across a row or down a column, for example), use Excel's Fill feature.

Using Fill to copy cells across adjoining cells

1. Select the cell that contains the content to be copied.

2. Point to the small square (fill handle) in the lower-right corner of the active cell (see Figure 13.8).

3. When your mouse turns to a black cross, drag though the cells into which you want to copy the cell content.

4. Release the mouse button and see your range of cells filled with the copied content, as shown in Figure 13.9.

Copy without the Clipboard by using drag and drop

Actually, the Clipboard is being used with this method, but you aren't formally invoking it. To copy a source cell or range to a target that is within visible range of the source, point to the edge of the selection (your mouse turns to a white arrow) and depress the Ctrl key. With the key held down, drag the range to the target area and release the mouse button, dropping the selected content in it's new location.

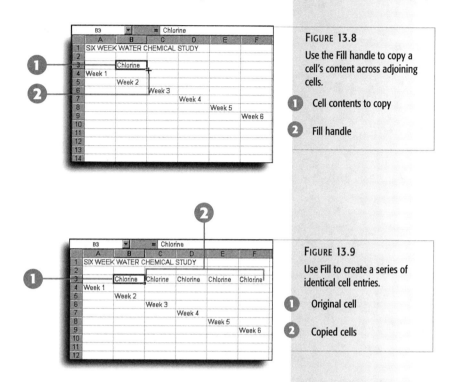

FIGURE 13.8
Use the Fill handle to copy a cell's content across adjoining cells.

① Cell contents to copy

② Fill handle

FIGURE 13.9
Use Fill to create a series of identical cell entries.

① Original cell

② Copied cells

Moving Cell Content

Copying cell content leaves the original cell intact and makes a duplicate entry in your target location. Moving, on the other hand, removes the content from the source and places it in the target area so that your content appears only once.

Moving (cutting from one place and pasting in another) can be performed by invoking the Clipboard or by dragging cell content from the source to the target. Select one of the following methods, choosing the one that's most appropriate for your situation:

- *Use the Clipboard.* This method is best used when your source (cells to be moved) and target (desired new location) are not simultaneously visible. Open the **Edit** menu and choose **Cut**, or right-click the source selection and choose **Cut** from the shortcut menu. You can also use the Cut button ✂ on the toolbar. Next, click in the target cell (or first cell in the target range), open the **Edit** or shortcut menu, and choose **Paste**. You can also use the Paste button on the toolbar 📋.

- *Use your mouse.* Without formally invoking the Clipboard, you can use the drag-and-drop technique to drag one cell or a range of cells from one place to another, moving the cell content. Select the source content—the cell or cells you want to move—and point to the edge of the selection. When your mouse turns to a white arrow, drag to the target cells and release the mouse button.

Deleting Cell Content

Removing cell content is very simple—select the cell or range of cells and press the Delete key on your keyboard. You can also select your cells, open the **Edit** menu, point to **Clear**, and then choose **Contents**.

If the data you want to delete is sandwiched between other data—rows above and below, columns to the left and right—you may want to give Excel instructions for what to do with the blank space that will be created by the deletion.

Deleting data with the Edit menu

1. Select the cells that you want to delete.

2. Open the **Edit** menu and choose **Delete**. The Delete dialog box opens (see Figure 13.10), offering two sets of options—one set pertaining to how to deal with the surrounding data and one set asking what you want to delete.

3. Click the option you want, and click **OK**.

If you want to retain your cell's content but need to delete formats that have been applied—currency or decimal formatting, for example—you can use Excel's **Clear** command.

FIGURE 13.10
Use the Delete dialog box to confirm your deletion and instruct Excel how to deal with surrounding data.

Deleting cell formats

1. Select the cells in which you want to remove formatting.

2. Open the **Edit** menu, point to **Clear**, and choose **Formats**.

Your cell or range contents remain, but any formatting that had been applied is removed. If, for example, you had applied currency formatting, your numbers remain in the cell, but dollar signs, commas, and any zero decimals disappear. The numbers return to General format. In the case of text, the text remains in the cell but returns to Excel's default Arial 10pt text.

Working with Columns and Rows

When you initially set up your worksheet, doing some planning—at least in your head—is helpful. You then enter the column headings and row labels for your data and enter your data in the cells where your columns and rows intersect.

What happens, however, if you forget a column or row? It's easy to forget a category or item and then have no place to put it within the data you've already entered. Excel makes it easy to add a blank row or column where you need one, moving the existing data aside to accommodate it. You can insert one column or row at a time, or insert several adjoining columns or rows all at once.

Inserting Columns and Rows

Adding a row or column requires selecting an existing row or column to tell Excel where to place the new one. If, for example (as shown in Figure 13.11), you forgot a saleswoman in column A, you can insert a row for her.

Inserting a row

1. Click the row number for the row below where you need a new, blank row. The entire row, across all 256 columns, is selected.

FIGURE 13.11

Select the row below where
you want your new row
inserted.

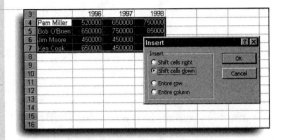

2. Open the **Insert** menu and choose **Rows**. The row you
   selected appears to move down, and a new, blank row is
   inserted.

To insert multiple rows, select the number of existing rows that
you want to add (starting with the row below your desired location for the new row) and perform step 2 above. Instead of a single row, however, you will see several new rows added, equal to
the number of rows you selected before issuing the command.

Adding a column or columns is equally simple. You can add one
or several columns to your worksheet.

Adding columns

1. Select the column to the right of where you want your new,
   blank column inserted. Be sure to click the column letter to
   select the entire column.

2. Open the **Insert** menu and choose **Columns**. A new, blank
   column appears to the left of your selected column.

To insert more than one column, select the number of existing
columns to the right of where you want your new columns to be
inserted, and follow step 2 above. The number of columns you
insert will be equal to the number of existing columns you
selected.

If you select a block of cells rather than an entire row or column
before issuing the **Insert Columns** or **Insert Rows** command,
the **Insert** menu contains the **Cells** command. When you
choose Cells, an Insert dialog box opens (see Figure 13.12), asking you to tell Excel which way to move the surrounding cells—
up, down, left, or right—to accommodate the new cells. Make

Context-sensitive commands

Excel is *context-sensitive,* meaning
that it is aware of what's going on
while you're working and offers only
the appropriate tools for the current
situation. When you want to add
columns, for example, you'll notice
that the **Rows** command is
dimmed in the **Insert** menu, and
Columns is available.

your selection and click **OK**. Note that you also can access this Insert dialog box by right-clicking the block of cells and choosing **I**nsert from the shortcut menu.

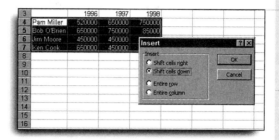

FIGURE 13.12

Inserting cells requires some direction from you to tell Excel where to move the surrounding cells.

Changing Column Width

Many times, the amount of text or numbers you type into a cell exceeds the default column width of 8.43 characters. When your content exceeds a column's width, the excess content spills over, appearing to fill the adjoining cell on the right. If you enter content into the adjoining cell, however, you'll see your overflow content truncated, or chopped off visually (the content is still there; it's just hidden). Figure 13.13 shows both situations. Either of these scenarios can be distracting, requiring you to widen the column so that all the content is visible within the column.

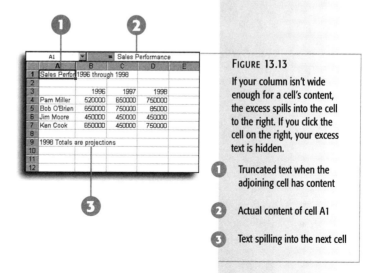

FIGURE 13.13

If your column isn't wide enough for a cell's content, the excess spills into the cell to the right. If you click the cell on the right, your excess text is hidden.

① Truncated text when the adjoining cell has content

② Actual content of cell A1

③ Text spilling into the next cell

Changing several column widths at once

You can change several column widths simultaneously by selecting the columns (drag through their column letters) and then double-clicking the boundary between any two of the selected columns. All the columns AutoFit to their widest individual entries. If you want to make all the selected columns a uniform width, drag a boundary between any of the two selected columns—all the columns snap to this new width.

Changing column width

1. Click the column letter at the top of the column that you want to widen.

2. Open the **Format** menu and choose **Column**. The submenu offers the following choices pertaining to column width:

   - **Width**. Choose this option to enter a specific number of characters for your column width. Click **OK** to close the Column Width dialog box.

   - **AutoFit Selection**. This command automatically widens (or narrows) the column to fit its widest entry.

   - **Standard Width**. This command opens the Standard Width dialog box, in which you can return an already-widened column to the default width of 8.43 characters or enter a new default of your own. If you set a new width, all the columns—not just the one you have selected—change to the new width. When using this dialog box, type your desired width and click **OK**.

For a faster, although less exact method for changing column width, use the mouse.

Changing column width with the mouse

1. Select the column to be changed by clicking its column letter.

2. Point to the boundary between the selected column letter and the letter to its right.

3. When your mouse pointer turns to a two-headed arrow (see Figure 13.14), click and drag the boundary to the right to widen the column or to the left to narrow it.

Changing Row Height

Altering the height of your rows is usually an aesthetic choice as opposed to a functional one. Changing column width is typically done to facilitate entry of cell contents, but changing row height is done to give your content more room and visually "open up" the cells. Row height can, however, affect a data-entry person's effectiveness by making it easier to read and edit content in the cell.

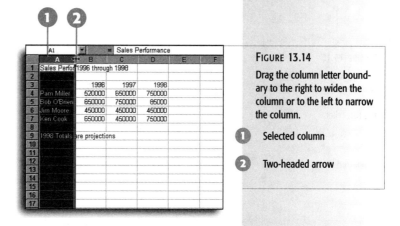

FIGURE 13.14

Drag the column letter boundary to the right to widen the column or to the left to narrow the column.

1 Selected column

2 Two-headed arrow

Adjusting row height

1. Select the row that you want to make taller or shorter by clicking its row number.

2. Open the **Format** menu and choose **Row**. The submenu contains the following options related to row height:

- **Height**. Enter a specific point size (the default is 12.75). A row's height is measured in points so that you can use the font size, also measured in points, as a guide. Click **OK** to close the Row Height dialog box.

- **AutoFit**. This selection makes your row the height it needs to be for the largest text in the row. If, for example, your row contains a cell or cells with 18-point text in them, the row will be AutoFit to 23.25 points. You will typically use this command to reset a row's height after adjusting manually.

You can also adjust your row height with your mouse.

Adjusting row height manually

1. Clicking a row number to select the row to be adjusted.

2. Point to the boundary between the row number button of the selected row and the row below it. Your mouse pointer turns to a two-headed arrow (see Figure 13.15).

Adjusting several row heights simultaneously

To make several rows taller or shorter at the same time, select the group of rows by dragging through their row numbers. Point to a boundary between row numbers of any two selected rows and drag down to make them all taller, or up to make them all shorter. All the rows in the selection adjust to the same height when you release the mouse button.

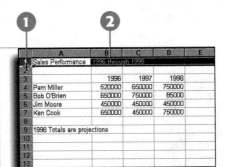

FIGURE 13.15

When your mouse turns to a two-headed arrow, drag your row boundary down to make the row taller.

1 Two-headed arrow

2 Selected row

3. Drag down to make the row taller, or up to make it shorter, and then release the mouse button.

Hiding Columns and Rows

After you enter your data into columns and rows, you may need to hide one or more of the columns or rows of data from view—for the sake of discretion when working with confidential or sensitive information or to keep from accidentally editing the column's or row's content.

Hiding columns or rows

1. Select the columns or rows to be hidden. They don't need to be contiguous columns or rows.

2. Open the **Format** menu, choose **Column** or **Row** (depending on which is selected), and then choose **Hide**. A thick line appears where the hidden row or column was when it was visible.

After your columns or rows are hidden, you can continue to work on the remaining visible worksheet content. To bring your columns or rows back into view, open the **Format** menu, choose **Column** or **Row** (depending on what you have hidden), and choose **Unhide**. The hidden columns or rows reappear.

Transposing Columns and Rows

After your worksheet is set up and your data entered, you may want to take your row data and show it in columns or take your

Hiding and unhiding columns and rows with the mouse

To hide a column with your mouse, reduce its width to 0.00 by dragging the column control button's seam to the left. Make the hidden column reappear by dragging the seam back to the right. To hide a row with your mouse, drag the row's control button seam up until the row has a height of 0.00. Drag back down to unhide the row.

column data and show it in rows. Switching columns for rows (or rows for columns) uses the **Transpose** option available through the **Paste Special** command. This process is typically performed to duplicate data and show it from a new perspective.

Transposing columns and rows

1. Select the columns you want to place in rows or the rows you want to place in columns.

2. Open the **Edit** menu and choose **Copy**.

3. Click in the first cell (upper left) of the area where you want to place the transposed data. The original location and this target area cannot overlap.

4. Open the **Edit** menu and choose **Paste Special**. In the Paste Special dialog box, click the **Transpose** check box and then click **OK** (see Figure 13.16).

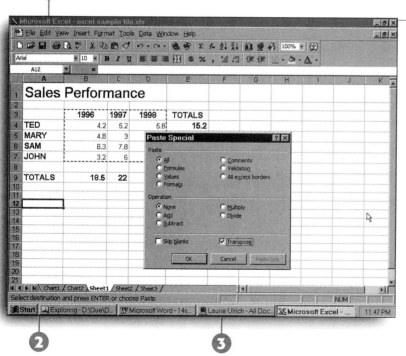

FIGURE 13.16

Copy your columns to the Clipboard and then paste them as rows elsewhere on your worksheet. You can also transpose rows, turning them into columns.

1 Selected column data

2 The first cell in the paste target area

3 Click the **Transpose** option.

After your rows or columns have been transposed, you can delete any redundant data, if desired. Figure 13.17 shows data that was in columns, now appearing in rows.

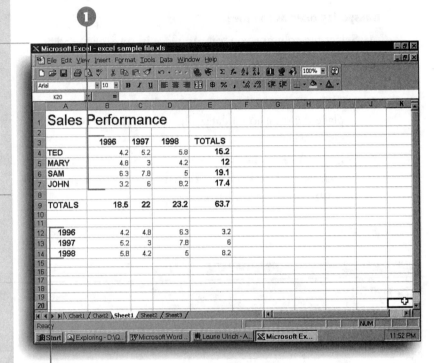

FIGURE 13.17

Changing data from columns to rows (or vice versa) gives you a different perspective on your data.

1 Original column data

2 Data transposed to appear in rows

Working with Worksheets

Working with a worksheet doesn't entail changing its content—it entails changing the worksheet's relationship to the workbook of which it is a part. A new, blank workbook starts with three blank worksheets—you can add more sheets (up to 16 total), rearrange them, copy them, delete them, and hide them. The power to control your worksheets gives your workbook more uses and gives you more flexibility.

Inserting and Deleting Worksheets

To add a new worksheet to your workbook, click the tab of the existing sheet that should precede it. For example, if you're adding a fourth sheet, click Sheet 3's tab to make it the active sheet. Then open the **Insert** menu and choose **Worksheet**.

To delete a worksheet, right-click the sheet tab and choose **Delete** from the shortcut menu. A prompt appears, reminding you that the sheet and all its contents will be deleted (see Figure 13.18). Click **OK** to confirm this and delete the sheet, or click **Cancel**.

FIGURE 13.18
This prompt gives you a chance to rethink and perhaps cancel your deletion of the selected sheet.

Just as you can copy cell content and use it somewhere else to save yourself retyping, you can copy an entire worksheet to another location within the current workbook or to another workbook altogether. This gives you the power to create duplicate sheets without the time and margin for error inherent in retyping your content.

Copying a sheet

1. Right-click the worksheets tab, and choose **Move** or **Copy** from the shortcut menu.

2. In the Move or Copy dialog box, click the **Create a copy** check box in the lower-left corner (see Figure 13.19).

FIGURE 13.19
The Move or Copy dialog box gives you options for moving or copying a selected sheet to a new position in the current workbook or to a completely different workbook.

Keep your target workbook open

If you plan to copy a sheet to another workbook, that workbook must be open when you initiate the **Move** or **Copy** command.

3. In the **To** book drop-down list, select from the list of open workbooks or select **(new book)** from the list. Choosing **(new book)** simultaneously creates a new workbook and places your sheet in it.

4. Select where to place your sheet among the other sheets in the **Before sheet** list box.

5. Click **OK** to copy your sheet to its new location.

You can also copy your sheet within the same workbook without using the Move or Copy dialog box. This process is faster and less complicated than the Move and Copy dialog box method, but can only be used for moving or copying a sheet within the current workbook.

Copying a sheet by dragging its tab

1. Click once on the sheet tab of the sheet you want to copy.

2. Press and hold the Ctrl key while dragging the sheet tab to the left or right. You'll notice a small black triangle appear to the left of the active tab, along with a small paper icon with a plus sign in it (see Figure 13.20).

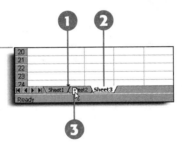

FIGURE 13.20

Use the Ctrl key as you drag your sheet tab to a new location, creating a copy of the selected sheet.

1 Small black triangle points to the new site of the copied sheet.

2 Sheet to be copied

3 Plus sign reminds you that you're making a copy.

3. When the small black triangle is pointing to the location where you want the sheet copied (in front of, after, or between existing sheets), release the mouse button. The copied sheet has the same name as the original, but with a (2) at the end of the name, as shown in Figure 13.21.

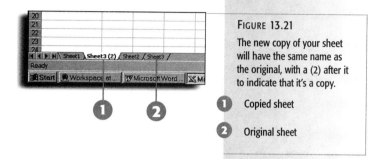

FIGURE 13.21

The new copy of your sheet will have the same name as the original, with a (2) after it to indicate that it's a copy.

1 Copied sheet

2 Original sheet

You can move a sheet by the same methods that a copy is made, with minor adjustments in the procedure.

If you're using the Move or Copy dialog box, don't check the **Create a copy** check box. If you're using the mouse to move the sheet, don't use the Ctrl key. Without the Ctrl key, no copy is made—you'll notice no plus sign in the paper icon as you drag the sheet tab.

Hiding and Displaying Worksheets

When people first hear that they can hide a worksheet, the common reaction is "Why?" Upon hearing some suggested reasons for hiding a sheet, the reaction is more of an "Aha!" because the capability to control what other users see in a workbook is very attractive.

Imagine that you work in the Human Resources department, and you have a workbook that contains all your employee data— one sheet has their names and addresses, another contains their work history, and another contains their insurance information. A fourth tab contains names with current salaries. Virtually all these tabs contain very sensitive information that doesn't belong in just anyone's hands.

So you can share your workbook with others, giving each person only the data they need without compromising the confidentiality of insurance or salary records, it's great to be able to hide the confidential sheets.

Hiding sheets also removes all possibility of the sheet's content being altered accidentally. If your data-entry people are entering

Renaming Sheets

After you copy a sheet, you will probably want to rename it— the (2) that appears next to the copied sheet's name doesn't really make the copy distinct from the original. To rename a sheet, double-click the sheet's tab and type a new name. If you want to add to the existing name, click at the end of the current name (after you've double-clicked the tab) and type the added text.

a list of new hires, you don't want them accidentally adding the new hires to a list of people who are no longer with the company. Hiding the sheet that lists former staff members will keep this from happening.

Hiding a worksheet

1. Select the tab of the sheet you wish to hide. You can select multiple tabs if you want to hide more than one sheet.

2. Open the **Format** menu, point to **Sheet**, and choose **Hide**. The tab disappears, leaving the sheet to its left selected.

To bring a hidden sheet back into view, click any of your remaining tabs and open the **Format** menu. Point to **Sheet** and choose **Unhide**. The Unhide dialog box opens, listing the hidden sheets for the current workbook (see Figure 13.22). Choose the sheet you want to unhide and click **OK**. If you've hidden multiple sheets, you must redisplay (unhide) them one at a time.

What's stopping the other user from displaying hidden sheets?

Nothing is stopping them. Any user who knows how to unhide sheets can do so. If you want to absolutely protect your sheets, copy the portion that the user can see to a new, blank workbook and give them that workbook only.

FIGURE 13.22

Choose which hidden sheet you want to unhide.

Enhancing the Appearance of Worksheets

Use fonts, borders, and colored shading

Use Excel's automatic formatting tools

Work with predesigned formats

Formatting Text and Numbers

Understanding the points font measurement system

Type is measured in *points*. An inch has 72 points, so each letter in a word that is formatted to 72 points is approximately 1" square. Text that is 18 points is 1/4 of an inch square, and 10-point text (Excel's default) is just over 1/8 of an inch square.

When you first begin to enter your worksheet content, you'll notice that Excel's default font is Arial, 10 points, following the design of the Blank Workbook template on which all blank worksheets are based. This font is chosen to create legible, plain worksheets that meet the basic needs of the average user. Although this default is a tidy font that's easy to read, it's not very exciting. You'll find that you can make your worksheets look more professional and create attention-grabbing effects by changing your fonts and applying formats to your text and numbers.

Changing Fonts

Fonts can be changed from the Formatting toolbar, which includes the most commonly used tools for changing the typeface, font size, style, and alignment. You can also use the Font dialog box for "one-stop-shopping" for all the available character formats you can apply to your worksheet content.

To apply any of the Formatting toolbar's formats to your worksheet content, select the cell or cells to which you want to apply the formats, and then click the appropriate button. Figure 14.1 shows a worksheet on which I formatted the title with Merge and Center [⊞], applied a different font [Arial ▾] and size [10 ▾] to the title text, and filled some cells with color [🖌▾] behind the content.

FIGURE 14.1

Apply formats throughout your worksheet to enhance it visually and draw attention to important details.

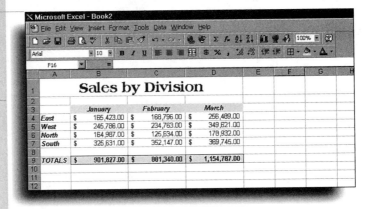

When formatting the appearance of cell content, you can use the **Format** menu's **Cells** command.

Formatting cells

1. Select the cells that you want to format. You can select an individual cell, a contiguous range (block) of cells, or two noncontiguous ranges.

2. Open the **Format** menu and choose **Cells**. The Format Cells dialog box opens with the **Font** tab displayed (see Figure 14.2).

3. Click the tab that contains the formats you want to apply, and make your selections within that tab. You can move from tab to tab, making selections in any or all of them.

4. Click **OK** to apply your settings and close the dialog box.

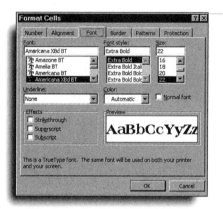

FIGURE 14.2

Enjoy one-stop-shopping for all the formats that can be applied to text in the Format Cells dialog box.

Aligning Text

Excel automatically aligns text to the left. You can quickly change the alignment of any text to center or right alignment by using the Center ▤ and Align Right ▤ toolbar buttons.

You can also use the **Format** menu to change the alignment of content in selected cells.

Aligning cell content with the Format menu

1. Select the cell or cells that you want to align.

2. Open the **Format** menu and choose **Cells**.

3. Click the **Alignment** tab (see Figure 14.3).

FIGURE 14.3

In the Format Cells dialog box, you can align your text both horizontally and vertically or apply a different orientation to your text.

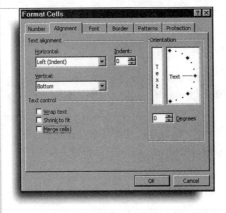

Don't go overboard with text formatting

Although it's fun and creative to apply fonts and styles throughout your worksheet, too many formats will make your worksheet look too busy and detract from its professional tone. Use no more than three fonts in any one worksheet, and keep your font sizes consistent throughout the sections of your data.

- **Horizontal**. Choose from seven different horizontal alignment formats.

- **Vertical**. By default, cell content is vertically aligned to the bottom of the cell. You can change the alignment to **Top**, **Center**, or **Justify**.

- **Text Control**. This section of the dialog box offers three option boxes, as described in Table 14.1.

- **Orientation**. This section of the dialog box enables you to rotate the text in your selected cells. Click along the edge of the clock-like semicircle or enter a number of **Degrees** to rotate your text (refer to Figure 14.3).

TABLE 14.1   **Text Control Options**

Name of Option	Effect On Selected Content
Wrap Text	For cells containing phrases or sentences, this option enables you to wrap the text in the selected cells. Cells containing wrapped text get taller rather than wider to accommodate long strings of text.
Shrink to Fit	If your column width or row height cannot be adjusted due to external requirements, choose **Shrink to Fit** to make the cell's contents fit without reducing the font size displayed on the Formatting toolbar.
Merge Cells	Use this option to make one large cell out of a selected range of cells.

4. After making your alignment selections, click **OK** to apply them and close the dialog box.

Applying Number Formatting

By default, Excel right-aligns your numeric content, based on the assumption that your numbers represent quantities—numbers of items in inventory, amounts of money, and so forth. You can apply visual formatting to your numeric content just as you would apply it to text—you can convert numbers to Currency Style or Percent Style % or you can insert commas with Comma Style . These styles are available from the Formatting toolbar because they're the most commonly applied.

To apply less common number styles or to change not only how your numbers look but how they work, you can also use the **Format** menu.

Applying number styles from the **F**ormat menu

1. Select the cells to be formatted. Your range can include text, and you can select entire columns or rows even if some of the cells don't contain numeric content.

2. Open the **Format** menu and choose **Cells**.

3. In the Format Cells dialog box, click the **Number** tab (see Figure 14.4).

4. Click to select one of the categories on the left side of the dialog box. A series of options for that category now appears on the right.

5. View the Sample as you make your selections, and then click **OK** to apply your formats and close the dialog box.

Help with categories

Descriptions of the categories appear at the bottom of the dialog box when a category is selected. Try clicking the categories to discover their use.

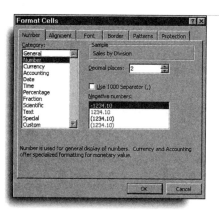

FIGURE 14.4

Apply currency, date, time, percentage, or fraction formats to your numeric content in the Format Cells dialog box.

Adding Emphasis with Borders, Shading, and Backgrounds

Your worksheet has a white background and black text, and although the worksheet's grid appears onscreen, it doesn't print unless you choose to include it in your print job. These defaults make for a visually boring worksheet, even if you apply character formats as discussed earlier in this chapter.

Applying borders and shading to the cells and a background to the entire worksheet gives your worksheet a professional, creative, "high tech" look and adds polish to your reports and printed presentations. In addition, the selective placement of these effects can help draw the reader's eye to important information and away from less significant content.

Working with Borders

Borders can be applied to one or all sides of a cell or range of cells. Borders are applied through the Border tool ▦▾ or through the **Border** tab in the Format Cells dialog box.

Using the Border Tool

Click the arrow next to the Border button ▦▾ to open a palette of border styles for any and all sides of a cell or range of cells (see Figure 14.5). The line styles are thick and thin, single and double, as shown in the squares in the palette.

Use your ToolTips to identify border buttons in the array

Point your mouse (without clicking) on any of the border buttons within the Border palette. A descriptive ScreenTip appears, taking the guesswork out of applying borders based solely on the appearance of the buttons.

FIGURE 14.5

The Border palette presents an array of 12 different borders that you can apply to a single cell or range of cells.

To apply a border to a cell or range of cells, select the cells and then click the arrow next to the Border tool. Click the button in the palette that contains the border you need. Figure 14.6 shows a thick bottom border applied to a range of numbers.

If you want to remove a border, select the cell or cells and choose the No Border button from within the Border palette.

Setting Custom Borders

If you need more control over the appearance and placement of your borders, use the **Format** menu to access more border options.

Customizing borders

1. Select the cell or cells to which you want to apply a custom border.

2. Open the **Format** menu and choose **Cells**. The Format Cells dialog box opens.

3. Click the **Border** tab (see Figure 14.7).

4. Choose your border options—the placement, style, and color of your lines.

5. Click **OK** to apply your border formats and close the dialog box.

> **Use borders sparingly**
>
> If you place borders all over your worksheet, they lose their visual impact and you risk confusing other users who view your worksheet onscreen or on paper. Use borders to draw attention to important cells and separate sections of your worksheet.

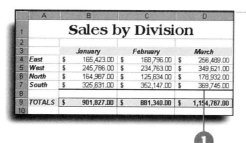

FIGURE 14.6

A thick bottom border works well at the foot of columns that are totaled.

① Thick border under numbers before totals

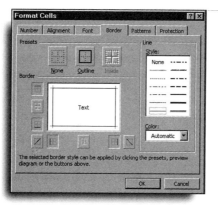

FIGURE 14.7

Choose the placement, style, and color of your borders in the Format Cells dialog box.

Applying Shading and Patterns

Another tool for adding visual impact and indicating important sections of your worksheet is shading. You can apply solid color fills to selected cells by clicking the Fill Color ![fill color icon] tool's arrow on the Formatting toolbar. A palette of 30 different colors appears (see Figure 14.8). Click the color you want to apply to your selected cells.

If you want to keep the palette open and available onscreen without having to click the Fill Color arrow again, tear the palette off the toolbar by dragging its title bar. Drag the now floating toolbar to a convenient location as you format the remaining parts of your worksheet.

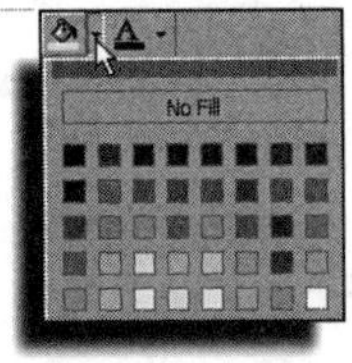

FIGURE 14.8
Apply solid colors to your selected cells with the Fill Color tool.

Just as you can apply solid colors to cells, you can also choose from a palette of patterns in the Format Cells dialog box that can be applied to cover cell content or fill in sections of empty cells for an interesting visual effect.

Applying patterned fills to cells

1. Select the cell or cells to be filled with a pattern.

2. Open the **Format** menu and choose **Cells** to display the Format Cells dialog box.

3. Click the **Patterns** tab (see Figure 14.9).

4. Click the **Pattern** drop-down list to see a palette of patterns and colors. You can apply both a color and a pattern by clicking a color first and then selecting a pattern.

5. To apply your pattern and color to the selected cells, click **OK**. The dialog box closes.

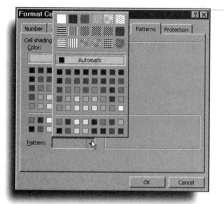

FIGURE 14.9
Click the **Pattern** button to see a palette of 18 different patterns that you can use to fill cells.

Using AutoFormat

You can apply all the visual formats (fonts, text and cell colors, borders, patterns) to your cells "a la carte" or use Excel's AutoFormat feature to apply them in predesigned, coordinated groups.

Using AutoFormat to format a worksheet

1. Select the cells to which you want to apply the AutoFormat. This is usually a large range within a worksheet, such as an entire section.

2. Open the **Format** menu and choose **AutoFormat**.

3. The AutoFormat dialog box opens, showing a list of table formats for your selected cells. Click any format on the left to see a sample of it on the right.

4. Click the **Options** button to see a list of the formats that are part of the selected AutoFormat (see Figure 14.10). You can turn these options on or off to control which ones will apply to your selected cells.

5. When you've selected your AutoFormat and made any changes to the Options, click **OK** to apply the formats and close the dialog box.

Figure 14.11 shows a worksheet with the **Colorful 2** AutoFormat applied.

Don't cancel out your own formatting with AutoFormats

If you've already put in time changing column widths and row heights to achieve a specific look for your worksheet, don't cancel out your existing formats when you apply AutoFormat to shade and apply borders to your cells. Turn off the **Width/Height** option box so that your current widths and heights are not changed when the AutoFormat is applied.

FIGURE 14.10

Choose from 17 different AutoFormats that apply fonts, shading, borders, and color to your worksheet with one simple command.

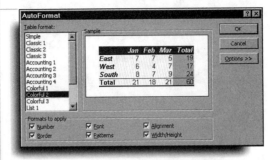

FIGURE 14.11

Your selected cells are formatted to match the sample in the AutoFormat dialog box.

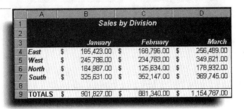

Applying Conditional Formatting

Excel's Conditional Formatting feature enables you to choose a set of formats—fonts, colors, borders, and shading—and apply them to cells that meet a set of criteria. For example, if you tell Excel to format all cells that contain numeric content exceeding a certain number (>5000, for example), all cells containing numbers greater than 5000 will be formatted as you indicate. Your criteria will be based on the need to draw attention to certain cells, such as sales totals exceeding quota.

Using conditional formatting

1. Select the range of cells in which you want Excel to look for data that meets your criteria.

2. Open the **Format** menu and choose **Conditional Formatting**.

3. The Conditional Formatting dialog box opens, displaying **Condition 1** (see Figure 14.12).

4. In the first list box, choose whether or not the criteria will apply to cells containing values you entered (**Cell Value Is**) or formulas (**Formula Is**).

5. In the second list box, choose the operator, such as between, greater than, less than, or equal to.

Office Assistant to the rescue!

Although the Office Assistant pops up at various times, his appearance during the use of the Conditional Formatting feature may be especially helpful. If you're new to the use of operators and conditions, click the option buttons that offer definitions of terms and concepts.

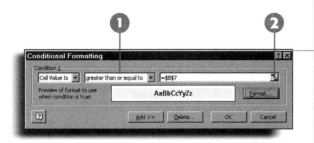

FIGURE 14.12

Set your formats and determine what conditions must exist for the formats to be applied. This tool makes it easy to draw attention to important numbers throughout your worksheet.

1 Operator

2 Collapse Dialog button

6. In the third box, click the **Collapse Dialog** button to shrink the dialog box. This enables you to choose the cell in your range that contains the value to be compared to your operator. If you chose **Between** as the operator, a fourth box is present for the second comparison cell.

7. After clicking to select the comparison cell, click the **Collapse Dialog** button again to re-open the dialog box.

8. If you require a second condition, click the **Add>>** button to open a dialog box to display **Condition 2**. You work with the same fields for the second condition as you did for the first. If a third condition is needed, click **Add>>** again to display **Condition 3**, again showing the same condition fields.

9. Click the **Format** button to open the Format Cells dialog box. Use any or all the tabs in this box (**Font, Border, Patterns**) to choose the formats that will be applied to the cells meeting your criteria.

10. Click **OK** to close the Format Cells dialog box.

11. In the Conditional Formatting dialog box, click **OK** to apply the formatting to any cells that meet your criteria.

Figure 14.13 shows cells that have been formatted because they met the criteria seen in Figure 14.12.

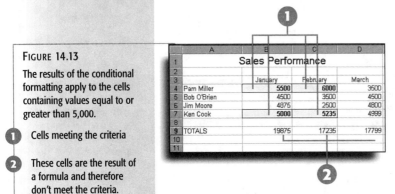

FIGURE 14.13
The results of the conditional formatting apply to the cells containing values equal to or greater than 5,000.

1 Cells meeting the criteria

2 These cells are the result of a formula and therefore don't meet the criteria.

Creating Worksheet Backgrounds

Instead of or in addition to any cell or range formatting, you can apply a graphic background to your worksheets. The use of a background adds visual interest and can create a polished, graphic look for your work.

Adding a background image to your worksheet

1. Click the worksheet tab to which you want to apply a background.

2. Open the **Format** menu, choose **Sheet**, and then choose **Background**.

3. The Sheet Background dialog box opens, giving you the opportunity to search your drives for graphics files to apply to the selected worksheet's background (see Figure 14.14). As you click graphic files, a preview is displayed.

FIGURE 14.14
Choose a graphics file to serve as your worksheet's background image.

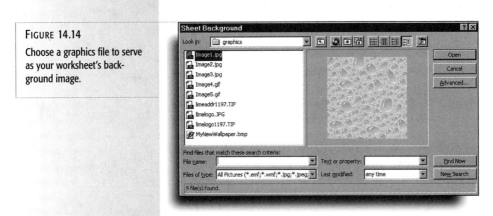

4. Choose a file and click **Open**. You can also double-click the desired file. The background is filled with the image, as shown in Figure 14.15.

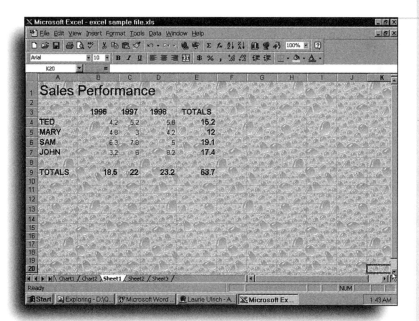

FIGURE 14.15

A background should enhance the overall look of your worksheet—choose an image that won't overwhelm your data and cell formatting.

Using Formulas and Functions

Calculating quickly with AutoCalculate

Writing formulas

Using cell names and labels in formulas

Using functions in formulas

Fixing worksheet errors

Getting Quick Answers to Simple Calculations

Calculations are why Excel exists. To perform calculations in a worksheet, you write formulas; to perform complex calculations, you use functions in your formulas (functions are built-in mathematical equations that save you time and effort).

To get really quick answers without writing a formula yourself, you have two options: AutoCalculate, which calculates cells you select but doesn't write a formula in the worksheet, and AutoSum, which writes a SUM formula for you in the worksheet.

Calculating Numbers Quickly Without a Formula

I can't find the status bar

If your status bar is missing, open the **Tools** menu and choose **Options**. On the **View** tab, choose the **Status bar** check box and then choose **OK**.

I don't see my AutoCalculate box

AutoCalculate only appears in the status bar when a function is selected *and* calculable cells are selected (for example, if the selected function is Sum but no cells with numbers are selected, AutoCalculate is hidden).

To calculate selected cells on-the-fly without writing a formula, you can use AutoCalculate.

Using AutoCalculate to Perform Quick Calculations

1. Select the cells you want to add up (or average, or count).
2. Look at the AutoCalculate box in the status bar shown in Figure 15.1.
3. To change AutoCalculate's calculation function, right-click the AutoCalculate box and choose a different function from the shortcut menu.

   You can select from six functions (**Sum, Average, Count Entries, Count Numbers, Minimum, Maximum**), or you can select **None** to turn the feature off.

Using AutoSum to Enter a Formula

If you need to quickly calculate a sum and want a permanent sum value that remains in the worksheet cell where you put it, you need to enter a sum formula in the cell. But you don't need to learn to write formulas yet—you can enter a formula that sums a group of numbers, without actually writing the formula yourself, by using the AutoSum button on the Standard toolbar.

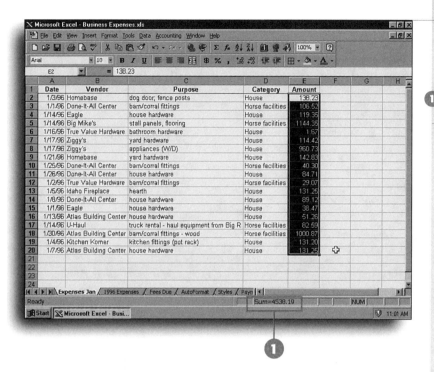

FIGURE 15.1

AutoCalculate calculates all selected cells, according to the function you select.

1 AutoCalculate

Using the AutoSum button to enter a SUM formula

1. Click a cell at the bottom of a column of numbers you want to sum, as shown in Figure 15.2.

2. On the Standard toolbar, click the AutoSum button ∑.

A SUM formula is written, and the cells Excel thinks you want to sum are surrounded by a moving border. If you want to sum different cells, drag the mouse pointer to select them on the worksheet.

3. When the cells you want to sum are surrounded by a moving border, press Enter.

The SUM formula is entered, the result is displayed in the cell, and the moving border disappears.

AutoSum is versatile

You can sum a row of numbers by placing the AutoSum formula at the end of the row. Or you can place the AutoSum formula anywhere on the worksheet and then drag to select the cells you want to sum.

FIGURE 15.2

AutoSum writes the formula
and guesses which cells, but
you can drag to select different
cells.

1 Moving border

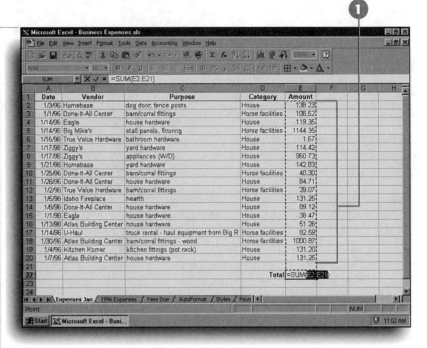

Understanding Cell References

A cell reference is the cell's address on the worksheet, given by column letter and row number. You can tell what a cell's reference is either by looking at the row and column that intersect at the cell or by selecting the cell and looking at the Name box (see Figure 15.3).

If you click in the upper-left corner of a worksheet, the Name box reads A1, which is that cell's reference: a combination of the column letter, A, and the row number, 1.

When you write formulas that include cells, the cells in the formula are identified by their references; for example, the formula =A1+B1 adds together the values stored in cells A1 and B1.

SEE ALSO

➤ *To learn more about creating cell names, see page 316*

FIGURE 15.3

Cells are identified and located by their cell references, or addresses. This cell's reference is A1—it's at the intersection of Column A and Row 1.

1 Name box

2 Cell A1 selected

Writing Your Own Formulas

You'll probably need to do more calculations in your workbooks than AutoSum can do for you, which means you'll need to learn how to write formulas.

A simple formula might consist of adding, subtracting, multiplying, or dividing cells. To enter an operator in a formula, type the operator's symbol, as detailed in Table 15.1.

Remember, all formulas begin with an equals sign (=), followed by whatever operators, cell references, and functions the formula requires.

TABLE 15.1 Arithmetic operators

Operator	Description
+ (plus sign)	Addition
– (minus sign)	Subtraction

continues…

TABLE 15.1   Continued

Operator	Description
* (asterisk)	Multiplication
/ (forward slash)	Division
^ (caret)	Exponentiation

All formulas can calculate cells in the same worksheet, on different worksheets, and even in different workbooks (which links the workbooks and worksheets together).

Writing a Simple Formula

You can write a simple formula that adds the values of two cells. To write a simple formula with other arithmetic operators, type another operator in place of the plus sign.

Writing a formula that sums the values in two cells

1. Click the cell where you want to display the results of the formula.

2. Type an equals sign (=).

3. Click one of the cells you want to add.

4. Type a plus sign (+).

5. Click the other cell you want to add (see Figure 15.4).

6. Press Enter.

The formula is complete.

Learning About Cell Reference Types

When you build a formula by clicking cells and ranges (as in the previous section), the cells have relative references. What the formula in Figure 15.4 really does is add the cell *two cells to the left* and the cell *one cell to the left* of the current cell because the references are relative to the cell that contains the formula. (If this seems confusing, wait a while. It will become clearer a bit later.)

Cells can have different types of references, depending on how you want to use them in a formula. First I'll explain the

---

Those symbols in the formula bar

When you write a formula, three symbols appear in the formula bar: an **x** (the Cancel button), a check mark (the Confirm button), and an equals sign (=). These symbols are for the keyboard-challenged and mouse-addicted among us. You can start a formula by clicking the equals sign. Then write your formula and click the check mark to complete it. If you change your mind, you can delete the formula by clicking the **x**.

Starting a formula in Excel

All Excel formulas begin with an equals sign (=).

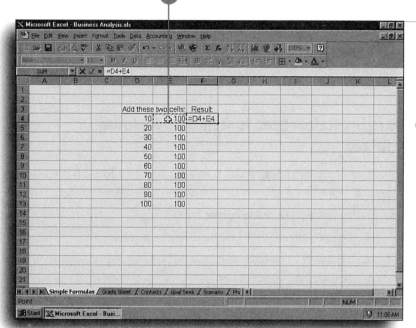

FIGURE 15.4

Start with an equals sign and build the formula by clicking the cells you want and typing the arithmetic operators between them.

1 Click a cell to add it to the formula.

terminology and how to create the different types, and then I'll show you how they work with actual examples (at which point they'll make more sense).

For any cell there is only one reference but four possible reference types: relative, absolute, and two mixed types. Dollar signs ($) in the reference determine the type.

For example:

- A1 is called relative.

- A1 is called absolute.

- $A1 and A$1 are called mixed.

An absolute cell reference is a fixed geographical point, such as a street address, "123 Cherry Street."

A relative cell reference is like a relative location, as in "one block west and two blocks south."

A mixed cell reference is a mixture of absolute and relative locations, as in "three blocks east on Hampton Avenue." A mixed cell reference can have an absolute column and a relative row, as in $A1, or a relative column and an absolute row, as in A$1.

The dollar signs designate the row and/or column as absolute—unchanging—within a reference. As you write formulas, the meanings of absolute, relative, and mixed will become more clear.

Changing References to Relative, Absolute, or Mixed

If you need to change a cell reference type in a formula, you can do this much faster than by typing in the dollar sign ($).

Cycling through the cell reference types

1. Double-click the cell containing the formula.

2. Within the formula, click the cell reference you want to change (see Figure 15.5).

FIGURE 15.5

Click in the cell reference and press F4 to change the reference type.

1 Click in the cell reference.

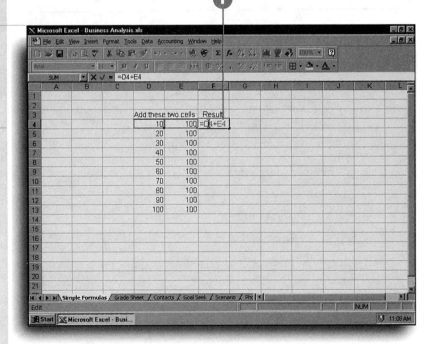

3. Press F4 until the reference changes to the type you want.

Pressing F4 repeatedly cycles through all the possible reference types.

4. Press Enter to complete the change.

Using AutoFill to Copy a Formula

When you write a formula that uses relative references, the references adjust themselves when you copy the formula. They do this because the formula is calculating cells that are located relative to the formula on the worksheet.

Understanding the concept of relative references

1. Write a formula that adds the cell to the left of the formula and the cell to the left of that cell (see Figure 15.6, where the formula in F4 adds cells D4 and E4).

2. Position the mouse pointer over the AutoFill handle (the small black box in the lower-right corner of the selected

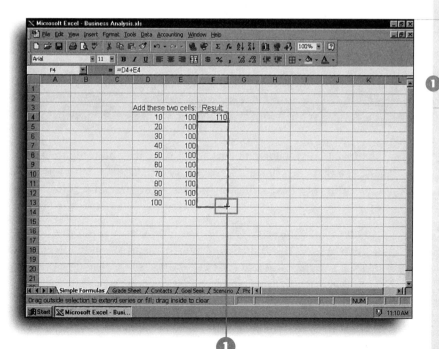

FIGURE 15.6

Copy a formula quickly by dragging the AutoFill handle.

1 AutoFill handle

Sideways, too

AutoFill also works horizontally, to copy formulas across a row.

cell). Then drag down to fill the formula down the right side of the table.

3. Release the mouse button after you've dragged to AutoFill all the cells down the side of the table.

The formula is copied to all the cells you dragged, as shown in Figure 15.7.

FIGURE 15.7

Relative references are self-adjusting when you use AutoFill to copy a formula.

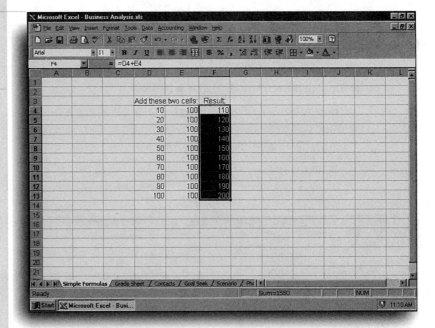

The formulas you copied by using AutoFill have adjusted themselves so that every formula adds the two cells to the left of it. The formulas are self-adjusting because they contain relative references.

In Figure 15.8, the same formula has been copied down the side of the table, but this time the formula contains absolute references. The references add cells D4 and E4 all the way down the column—which in this example is quite useless.

But suppose you want every formula to add the two cells to the left of it (relative references) to the value in cell A1 (an absolute reference). In this case, an absolute reference for cell A1 ensures that the correct values are calculated in every copy of the formula (see Figure 15.9).

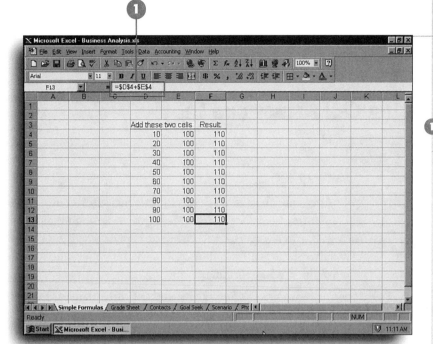

FIGURE 15.8

Absolute references do not adjust when you copy a formula; they always calculate the same cells.

① Absolute references

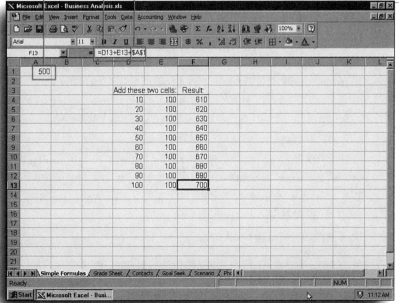

FIGURE 15.9

In these formulas, the relative references adjust, and the absolute reference always refers to the same cell.

① Each formula includes this cell as an absolute reference.

② Relative references

③ Absolute reference

Mixed references allow a formula to refer to cells that have relative row references within an absolute, or unchanging, column (as in $A1) or relative column references within an absolute, or unchanging, row (as in A$1).

Using Cell Names and Labels

Why would you want to use cell names? Here are some good reasons:

- Any formula is easier to read and understand if you use cell names and labels in place of cell references (for example, the formula =tax+subtotal is easier to understand than =H32+H33). After you create cell names or labels, Excel automatically uses the cell name instead of the reference when you use the cell in a formula.

- If you name your cells and ranges and use those names in your formulas, you reduce your chances of inadvertently using the wrong cell reference in a formula.

- You don't have to worry about relative and absolute reference types because no matter where you move or copy a formula or its named cells, the formula finds and calculates the correct cell values.

A cell name can be almost anything you create, as long as it's not an existing cell reference (for example, you can name a cell "rate" or "January" or "Fred", but not "FY1998" because that's the intersection of column FY and row 1998). Cell names use absolute cell references for identification, so using a name in a formula is just like using an absolute reference, but easier to read.

A cell label is similar to a cell name but is a row or column label with which Excel automatically identifies cells in a formula. I'll show you how to create and use cell names and labels to make your formulas easier to understand.

Here are the rules for cell names:

- They must start with a letter or an underscore (_).

- They can't include spaces (use an underscore instead). Better yet, use initial capitals to separate words, as in "FirstName."

(Names are not case-sensitive, so you don't have to remember to type the capital letters in your formulas—but the initial capitals make the name easier to read.)

- They can't include periods (.). Periods are allowed but can interfere with VBA programming code, which uses periods to identify objects.

- They can't be longer than 255 characters (but really, that's way too long to be practical, anyway).

- They can't include hyphens or other punctuation marks (if Excel won't let you create the name, a punctuation mark may be the problem).

Naming Cells

The fastest methods for naming cells are the Name box and the Create Names dialog box. Each is more convenient in particular situations; I'll show you how and when to use each procedure.

Using the Name Box

The Name box is the fastest way to name a cell or range if you're only creating one name or if the name is not already a label or table heading on the worksheet. For example, on my Phone List worksheet, I named the entire table "Contacts" so that I can get to it quickly from anywhere in the workbook (see Figure 15.10).

Naming cells or ranges by using the Name box

1. Select the cell or range you want to name.

2. Click in the Name box shown in Figure 15.11. The reference in the Name box is highlighted for renaming.

3. Type the name and press Enter.

   When the named range is selected, the name appears in the Name box (see Figure 15.12).

4. To select the range, click the down arrow in the Name box, and then click the range name.

FIGURE 15.10

After the range is named, I can select it quickly by clicking its name on the Name box list.

1 Name box

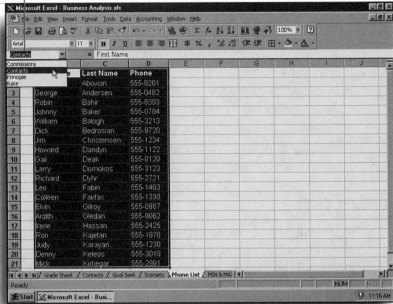

FIGURE 15.11

One click in the Name box highlights it for naming.

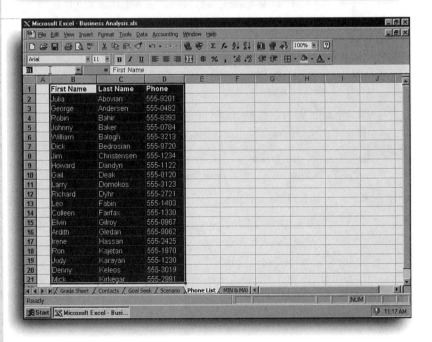

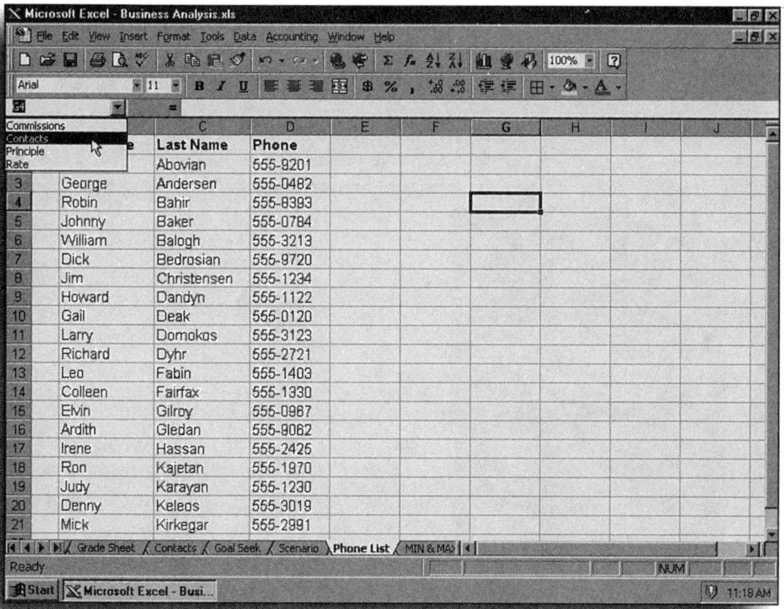

FIGURE 15.12

When a named range or cell is selected, the name appears in the Name box.

Using the Create Names Dialog Box

The Create Names dialog box is quicker if the names you want to use are already in place on the worksheet as row or column labels. For example, on my Phone List worksheet, I named each column in my "Contacts" range with its column heading. The Create Names dialog box creates all four names at once.

Creating names by using the Create Names dialog box

1. Select the range you want to name, including the headings on the top, left, bottom, or right edges of the range (see Figure 15.13).

2. Open the **Insert** menu, point to **Name**, and then click **Create**.

3. In the Create Names dialog box shown in Figure 15.14, mark or clear check boxes as needed so that only the appropriate check boxes are checked (in this example, only the **Top row** check box should be marked).

4. Click **OK**.

   The names are created, and you can select any of the ranges by clicking its name in the Name box list.

Deleting names you no longer need

Deleting names you don't need makes it easier to find the names you do need because the list stays short and manageable. To delete a cell or range name, open the **Insert** menu, point to **Name**, and click **Define**. Then select the name you want to delete, and click **Delete**.

FIGURE 15.13

To create names, select the range and include the headings or labels.

1 These headings become range names.

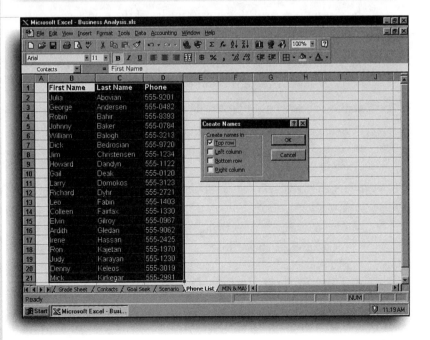

FIGURE 15.14

Select the headings you want Excel to use as range names.

Writing Formulas with Named Cells

Using cell and range names in a formula is quite easy and makes the formula easier to read and understand.

Using cell and range names in a formula

1. Click in the cell where you want to display the result of the formula.

2. Type your formula, beginning with an =.

3. Where you need to insert a name, type the name. You can also open the **Insert** menu, point to **Name**, click **Paste**, and then double-click the name in the list.

4. Complete the formula by pressing Enter. A formula with cell names instead of references might look like the one in the Formula bar in Figure 15.15.

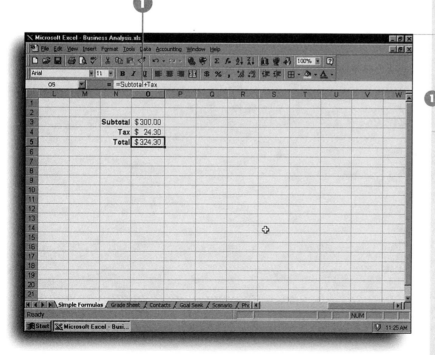

FIGURE 15.15

Names make formulas easier to understand.

1 Names instead of cell references

Writing Formulas with Labels

Should I use labels or names?

Labels are convenient as long as the formulas are positioned close to the table so Excel knows which labels are referred to in the formula. But if the formula is not lined up with the columns or rows the labels identify, the labels won't work and you need to create names instead.

If your data has row and column labels, you can use them in formulas just like names, but without first creating names.

In Figure 15.16, the table has column headers that I can use in formulas without first creating names with them.

Writing a formula with labels

1. Click a cell in line with the labeled columns and rows you want to use in the formula.

2. Type your formula, and type labels where the cell references are needed, as shown in Figure 15.16.

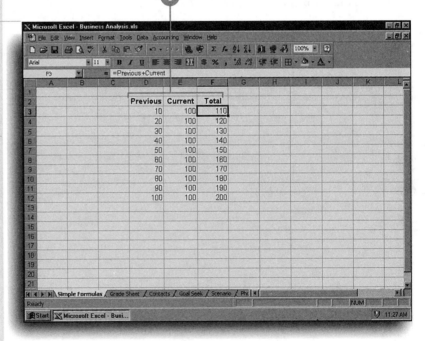

FIGURE 15.16

Labels are quick and convenient when your formulas are lined up with labeled rows and columns.

❶ Column labels

Using Functions in Formulas

Not all calculations are simple. Fortunately, Excel can handle tremendously complex calculations for you.

Functions are built-in formulas that perform complex math for you—you enter the function name and any *arguments* (extra information) the function requires, and Excel performs the calculations. SUM and AVERAGE are examples of simple, straightforward functions; PMT and VLOOKUP are examples of common but more complex functions that I'll show you how to use.

Excel comes with a slew of functions—some you'll use all the time, and some you'll only be interested in if you're an electrical engineer or nuclear physicist. Functions have specific names, such as SUM or AVERAGE or BETADIST, and function names must be spelled correctly or Excel won't recognize them. Fortunately, Excel provides dialog boxes that do the spelling for you and help you fill in the arguments each function requires.

Writing a Formula by Using Functions

Using the Paste Function dialog box to write a formula

1. Click in the cell where you want the results of the formula to appear.

When you use the Paste Function dialog box and the Formula palette, you don't need to type an equals sign first because Excel inserts it for you.

2. On the toolbar, click the Paste Function button [fx].

The Paste Function dialog box appears, as shown in Figure 15.17. The Office Assistant may appear along with the Paste Function dialog box; click the **No, don't provide help now** button, and he'll go away.

3. Click a category of functions and then double-click the function you want.

Each category has a different set of functions from which you can choose, which makes it easier to find the function you want. If you don't know which category your function is in, try **Most Recently Used** (a short list of recently used functions) or **All** (a long list of every function available).

The Formula palette opens to help you complete the function, as shown in Figure 15.18.

This formula thing is in my way

You can drag the Formula Palette, the dialog box where you supply arguments for the formula, elsewhere on the worksheet to move it out of your way. To move it, click anywhere on the palette and drag it with the mouse.

FIGURE 15.17

The Paste Function dialog box
briefly explains the selected
function.

1 Function explanation

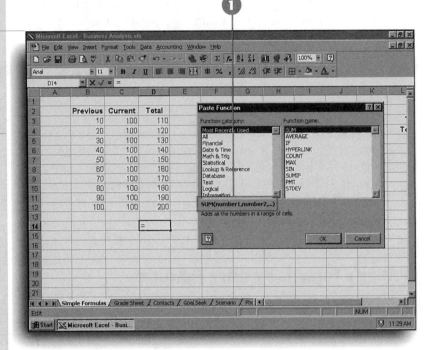

Writing your own formulas

When you get comfortable with a
formula, it's often faster to write it
yourself, but you must spell the
function name correctly. Here's a
tip: Type the function name in
lowercase letters. If it's spelled correctly, Excel converts it to uppercase
after you press Enter (for example,
sum is converted to SUM); but if
it's spelled incorrectly, Excel won't
convert it to uppercase—your clue
that it's misspelled.

4. Click in the Argument box and read the description of the
   argument to figure out what information is needed.

5. Click or drag worksheet cells to fill in arguments (if the
   arguments call for cell references).

   To shrink the Formula palette so it doesn't cover worksheet
   cells you want to select, first click the Collapse dialog button
   at the right end of the argument. Select the worksheet cells,
   and then click the Expand dialog button (at the right end of
   the collapsed Argument box) to display the Formula palette
   again and continue building your function.

6. Click **OK**.

   The function is built and the formula is complete.

This is the basic procedure; now I'll show you how to use the
procedure to write the specific, common, and useful worksheet
formulas shown in Table 15.2.

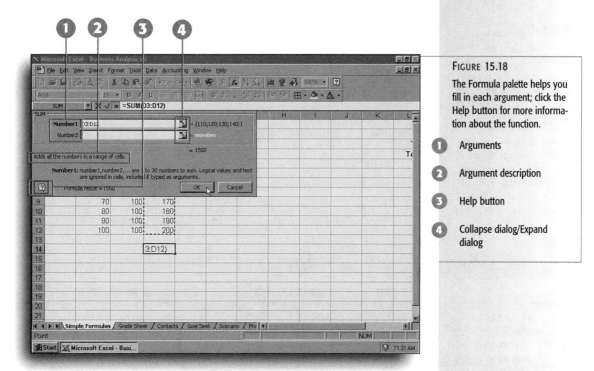

FIGURE 15.18

The Formula palette helps you fill in each argument; click the Help button for more information about the function.

1 Arguments

2 Argument description

3 Help button

4 Collapse dialog/Expand dialog

TABLE 15.2   Common and useful worksheet functions

Function	Purpose
SUM	Add together the values in a selected range.
MIN	Find the minimum value in a selected range.
MAX	Find the maximum value in a selected range.
AVERAGE	Average the values in a selected range.
PMT	Calculate the payment for specific loan terms.

Implementing Some Common and Useful Functions

In this section I'll show you examples of the functions in Table 15.2, with suggestions about where they're useful in real life.

Using mock data

When you first write a formula, you'll want to test it to be sure it's calculating properly (that is, you want to be sure you entered all the arguments correctly and the results are accurate). To test your formulas, enter mock data (phony numbers) in the worksheet. Use mock data that's simple: short text that's quick to type and round numbers so you can do the math in your head and know quickly whether the results are accurate.

This short list of functions is just a few of the hundreds of functions available in Excel. If you explore the list of functions in the Paste Function dialog box, you'll find functions that will calculate sine, cosine, and tangent; the actual value of Pi; lots of accounting and engineering equations; logarithms; binomials . . . it's nearly endless. But I'm only going to show you the functions that you will most likely want to use.

SUM

The SUM function is universally useful: it adds up all the numbers in a selected range. A good place for the SUM function is at the end of a list of numbers, such as the list in Figure 15.19.

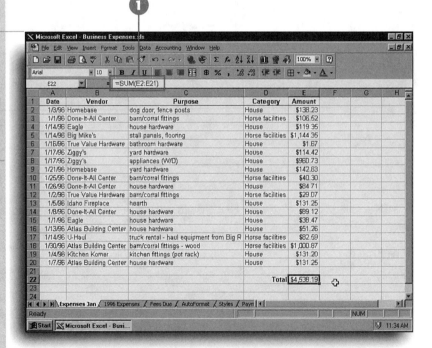

FIGURE 15.19

Although below the list is a convenient—and conventional—place, you can put the formula anywhere you want on the worksheet.

1   The new formula

Writing a SUM formula

1. Click in the cell where you want to place the formula.

2. Type =.

3. Type sum(.

4. On the worksheet, drag to select the cells you want to add together (in this example, the range E2:E20).

5. Type).

6. Press Enter.

The formula is complete. If you spelled the function name, SUM, correctly, Excel converted it to uppercase letters.

When you drag cells to insert them in a formula, Excel uses relative references; so if you copy this formula to another cell, the results change because the relative references adjust themselves.

If you drag the cell to move it elsewhere on the worksheet, on the other hand, the formula retains its original references and the results remain accurate. If this gets confusing and you want to be sure the references remain the same, you can change the references to absolute types.

SEE ALSO

➤ *To learn more about cell references, see page 308*

MIN

The MIN function returns the minimum, or lowest, value in a range of numbers. Of course, if your range is a single column of numbers, you can also find the smallest value by sorting or filtering the list, but if your range is a large table of numbers like the one in Figure 15.20, the MIN function comes in handy.

Writing your own formula with the MIN function

1. Click in the cell where you want to place the formula.

2. Type =.

3. Type min(.

4. On the worksheet, drag to select the cells in which you want to search for a minimum value (in this example, the range B3:M11, all the numbers in the table).

5. Type).

6. Press Enter.

The minimum value in the table is 1006, and it would have taken a bit more time to find it yourself.

Changing the reference type

Here's how to quickly change a cell's reference type: Double-click the cell to show the formula and then click the reference. Then press F4 until the type cycles to the type you want, and press Enter.

FIGURE 15.20

The MIN function finds the minimum value in the selected table of data; it's a real time-saver if the table is large.

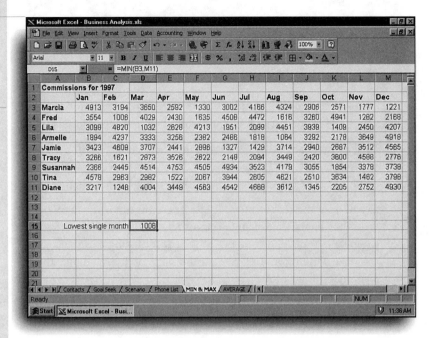

Because the minimum value is the result of a formula, it continues to find the minimum value automatically, even if I change the numbers in the table.

MAX

The MAX function is the opposite of the MIN function and works exactly the same way, but it finds the largest value in a selected range of cells. To write your own formula with the MAX function, you can follow the previous procedure for the MIN function but substitute MAX for MIN. To write a MAX formula by using the Formula palette, use the following procedure.

Writing a formula with the MAX function by using the Paste Function dialog box

1. Click the cell where you want to enter the formula.

2. Click the Paste Function button. f_{*}

   The Paste Function dialog box appears, as shown in Figure 15.21.

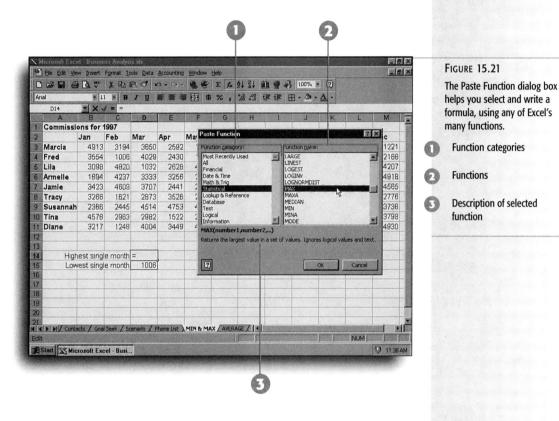

FIGURE 15.21

The Paste Function dialog box helps you select and write a formula, using any of Excel's many functions.

1. Function categories

2. Functions

3. Description of selected function

3. To narrow your range of choices, click a function category in the **Function category** list. (If you know the name of the function you want but don't know what category to find it in, click **All**.)

4. Scroll through the list of functions on the right side of the dialog box and double-click the function you want (in this example, I've looked up the **MAX** function in the **Statistical** category).

5. The Formula palette appears for the function you double-clicked (in this case, the MAX function, as shown in Figure 15.22).

6. Highlight or delete any value in the **Number1** argument and enter the entire table range by dragging to select the cells. In this example, the table range is A2:M11 (but I previously named this range "Commissions," so when I select the range, Excel inserts the range name, as shown in Figure 15.23).

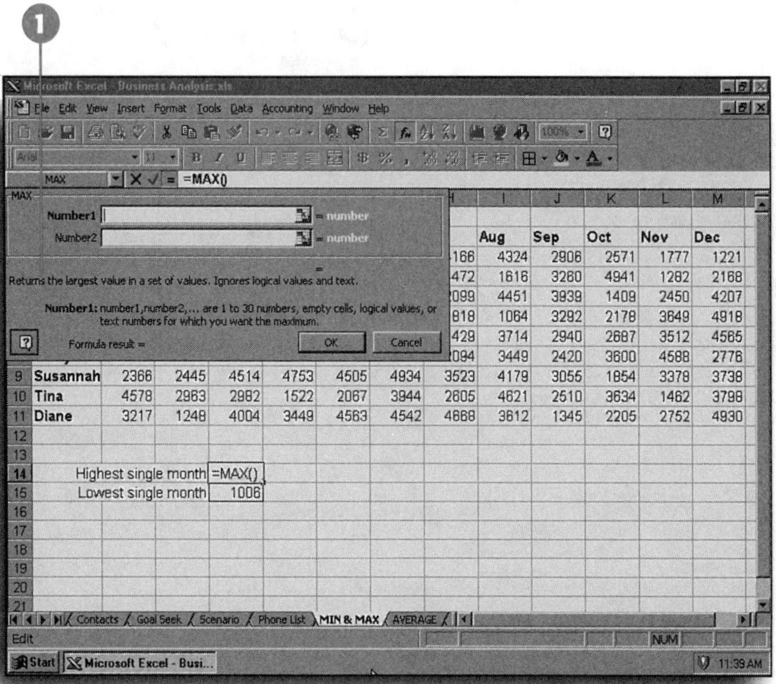

FIGURE 15.22

The Formula palette for the selected function explains each of the arguments.

❶ Explanation of selected argument

Making the MAX and MIN functions more useful

When you use the MAX or MIN function to determine the highest or lowest value in a large table, you still have to search to find that value among all those numbers. You can make the value jump out visually by combining the MAX or MIN function with Conditional Number Formatting, which formats the number in the table with any formatting you choose.

If the Formula palette is in your way, you can drag it out of your way to make the range easier to select. Or you can click the Collapse dialog button (refer to Figure 15.18) to minimize the dialog box, select your range, and then click the Expand dialog button (refer to Figure 15.18) to return the Formula palette to normal size.

7. Click **OK**.

The formula is complete, and the maximum value in the range, 4941, is displayed (see Figure 15.24).

SEE ALSO

➤ *To learn more about conditional number formatting, see page 300*

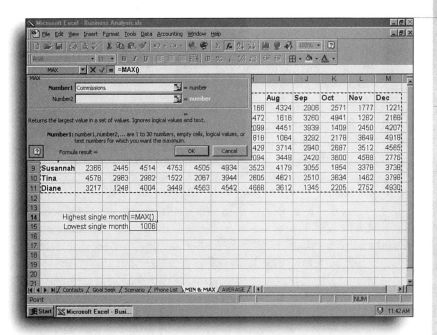

FIGURE 15.23

Using a range name such as "Commissions" instead of cell references makes the formula more understandable.

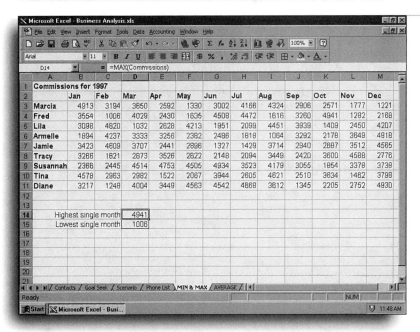

FIGURE 15.24

Whether you use the Paste Function dialog box and Formula palette or write the formula yourself, the result is the same.

AVERAGE

The AVERAGE function is another common and easy-to-use function. It's as simple to write as the SUM, MIN, and MAX functions, so I'll demonstrate it without using any dialog boxes.

Here's the important thing to know about the AVERAGE function: It gives a more correct result than you'll get by adding cells and dividing by the number of cells. When I first began using Excel, I didn't know about functions, so I calculated averages by adding the cells together and then dividing by the number of cells, but occasionally I got very wrong answers! If a cell didn't have a value in it, my method averaged that cell as a zero, but the AVERAGE function adds the cells in the selected range and then divides the sum by the number of values, so any blank cells are left out of the calculation. The comparison is shown in Figure 15.25 (I created cell comments that show the formulas for each cell.).

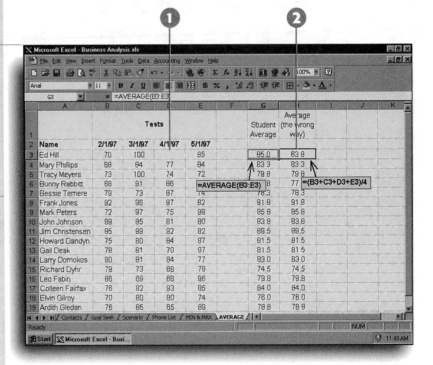

FIGURE 15.25

Adding and dividing won't always give the correct average, but the AVERAGE function will.

1 Ed Hill skipped this test.

2 His resulting add-and-divide average is wrong.

Writing a formula by using the AVERAGE function

1. Click in the cell where you want to place the formula.

2. Type =AVERAGE(.

3. In the worksheet, drag the range of cells you want to average (or type the range name or label).

4. Type a closing parenthesis,).

5. Press Enter.

PMT

If you're shopping for a house, car, boat, or anything else expensive enough to require a loan, a key bit of information you want to know is how much the monthly payment will be. The PMT function will figure it out for you quickly if you provide the annual interest rate, number of monthly payments, and total loan amount.

Figure 15.26 shows the PMT formula (in the formula bar) filled out with the appropriate cells in the worksheet. If you use cell references or named cells in the formula instead of numerical values, you can experiment with the formula results by changing the input values on the worksheet.

Fixing Worksheet Errors

Errors seem to sneak into the most scrupulously designed worksheets, but you can look up the usual causes of a particular error and then fix it.

To figure out why you have an error message where you've entered a formula, begin by checking the formula for typing and spelling mistakes. If typing and spelling don't appear to be a problem, look up the error message and potential solution in Table 15.3.

I'm borrowing negative money?

Because your payments eventually reduce the loan amount to zero, either the payments must be positive values and the loan amount negative, or your payments must be negative values and the loan amount positive. In this example, I typed the minus sign next to the function argument so that all the cell values appear to be positive. However, you can also enter a negative value for the loan amount, in which case the payments will appear as positive. You can also enter the loan amount as a positive value and your payments will show up as negative.

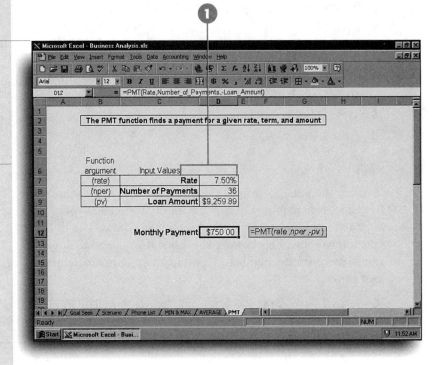

FIGURE 15.26

Use the PMT function to calculate how large a loan you can afford.

1 Name cells with the **Insert**, **Name**, **Create** menu command.

TABLE 15.3   **Error values**

This Error:	Means This:	To Fix It, Do This:
#####	The column isn't wide enough to display the value.	Widen the column.
#VALUE!	Wrong type of argument or operand (for example, calculating a cell with the value #N/A).	Check operands and arguments; make sure references are valid.
#DIV/0!	Formula is attempting to divide by zero.	Change the value or cell reference so that the formula doesn't divide by zero.
#NAME?	Formula is referencing an invalid or nonexistent name.	Make sure the name still exists or correct the misspelling.
#N/A	Most commonly means no value available or inappropriate arguments were used.	In a lookup formula, be sure the lookup table is sorted correctly.

This Error:	Means This:	To Fix It, Do This:
#REF!	Excel can't locate the referenced cells (for example, referenced cells were deleted).	Click **Undo** immediately to restore references, and then change formula references or convert formulas to values.
#NUM!	Incorrect use of a number (such as SQRT(–1)), or formula result is a number too large or too small to be displayed.	Make sure arguments are correct, and make sure the result is between –1*10307 and 1*10307.
#NULL!	Reference to intersection of two areas that do not intersect.	Check for typing and reference errors.
Circular	A formula refers to itself, either directly or indirectly.	Click **OK.** Then look at the status bar to see which cell contains the circular reference.

Displaying Worksheet Data in Charts

Create charts to graphically display your worksheet's numeric data

Use the Chart Wizard to customize your chart

Edit your data and see it reflected in the chart

Move, resize, and delete your charts

Change the appearance of chart elements

Add and format chart text

Format the colors and placement of chart elements

Edit the chart's data source and range

Creating Charts with the Chart Wizard

Even if you're excited about what your worksheet's numbers represent—money or sales, for example—rows and columns of numbers can be pretty boring to look at. In addition to being dull, numbers can also be confusing. Many times, the person who designs and maintains the worksheet is the only person who understands how it works or what it shows. Expressing the worksheet's numeric data in the form of a chart can clear up all the confusion.

Just as clip art and graphics in a document or presentation are visible proof that "A picture's worth a thousand words," charts prove the saying as well. Figure 16.1 shows a simple worksheet that stores and totals sales figures for a company. Figure 16.2 shows that same data expressed in the form of a chart. Which one immediately tells you which salesperson sold the most in 1997? Can you tell at a glance? Which one is easier to look at?

Charts (also known as graphs)

Many people refer to charts as "graphs"–an older term for manually created charts that were plotted by hand on graph paper.

FIGURE 16.1

This raw numeric data shows the data in black and white. You have to read the whole chart, however, to get the "big picture."

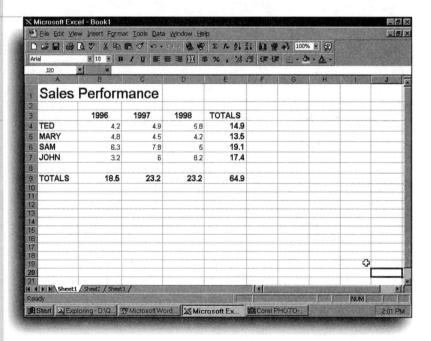

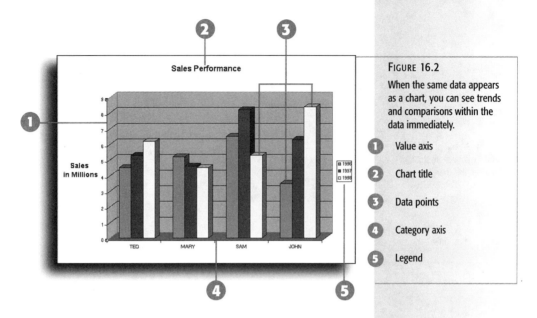

FIGURE 16.2
When the same data appears as a chart, you can see trends and comparisons within the data immediately.

1 Value axis

2 Chart title

3 Data points

4 Category axis

5 Legend

Excel gives you a very friendly tool for creating your charts, called the Chart Wizard, which takes you step by step through the process of building a chart. Each step includes questions or options that you can handle as you see fit, based on the content of your data and the needs of your audience.

Using the Chart Wizard requires that you have the data that will be used in your chart and that the data is open. If the data is in one workbook and you want your chart to be in another, both workbooks must be open.

Selecting a Data Source

Before you start the Chart Wizard, select your data. Be sure to leave out any text that doesn't directly identify your numbers, and leave out any numbers that you don't want plotted on the chart. Figure 16.3 shows the data selected for a chart.

After selecting your data, click the Chart Wizard button 📘 on the toolbar, or open the **Insert** menu and choose **Chart**.

Charts illuminate your data

Many times the person who enters data into a worksheet is so familiar with the data that he doesn't provide a lot of parenthetical information, such as formatting numbers for currency to show that the numbers represent money. Charts (and the titles, legends, and other features) help illustrate these points to those less familiar with the data.

Chart your finances with the Financial Manager

In addition to Excel's Chart Wizard, you can use the Small Business Financial Manager to create financial charts that depict the performance of your investments.

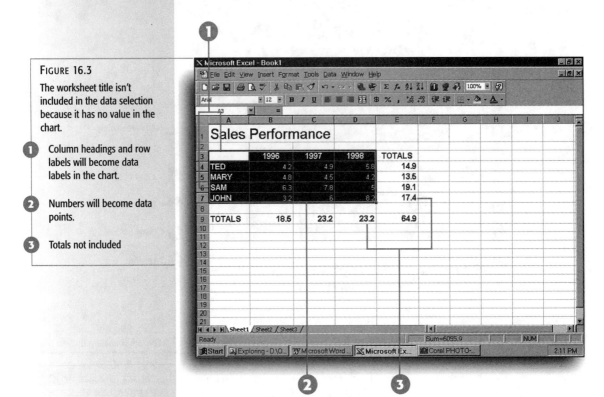

FIGURE 16.3

The worksheet title isn't included in the data selection because it has no value in the chart.

1 Column headings and row labels will become data labels in the chart.

2 Numbers will become data points.

3 Totals not included

Office Assistant pops up to offer help

If it's your first use of the Chart Wizard and you haven't modified your Help options in any way, the Office Assistant appears as soon as you begin the Chart Wizard. If you're feeling hesitant about the charting process, take advantage of the Office Assistant's offer to help by clicking the **Help with this feature** button.

Choosing a Chart Type

The first step (out of a total of four) in the Chart Wizard is selecting a **Chart Type**. There are 14 **Standard types** and 20 **Custom types**. Figure 16.4 shows the Chart Wizard dialog box, with Step 1 displayed.

How do you know which chart type is best for you and your data? Table 16.1 contains a list of common chart types and explains the types of data or situations for which they're best suited.

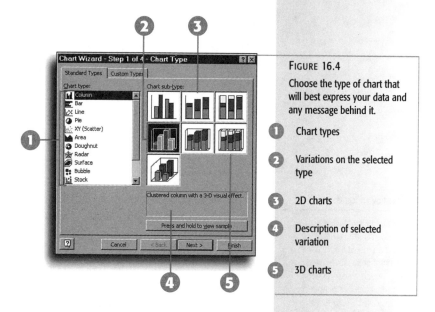

FIGURE 16.4

Choose the type of chart that will best express your data and any message behind it.

1   Chart types

2   Variations on the selected type

3   2D charts

4   Description of selected variation

5   3D charts

TABLE 16.1   Understand common chart types

Chart Type	Common Uses
Column	Vertical columns compare values. If the columns are shown in chronological order, the height of the bars can show a trend. Best used for data that compares values over months or years and between people or organizations. A column chart is one of the few chart types that can both compare and show trends.
Bar	This bar chart works like a column chart, but the bars are horizontal, decreasing its visual impact for showing trends.
Line	Each number in your data is plotted as a point on the line. The lines, if showing chronological data, can show trends over time. If there is more than one line, the lines can be visually compared to one another. Plot your sales over several months or years, and use a line chart to show the peaks and valleys in your sales history. This type of chart is good for demonstrating seasonal fluctuations.
Pie	A pie chart shows how much various people, departments, or divisions contributed to a total, although the total is not part of the data. Pies are good charts for showing how much of your total sales come from which products or services.

continues...

TABLE 16.1 **Continued**

Chart Type	Common uses
Scatter	Use a scatter chart to show survey results and similar data. Scatter charts show frequency of responses or results in tests. Different-colored dots scattered over the chart can be compared to one another (how many blue dots versus how many red dots).
Area	Overlapping areas show comparisons over time. Stacked area charts compare two or more values over time.

Basic charting concepts

Each number in your data is a potential bar, column, pie slice, or dot on a chart, called a *data point*. Each group of points (over three years for one salesperson or over one year for all the salespeople, for example) is called a *data series*. Most charts can display several data series. The pie chart, however, can display only one series at a time.

For each chart type you click, you'll see an array of variations—2D and 3D versions, some with and without certain accessories. When you click each of the chart variations for your selected type, a description appears, defining that variation's uses and features. If the description doesn't paint a complete picture for you, click the **Press and hold to <u>v</u>iew sample** button to convert the selected variation to show your data. When you find the chart type and variation that best meets your needs, click the **<u>N</u>ext** button.

The **Custom Types** tab shown in Figure 16.5 contains variations on the Standard types, most of which pertain to colors and graphics effects you can add to the more "vanilla" charts available in the **Standard** tab. As you click each of the custom chart types, a sample appears on the right, containing your data. If you prefer to use one of these types instead of a Standard chart, click the one you want and then click the **<u>N</u>ext** button to apply your selection and continue with the Chart Wizard.

FIGURE 16.5

The chart types on the **Custom Types** tab give you graphics alternatives to the common Standard types.

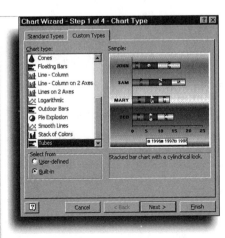

Editing Your Data Range

Step 2 in the Chart Wizard asks you to confirm or change the data range for your chart. If you didn't select the range before starting the Wizard, you must do so now. You can also take this opportunity to change the range you selected.

Changing your chart's data range

1. In the Step 2 dialog box (Chart Source Data), click the **Collapse Dialog** button at the right end of the **Data range** text box (see Figure 16.6). The Wizard dialog box shrinks down to a single line that displays your current range and the Wizard title bar. If you have a range currently selected, it appears on your worksheet with a dashed, animated border around it (see Figure 16.7).

Choosing a data range in another workbook

If your intended data range is in another workbook, click the **Collapse Dialog** box to shrink the Wizard and then open the **Windows** menu. Choose the workbook that contains your source data. Select the data (a dashed, animated border appears around it) and click the **Collapse Dialog** box again to redisplay the Wizard. You are back in your original workbook, with your data range selected.

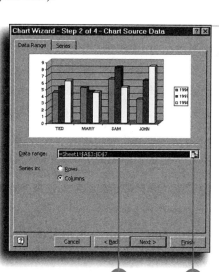

FIGURE 16.6

Click the Collapse Dialog button to shrink your Data Range dialog box and select or change the range of cells that contains your chart data.

①   Current selected range

②   Collapse Dialog button

2. Click and drag through the cells on your worksheet that should be included in the chart. The dashed, animated border now appears around your new range.

3. Click the **Collapse Dialog** button again to redisplay the entire Wizard dialog box.

4. Click **Next** to continue to Step 3.

FIGURE 16.7

While you're selecting your range, the Wizard box shrinks to get out of the way. Your selected range has a dashed, animated border.

1 Wizard dialog box

2 Selected range

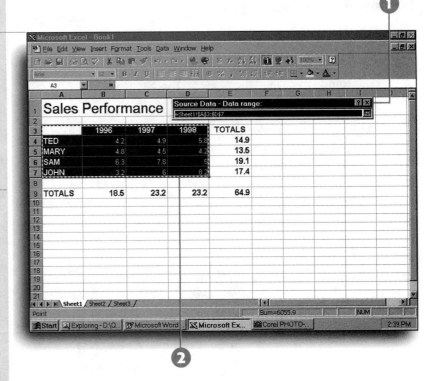

The **Series** tab in Step 2 of 4 gives you yet another way to add and remove series ranges in your chart (see Figure 16.8). Use this tab and its three separate Series boxes and Collapse Dialog buttons to redirect the Chart Wizard to a different or additional data range for your legend and/or category axis.

Exploring Your Chart Options

When you proceed to Step 3 (Chart Options), your chart is already built for you, based on the defaults for the chart type variation you selected in Step 1. You could click **Finish** right now, and your chart would be complete. Step 3, however, offers you the chance to play with your chart's defaults and add, delete, or format various chart elements. Figure 16.9 shows the Step 3 dialog box with a chart ready for customizing.

Choosing your chart's informational perspective

The **Data Range** tab contains two option buttons, **Rows** and **Columns**, which enable you to choose which data will appear in your legend and which will appear in your category axis. Click the options and view the change in the sample chart, remembering that whatever data appears in the category axis is the most immediately visible and dynamic for your reader.

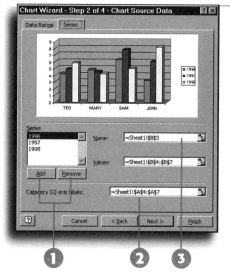

FIGURE 16.8

Use the **Series** tab to select individual data series for your chart, legend, and category axis.

1 Add and remove columns or rows that contain charted data.

2 Data series appearing on the category axis

3 Data series appearing in legend

To view or change your Chart Options, click the tabs in the Step 3 dialog box. The tabs give you the capability to add and edit parts of your chart, making it more informative and easier to read.

Titles

Titles help your audience understand what information is included in your chart. You can add a chart title and titles for your category and value axes (see Figure 16.10).

Click to activate your cursor in any of the title boxes. After typing the title, press the Tab key to move to the next title box. As you enter your titles, you'll see them appear in the preview on the right side of the dialog box.

Axes

Your *axes* are the lines along which your data is plotted. The **Axes** tab displays options for your category and value axes. By default, the data in your range's first column appears in the category axis and your numeric amounts are plotted along the value axis. Figure 16.11 shows the **Axes** tab in Step 3 of the Chart Wizard.

Make your titles informative, not redundant

Many users feel compelled to add titles even if the titles are repetitive of the category and value axis labels. Titles take up room on your chart, so apply them only when their content is informative to the reader.

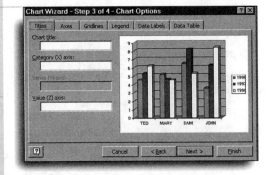

FIGURE 16.9

In Step 3 of 4, you can add and edit the elements of your chart—titles, labels, gridlines, and your legend.

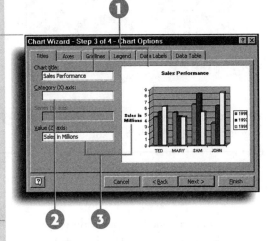

FIGURE 16.10

Axis titles tell your audience if the values in your value axis represent dollars or units.

1 Chart title

2 Category axis title left blank because data labels already explain that axis

3 Value axis title

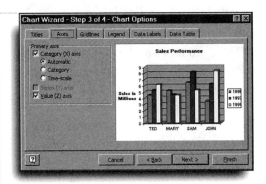

FIGURE 16.11

Choose to turn your axis labels on or off on the **Axes** tab.

Gridlines

Gridlines help the reader visually follow the chart from the data points to the value axis. Gridlines normally start at the tick marks (notches) on the value axis and continue horizontally across your chart, behind the bars, lines, or columns. Figure 16.12 shows the default gridlines in place on the preview chart and displays your options for adding and deleting horizontal and vertical gridlines.

When it comes to gridlines, less can be more

By default, only the gridlines at your major value axis tick marks are turned on. Adding the minor gridlines can make a chart too busy, creating a striped pattern in the background that makes reading the chart difficult.

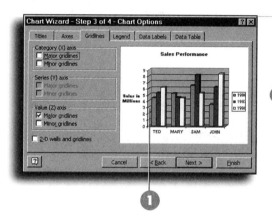

FIGURE 16.12

Add or delete gridlines to enhance your chart's readability.

1 Major tick marks on value axis

Legend

A legend on a chart works like a key on a map, identifying the unlabeled elements. In the chart in Figure 16.13, the legend links the column colors to the years in which the sales were made.

Use the Legend tab to turn your legend off or on and to choose the placement of your legend on the chart.

Move your legend to a new position

For column charts, the default position is **Right**, although **Bottom** is a popular choice because it takes up less room on the chart. The legend can be moved manually after the chart is created, but it is easier to let the Wizard do it through the **Legend** tab.

Data Labels

Data labels provide the exact figures that your bars, lines, and slices represent (see Figure 16.14). If it's imperative for your readers to know the exact amount that the data points represent, turn on the **Show value** data labels option. The **Show label** option usually just repeats the labels in the category axis.

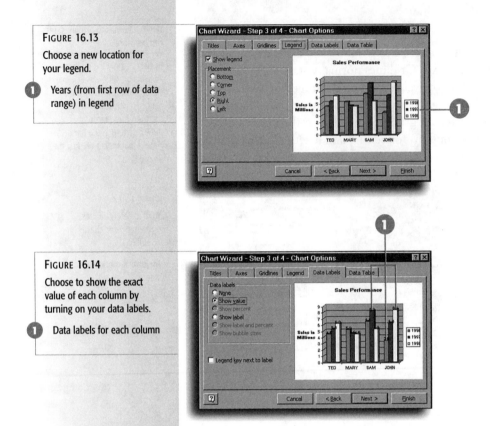

FIGURE 16.13

Choose a new location for your legend.

① Years (from first row of data range) in legend

FIGURE 16.14

Choose to show the exact value of each column by turning on your data labels.

① Data labels for each column

Data Table

If you want your chart to be accompanied by the data from your data range, click the **Show data table** option on the **Data Table** tab. When the Data Table is turned on, you can choose whether to **Show legend keys** in the table (see Figure 16.15).

Adding Your Chart to the Workbook

After you make your changes to your Chart Options, click **Next** to move to the last step in the Chart Wizard, **Chart Location** (see Figure 16.16).

You have two choices for the location of your new chart:

- **As new sheet**. Choose this option if you want your chart to be big, the size of a full page. A new sheet tab called Chart1 is added to your workbook. If you want to rename the tab at the same time that you create the chart, type the name of your choice into the box, and that name will appear on the tab.

- **As object in.** If you want your chart to be in a floating graphics box on the same sheet as your data, click this option. You can choose to place the chart on any sheet within your workbook (although the sheet containing your data is the default). Click the drop-down arrow to see a list of your sheets, and click one to select it.

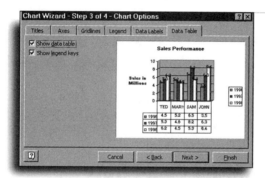

FIGURE 16.15

Instead of labeling your columns with Data Labels, add a Data Table to show all the data that went into your chart.

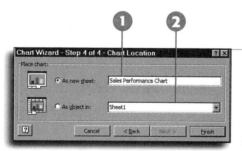

FIGURE 16.16

Choose where to create your new chart—on its own sheet or on an existing sheet in the workbook.

1 Type sheet name here or accept default "Chart1."

2 Choose one of the workbook's existing sheets.

Make your selection and click the **Finish** button to create your chart. Your complete chart appears (see Figure 16.17), ready for immediate use or reformatting if necessary. Use the Chart toolbar (which appears whenever your chart is active) to access common chart-formatting tools.

FIGURE 16.17

The result of your completion of the Chart Wizard process is a finished chart, formatted with your titles, labels, and legend.

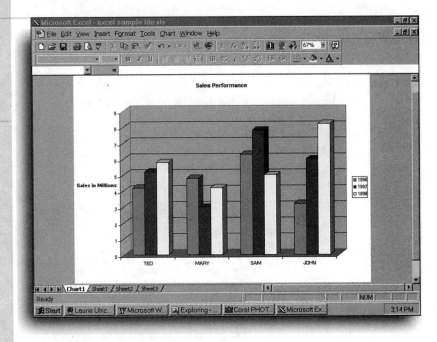

Protecting your chart from changes to the data

If you wish to protect the chart you created from any changes that might be made to the data that was used to create it, select the chart (click the chart sheet or in your worksheet) and open the **Edit** menu. Choose **Copy** to create a duplicate of the chart. Go to another workbook, and from that workbook's **Edit** menu, choose **Paste**. There will be no link between the copy and the original data.

Edit chart data by editing the chart?

If (and only if) you're using a 2D chart type, you can drag your chart's bars or columns to new heights (making them shorter or taller) and change the chart's data as a result. Click and drag the bar or column with your mouse and release it at the desired level. Check your data source—you'll see the new data reflected there.

Editing Chart Data

Because your data resides in the same workbook as your chart, the data and your chart are inexorably linked. If you change the data in the cells that make up your chart's data range, the corresponding parts of the chart change also.

Editing your chart's data

1. Display your chart's data by clicking the sheet that contains the data.

2. Click in the cell that you wish to change—an amount or name, for example.

3. Type the new text or value and press **Enter** (see Figure 16.18, showing Ted's 1997 sales changed to 5.2) to confirm your change in the worksheet and update your chart to reflect the change.

4. Click the sheet that contains your chart, or if the chart is on the same sheet as the data, scroll as needed to display the chart. Note how the change you made has altered the chart's content. Figure 16.19 shows the change as it is reflected in the chart.

FIGURE 16.18
Change your data cell by cell
as needed.

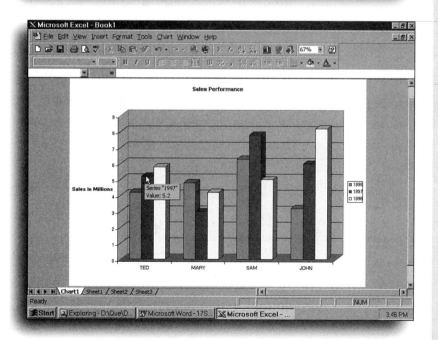

FIGURE 16.19
The chart's content is changed
to reflect the new data.

Deleting Your Chart

If your chart was placed on a separate sheet, deleting the chart requires the deletion of the sheet. Right-click the chart sheet tab and choose **Delete** from the shortcut menu. Click **OK** in the confirmation box.

If you added your chart to a worksheet, click the object (handles appear around the chart) and press the **Delete** key on your keyboard. The chart disappears.

Changing Chart Appearance

Many times the chart you initially create with the Chart Wizard is exactly what you need and doesn't require any editing at all in terms of its appearance or content. There will be times, however, when your data changes or you see the need to make cosmetic changes in your chart. "Cosmetic" changes can be anything from the fonts in your titles to the colors of your bars, lines, or pie slices.

Making changes is simple, as long as you are careful to select the right chart element. When it comes to charts, Excel's menus and toolbars are context-sensitive—depending on which part of your chart you have selected, the menu commands and toolbar buttons change to offer you the right tools for the job you need to do.

Which parts of your chart (chart elements) can you change after the chart is created? Virtually all of them. The parts of your finished chart are labeled in Figure 16.20.

Your chart consists of several parts, each of which can be formatted to meet your needs. Understanding what data these parts represent and what jobs they perform in your chart helps you make effective formatting choices.

FIGURE 16.20

Any part of your chart can be formatted—change colors or fonts and move or delete the chart's elements to suit your needs.

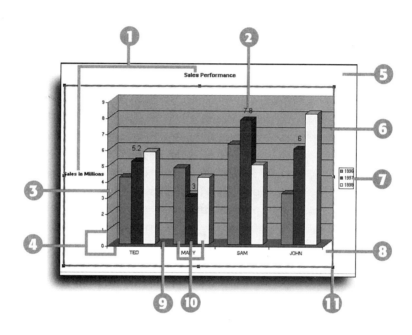

1. Titles
2. Data labels
3. Wall
4. Axes
5. Chart area
6. Gridlines
7. Legend
8. Plot area (selected)
9. Floor
10. Data series
11. Handles of selected plot area

- *Data series*. You can change the color of the bars, lines, or areas in any data series. Remember that a data series is any column or row within your source data.

- *Axes*. Edit the fonts used in axis labels or the color of the axis line itself. For the value axis, edit the number of tick marks that show increments in your range of values.

- *Fonts*. Change the typeface, style, and size of any text—in your titles, axis labels, legend, or data labels.

- *Plot area*. This is the whole background of the chart and the space around it. You can fill this area with a solid color or a pattern or choose from various special fill effects.

- *Chart area*. This is the area behind and beyond your chart's plot area. If your chart is on a workbook sheet along with your data, the chart area is significantly smaller than if your chart is alone on its own sheet. You can apply colors or other fills to your chart area, instead of, or in addition to, plot area fills.

- *Walls and floors*. In 3D bar, column, area, and line charts (or any chart that has a vertical and horizontal axis), you can change the color of the wall along the value axis or the floor along the category axis.

- *Legend*. Delete it, move it, or change the font for your legend text. The placement of your legend can be key to showing people that it's important information.

- *Titles*. Delete, move, or change title text by reformatting the font, size, and color. Enlarge the text boxes that contain your titles to allow text to spread out, or force the text to wrap by making the box smaller.

- *Gridlines*. Add them, remove them, or change the line style or thickness. The color of your gridlines can also be changed. Gridlines help your readers visually follow the values of each data point back to the value axis.

- *Data labels*. Add labels to your data points, showing the exact value that the point represents. The value from your data source can be displayed, or a percentage of the total series can appear as part of the label.

Formatting a Data Series

Most charts can display several data series simultaneously, enabling you to pick one series at a time and format it. Pie and doughnut charts can only display one series at a time, so you cannot edit an individual data series for these types of charts— you edit the sections of the one series depicted. For charts that do contain multiple series, you must select the series you wish to format by clicking it with your mouse.

In bar and column charts, you select a series by clicking one of the bars or columns in the series (see Figure 16.21). All the bars or columns in the series become selected, with each of the bars or columns in the series having its own set of handles around it, showing that it is selected. To select a data series in an area or line chart, simply click the area or line that you wish to format.

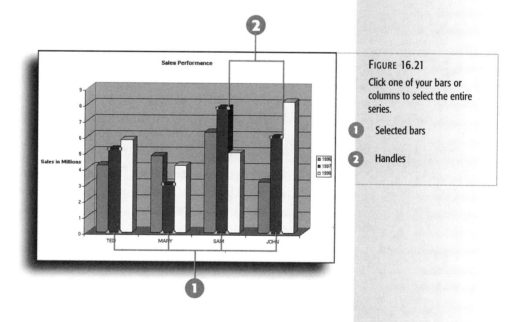

FIGURE 16.21

Click one of your bars or columns to select the entire series.

① Selected bars

② Handles

After you select the series, the **Format** menu changes, offering a **Selected Data Series** command. This command opens the Format Data Series dialog box, enabling you to apply colors and patterned fills to your selected data series. The **Fill Color** and **Font Color** buttons on the Formatting toolbar also affect only the selected series.

Color changes are made for aesthetic and functional reasons. Perhaps you want to apply a pattern to one of your chart's data series to make it stand out. Whatever your reason, changing the color of a data series can be performed in several ways, assuming first that the series is selected:

- Click the **Fill Color** icon on the Formatting toolbar. Choose from an array of colors by clicking the drop-down arrow to the right of the button. Click one of the colors in the array to apply the color to the selected element.

- Open the **Format** menu and choose **Selected (Element Name)**, where the element name is whatever you have selected on your chart at the time—remember that this menu command is context-sensitive. The Format Data Series dialog box opens, and from the **Patterns** tab, you can choose from a variety of colors and fill effects (see Figure 16.22).

- Click the **Format Selected Object** button on the tool-bar. This button is context-sensitive—whichever chart feature you have selected, click this button to open a Format dialog box with options for formatting that aspect of your chart. If a data series is selected, the Format Data Series dialog box opens, displaying options for changing the series' color (among other attributes).

- Double-click the data series. This automatically opens the Format Data Series dialog box. You can double-click any element in your chart to open the Format dialog box for that element.

- Right-click any bar, column, slice, or line in your data series and choose **Format Data Series** from the shortcut menu. This technique can be used on any element of your chart to open the appropriate dialog box for the object selected.

When you click the **Fill Effects** button in the Format Data Series dialog box, you can choose to apply a **Gradient, Texture, Pattern**, or **Picture** fill to your selected series' bars, columns, or area. These fills can add great visual interest to your chart, which is especially useful if it will be part of an onscreen presentation (using PowerPoint) or printed in color on paper (see Figure 16.23).

You'll be seeing the Patterns tab again

Even though it's within the Format Data Series dialog box when you're formatting a data series, this **Patterns** tab will appear in the Format Plot Area, Format Chart Area, and Format Walls (among others) dialog boxes depending on which item in your chart is selected. The same color, pattern, gradient, texture, and picture options will be offered.

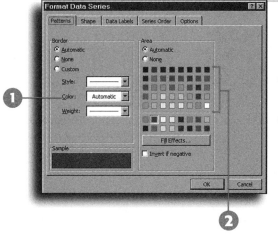

FIGURE 16.22

Use the Format Data Series dialog box to change colors of your bars, lines, or pie slices.

① Choose a color and/or line style for your border.

② Select a solid color for your data series.

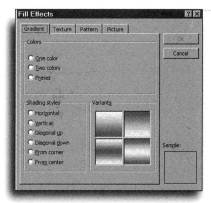

FIGURE 16.23

More elaborate fills can be applied through the Fill Effects dialog box.

To apply the special fill effects, click the tab of the effect you wish to apply and choose the style you want to use. Table 16.2 describes the different fill effects and the options for each one.

TABLE 16.2   Understand your Fill Effects options

Click This Tab	To See These Options
Gradient	Choose **One color**, **Two colors**, or from a variety of attractive **Preset** gradients. When you choose Two Colors or Preset, additional options for them are displayed. The bottom half of the dialog box shows the **Shading styles** and **Variants**, allowing you to pick the direction that the gradient's shading will flow.

continues…

TABLE 16.2   **Continued**

Click This Tab	To See These Options
Texture	Select one of 24 textures, ranging from **White Marble** to **Paper Bag**. These textures print best in color, although some of the more monochrome textures will look okay if your printer has a resolution of 6 dpi or better.
Pattern	Choose from 48 different two-color patterns, ranging from stripes to checkerboards. You can select the **Foreground** and **Background** colors for the pattern by clicking the color list boxes and selecting a color from the array.
Picture	Pictures are only available if you chose to install them when you installed the Office software. You can click the **Select Picture** button to choose from other graphics files that may be on your computer, choosing files in any standard graphics file format (JPEG, TIF, WMF, BMP). When your picture is selected, choose how it will be applied to the bar, column, or area by utilizing the **Format** and **Apply to** options.

Apply colors and fills with care

Remember that when it comes to formatting to draw attention to certain areas of your chart, using too many attention-getting formats will defeat your purpose. Use colors and fills for your cells sparingly so that when you do use them, they create visual impact. Increase legibility by avoiding busy patterns or dark colors behind your text.

After selecting your fill effect, click **OK** to return to the Format Data Series dialog box. Then click **OK** to apply the fill to your selected series. Figure 16.24 shows a reformatted column chart with patterns and gradient fills applied to the data series.

Adding Data Labels

Data labels help your reader identify the value or name represented by plotted data points. To add data labels to your chart, follow these steps:

Applying data labels to an entire chart

1. Click anywhere on your chart to make it the active element in your worksheet. If your chart is on its own sheet, click that sheet tab to activate the chart.

2. Open the **Chart** menu and choose **Chart Options**. The Chart Options dialog box opens.

3. Click the **Data Labels** tab. A series of six label options appears, along with a sample box to show you the effects of whichever option is selected (see Figure 16.25). You'll see that some of the options are dimmed—only those applicable to your type of chart are available for selection.

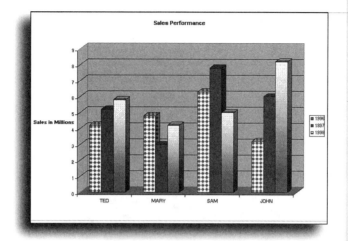

FIGURE 16.24

Apply a pattern fill to one or more of your data series to help differentiate your chart's columns.

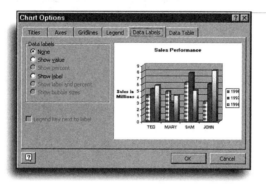

FIGURE 16.25

On the Data Labels tab in the Chart Options dialog box, you can apply names and values to your plotted data points for further clarification.

4. Click the option you want to apply, and check the sample to make certain you've achieved the desired effect.

5. If desired, click the **Legend key next to label** check box to reiterate your legend colors next to each label. This option is dimmed if the **None** label option is selected.

6. Click **OK** to apply your labels and close the dialog box.

After you add your data labels, you can move them by dragging the text boxes onscreen. Click any one of the labels and drag it to a new location. The labels must be dragged one by one.

If you find that you must move all your data labels, you may want an alternative to dragging each one individually. Try aligning the labels on an angle by using the **Alignment** tab in the **Format Data Labels** dialog box. Adjust the **Orientation** to

Which labels are best?

In bar, column, and area charts, the category axis already contains the data labels (names), so **Show value** is the best choice. When you're working with pie or doughnut charts, **Show percent** is a good choice, because the chart is showing one data series and each point in it is a fraction of the whole.

45 degrees (or any other angle you prefer) and click **OK**. The result appears in Figure 16.26.

FIGURE 16.26

If your labels are too close to your data points, try placing them at an angle for increased visibility.

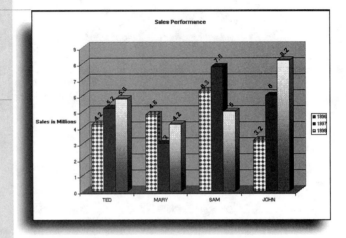

The font of your data labels can also be formatted—you can choose a new typeface, size, or color for your label text.

Formatting data label text

1. Click any one of your data labels to select all the labels for that data series (see Figure 16.27). Handles now appear around each label.

FIGURE 16.27

Handles appear around all your data labels when you click any one label in the series with your mouse.

1 Selected data labels

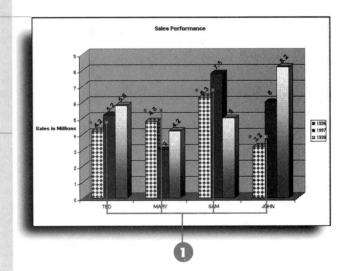

2. Open the **Format** menu and choose **Selected Data Labels**. The Format Data Labels dialog box opens.

3. Click the **Font** tab (see Figure 16.28). Choose a new font, size, style (bold, italic), underline style, or color for your text. You can even apply a background color to the label text boxes to help them stand out.

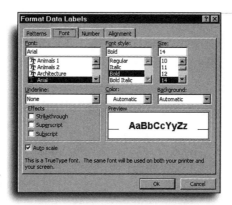

FIGURE 16.28
Change your data label's font, size, or color for added visual impact and legibility.

4. After making your selections, click **OK** to apply them.

If your data point values represent money, you may want to apply a currency format to the numbers—even if the fact that the values are money is stated on the value axis or in your chart's titles.

Applying currency format to data values

1. With your labels selected, open the **Format** menu and choose **Selected Data Labels**.

2. Click the **Number** tab (see Figure 16.29).

3. Choose **Currency** from the categories and select a format for your negative numbers and the number of decimal places you want to see. If you're working with non-U.S. dollars, choose a currency symbol.

4. Click **OK** to apply the currency format to your labels and close the dialog box.

Automatic scaling of your data label text

Click the **Auto scale** check box in the Format Data Labels dialog box so that if you resize your chart, the data labels will be resized with it, remaining in their current proportions to the rest of the data points (bars, columns, pie slices).

Other number formats

The **Number** tab in the Format Data Labels dialog box offers 12 different number formats, including **Percentage**, **Fraction**, and **Special** (which can be applied to zip codes or social security numbers). Each category has its own set of options for customizing the application of that format.

FIGURE 16.29

Choose from up to 12 number formats and apply the one you need to your data labels.

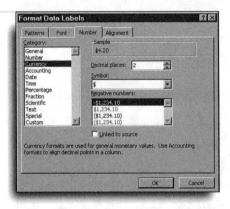

Applying and Formatting Axis Titles

If you forgot to add titles to your chart during its creation, it's easy to add them later. You can add a title for the entire chart or a title for one or both of your axes. Titles help your readers understand the nature of the information being charted and provide important information that might not be obvious in the chart itself. Figure 16.30 shows a chart with all three titles applied (chart, value axis, and category axis).

FIGURE 16.30

Titles make your chart's content clearer and provide useful information for the reader.

1 Chart title

2 Axis titles

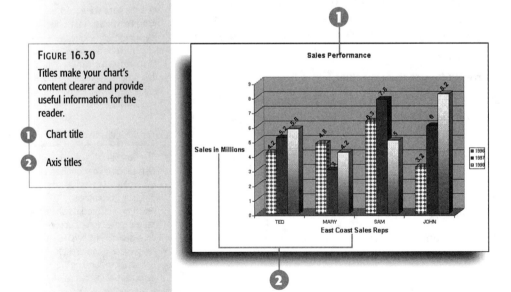

Adding chart and axis titles

1. With your chart selected in the worksheet or on its own sheet, open the **Chart** menu and choose **Chart Options**.

2. The Chart Options dialog box opens. Click the **Titles** tab (see Figure 16.31).

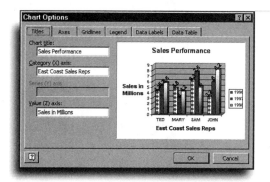

FIGURE 16.31
Add your titles to the entire chart and the appropriate axes.

3. Click in one or all three of the available title boxes, and type your titles. Keep the titles short and to the point.

4. Click **OK** to apply your titles and close the dialog box.

After you add titles (or if you had already included titles in your chart as originally created), you may wish to change the appearance of the text—apply a different font, make the text bigger or smaller, or change its color. The simplest way to do so is to first click the title you wish to format. When you see handles appear around the title text, choose the Font [Arial ▾], Font Size [10 ▾], and Font Color [**A** ▾] of your text from the Formatting toolbar. You can also apply the Bold [**B**], Italic [*I*], and Underline [U] styles if desired.

If you prefer to use a dialog box for your text formatting, select your title and open the **Format** menu. Choose **Selected Chart Title** (or **Selected Axis Title**, depending on which type of title is selected), and click the **Font** tab. Make your formatting selections and click **OK**.

> **Why aren't all the title boxes available?**
>
> If a particular title box is dimmed, it's because that particular axis or series is not part of your active chart's type.

Changing the Appearance of Gridlines

Gridlines are essential to most types of charts that have both a vertical and horizontal axis, such as bar, column, line, and area charts. The gridlines help the reader follow the data points back to the value axis to see what amount is represented by the plotted point. Figure 16.32 shows a chart with horizontal guidelines.

FIGURE 16.32

Make sure your bar, column, line, and area charts have gridlines to help your readers identify the values represented by your data points.

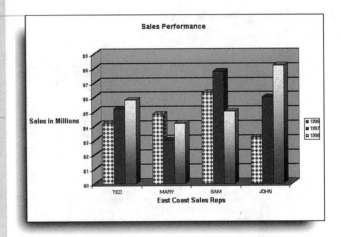

Adding Gridlines

Sometimes the use of data labels that show the numeric value of your data points negates the need for gridlines. In cases where data labels are not used, however, you'll definitely want to add gridlines to your chart. You may also want to format their appearance for the greatest visual impact.

Applying gridlines to your existing chart

1. If your chart has no gridlines, select the chart by clicking anywhere on it. From the **Chart** menu, choose **Chart Options**.

2. Click the **Gridlines** tab in the Chart Options dialog box (see Figure 16.33).

3. Click in the **Major gridlines** boxes to choose to insert vertical—**Category (X) Axis**—gridlines or horizontal—**Value (Z) Axis**—gridlines.

4. Turn on the **Minor gridlines** options in either or both selected axes to increase the frequency of the gridlines on your chart.

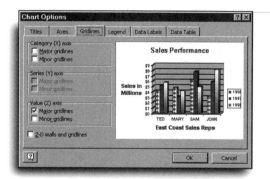

FIGURE 16.33

Choose which axes to use for your gridlines, and determine the number of gridlines to be added.

5. Click the **2-D walls and gridlines** option if you are using a 3D chart type and you don't want the gridlines to have to wrap around the value axis wall of your chart.

Formatting Gridlines

After you add your gridlines, you may want to make them thicker, change their color, or change the number of gridlines that appear on the chart.

Formatting gridline appearance

1. In your active chart, click any one of your chart's gridlines. Handles appear at both ends of the gridline on which you clicked.

2. Open the **Format** menu and choose **Selected Gridlines**. This opens the Format Gridlines dialog box. You can also double-click the gridline to open this dialog box.

3. Click the **Patterns** tab to change the **Style**, **Color**, and **Weight** of the gridlines. Click the **Custom** option to activate these areas of the dialog box (see Figure 16.34).

4. Click the **Scale** tab (see Figure 16.35) to adjust the number of gridlines by adjusting the intervals at which the gridlines appear and to change the top and bottom numbers on your value axis. Table 16.3 explains the scale settings.

Avoid using minor gridlines

In most charts, the use of minor gridlines creates the appearance of a striped background instead of creating informative lines to help your reader interpret the chart.

Double-click a chart element to open a formatting dialog box

You can quickly open the formatting dialog box for any chart element by double-clicking the element. This can save you the extra step of choosing the command from the **Format** menu. The downside of this technique is that you may accidentally double-click the wrong element and then have to close the dialog box and try again.

FIGURE 16.34

Choose the line style, color, and thickness of your gridlines.

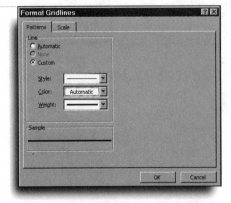

FIGURE 16.35

On the Scale tab, you can set the frequency of your gridlines.

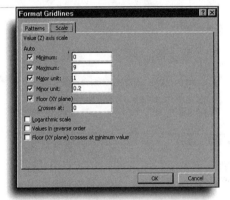

TABLE 16.3   **Understand your gridline scale options**

Option	Uses and Effects
Minimum	For most data, this is set to zero. If your data contains negative numbers, the lowest negative number becomes the minimum value.
Maximum	This number is normally higher than your data's highest value so that the bar, column, or line doesn't meet the top of the chart. If the **Auto** check box is checked, the number comes from your data's values. You can adjust this number to any value you want by removing the **Auto** check mark and typing the desired number in the box to the right of the option.
Major unit	This option determines the intervals at which your major gridlines appear. The higher this number, the fewer gridlines you'll have on your chart. Remove the **Auto** check mark to enter your own number.

Option	Uses and Effects
Minor unit	If you are using minor gridlines, you can adjust the number of minor lines your chart contains. Keep this number as low as possible to avoid making the chart too "busy" and hard to read. If you wish to adjust this number, clear the **Auto** check mark first.
Floor (XY plane) Crosses at	This number is the value across which your category axis is drawn. If you're using negative numbers, you may want to make sure this is set to zero so you have a clear baseline that quickly shows the difference between your positive and negative data points.
Logarithmic scale	Not commonly used, this feature converts your value axis scale to the tenth power.
Values in reverse order	This option flips your value axis so that zero (or your lowest value) is at the top.
Floor (XY plane) crosses at minimum value	If you want to make sure that the category axis crosses your value axis at the lowest value, check this box. With this box checked, whatever you change your minor unit to will become the point at which the axes cross. This option overrides the previous floor option.

5. Click **OK** to apply your changes to the appearance and frequency of your gridlines.

Adding and Formatting a Legend

By default, every chart that is created by the Chart Wizard has a legend. If you turned the legend off while creating the chart, you can easily turn it back on.

Turning your legend back on

1. Select your chart and open the **Chart** menu. Choose **Chart Options**.
2. Click the **Legend** tab (see Figure 16.36).
3. Click the **Show legend** option and click **OK**. Your legend appears in the default position, which is usually the right side of the chart.

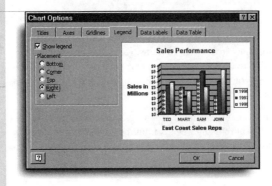

FIGURE 16.36

Turn your legend on by choosing **Show legend** from the Chart Options dialog box.

What else can you change about your legend?

You can change the appearance of your legend's text by clicking the **Font** tab in the Format Legend dialog box. You can also click the **Patterns** tab to choose a border color and style (for the border of the legend box) and apply a fill color or effect to the legend background.

After adding a legend (or if your chart already had one), you can change its position and size in two ways:

- Click and drag the legend to a new place on the chart. When you click the legend, handles appear. Use them to resize the legend box.

- Click the legend, open the **Format** menu, and choose **Selected Legend**. Choose a placement option (**Bottom**, **Corner** (upper right), **Top**, **Right**, or **Left**). Using this method automatically resizes the box to fit the new location.

Formatting Chart Axes

Your chart axes are perhaps the most important parts of your chart. They are created by the columns and rows in your source data, and their text and numeric content help your readers understand the data being charted.

Formatting chart axes

1. Select the axis you wish to format. To select the category axis, click the horizontal line across the bottom of your chart. To select the value axis, click the vertical line on the left (or sometimes right) side of your chart. Figure 16.37 points out both axes and shows the category axis selected.

2. From the **Format** menu, choose **Selected Axis**.

3. Choose the tab that contains the feature you wish to change—color and lines (**Pattern**), text (**Font** and **Alignment**), or number formats (**Number**). All these tabs have been discussed in previous sections of this chapter.

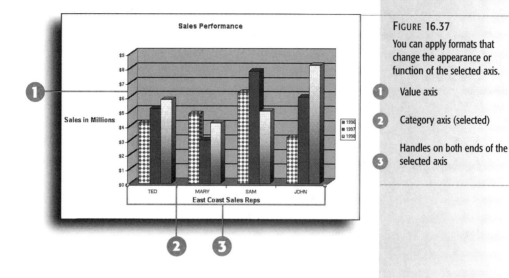

FIGURE 16.37

You can apply formats that change the appearance or function of the selected axis.

1 Value axis

2 Category axis (selected)

3 Handles on both ends of the selected axis

4. To change the frequency of tick marks or gridlines along your axis, click the **Scale** tab. Figure 16.38 shows the Format Axis dialog box with the **Scale** tab selected for the category axis.

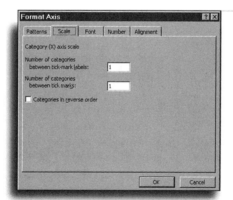

FIGURE 16.38

Choose the number of tick marks (and therefore potential gridlines) on your axis through the **Scale** tab.

5. Depending on the axis you have selected, the scale options differ. Make your selections and click **OK** to apply them and close the dialog box.

Figure 16.39 shows the value axis scale options, the same ones we saw when formatting the scale of gridlines. Refer to the section on "Formatting Gridlines" earlier in this chapter for an explanation of the options on this tab.

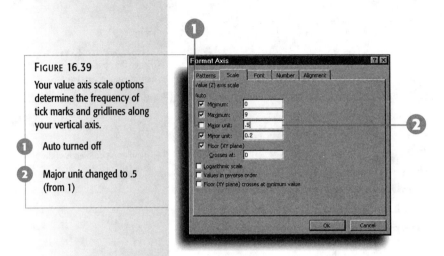

FIGURE 16.39

Your value axis scale options determine the frequency of tick marks and gridlines along your vertical axis.

1 Auto turned off

2 Major unit changed to .5 (from 1)

Changing Chart Types

The most major change you can make to your chart is to change its type. Some changes of type merely change a 2D chart to a 3D, or vice versa. Some changes are more drastic, however, and result in an entirely different view of the charted data. Changing chart types may require reselection of the data source (range of cells to be charted), which is discussed in the next section of this chapter.

Changing your chart type is simple and opens a dialog box you will recognize from the Chart Wizard as Step 1 of 4. You'll employ the same criteria for selecting a chart type now as you did when you originally created your chart—ask yourself the following questions:

- What type of data will the chart depict?
- Does the data include several categories (divisions, departments, products) or just one data series?
- Which type of chart will express it best?
- If this is a change of types, what was wrong with the original type?

After answering these questions, you're ready to select a chart type. You can use the Chart Type dialog box to help you answer the questions and make your decision.

Changing chart types

1. Click your chart to select it. Figure 16.40 shows the chart we're starting with in this example.

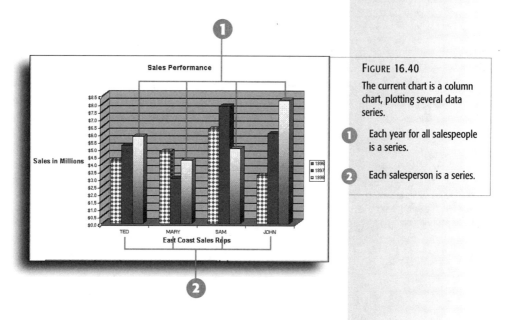

FIGURE 16.40

The current chart is a column chart, plotting several data series.

1 Each year for all salespeople is a series.

2 Each salesperson is a series.

2. From the **Chart** menu, choose **Chart Type**. The Chart Type dialog box opens (see Figure 16.41).

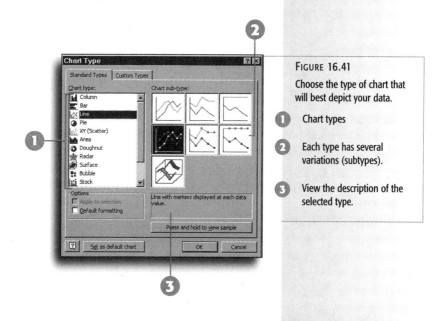

FIGURE 16.41

Choose the type of chart that will best depict your data.

1 Chart types

2 Each type has several variations (subtypes).

3 View the description of the selected type.

Change chart types quickly with the Chart toolbar

Use the Chart Type button [icon] on the Chart toolbar to quickly change your chart type to one of 18 different 2D and 3D types. Click the button and select one of the types from the palette. The downside of this faster method is that your data and the new chart type may not be compatible—you may end up having to reselect a data source or reformat the chart to make it look right.

3. Choose from 14 **Standard types** and 21 **Custom types**. Each one has a description and may also offer suggestions (within the description) of potential uses for the selected chart type.

4. Click the **Press and hold to view sample** button (on the **Standard types** tab only) to see the sample with your data. This can be very helpful.

5. After you select a type, click **OK** to apply the new chart type to your data. Your chart, with its current formatting, changes to the new type. Figure 16.42 shows the chart from Figure 16.41 changed to a line chart.

FIGURE 16.42

A chart type that fits the data is selected, showing a trend in sales for four divisions.

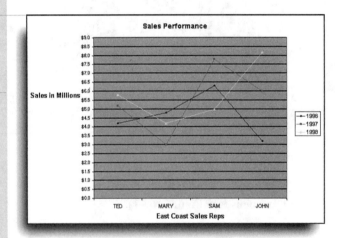

Changing Your Data Source

Changing your data source may require additional chart formatting

When changing your data source, keep in mind that the change you make may create a conflict with the type of chart you're currently using or may result in your having to reformat the chart's elements to match the needs of the data.

If your data source is wrong for your needs, it's usually immediately apparent—a data series is missing, or one you didn't want to include appears in the chart—and you must change the range of cells included in your chart.

Changing your data source

1. Click anywhere on your chart to select it. It doesn't matter if a particular element is selected.

2. From the **Chart** menu, choose **Source Data**. The Source Data dialog box opens (see Figure 16.43).

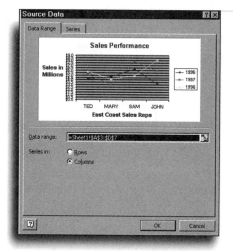

3. On the **Data Range** tab, click the **Collapse Dialog** button to shrink the dialog box. This exposes the range of cells currently selected for your chart. An animated border appears around the cells (see Figure 16.44).

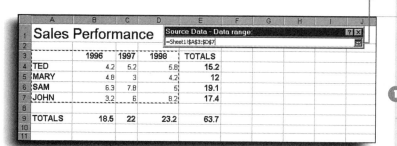

FIGURE 16.44
Shrink the Source Data dialog box to expose your current source data.

❶ Collapse Dialog button

4. Click and drag through the cells you now want to chart—this can be the existing range plus or minus some cells, or a completely different range of cells in another sheet or elsewhere on the same sheet. Figure 16.45 shows a selected single data series from the original multiple-series range.

FIGURE 16.45

Drag through your desired range of cells to select your new source data.

1 A single data series is selected.

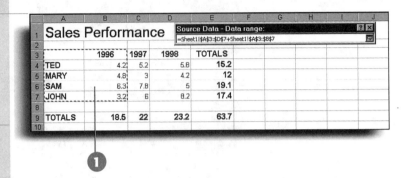

Selecting a range in another workbook

If your desired range of cells is in a different workbook than the one that will contain the chart, open that workbook before beginning this process. When you get to Step 4, choose the source workbook from your active workbook's Window menu. Select the desired cells, and click the **Collapse Dialog** button to continue.

5. When the desired range is selected, click the **Collapse Dialog** button again, and then click the **OK** button to chart the new range.

Figure 16.46 shows the data from Figure 16.41 reflected in a pie chart. The legend has been removed and data labels showing percentages and names have been added.

FIGURE 16.46

Changing the data source enables you to change your chart type.

1 Single data series expressed in one pie

2 Data labels show percentage of the whole pie represented by each data point.

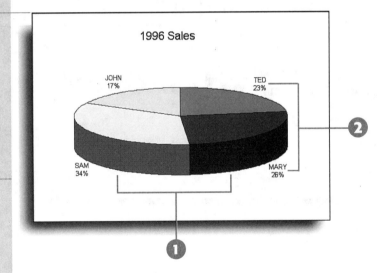

Managing Lists as Databases

Creating Lists

Sorting out the terminology

In Excel, the terms "list," "database," and "table" mean the same thing: a rectangular block of data that all pertains to a single subject (for example, contact information), in which each column, or *field*, contains the same kind of data (for example, last name or phone number), and each row, or *record*, contains all the fields of information for a specific entry (for example, Mary Smith).

In Excel, a list is an organized rectangular block of data. Figure 17.1 shows a list—it has a row of column headings across the top, telling you what kind of data is in each column, and below the column headings are rows of list data.

You create lists whenever you enter data in an organized manner; for example, a telephone roster with a column for names and a column for phone numbers is a list. There's nothing special about entering a list—normal worksheet data entry techniques are all you need. What makes data a list is the way it's organized. And after you've organized your data into a list (or table or database), you can organize and reorganize it by adding and deleting data and by sorting, filtering, and so forth.

Creating a List with a Data Form

Adding columns to the table

To add more columns to a table, you must enter them directly in the worksheet; when you next create a data form for that table, the new column headings appear in the form.

A data form is like a window into a table—a window that shows only one record at a time. Some folks find entering data in a form one record at a time to be less confusing than entering data in a big table. You can create a data entry form instantly if you have entered column headings for your table or list.

An Excel data form is not a permanent object; you create a data form whenever you need to use it (and because it's always created fresh, it always shows the current column headings).

Creating or opening a data form for a list

1. Be sure your table or list has column headings and at least one row of data already entered.

2. Click any cell within the table.

3. Open the **Data** menu and choose **Form**.

   A data form is created for the table, as shown in Figure 17.1.

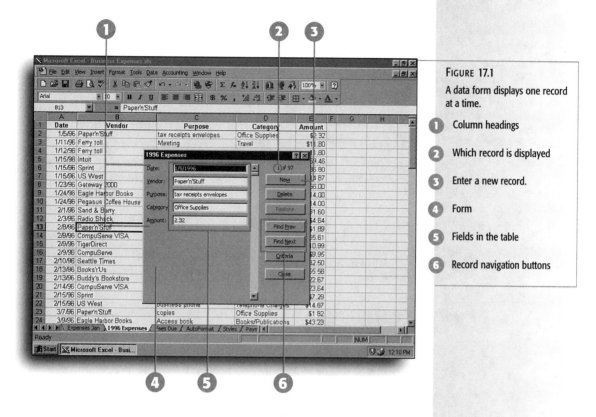

FIGURE 17.1

A data form displays one record at a time.

1 Column headings

2 Which record is displayed

3 Enter a new record.

4 Form

5 Fields in the table

6 Record navigation buttons

Editing a List with a Data Form

To edit a list with a data form, first follow the procedure described previously in the section, "Creating or opening a data form for a list." Then navigate to the record you want to edit, and select and change the data. You can navigate by using these techniques:

- Click the **New** button to start a new record.

- Press Tab (to go to the right) and Shift+Tab (to go to the left) to move from field to field in the displayed record.

- Press Enter to move to the next record in the table or to start a new record if the last record in the table is displayed.

- Click the **Find Next** button to move to the next record in the list.

- Click the **Find Prev** button to move to the previous record in the list.

- Click the **Delete** button to delete the displayed record and then click **OK** to confirm the deletion. The record is deleted, and the remaining records move up to fill in the blank space left by the deleted record. You can delete only one record at a time from within a data form; to delete several records at once, use normal worksheet editing techniques instead of a data form.

- Click the **Restore** button to undo changes you've just made (but click it before you move to another record in the list, or this won't work).

- Click the **Close** button to close the data form. New record(s) are added at the end of the table.

SEE ALSO
> *To learn more about formatting lists to enhance their appearance, see page 292*

Sorting Lists

Any list is just a sea of data until you organize it to render it useful or meaningful. Your first line of defense against a jumble of disorganized data is to sort it.

In this section you'll find procedures for sorting lists and tables by a single column, called a sort key, and by two or more columns, or keys.

Sorting a List by a Single Column

What if I want to sort just one column?

To sort a single column in a table without sorting the attached data along with the column, select all the cells in the table column before sorting. Only that column is sorted, and the other columns are unchanged.

When you sort a list, you arrange a specific column, or *field*, in the list in an ascending or descending order. The field you sort on is also known as a sort key. All the attached data in the table is sorted along with the specific column. For example, if you sort a contacts list in the Last Name column, the columns for First Name, Phone, and Address get sorted along with the Last Names, and the records of data remain intact.

Any data in cells adjacent to the list gets sorted with the records in the list, and data in cells separated from the list by a blank row or column is not included in the sort. This means that you can have two lists on a worksheet and sort them independent of one another, as long as they are separated by a blank row or column.

Sorting a list quickly by a single key

1. Click in the table column (the field) you want to sort by. In Figure 17.2, I'm going to sort the list by Last Name.

Don't select more than one cell—just click in the table column.

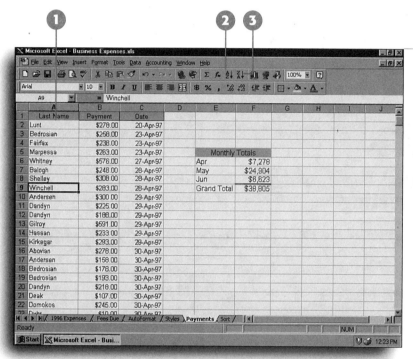

FIGURE 17.2

Because these tables are separated by a blank column, only the list I clicked in will be sorted.

1 Click in column.

2 Sort ascending

3 Sort descending

2. On the Standard toolbar, click a Sort button:

- To sort in an ascending order (1–10 or A–Z), click Sort Ascending ![Sort Ascending button].
- To sort in a descending order (10–1 or Z–A), click Sort Descending ![Sort Descending button].

The list or table is sorted, as shown in Figure 17.3.

Sorting a List by Two or Three Columns

In Figure 17.4, I've got a table of nationwide sales results for baseball caps. I want to compare the sales for each color—red and black—and see if different target audiences have different cap color preferences.

FIGURE 17.3

The whole list is sorted along with the column I clicked in (Last Name).

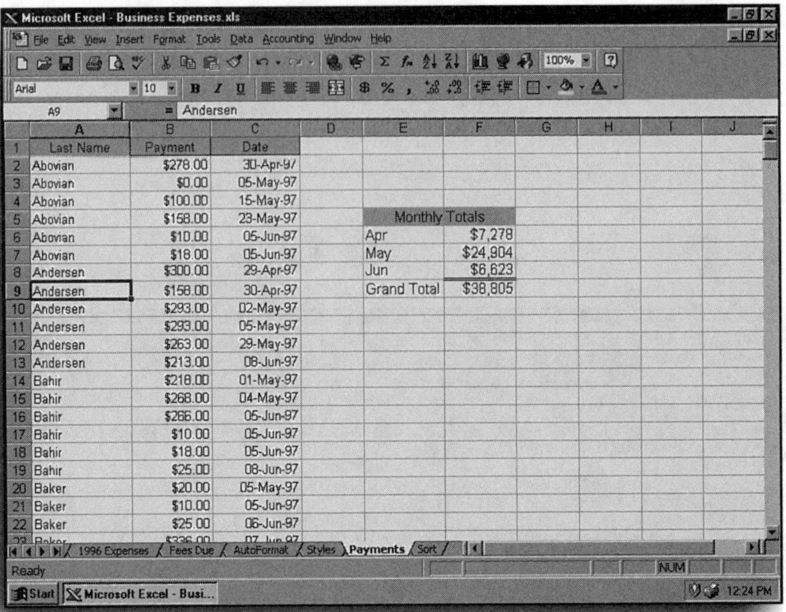

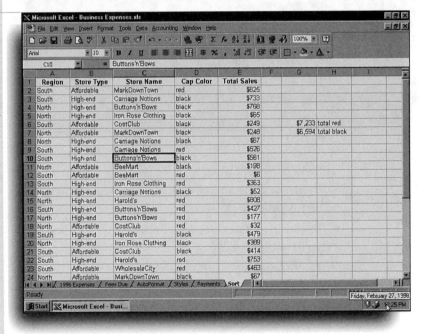

FIGURE 17.4

This data needs to be sorted by Store Type, and by Store Name within Store Type, and then by Cap Color within Store Name.

The data was entered in a random order, and now I need to sort it to make sense of it. I'll sort it by Store Type (High-end or Affordable), then by the actual Store Name, and then by Cap Color.

Sorting a list by two or three keys

1. Click any cell in the table.

2. Open the **Data** menu and choose **Sort**.

   The Sort dialog box appears, as shown in Figure 17.5.

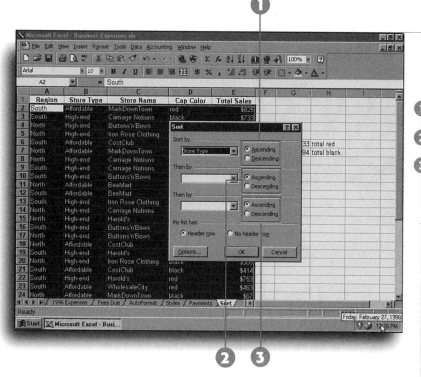

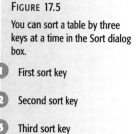

FIGURE 17.5

You can sort a table by three keys at a time in the Sort dialog box.

1 First sort key

2 Second sort key

3 Third sort key

3. In the **Sort by** box, click the down arrow and then click the top-level sort key (in this case, the **Store Type** field).

4. Click an option button for the sort order you want (in this case, **Ascending**).

5. In the first **Then by** box, choose the second-level sort key (in this case, **Store Name**) and a sort order.

6. In the second **Then by** box, choose the third-level sort key (in this case, **Cap Color**) and a sort order.

The completed dialog box for this example is shown in Figure 17.6.

FIGURE 17.6

The Sort dialog box is ready to sort the table by three keys.

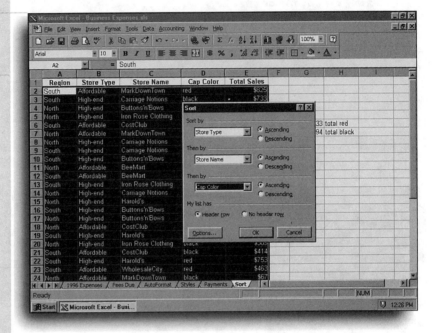

FIGURE 17.6

The Sort dialog box is ready to sort the table by three keys.

Header row or no header row?

A header row is a row of column headings at the top of a list. Normally Excel figures out whether your top row is headings or part of the list and selects the correct option for you; but if your headers and list are all text or all numbers, Excel may guess wrong and sort the headings into the list. If your headings disappear after you sort, undo the sort and then sort again, but this time select the **Header row** option, which tells Excel to leave the

7. Click **OK**.

The table is sorted by the keys you set in the Sort dialog box; for this example, my sorted table is shown in Figure 17.7.

Undoing a Sort and Returning the List to Its Former Arrangement

You may want to sort a list for temporary information without keeping that sort order. You can use a couple of methods to return a sorted list to its original sort arrangement.

The simplest way to undo a sort and return the list to its former arrangement is to click the Undo button on the Standard toolbar.

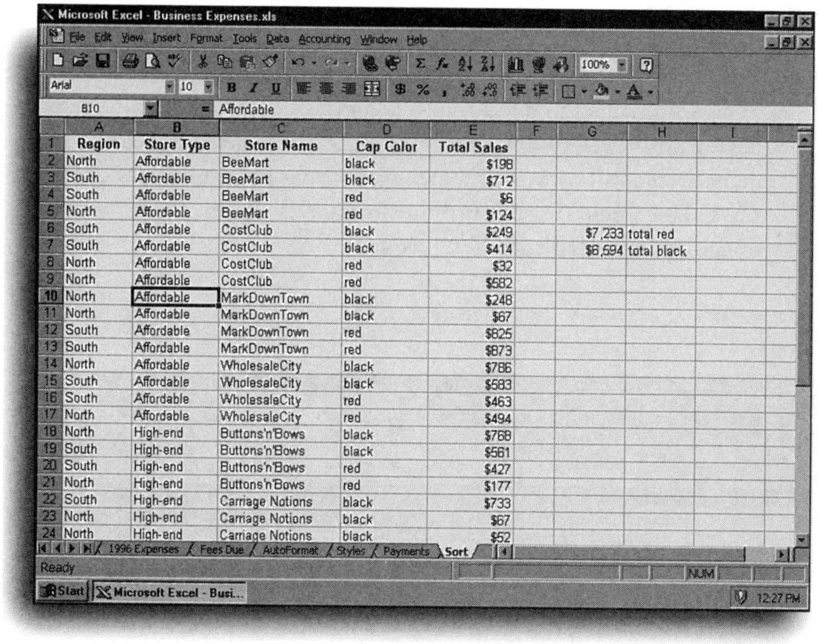

FIGURE 17.7

This table is sorted by Store Type, then by Store Name, and then by Cap Color.

Here's a way to be able to return to a presort arrangement after performing lots of data manipulation in a table. Before you begin to sort, insert a column of numbers, sorted in ascending order, somewhere in the table (insert a column and use AutoFill to enter the numbers). Then ignore the new column while you work with the table. When you need to return the table to its initial sort order, sort the number column you inserted.

Filtering Records

If you've got a large table of data and you want to focus on particular records, or rows, within the table, you can *filter* the table to show only those records and hide all others.

You can also use filters to extract, or pull out, specific records and paste them onto another worksheet (or into another file, such as a Word document).

The easiest, fastest way to filter a list is by using AutoFilter. You can filter a list by looking for a specific entry in a single field (for example, a specific city in a City field) or by looking for multiple criteria (such as expense amounts greater than $100 in a specific expense category).

New terms

Field is the common term for a column of data in a table, and record is the common term for a row of data in a table. You'll see these terms a lot, both in this book and in Excel's Help files.

Filtering a List on a Single Criterion

I'm the treasurer for a local organization, and the table in Figure 17.8 is similar to a table I use to keep track of which members have paid their fees. It's a fairly long list, and I want to see at a glance who still owes a balance. By filtering the nonblank cells in the Balance field, I use AutoFilter to hide everyone who's paid up and show only those who owe fees.

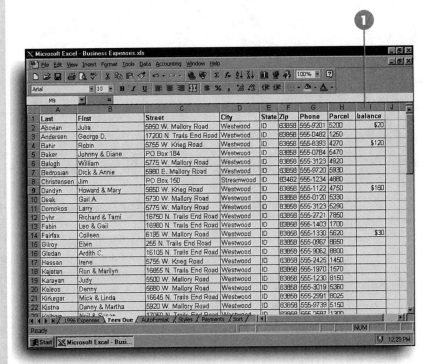

FIGURE 17.8

By hiding the records with blank cells in the Balance column, I can see a list of people who still owe money.

1 Filter nonblanks

Filtering a table with AutoFilter

1. Click any cell in the table.

2. Open the **Data** menu, point to **Filter**, and choose **AutoFilter**.

    Small gray Filter arrows appear at the top of every column in the table, as shown in Figure 17.9.

3. Click a Filter arrow in the field where you want to set filter criteria (in this example, the Balance field, as shown in Figure 17.10).

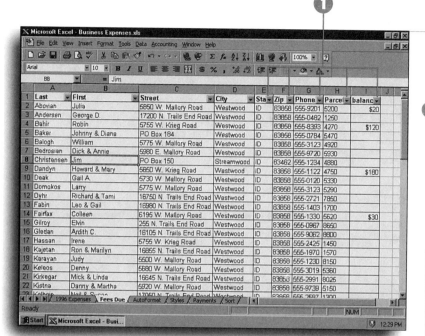

FIGURE 17.9

AutoFilter operates by means of small gray Filter arrows at the tops of the columns.

1 Filter arrows

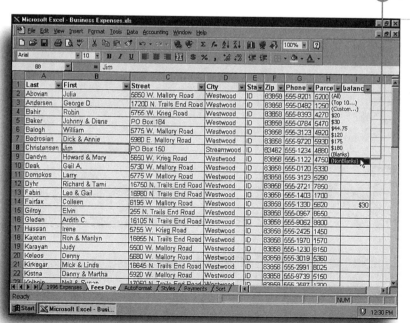

FIGURE 17.10

The Filter arrow drops a list of criteria found in that field.

1 Filter criteria

4. Click the criterion you want to filter on (in this example, I'm filtering on nonblanks).

Records with the criterion you choose are displayed, and all others are hidden, as shown in Figure 17.11. The Filter arrow in the active-filter field is blue, which helps you remember where you set criteria.

5. To keep AutoFilter on but remove the filter criteria, click the Filter arrow and then click **(All)**.

The **(All)** choice is at the top of the criteria list; you may need to scroll up the list to find it.

To remove the filter and display all records, open the **Data** menu, point to **Filter**, and choose **AutoFilter** to turn off AutoFilter.

FIGURE 17.11

Filtering the table shows me at a glance who still owes what.

1 Active filter (blue arrow)

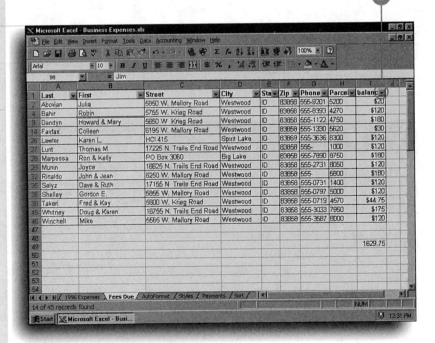

Filtering a List on Multiple Criteria

Sometimes you need more complex filter criteria, as I want in the expenses list in Figure 17.12.

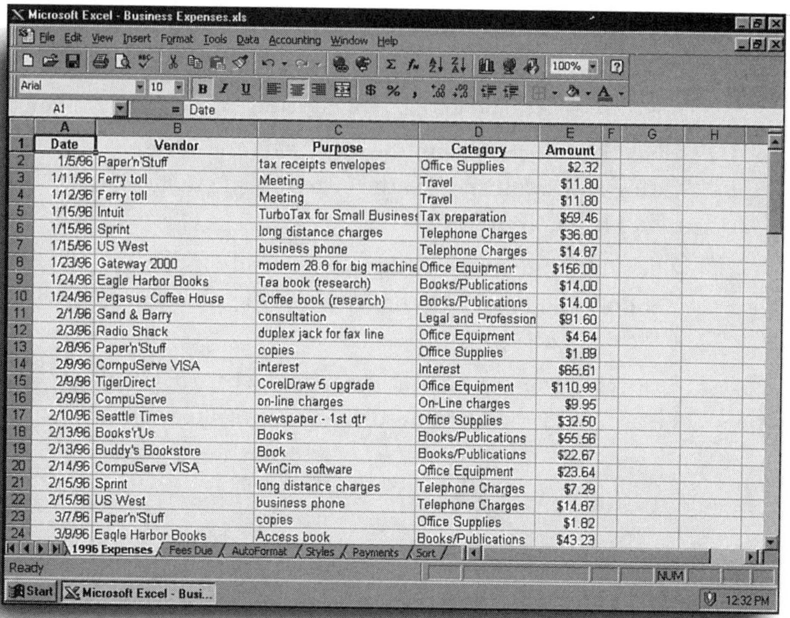

FIGURE 17.12

Filtering helps me understand better where I spent my year's expenses.

Here are several ways to narrow a filter and make it even more specific (all are covered in the following sections):

- *Filter on two different fields.* For example, I want to see the expenses for Office Supplies, specifically for the Paper'n'Stuff vendor.

- *Filter on two criteria in the same field.* For example, I want to see what I spent at Buddy's Bookstore or at Books'r'Us, both in the Vendor field.

- *Filter on a criteria range.* For example, I want to see a filtered list of all my expenses in January.

- *Filter on the highest or lowest numbers in a number field.* For example, I want to see the five highest expense amounts for the year.

Filtering on Two Different Fields

I'm trying to get my budget under control, and Excel can help me. To start with, I want to see the expenses for Office Supplies, specifically for the Paper'n'Stuff vendor.

Filtering on two different fields

1. Click anywhere in the table. Then open the **Data** menu, point to **Filter,** and choose **AutoFilter.**

2. Click the Filter arrow in the first field (in this case, **Category**) and then click the criterion you want (in this case, **Office Supplies**).

3. Click the Filter arrow in the second field (in this case, **Vendor**) and then click the criterion you want (in this case, **Paper'n'Stuff**).

I'm starting to get a better idea about what's happening. Figure 17.13 shows the results of my two-field filter.

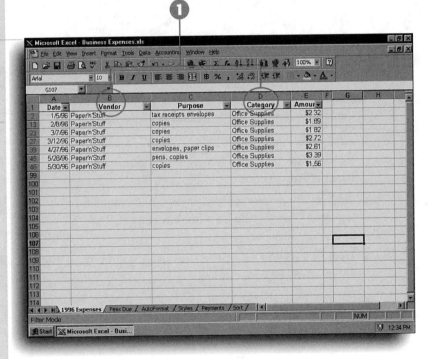

FIGURE 17.13

To filter on two fields, select a filter criterion in each field.

1 These two fields are filtered.

Filtering on Two Criteria in the Same Field

Next, I want to see what I spent at Buddy's Bookstore and Books'r'Us, both in the Vendor field. This filter requires that I set up an OR criterion in the Vendor field to show every record where the vendor is either Buddy's Bookstore OR Books'r'Us.

Filtering on two criteria in the same field

1. Click in the table. Then open the **Data** menu, point to **Filter**, and choose **AutoFilter**.

   If AutoFilter is already turned on, be sure all other AutoFilter criteria are removed (all AutoFilter arrows should be black).

2. Click the Filter arrow in the Vendor field and then click **(Custom . . .)**.

   The Custom AutoFilter dialog box appears, as shown in Figure 17.14.

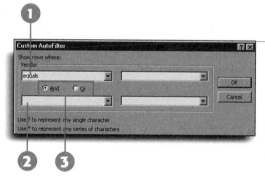

FIGURE 17.14

Set up complex filter criteria in the Custom AutoFilter dialog box by selecting items from the drop-down lists.

① First criterion

② Second criterion

③ And/Or

3. In the upper-left box, select a comparison operator from the list (in this example, **equals**).

4. In the upper-right box, select a value from the field (in this example, **Buddy's Bookstore**).

5. Click the **Or** option button.

6. In the lower boxes, select a comparison operator and field value (in this example, **equals** and **Books'r'Us**).

   The Custom AutoFilter dialog box in Figure 17.15 is set up to run this filter.

7. Choose **OK**.

   This was helpful. The results of my filter are shown in Figure 17.16.

An OR operator or an AND operator?

An OR operator displays records that meet either of the criteria; it reads "Show me any entry that is either X OR Y." An AND operator displays records that meet both of the criteria; it reads "Show me any entry that is both X AND Y." If you create an AND filter and get no records displayed, you probably want an OR filter instead.

FIGURE 17.15

This OR filter will display
records for both bookstores.

1   OR option

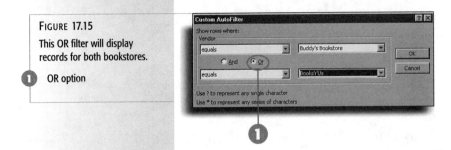

FIGURE 17.16

The results of my OR filter:
All vendors that are Buddy's
Bookstore OR Books'r'Us.

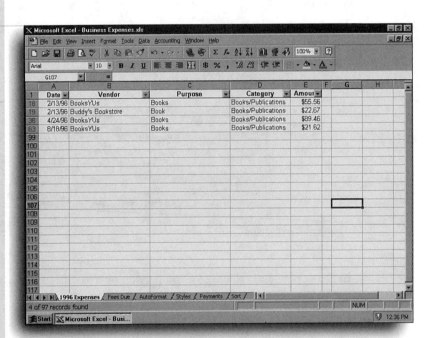

Filtering on a Criteria Range

Trying to get the whole picture, I want to see a filtered list of all
my expenses in January. This is an example of an AND filter:
Show all records where the Date value is greater than or equal to
1/1/96 AND less than or equal to 1/31/96.

Filtering on a criteria range

1. Click in the table. Then open the **Data** menu, point to
   Filter, and choose **AutoFilter**.

   If AutoFilter is already turned on, be sure all other
   AutoFilter criteria are removed.

2. Click the Filter arrow in the Date field and then click **(Custom . . .)**.

The Custom AutoFilter dialog box appears.

3. In the upper-left box, select a comparison operator from the list (in this example, **is greater than or equal to**).

4. In the upper-right box, type the beginning date (in this example, 1/1/96).

5. Be sure the **And** option button is selected.

6. In the lower boxes, select a comparison operator (in this example, **is less than or equal to**) and type a field value (in this example, 1/31/96).

Figure 17.17 shows the Custom AutoFilter dialog box set up to run this filter.

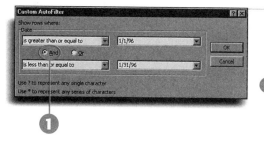

> **Excel sees your dates as serial numbers**
>
> If you open the Custom AutoFilter dialog box again to set a different filter, you might be curious about why there are five-digit numbers where you entered dates. Excel has converted the typed dates into date serial numbers, which is how Excel keeps dates in calendar order. Pay no attention to the serial numbers–continue to type your dates as dates, and Excel will figure it out.

FIGURE 17.17

This complex criteria displays records with balues between two dates–greater than another.

1 AND option

7. Choose **OK**.

The results of my AND filter are shown in Figure 17.18.

SEE ALSO

➤ *To learn more about formatting dates, see page 295*

Filtering on the Highest or Lowest Numbers in a Number Field

Finally, I want to see the five highest expense amounts for the year.

Filtering on the highest or lowest numbers in a number field

1. Click in the table. Then open the **Data** menu, point to **Filter**, and choose **AutoFilter**.

If AutoFilter is already turned on, be sure all other AutoFilter criteria are removed.

FIGURE 17.18

Blue row numbers indicate that the table is filtered and many rows are hidden.

1   Blue row numbers

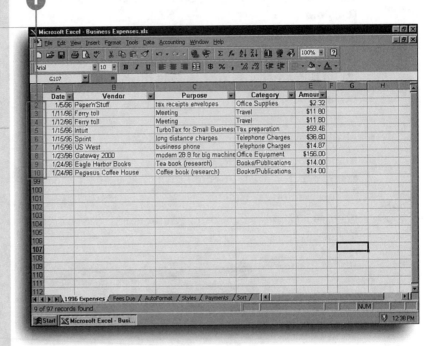

2. Click the Filter arrow in a number field (in this case, the **Amount** field) and then click **(Top 10...)**.

The Top 10 AutoFilter dialog box appears, as shown in Figure 17.19.

FIGURE 17.19

I've set up the Top 10 AutoFilter dialog box to show the five highest amounts in my expenses table.

3. In the left-most box, select **Top** or **Bottom** (for this example, I selected **Top**).

4. In the center box, type or scroll to the number of records you want to display (in this case, **5**).

5. In the right-most box, select **Items** or **Percent**. I selected **Items**; **Percent** would show me amounts that fall within the Top 5 percent of the list, but I'm not interested in percentages.

6. Choose **OK**.

The results are shown in Figure 17.20.

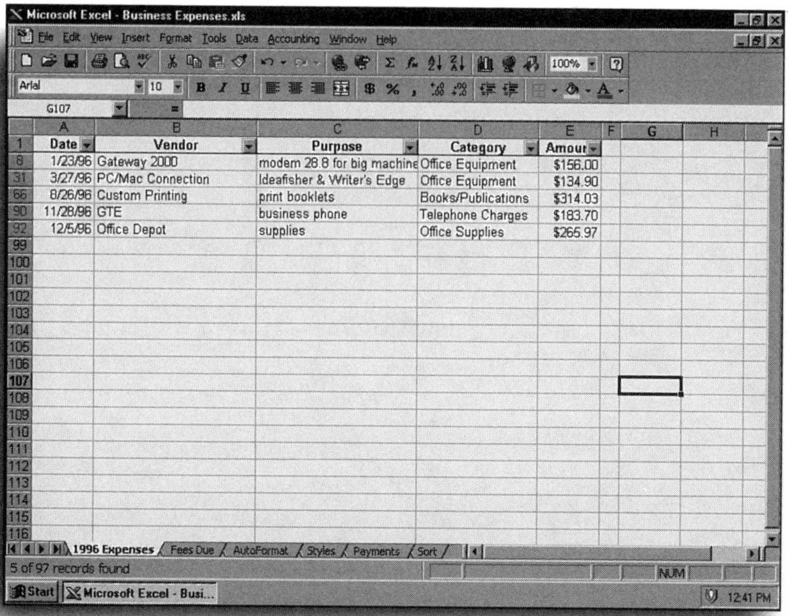

FIGURE 17.20
My top five individual expense
items for the year; if I'd sorted
by **Amount** before filtering,
they'd be displayed in sorted
order too.

Calculating Filtered Records

Viewing a filtered list is a good beginning, but calculations give you more information about the table. For example, I'd like to know what my average telephone charge from Sprint was. I can get that by using the SUBTOTAL function with my filtered list.

If I use the SUM or AVERAGE functions, the entire table is calculated rather than the records I display with a filter.

If I use the SUBTOTAL function, the formula calculates the filtered, displayed records only, rather than the entire table—that's what I want here.

The SUBTOTAL function can calculate several different functions, depending on the arguments you enter. The *SUBTOTAL (function_num,Ref1)* function requires a number in the *function_num* argument that determines what specific calculation it performs. Table 17.1 shows the possible SUBTOTAL *function_num* arguments and their corresponding calculations.

Fast, temporary calculations

To get a quick, impermanent calculation of filtered records, use AutoCalculate. Filter the list, and then select the cells you want to sum (or average or whatever) and look at the AutoCalculate box on the status bar. AutoCalculate only calculates visible (non-hidden) cells.

AutoSUBTOTAL?

If you use the AutoSum button to create a SUM formula when the table is filtered, a SUBTOTAL formula is created instead of a SUM formula, but the new SUBTOTAL function calculates a sum. If you want the SUBTOTAL function to calculate an average instead of a sum, you need to change the calculation argument in the SUBTOTAL function.

TABLE 17.1   SUBTOTAL Arguments and Calculations

This Argument	Performs This Calculation
1	AVERAGE
2	COUNT
3	COUNTA
4	MAX
5	MIN
6	PRODUCT
7	STDEV
8	STDEVP
9	SUM
10	VAR
11	VARP

For this example, I'm going to set up a SUBTOTAL formula that averages the filtered values in the Amount field of my expenses list.

Calculating a filtered list with the SUBTOTAL function

1. Click in a cell below the list where you want to display the result of the formula.

2. On the toolbar, click the Paste Function button f_x.

3. In the **All** or **Math & Trig** category, double-click **SUBTOTAL**.

   The SUBTOTAL formula palette appears, as shown in Figure 17.21.

4. In the **Function_num** box, type 1.

   1 is the argument that tells SUBTOTAL to calculate an average; for a different calculation, look up the argument in Table 17.1.

5. In the **Ref1** box, type the range to calculate (in this case, type the range E2:E98 in the **Amount** column).

6. Choose **OK**.

Yes, it matters where you put the formula

If you click in a cell next to the list, the cell will probably be hidden when you filter the list, but a cell below the list will still be visible when you filter the list.

It could be easier . . .

The only difficult part of the SUBTOTAL function is figuring out what calculation argument to use; maybe in the next version of Excel, Microsoft will make the arguments available in the dialog box instead of making us plow through the layers of Help files to find them. In the meantime, refer to Table 17.1 to find the argument you need quickly.

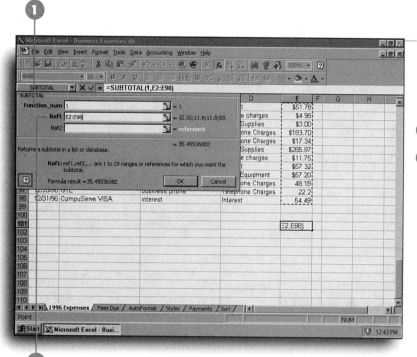

FIGURE 17.21

This SUBTOTAL formula palette is set up to average whatever cells are displayed in the Amount column.

1 Calculation argument

2 Range to calculate

The SUBTOTAL formula calculates an average for the Amount cells that are displayed. Figure 17.22 shows the SUBTOTAL formula and the list filtered for my Sprint charges.

When you finish working with filtered data, you can leave the filter on or turn it off. To turn it off, open the **Data** menu, point to **Filter**, and choose **AutoFilter**.

SEE ALSO

➤ *To learn more about writing formulas, see page 309*

➤ *To learn more about using functions, see page 322*

FIGURE 17.22

Every time I change the filter, the SUBTOTAL formula recalculates an average for the displayed cells.

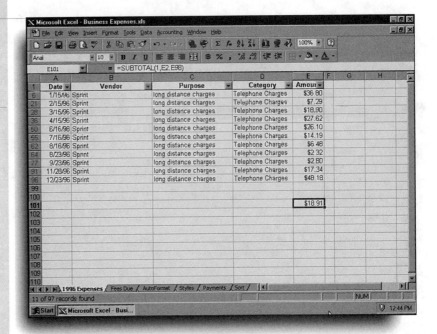

Using Outlook to Organize Your Email and Your Time

Getting to Know Outlook

Displaying toolbars

Repositioning toolbars

Adding, deleting, and modifying shortcuts

Adding and removing shortcut groups

Managing Outlook folders

Creating new folders

Archiving folders

Setting Outlook options

Introducing Outlook 97

You don't have to be well organized to use Outlook, but you do have to *want* to be well organized. So read on at your own risk. After you start using Outlook, the days of missed appointments, forgotten-to-do items, and address books made of cocktail napkins and matchbook covers are over. You'll be so organized you won't know what to do with all the your new-found leisure time.

If this sounds good, the first thing you should do is familiarize yourself with the basic Outlook features. To begin with, Outlook is a Personal Information Manager. Its job is to do, electronically, the same thing that many of its paper-based cousins—the daily planners and organizers—do with pen and ink. The big difference is that Outlook provides so many more options and features that there's really no comparison. As a matter of fact, you can create a hard copy of Outlook information any time you want, so with Outlook you can have the best of both worlds.

As to what Outlook actually does . . . well, it's really quite simple—everything. That may be a slight exaggeration, but it's close to the truth when it comes to information management. Outlook enables you to send and receive email, keep track of appointments, maintain contact information, journalize phone calls and correspondence, organize to-do lists, and more.

The Outlook Window

Of course, the first thing you have to do is launch Outlook and get it up and running. You can either double-click the Microsoft Outlook icon on the desktop or click the **Start** button on the Windows 95 taskbar and select Microsoft Outlook from the **Programs** submenu.

By default, Outlook is set to use the original profile (Internet Mail) every time you start Outlook. However, if you create different profiles, you can instruct Outlook to use a different profile or to ask you which profile to use each time you launch the program.

You can create user profiles by opening the Control Panel (click the taskbar **Start** button, then **Settings**, and then **Control**

What's in a profile?

An Outlook profile is a group of individualized settings that determines how Outlook operates for a particular user. Unless you use multiple information services or have multiple users on the same computer, you probably won't need to worry about setting up different profiles.

Panel) and double-clicking the Mail and Fax icon to open the Internet Mail Settings Properties sheet. Click **Show Profiles** to open the Mail and Fax dialog box. Click the **Add** button to open the Inbox Setup Wizard. Follow the Wizard steps to create a new profile.

Changing the default profile options

1. Start Outlook and from the **Tools** menu, choose **Options** to open the **Options** property sheet.

2. Click the **General** tab and move to the **Startup Settings** options.

3. If you want Outlook to ask you which profile to use each time you start the program, select **Prompt for a profile to use**. Otherwise, choose a default profile to start with from the **Always use this profile** drop-down list.

4. Click **OK** to return to the active Outlook folder.

Understanding the Outlook Window

The easiest way to familiarize yourself with Outlook is to take a quick tour of the Outlook window and its basic features. As you can see in Figure 18.1, the opening window consists of a menu bar, a toolbar, an Outlook Bar full of shortcuts, and an information viewer.

These are the basic tools that enable you to access and utilize Outlook features. When you understand how they work, you'll be well on your way to becoming the captain of your information.

Menus and Toolbars

Menus and toolbars are common to all Windows programs. And it's fortunate that they are common because these wonderful creations hold most, if not all the program commands that are available to you. To activate a command, you simply select a menu item or click a toolbar button.

You can't customize the Outlook toolbars, but you can manipulate them to some extent. To begin with, there are actually three toolbars, although only two appear by default. The first is the

Do you really want to use Microsoft Word as your email editor?

If you have Microsoft Word installed, the very first time you open Outlook, it asks if you want to use Word as your email editor. Although Outlook has its own email editor, it doesn't have the extensive editing features of Word. I personally find that Word's profusion of tools is overkill for composing email. However, if you try Word and don't like it, you can revert to the Outlook editor by deselecting **Use Microsoft Word as the e-mail editor** in the **E-mail** tab of the Options dialog box.

FIGURE 18.1

The Outlook main window provides easy access to all the information management tools.

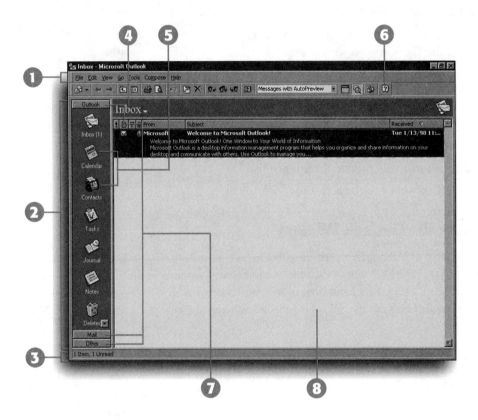

FIGURE 18.1

The Outlook main window provides easy access to all the information management tools.

1 Menu bar

2 Outlook Bar

3 Status bar

4 Current folder

5 Shortcuts

6 Toolbar

7 Shortcut groups

8 Information viewer

menu bar, which is really a toolbar that holds menu items instead of buttons. The second is the Standard toolbar. And the third, which is hidden by default, is the Remote toolbar shown in Figure 18.2.

FIGURE 18.2

The Remote toolbar comes in handy for managing your remote mail connections.

The Remote toolbar houses the commands with which you access remote mail.

The menu bar and the Standard toolbar contain different commands, depending on the Outlook folder you're in.

Displaying Toolbars

There may be times when you want to see both Outlook toolbars on the screen, and other times when you prefer to remove them. Fortunately, Outlook provides you with the means to display the toolbars or hide them with a couple of mouse clicks.

Showing or hiding Outlook toolbars

1. Open the **View** menu and choose **Toolbars** to access the **Toolbars** submenu.

2. Add a check mark to select the toolbar(s) you want to display, or remove a check mark to deselect the toolbar(s) you want to hide.

You can also right-click a blank spot in the toolbar area (to the right of the toolbar or menu bar) to access the Toolbars menu.

Repositioning Toolbars

Although the Microsoft programmers think that toolbars belong at the top of your application window, you don't have to agree. If you don't, the solution is easy—put them where you want them.

Putting toolbars in their place

1. Position your mouse pointer over the toolbar handle (the vertical bar at the far left side).

2. Drag the toolbar to a new location. If you want the toolbar docked (the default menu bar and Standard toolbar are docked at the top), drag it to the desired side.

3. Drop the toolbar to anchor it in the new spot. If you drop a toolbar in the middle of the window, it becomes a floating toolbar. The Remote toolbar shown in Figure 18.2 is a floating toolbar.

You can turn a docked toolbar into a floating toolbar by double-clicking the toolbar handle. If you then decide to redock it, you can double-click the floating toolbar's title bar. You can also change the position of docked toolbars by dragging them around. For example, if you decide that you want the Standard toolbar above the menu bar, all you have to do is drag the menu bar below the Standard toolbar and drop it. The two toolbars will immediately change places.

The Information Viewer

The information viewer displays the contents of the currently selected folder. Whether it's email messages, to-do lists, appointments, or folders and files, they all appear in the information viewer. The folder banner above the information viewer contains the name of the current folder so you always know where you are.

When viewing folders with columns, you can add, delete, and move the columns. The only other thing you can do to the information viewer is resize it. To change its size, drag the left border to the left or right. You can also enlarge it by removing or repositioning toolbars. To provide even more space for the information viewer, you can hide the status bar that appears at the bottom of the Outlook window by removing the check mark from the **Status Bar** item on the **View** menu. To unhide the status bar, open the **View** menu and add a check mark to the **Status Bar** item.

The Outlook Bar

The Outlook Bar is one of my favorite Outlook tools. It makes navigating through the program a snap—simply click a shortcut icon to jump to the associated folder. And, unlike the toolbars, the Outlook Bar is very customizable, allowing you to move shortcuts around, add new ones, delete old ones, and even create new shortcut groups. In addition, you can add shortcuts for other items on your system, including drives and folders, thereby enabling you to use Outlook as your command center for much of what you do.

The Outlook Bar is composed of three shortcut groups, Outlook, Mail, and Other, that contain shortcut icons for the various Outlook features, as well as My Computer, My Documents, and Favorites. To access an Outlook feature, just click the appropriate icon, and Outlook immediately switches to that window.

The following shortcuts are available:

TABLE 18.1 Standard Outlook shortcuts

Group	Shortcut	Description
Outlook	Inbox	The container that holds all incoming email messages until you file or delete them.
	Calendar	The Outlook calendar window that contains your appointment book, a monthly calendar, and a taskpad for tracking to-do items.
	Contacts	Your contact address book. Fill it up with names, addresses, phone numbers, and more.
	Tasks	This is where you take care of serious to-do list organizing.
	Journal	Keep track of documents, phone calls, correspondence, and more in the Outlook Journal.
	Notes	Handy sticky notes that you can use to keep track of odds and ends.
	Deleted Items	Outlook's very own recycle bin. After you trash an item, you can still retrieve it (unless you empty the Deleted Items folder).
Mail	Inbox	Because the Inbox is such an important part of your information management system, it appears both in the Outlook group and in the Mail group. It's the same Inbox regardless of which shortcut you use to access it.
	Sent Items	If you set your email (Sending) options to retain a copy of all email you send, this is where Outlook stores it. This option is turned on by default.

continues...

TABLE 18.1	**Continued**	
Group	**Shortcut**	**Description**
Mail	Outbox	I like the Outbox, especially because it has saved me from myself on several occasions. It holds outgoing email until you give the okay to send it. There have been a couple of times when I incorrectly addressed a piece of email that I was able to catch and correct only because it first went to the Outbox.
	Deleted Items	Same as Deleted Items in the Outlook group.

The shortcut groups are easy to use. Click the group name in the Outlook Bar, and the entire group slides up or down (depending on its current location) revealing the available shortcuts.

If you decide you need more workspace in the Outlook window, you can resize the Outlook Bar by dragging its right border. Place your mouse pointer over the right border until the pointer changes to a double-headed arrow, and then drag left or right. For those times when resizing the window isn't enough, you can hide the Outlook Bar altogether.

Hiding the

1. Position your mouse pointer on the Outlook Bar background or on a shortcut group title bar.

2. Right-click to open the shortcut menu.

3. Select **H**ide Outlook Bar.

To show the Outlook Bar, open the **V**iew menu and choose **O**utlook Bar.

Adding and Deleting Shortcuts

The default Outlook shortcuts are set up for the "average" user. However, most of us are not average and, therefore, want things set up a little differently than the next user. Suppose you never use the Notes feature but you're always accessing My Computer. Why not get rid of the Notes shortcut and replace it with the My Computer shortcut? Outlook lets you add and delete shortcuts with a couple of mouse clicks, so there is no reason not to do it.

Adding a shortcut to the Outlook Bar

1. Open the **File** menu and choose **Add to Outlook Bar** to open the Add to Outlook Bar dialog box shown in Figure 18.3.

FIGURE 18.3
You can add Outlook folders, system drives, and even system folders to the Outlook Bar.

2. Open the **Look in** drop-down list and choose the location from which to add an item. Your choices are **Outlook** and **File System** (system drives and files).

3. Select the folder or drive from the **Folder** name list box. The **Folder name** drop-down list retains a history of recently selected items from which you can choose as well.

4. Click **OK** to add the shortcut to the bottom of the active shortcut group and return to Outlook.

If you can't see the new shortcut in the Outlook Bar, use the down-arrow icon to scroll down through the group.

Removing a shortcut from the Outlook Bar

1. Place your mouse pointer on the shortcut icon you want to delete.

2. Right-click to view the shortcut menu shown in Figure 18.4.

3. Select **Remove from Outlook Bar**. Before deleting the shortcut, Outlook requires confirmation from you.

4. Click **Yes** if you're sure you want to delete this shortcut.

5. Click **No** if you've changed your mind or attempted to delete this shortcut by mistake.

Taking a shortcut to adding shortcuts

Any time you want to add a shortcut quickly, place your mouse pointer on the background area (not on an icon) within the Outlook toolbar, and right-click. Then select **Add to Outlook Bar** from the shortcut menu.

FIGURE 18.4
Right-clicking a shortcut
provides a variety of options.

As soon as you return to Outlook, the shortcut is gone (unless
you selected **No** in the last step).

Modifying Shortcuts

It's great to be able to add or delete shortcuts, but that's not
always the best solution. Sometimes you may just need to
rearrange things. Perhaps you use the Deleted Items shortcut so
much that it would be handier if it were right under the Inbox.
The solution is simple—move it up.

Repositioning a shortcut on the Outlook Bar

1. Place your mouse pointer over the shortcut you want to
    move.

2. Click and hold down the left mouse button.

3. Drag the shortcut to its new location. You can reposition
    the shortcut anywhere you see the thick black line (see
    Figure 18.5).

FIGURE 18.5
You can drop the shortcut
wherever the black line
appears.

4. Release the left mouse button to drop the shortcut when
    you decide on a new location.

If you want to move the shortcut to a different group, drag the
shortcut to the new group, and scroll through the icons until
you find the desired location.

As you add more and more shortcuts to the Outlook Bar, it
becomes rather tiresome having to scroll through them all to get
the one you want. If you find yourself in this situation, you may
want to change the size of the icons so you can fit more on the

screen at one time. One nice thing about this feature is that you can make the change on a group-by-group basis as needed.

Changing the size of the shortcut icons

1. Open the shortcut group for which you want to change the icon size.

2. Place your mouse pointer on the background of the Outlook Bar.

3. Right-click and select **S̲mall Icons** from the shortcut menu. To go from small to large, simply select **Lar̲ge Icons**.

The change is instantaneous and quite effective, as you can see in Figure 18.6

FIGURE 18.6

If your eyesight can handle it, small icons conserve valuable desktop real estate.

One other change you can make to shortcuts if you so desire is to rename them. For example, if you decide that Deleted Items is too tame for you and the folder should really be called The Terminator, you can make the name change in a flash.

A shortcut by any other name . . .

1. Place your mouse pointer over the shortcut you want to rename.

2. Right-click and select **R̲ename shortcut** from the menu. The shortcut name is immediately highlighted.

3. Type in the new name (see Figure 18.7).

FIGURE 18.7

Try to keep shortcut names brief to save space.

4. Press Enter to save the new name.

Keep in mind that this operation only renames the shortcut icon, not the actual folder to which the shortcut points. Even if you rename the Deleted Items shortcut to The Terminator, the folder that appears when you click it is still called Deleted Items. To change a folder name, right-click the folder in the Folder List and select **Rename [*folder name*]** from the shortcut menu. Type in the new name and press the Enter key.

Adding and Removing Shortcut Groups

Shortcut groups are handy for organizing related shortcuts. If the three that come with Outlook turn out to be insufficient for your needs, you can create a new group.

Adding Shortcut groups to the Outlook Bar

1. Position your mouse pointer over the background area of the Outlook Bar.

2. Right-click and select **Add New Group** from the shortcut menu.

3. A new shortcut group is added to the bottom of the Outlook Bar (see Figure 18.8).

4. Type in the name for the new group and press Enter.

FIGURE 18.8

New shortcut groups appear at the bottom of the Outlook Bar.

To remove a shortcut group, use the steps for adding a group but select **Remove Group** instead. As with the shortcuts themselves, you can rename a shortcut group.

Renaming a shortcut group

1. Place your mouse pointer on the background or title bar of the group whose name you want to change.

2. Right-click and select **Rename Group** from the shortcut menu.

3. Type in the new name for the group and press Enter.

Shortcuts and shortcut groups offer you an easy way to get around in Outlook. By customizing them, you can design an Outlook Bar that truly suits your needs.

Cleaning up the Outlook Bar

To begin with, try resizing your Outlook Bar icons so they're small (right-click the Outlook Bar background and select **Small Icons**). I find them much easier to see and use simply because the large icons create too much clutter. If you agree, do what I did and eliminate the Mail group and the Other group by dragging the shortcuts from both into the Outlook group. With small icons selected, these all fit very nicely in one group. Then remove the Mail and Other groups by right-clicking on each one (on either the title or the background) and selecting **Remove Group**. Now when you add new groups (Business, Personal, or whatever), you'll have plenty of room for them.

Managing Outlook Folders

The basis of Outlook's information management system is folders, which means everything in Outlook revolves around folders. Each Outlook module is a folder. All the shortcuts in the Outlook Bar point to folders. You can add, delete, move, copy, and rename folders.

The first thing you must understand about Outlook folders is that they are a little different from the folders you find in Windows Explorer. Some Outlook folders—such as the mail folders (Inbox, Sent, and so on)—can hold individual items (email messages). Other folders—such as Calendar—hold the entire module, which, in the case of Calendar, includes the calendar, the appointment book, and a small to-do list.

You can place items from one folder type into another, but the results may not be exactly what you'd expect. Generally what happens is that the item you attempt to store is converted to the item type normally stored in the target folder. For instance, if you place a task in an email folder, you end up with an email message that includes the task information. Drop an email message into a note folder, and you end up with a new note that contains the email message information.

The folder hierarchy begins with Personal Folders. Each of the Outlook modules is a subfolder of Personal Folders. The same is true of new folders you add. You can see the existing folders at any time by opening the Folder List shown in Figure 18.9.

FIGURE 18.9

The Folder List gives you a Windows Explorer-like view of the Outlook folders.

You can open the Folder List by using one of the following methods:

- Open the **View** menu and choose **Folder List**.
- Click the Folder List button on the Standard toolbar.
- Click the current folder name on the folder banner. Use this option to toggle the folder list on and off for a quick peek, as the list drops over the information viewer and obscures whatever you're working on.

To access individual folders, you can either use the shortcut in the Outlook Bar (if a shortcut exists) or click the desired folder in the Folder List.

Creating New Folders

When you begin using Outlook, you start with a bare-bones framework that takes care of the basic tasks and nothing more. As you utilize more and more features, you'll find that the initial handful of folders just isn't enough to organize all your information.

The first place you'll probably encounter a need for new folders is in organizing your email. Just as with your paper correspondence, you'll want to retain copies of important email messages. And like your hard-copy correspondence, you'll find messages much easier to retrieve if you file them in separate, clearly labeled locations with other, related messages. In Outlook, that location is a folder.

Creating new Outlook folders

1. Open the **File** menu, point to **New**, and choose **Folder** to open the Create New Folder dialog box (see Figure 18.10).

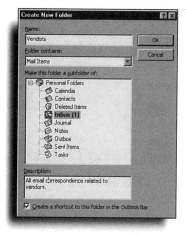

FIGURE 18.10
You can add a new folder to any existing folder.

2. Enter a label for the new folder in the **Name** text box.

3. Click the down arrow next to the **Folder contains** drop-down list and choose the type of items for the new folder. Your choices include **Appointment Items**, **Contact Items**, **Journal Items**, **Mail Items**, **Note Items**, and **Task Items**.

4. In the **Make this folder a subfolder of** list box, select the Outlook folder in which to create the new folder. If you want it to be at the same level as the default folders (Inbox, Calendar, and so on), choose **Personal Folders**.

5. Decide whether or not you want a shortcut to this folder in the Outlook Bar. Then select or deselect the **Create a shortcut to this folder in the Outlook Bar** check box, accordingly.

Keeping folders in line

When you create new folders, save yourself time and aggravation by planning a logical hierarchy before you start. For example, if you're creating folders to hold email, put them under the Inbox. If you're going to keep track of vendor email, create separate folders for each vendor under a Vendor folder in the Inbox.

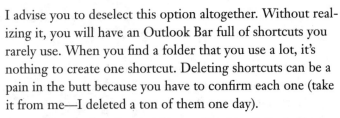

Other ways to open the Create New Folder dialog box

- Click the down arrow to the right of the New button on the Standard toolbar, and select **Folder** from the drop-down menu.

- Press Ctrl+Shift+E.

- Right-click the folder banner and select **Create Subfolder** from the shortcut menu.

I advise you to deselect this option altogether. Without realizing it, you will have an Outlook Bar full of shortcuts you rarely use. When you find a folder that you use a lot, it's nothing to create one shortcut. Deleting shortcuts can be a pain in the butt because you have to confirm each one (take it from me—I deleted a ton of them one day).

6. Click **OK** to add the new folder and return to Outlook.

As you can see in Figure 18.11, the new folder immediately appears as a subfolder of the folder you selected in the Create New Folder dialog box.

FIGURE 18.11

The new folder appears below and to the right of the parent folder.

Using Outlook Folders

Before you can use folders, you've got to be able to get at what's inside. With Outlook, you actually have a few ways to open a folder. You can click the folder's Outlook Bar shortcut (if it has one), click the folder name in the Folder List, or right-click it in the Folder List and select **Open Folder** from the shortcut menu. You can even open a folder in an entirely new window by selecting **Open in New Window**.

Moving Folders

Even if you plan your folder hierarchy logically, there will still be times when you need to rearrange your Folder List. When that happens, all you have to do is drag the folders from their original location and drop them in a new spot. However, as your Folder List grows, it may be easier to use the folder move command.

Rearranging folders with the Move command

1. Highlight the folder in the Folder List that you want to move.

2. Open the **File** menu, point to **Folder**, and choose **Move** [*folder name*] to open the Move Folder dialog box shown in Figure 18.12.

FIGURE 18.12

The **Move** command let's you pick the new location for the selected file.

3. Choose the folder into which you want to move the selected folder.

4. Click **OK** to complete the move and return to Outlook.

If you decide, in the middle of the move, that what you really need is a new folder into which to move the existing one, you can create one by clicking the **New** button. This opens the Create New Folder dialog box. Then follow the steps outlined earlier in this chapter for creating new folders.

Copying Folders

Sometimes moving the folder is not the answer, but copying it may be. Suppose, after you create a Vendor folder in the Inbox and add subfolders for each vendor, you decide you need an identical set in the Sent folder. You could move to the Sent folder and start from scratch. Or you could copy the original Vendor folder and its subfolders to the Sent folder.

Copying Outlook folders

1. In the folder list, highlight the folder you want to copy. Remember all subfolders, as well as folder contents, will be copied along with the parent folder.

2. Open the **File** menu, point to **Folder**, and choose **Copy** [*folder name*] from the menu bar to open the Copy Folder dialog box (see Figure 18.13).

3. Choose the folder to which you want the highlighted folder(s) copied. To create a new parent folder, click **New**, and follow the steps in the earlier exercise on creating a new folder.

FIGURE 18.13

You can copy an entire set of folders in a single operation.

4. Click **OK** to complete the copy and return to Outlook.

You can also open the Copy Folder dialog box by right-clicking the folder to copy and selecting **Copy** [*folder name*] from the shortcut menu.

Deleting Folders

Caution: Deleting a folder is an irreversible action

When you delete a folder, everything—including its contents and any subfolders (and their contents)—is permanently and irretrievably erased. Unlike individual items that make a stopover in the Deleted Items folder, deleted folders are terminated on the spot.

When you no longer need a folder, there's no point in keeping it around to clutter things up. Getting rid of an unwanted folder is actually pretty simple. Highlight the intended victim in the Folder List and press Delete. The folder, its contents, and any subfolders are instantly deleted.

In addition to deleting folders in the Folder List, you can drag a folder to the Deleted Items shortcut on the Outlook Bar; however, this has the same effect as pressing the Delete key. Nothing is stored in the Deleted Items folder. A third way to delete folders is by right-clicking the folder and selecting **Delete** [*folder name*] from the shortcut menu. Or you could highlight the folder and click the Delete button ⊠ on the Standard toolbar.

Archiving Folders

One of the advantages to Outlook is that it makes it easy to store all your information. One of the disadvantages of Outlook is that it makes it easy to store all your information. Confused? Well, don't be. The problem is that because it's so easy to store information, after a while you can end up with an unmanageably large amount of data. Fortunately, Outlook provides for that likelihood by enabling you to archive information.

When you archive an Outlook folder, you are merely transferring certain pieces of data to an archive folder for storage. It's kind of like putting the holiday ornaments and trimmings in the attic or basement; you get them out of the way until you need them again. The nice thing about folder archiving is that you can set the rules for when and how archiving is done. You can either set the parameters and let AutoArchive take care of the rest, or you can manually archive whenever the mood strikes you.

Before you set the AutoArchive options for individual folders, you need to set the global (Outlook-wide) AutoArchive options.

Establishing Outlook's AutoArchiving rules

1. Open the **Tools** menu and choose **Options** to open the Options dialog box.

2. Click the **AutoArchive** tab to view the AutoArchive options, as shown in Figure 18.14.

FIGURE 18.14

The options you set here will apply to all folders in Outlook.

3. Place a check mark in the box to select **AutoArchive every *xx* days at startup**. If you remove the check mark from this option, AutoArchiving is turned off.

4. In the spin box, enter the number of days between AutoArchives.

5. Remove the check mark in the **Prompt before Auto-Archive** check box if you want Outlook to perform an AutoArchive *without* notifying you.

6. Remove the check mark from **Delete expired items when AutoArchiving (e-mail folders only)** if you want to retain email items in the original folder even after you AutoArchive. This would make sense if you are using AutoArchive as a method of backing up your email folders rather than cleaning them out.

7. In the **Default archive file** text box, enter the location and folder name where AutoArchive should store archived information. You can click the **Browse** button to locate the folder.

8. Click **OK** to save the settings and return to Outlook.

After you establish the global settings, it's time to move on to the individual folders themselves. Chances are, some information will be more time-sensitive than other information, so you'll want to set up the AutoArchiving parameters a little differently.

Using AutoArchive to keep your folders current

1. Highlight the folder in the Folder List.

2. Right-click the folder and select **Properties** from the shortcut menu to open the folder Properties dialog box.

3. Click the **AutoArchive** tab to view the AutoArchive options, as shown in Figure 18.15.

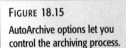

FIGURE 18.15

AutoArchive options let you control the archiving process.

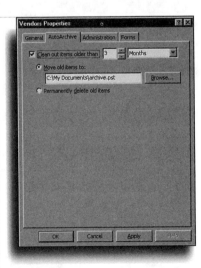

4. Place a check mark in the **C**lean out items older than check box to turn on AutoArchiving.

5. Enter the age of items to be archived. Anything that has resided in the folder for the length of time indicated (or longer) will be archived when AutoArchive activates.

6. If you want to retain items that have reached the indicated age, select **M**ove old items to. Then enter the location of the file in which to store them.

7. If you want to permanently get rid of anything that hits the age limit, select **Permanently delete old items.**

8. Click **OK** to save the new settings and return to Outlook.

For times when files are getting too cluttered and you just can't wait for AutoArchiving to do its thing, you can take over and do the archiving yourself.

Taking archiving into your own hands

1. Highlight the file you want to archive.

2. Open the **File** menu and choose **Ar**chive to open the Archive dialog box shown in Figure 18.16.

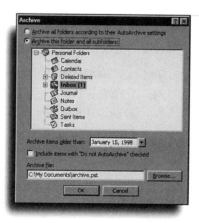

FIGURE 18.16
You can manually archive one or all your folders.

3. Set the archive options to suit your archiving needs.

   The following archiving options are available:

   - **A**rchive all folders according to their AutoArchive settings. This option forces an AutoArchive immediately rather than waiting for the prescribed time.

- **Ar̲chive this folder and all subfolders**. Select a folder from the list. The selected folder and all its subfolders will be archived.

- **Archive items o̲lder than**. Set the age limit for items to be archived by entering a cutoff date. Any items created prior to that date will be archived. Click the down arrow to access the pop-up calendar for easy date selection.

- **I̲nclude items with "Do not AutoArchive" checked**. You can shield individual Outlook items from Auto-Archiving by marking them "Do not AutoArchive." Checking this option in the Archive dialog box over-rides the Do not AutoArchive command and includes these items in this manual archive.

- **Archive f̲ile**. Enter the location and file in which the archived information is to be placed.

4. Click **OK** to archive the selected folder.

Anytime you want to retrieve archived information (as long as you have not selected **Permanently d̲elete old items**) in the folder's AutoArchive options, you can do so by opening the AutoArchive folder. By default, the AutoArchive folder is C:\My Documents\archive.pst.

Digging out archived information

1. Open the T̲ools menu and choose **Ser̲vices** to open the Services dialog box shown in Figure 18.17.

FIGURE 18.17

Address Books and Personal Folders are two of the available Outlook services.

2. Click the **A**_d_**d** button to open the Add Service to Profile dialog box (see Figure 18.18).

FIGURE 18.18

Other Outlook services include fax and mail.

3. Select **Personal Folders** and click **OK** to open the Create/Open Personal Folders File dialog box.

4. Use the **Look** _i_**n** drop-down list to locate the archive file (C:\My Documents\archive.pst) if you retained the default settings shown in Figure 18.19.

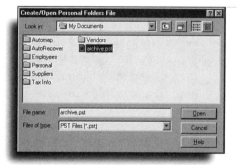

FIGURE 18.19

Use the Create/Open Personal Folders File dialog box to find your archive file.

5. Click **Open** to access the Personal Folders property sheet shown in Figure 18.20.

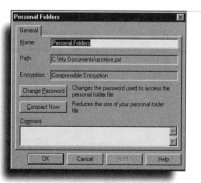

FIGURE 18.20

The Personal Folders property sheet lets you change the name, add a password, or compress the stored files.

6. Make any necessary changes to the archive file properties and click **OK** to return to the Services dialog box. For example, you might want to change the name from Personal Folders to Archives.

7. Click **OK** again to add the archive folder to the Folder List as a new set of Personal Folders (see Figure 18.21).

FIGURE 18.21

The new Personal Folder (Archives) appears in the Folder List on the same level as the original Personal Folders.

8. Use the archive folders as you would any other folders.

When you finish perusing and using the archive files, you can get rid of them by returning to the Services dialog box, selecting the folder, and clicking **Remove**. Don't worry about deleting the archived information. Removing a service doesn't affect the original file; it only eliminates it from the Folder List.

Setting Outlook Options

The extensive features provided by Outlook necessitate an equally extensive set of options so different users can get the most out of each feature. You can access Outlook options by opening the **Tools** menu and choosing **Options** to open the Options dialog box shown in Figure 18.22.

Each of the Options tabs contains options related to that Outlook feature:

- **General**. You'll find everything from adding sounds to setting the phone-dialing options here.

- **E-mail**. Have Outlook alert you with sights and sounds when new email arrives. You can even change the email editor you use.

FIGURE 18.22

Outlook has a variety of options to suit the needs of a wide range of users.

- **Sending**. This one includes tracking options, what to do with sent messages, and which font types will be used in email messages you compose.

- **Reading**. Indicate whether or not to include the original message text when you reply to or forward an email message, select the font types to be used in replies, and more.

- **Calendar**. Customize your standard work week (not everybody works Monday through Friday, 9 to 5). Add international holidays to your calendar.

- **Task/Notes**. Set reminder options or choose colors for different types of tasks and notes.

- **Journal**. Outlook will include all kinds of things in the journal if you give it the word.

- **Reminders**. Set some general options that apply to all reminders.

- **Spelling**. Set up the rules for how Outlook handles spell-checking tasks.

- **AutoArchive**. You decide how and when AutoArchiving is done.

- **Manage Forms**. If you create custom forms (such as email forms, contact forms), this is where you can determine how they're shared if you're on an Exchange Server network.

After you set your options, click **OK** to save the new settings and return to Outlook. Some of the options will only apply if you're on an Exchange network (email options, in particular), so don't be surprised if you set an option and it doesn't work. For example, email tracking options are useless unless you're on an Exchange Server network. The same goes for message formatting. Only recipients on your Exchange Server network will appreciate any fancy fonts you use in your email.

If you are finished using Outlook for now, exit by clicking the Close button (x in the upper-right corner) or by choosing **Exit** from the **File** menu. If you are using Outlook on a network, you also can log off as you exit Outlook by choosing the **File** menu and selecting **Exit and Log Off**.

Keeping in Touch with Email

Introducing Email

Getting a handle on email basics

Learning to use email will probably be a little easier if you understand the fundamentals. First of all, *email* stands for electronic mail, which is appropriate because it is an electronic message sent from one computer to another via a network. The network can be either a cabled network of the type found within large companies, or a telephone network, such as the Internet or America Online.

Using email requires three things: an email program to compose, send, and receive messages; a network to carry the email messages; and someone on the other end who uses a compatible email program and has access to the same network.

One last thing. Having access to the same network does not necessarily mean being tied into it but simply having the means to transmit information to it. For example, you don't have to be on America Online to send email to someone who is, as long as you have an Internet email account. The two accounts can communicate with each other. Unfortunately, you can't use Outlook as your email software if your only access to a network is through AOL or another proprietary network.

Over the last 150 years, a number of improvements in communication have revolutionized the way we transmit information, and email ranks right up there with the telegraph and the telephone. After you begin using email, you wonder how you ever got along without it. It's fast (most of the time), efficient, convenient, and so reasonably priced that it's almost a steal.

Realizing the importance of email, the Microsoft programmers made email features the centerpiece of Outlook. When you open Outlook, the first folder you see is the Inbox (unless you change the startup option). An entire shortcut group is dedicated to email tools. And no matter where you are in Outlook, you can create an email message by pressing Ctrl+Shift+M.

Outlook provides the email software. If you have access to a network and someone to write to, you're all set.

Setting up Internet Email

Even if you have access to a network through an Internet Service Provider (ISP) or a company network, you'll still have to let Outlook know about it. If you're on a company network, you should get your system administrator to assist you in setting up the Outlook mail feature. If you use your modem to dial into an Internet email account, you can set up Outlook yourself with a minimum amount of hassle; however, you will need a couple of things.

First of all, you must have a Dial Up Networking (DUN) connection established in Windows 95. Your ISP should have provided instructions and the necessary information for creating the DUN connection. You will need some of that same information when you add Internet Mail to your Outlook services, so make sure it's available before starting. You'll need to know your email address, your Internet mail (incoming) server, and your account name, password, and SMTP (outgoing) mail server. As soon as you've got this information together, you're ready to set up Internet email in Outlook.

Adding an Internet email service to Outlook

1. Open the **Tools** menu and choose **Services** to open the Services dialog box shown in Figure 19.1.

FIGURE 19.1

Initially, the only services installed in Outlook are the Outlook Address Book and Personal Folders.

2. Click the **Add** button to open the Add Service to Profile dialog box (see Figure 19.2).

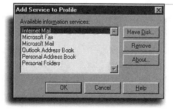

FIGURE 19.2

Outlook information services include mail and fax (if you installed faxing with Windows 95).

3. Select **Internet Mail** and click **OK** to open the Internet Mail properties sheet shown in Figure 19.3.

4. Fill in the information on the **General** tab. For a brief explanation of each field, click the Help button.

5. Click the **Advanced Options** button and enter your SMTP server name, if you have one. For most users the default settings for **Message Format** are fine, so you can ignore the Message Format button.

6. Click the **Connection** tab to view the connection options, as shown in Figure 19.4.

FIGURE 19.3

Setting up the Internet Mail service is a snap if you've got your account information handy.

FIGURE 19.4

You can choose between a network and a modem connection, depending on how you access the Internet.

7. Select **Connect using the modem**.

8. Choose the dial-up connection from the **Dial using the following connection** drop-down list.

9. Place a check mark in the **Work off-line and use Remote Mail** option. If you leave this unchecked, Outlook automatically connects at regular intervals (click **Schedule** to set the interval) and sends and receives any email that is available.

10. Click **OK** to save the settings. A dialog box appears, informing you that you have to exit Outlook by using the **Exit and Log Off** command before the new service will be available for use. Click **OK** to proceed.

11. Click **OK** to close the Services dialog box, which now displays Internet Mail as one of the services. Then exit Outlook by using the **Exit and Log Off** command on the **File** menu.

12. Start Outlook again and you're ready to send and receive email, using the new Internet Mail service.

If you have two separate Internet accounts you can use both from within Outlook by setting up separate Internet Mail services. However, to make it work you'll have to download and install the Internet Mail Enhancement Patch (IMEP). By the way, the patch also seems to improve Outlook's capability to automatically retrieve email.

Automatic Email Problems

You might want to think twice about automatic Internet Mail transferring. I've found that more often than not, Outlook has difficulty making the automatic connection. It then proceeds to ignore the fact that there's no connection and tries to send all mail in the Outbox anyway. After a lengthy and unsuccessful (no connection) attempt, Outlook claims that it has sent the email, and immediately transfers it from the Outbox to the Sent folder. To really send it, you have to go to the Sent folder, open each email message, open the **Tools** menu, and choose **Resend This Message**. You then have to log on manually and send everything.

By the way, dragging the unsent email message into the Outbox won't do the trick. You still have to open the **Tools** menu and choose **Resend This Message**.

Using the Address Book

Okay, now that you've got Outlook installed and your Internet Mail (or your company network) service set up, you're ready to begin emailing. However, you might want to take care of one more thing before proceeding—setting up an Address Book to hold email addresses and other contact information.

Just like its paper counterpart, an electronic address book holds contact information such as names, addresses, and phone numbers. Unlike its paper counterpart, an electronic address book enables you to use, manipulate, and search the contact information in a variety of ways.

If you're using the Contacts folder to store your address information (including email addresses), you're all set, because Out-look automatically creates an Outlook Address Book for you as soon as you enter a contact whose information contains an email address (or a fax number). If, however, you are not planning to use the Contacts folder to keep contact information (some folks just use Outlook for email and scheduling or some other combination of features), you'll have to set up a Personal Address Book.

Installing the Personal Address Book

1. Open the **Tools** menu and choose **Services** to open the Services dialog box.

2. Click the **Add** button to open the Add Service to Profile dialog box shown in Figure 19.5.

FIGURE 19.5

Your Personal Address Book is considered an information service by Outlook.

3. Select **Personal Address Book** from the list of available services.

4. Click **OK** to open the Personal Address Book properties sheet seen in Figure 19.6.

5. Change the name, location, or file name of the new address book if you want. Otherwise, accept the defaults as they are.

6. From the **Show names by** area, select the option you want to use.

7. Click the **Notes** tab and enter any miscellaneous or descriptive information you would like to include about this address book.

8. Click **OK** to save the settings and return to the Services dialog box. Before you get to the Services dialog box, another dialog box informs you that you will have to log off

and back on before the new service will be functional. Click **OK** to continue.

FIGURE 19.6

You have to tell Outlook where to put the new Address Book.

9. Click the **OK** button on the Services dialog box to return to Outlook.

10. Open the **File** menu and choose **Exit and Log Off** to close Outlook.

11. When you restart Outlook, your new Personal Address Book is ready to use.

Of the two types of address books Outlook offers, the Personal Address Book is the only one in which you can actually add and remove names. The Outlook Address Book is created automatically from Contacts entries, so the only way to modify it is by changing the information in the Contacts folder.

Adding New Entries in the Personal Address Book

After you've got a Personal Address Book set up, the next step is to fill it up with email addresses. You can do this in a few different ways—manually enter them, enter them directly from incoming email, or import them from a source outside of Outlook.

Entering Addresses by Hand

The method for manually entering addresses is pretty straightforward. You open the Personal Address Book, select a new address form, and fill it out.

Make the Personal Address Book your main address book

Because the Outlook Address Book is created automatically, it is also the first address book used when you access the Address Book to search, add, or remove an address book entry. To make the Personal Address Book your primary address book, open the **Tools** menu and select **Services**, click the **Addressing** tab, and then choose **Personal Address Book** from the **Show this address list first** drop-down list. This option will not be available when you add the Personal Address Book to Services until after you have logged off of Outlook and signed back on. Click **OK** to exit the dialog box.

Adding a new email address to the Personal Address Book

1. Open the **Tools** menu and choose **Address Book** to open the Address Book (see Figure 19.7). You can also press Ctrl+Shift+B or click the Address Book icon on the Standard toolbar in the Inbox window.

FIGURE 19.7

You can search for existing names, add new ones, or delete obsolete entries.

2. Open the **File** menu and choose **New Entry** to open the New Entry dialog box shown in Figure 19.8. You also can click the New Entry button on the Address Book toolbar.

FIGURE 19.8

You have several choices for creating a new address book entry.

3. Choose Internet Mail Address from the **Select the entry type list**.

Entry type choices include

- **Internet Mail Address.** Use this type for anyone who has an Internet email address. This includes people on services such as America Online, Prodigy, and CompuServe because you exchange email with them via the Internet.

- **Other Address.** Use this for non-Internet email addresses. You probably won't have much use for this type because anyone on a company network will have a company address book that is updated regularly by the system administrator.

- **Personal Distribution List**. This type is used to create groups of email addresses. You would use this if you routinely send exactly the same email to multiple recipients. It works great for sending out notices to club members or project information to coworkers on the same team.

4. Click **OK** to open the New Internet Mail Address Properties sheet shown in Figure 19.9. The **SMTP - Internet** tab is selected by default.

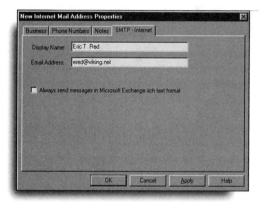

FIGURE 19.9
You can enter contact information other than name and email address.

5. Enter the person's name in the **Display Name** text box.

6. Enter the person's email address in the **Email Address** text box.

7. Ignore the **Always send messages in Microsoft Exchange rich text format** check box, which only works if you and the recipient are on the Exchange Server network (in which case you wouldn't be setting him up with an Internet address).

8. Enter any additional contact information you want by selecting the appropriate tab and filling out the form.

9. Click **OK** to save the new entry and return to the Address Book. The new entry appears in the list.

10. Press Alt+F4 to close the Address Book and return to Outlook. You can also click the Close button (x in the top-right corner) or from the **File** menu choose **Close**.

Using Incoming Email to Enter Addresses

One quick and easy way to enter addresses into the Personal Address Book is by using mail that you've received. You don't even have to open the Personal Address Book to do it.

Entering an address from an existing email message

1. Open the email message from which you want to extract the address.

2. Place your mouse pointer over the **From** header in the message (see Figure 19.10).

FIGURE 19.10

The From header includes the sender's email address.

3. Right-click and select **Add to Personal Address Book** from the shortcut menu (see Figure 19.11). The address is automatically added to the Personal Address Book.

FIGURE 19.11

You can do a number of things with the message header.

4. Close the message to return to Outlook.

You may want to open the address book and check the new entry. Depending on how the sender has set up his or her email program, the header (and therefore, your new entry) may contain only a first name plus the email address, or possibly just the email address and no name.

Importing Email Addresses

If you're switching to Outlook from another email program or want to add contacts from another personal information manager, you can import the data into the Personal Address Book (or the Contacts folder). You can even import data from another Exchange or Outlook Personal Address Book if you want to consolidate information.

From the **File** menu choose **Import and Export**, which opens the Import and Export Wizard seen in Figure 19.12.

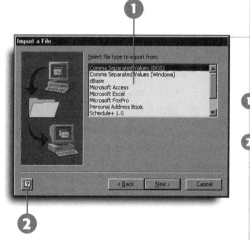

FIGURE 19.12

You have a variety of import sources from which to choose.

① File types that can be imported

② Click for Help.

Follow the steps in the Wizard to import the data. For assistance with using the wizard, click the Help icon in the lower-left corner.

Creating Email Groups

One of the reasons you bought a computer, I'm sure, is to make your life easier. Although there may be times when you have serious doubts about your decision, there are other times when you're thankful that you took the plunge. The capability to create groups of email recipients with the Outlook Personal

Distribution List option is one of those things that makes you think twice about dropping your monitor out a three-story window on a bad computer day.

A distribution list is a group of email addresses all gathered under one heading so you can use it to send a single email message to multiple recipients. For example, send your customers or vendors a change in your hours, address, or phone number by creating one email message and addressing it to the group. No more creating multiple identical messages and individually addressing them to each recipient.

Creating a Personal Distribution List

1. Open the **Tools** menu and choose **Address Book** to open the Address Book. You also can click the Address Book button 📇 on the Standard toolbar.

2. Open the **File** menu on the Address Book menu bar and choose **New Entry**. Or you can click the New Entry button 🔲 on the toolbar.

3. Choose **Personal Distribution List** from the **Select the entry type** list and then click **OK** to open the New Personal Distribution List Properties sheet (see Figure 19.13).

FIGURE 19.13
You can add as many individual addresses to a Personal Distribution List as you want.

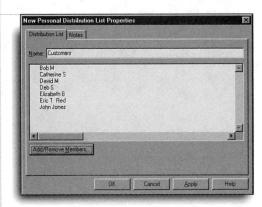

4. Type a name for the Personal Distribution List in the **Name** text box.

5. Click the **Add/Remove Members** button to open the Edit Members of [*Personal Distribution List name*], as shown in Figure 19.14.

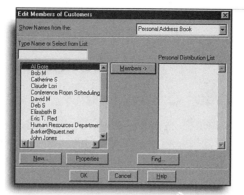

FIGURE 19.14
You can select existing address book entries or create new ones on the spot.

6. Highlight the names to include on the Personal Distribution List and click the **Members** button to add them. You can highlight multiple names by holding down the Shift key (adjacent entries) or Ctrl key (nonadjacent entries) while highlighting. You can use different address books by choosing from the **Show Names from the** drop-down list. To add a brand new name to the distribution list, click the **New** button and enter the appropriate information.

7. Click **OK** to return to the New Personal Distribution List Properties sheet, which now includes the selected names.

8. Click **OK** to return to the Address Book. The new Personal Distribution List appears in the address list with an icon indicating that it is a Personal Distribution List (see Figure 19.15).

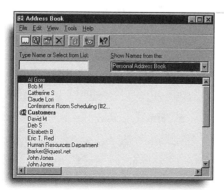

FIGURE 19.15
The icon of a man and woman indicates the entry is a Personal Distribution List.

9. Press **Alt+F4** or click the Close (x) button to close the Address Book and return to Outlook.

You can create as many Personal Distribution Lists as you need.

Editing Existing Entries

People move, phone numbers change, businesses close their doors. It's all part of life, and if a particular change happens to be part of your life, you'll want to update your Personal Address Book to reflect the new information.

Modifying Personal Address Book entries

1. Open the **T**ools menu and choose **Address B**ook to open the Address Book. You also can click the Address Book button on the toolbar.

2. Right-click the entry you want to edit to open its properties sheet. It doesn't matter whether it's a single name or a Personal Distribution List.

3. Make the necessary changes and click **OK** to return to the Address Book.

4. Repeat the process for each entry you want to change.

5. Press Alt+F4 or click the Close (x) button to close the Address Book and return to Outlook.

If you want to delete an entry, highlight it and press Delete or click the Delete button on the toolbar.

Composing Email

Now that you've got the preliminaries under your belt, it's time to get down to the real stuff—actually creating an email message. If you can type (even if you only hunt and peck), you'll be composing email messages in no time.

An email message consists of several elements:

- *Header*. The header includes the **To** button and field (the recipient), the **C**c button and field (send copies to these people), and the **Subject** field (what's this email about?). There is an optional fourth field, **Bcc**, that allows you to send "blind" copies. Unlike the name(s) in the **C**c field, nothing in the **Bcc** field appears on the message sent to the original recipient(s).

- *Options*. Except for the **Importance** and **Save sent message to** options, none of the other options work unless you're on an Exchange Server network. The Importance options work on some Internet email, but not all. You'll have to experiment to find out.

- *Message body*. That's the big, blank window under the **Subject** field. Fill it up with whatever you've got to say.

One of the nice things about Outlook is that you can create an email message from any folder by pressing Ctrl+Shift+M.

Creating a New Email Message

Creating an email message is easy. All you have to do is open a new form, add a recipient or two, enter a subject, type your message, and send it on its way,

Composing an email message

1. Open the **File** menu, point to **New**, and choose **Mail Message** to open a new Message form (see Figure 19.16). You also can click the New Mail Message button 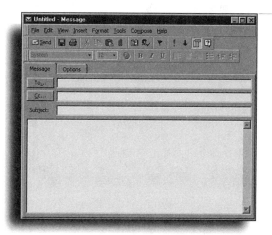.

2. Click the **To** button to open the Select Names dialog box shown in Figure 19.17. Or, if you know the person's email address, you can simply enter it in the **To** field.

Using shortcut keys in Outlook

One shortcut key cuts across all the boundaries. You can always open a new form specific to the folder you're in by pressing Ctrl+N. Therefore, if you're in the Inbox, pressing Ctrl+N opens a new email form; if you're in the Contacts folder, pressing Ctrl+N opens a new contact form; in the Calendar folder, it opens a new appointment form, and so on.

FIGURE 19.16

The message form menu bar and toolbar offer lots of options for managing email messages.

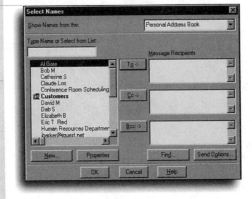

FIGURE 19.17
The Select Names dialog box displays names from the selected address book.

Get the most mileage out of the subject field

It may be tempting to ignore the subject field or use it haphazardly. However, the ease with which email can be generated means that most people receive a ton of it, much of which is "junk." As a result, many people use the subject field in determining which email to open first (if at all). If you want your email to get read, include a brief, accurate, and interesting subject line.

3. Select the recipient name(s) and click the **To** button to add them to the **To** field. Do the same for any **Cc**'s or **Bcc**'s you want to include as well.

4. Click **OK** to return to the new Message form. The names you selected now appear in the appropriate field.

5. Enter a short description of the message in the **Subject** field.

6. Type your message in the message body text box to complete the email (see Figure 19.18).

FIGURE 19.18
You can include any combination of individual and Personal Distribution List names in the **To** field.

7. Click the **Options** tab to see the available message options. Keep in mind, however, that unless you're on an Exchange Server network, only the **Importance** and **Save sent message to** options will work.

8. Click the **Send** button to send the message or place it in the Outbox, depending on the email service you're using.

If you're on a network, the message is sent immediately. If you're using Internet email, the message is placed in the Outbox until you sign on and check your mail.

Using Drag and Drop to Create Email Messages

Outlook has a very handy feature that enables you to create an email message from any folder by dragging a folder item to the Inbox and dropping it. Like magic, a new message form opens with the folder item inserted in the appropriate place.

For example, suppose you're in the Calendar folder, reviewing your appointments for the week, when you notice an important meeting and would like to remind everyone to attend. You could open a new message form, type something about the meeting in the Subject field, and then enter the meeting specifics in the message body. Or simpler—you could drag the appointment from the Calendar and drop it on the Inbox shortcut in the Outlook Bar or the Inbox folder in the folders list. The resulting email message contains the appointment information (see Figure 19.19). All you have to do is add the recipient(s) and send it.

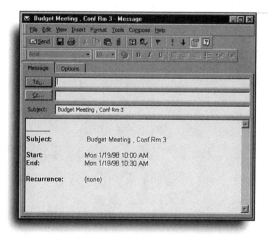

FIGURE 19.19

Creating email with drag and drop can be a great time-saver.

You can use the same drag-and-drop method from any Outlook folder. Of course, the results will vary depending on the folder. When you drag and drop a contact to the Inbox, a message form is created with the contact's email address (if she has one) in the To field. Using a task is similar to an appointment in that the task information is included in the **Subject** field and the message body. Experiment with it to see how it works in the other folders.

Formatting an Email Message

Text formatting is a feature of most word processors and text editors that enables you to spruce up your documents and, in the case of Outlook, your email messages. You can change the fonts, font sizes, font styles, font colors, and more.

Unless you're exchanging email with someone on an Exchange Server network, there's little point in using the formatting features. They do not carry over in Internet email, even if both the sender and the receiver are using Outlook.

You can apply formatting to the message text by highlighting the text you want to modify and using the appropriate buttons on the Message Formatting toolbar (see Figure 19.20).

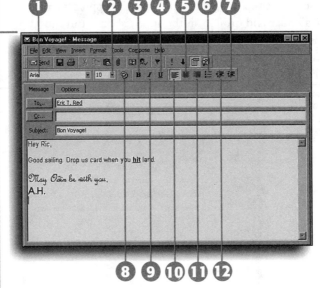

FIGURE 19.20

The Outlook email editor provides basic text-formatting features.

1 Font

2 Font size

3 Bold

4 Underline

5 Align center

6 Bullets

7 Increase indent

8 Font color

9 Italic

10 Align left

11 Align right

12 Decrease indent

If you're using Word Mail as your email editor, you'll find that you have a lot more formatting options, including styles, borders, shading, and backgrounds.

SEE ALSO

➤ *To learn more about text formatting, see page 103*

Adding Attachments to an Email

If the value of email is determined by how much information you can transmit, it becomes priceless when you begin attaching files. Rather than just telling a customer about a new product, why not show them by adding a picture? Don't like the budget report you just received? Then annotate it, revise it, and send it back to the original author. Got a deadline to meet? Do what I do—attach the chapter to an email message and send it to your editor.

It's actually pretty simple.

Including attachments with email messages

1. Create your email message, following the steps outlined earlier in this chapter.

2. Open the **Insert** menu on the Message menu bar (see Figure 19.21).

FIGURE 19.21
You have several choices for file attachments.

3. Select the attachment type from the **Insert** menu. For this example, we'll attach a file.

You can insert any of the following items in an Outlook email message:

- **File**. You can attach any computer file, including a text, graphic, or spreadsheet file, just to name a few.

- **Item**. This selection allows you to insert an Outlook item, such as a contact, an existing email message, or an appointment, in an email message.

- **Autosignature**. If you've created an autosignature, you can use this selection to include it in the message at the cursor location. An *autosignature* is text that you create for ending messages. Many people include their name and company information, or sometimes a personal quote.

- **Object**. Objects can be Office documents, clip art, WordArt, or video or sound clips. The selection is extensive. You can even create new objects to include in your email.

4. Locate the file to attach, using the Insert File dialog box shown in Figure 19.22.

FIGURE 19.22

Search your hard drive(s) for the file to insert in your email message.

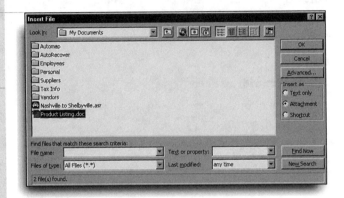

5. Highlight the file to include and click **OK** to return to the email message, which now contains the file (see Figure 19.23).

FIGURE 19.23

An attached file appears at the cursor as an icon with the file name below it.

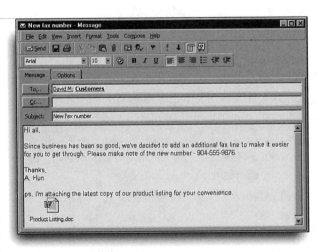

6. Repeat the process for as many attachments as you want to include.

You can add any combination of attachments to an email message; however, you should keep in mind that many Internet email accounts have a space limit. If you send multiple large files, the recipient may not be able to receive the message if his mailbox is too small to accommodate the combined size of all the attachments.

Sending Email

After you create your message, do your formatting, and attach any necessary files, you're ready to log on and send (and receive) your email. Again, this applies to Internet Mail, not network mail (which is generally sent and received automatically).

If you set up your Internet Mail to automatically send and receive, you don't have to do anything. Outlook will dial into your ISP and check your mail according to the schedule you established.

If, on the other hand, you're going to get your mail manually, you can either dial out yourself, using your dial-up networking connection, or you can let Outlook do it for you. My experience with letting Outlook dial out has not been good. Too frequently, it can't make the connection and tries to send mail anyway. Consequently, I do my own dialing.

To let Outlook do the dialing, all you have to do is open the **Tools** menu and choose **Check for New Mail.** Outlook will do the rest. You'll notice a second menu item called **Check for New Mail On**. Outlook does not support multiple Internet Mail accounts unless you have the Internet Mail Enhancement Patch (IMEP) installed, so this option functions the same as the **Check for New Mail** option.

If you want to be a little more choosy about how you get your mail, you can use Remote Mail. Open the **Tools** menu, point to **Remote Mail**, and choose **Connect** to use the Remote Connection Wizard to get your mail. (If you don't see **Remote Mail** on the **Tools** menu, click a mail folder first, such as the Inbox shortcut on the Outlook Bar.)

Remote mail offers the following options:

- **Retrieve and send all new mail**. Sends all mail currently in the Outbox and retrieves all mail in your Internet Mail mailbox.

- **Do only the following**. Here you can choose to download only the headers of the messages in your Internet Mail mailbox so you can see what's waiting for you before downloading. If you previously downloaded headers, you can indicate which messages to retrieve. You can also select individual outgoing messages to send and hold others for a later connection.

Receiving Email

Receiving email is the flip side of sending. If you use the **Check for New Mail** option, you receive your email during the same session in which you send it. If you use **Remote Mail**, you receive only those messages that you select for downloading. However you get your incoming mail, there are a number of things you can do after you receive it. You'll probably want to read it. You may want to reply to it or forward it to someone else. If the message has an attachment, you'll have to either open the attachment or save it to your hard disk. Finally, you'll probably want to store the message or delete it.

Reading Messages

Incoming email messages are automatically deposited in your Inbox, which you can open by clicking the Inbox shortcut on the Outlook Bar. The message information for each new message appears in bold, and the first few lines of the message are shown (unless you turn off AutoPreview) under the message information. After you open a message and close it, both the bolding and the preview disappear. The quickest way to open a message is to double-click it. That's all there is to it. After you've read the message, you can close it by pressing Alt+F4.

Responding to Messages

Very often an incoming message requires (or deserves) a response. Rather than closing the original message and creating a new message, you can let Outlook do the work.

Automating replies to email messages

1. Open the message by double-clicking it.

2. Click the **Reply** button on the message form Standard toolbar to open a new message form with the original message in the message text box (see Figure 19.24).

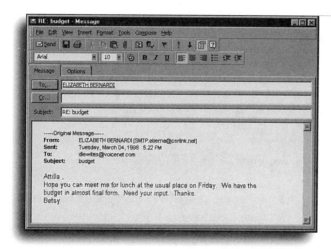

FIGURE 19.24
Outlook creates a new message form with everything filled in for you.

3. Type your reply above the original message information. If you prefer to delete the original message, or parts of it, select the text and press Delete.

4. Click **Send** to place the reply in the Outbox.

If the original message was sent to multiple recipients, you can send the same reply to each of them by using the **Reply to All** button.

By default, Outlook includes the original message in your reply. You actually have a few choices as to how you want the reply formatted.

Changing the reply options

1. Open the **Tools** menu and choose **Options** to open the Options dialog box. Be sure to access the **Tools** menu from the Outlook window, not the message form window.

2. Click the **Reading** tab to view the reading options shown in Figure 19.25.

FIGURE 19.25

The reading options enable you to determine how Outlook handles replies and forwarding.

3. Select the desired **When replying to a message** option from the drop-down list.

   The following options are available:

   - **Do not include original message**. The header and subject are filled out, but the message body is totally blank.

   - **Attach original message**. This includes the original message not as text but as an attachment.

   - **Include original message text**. To include the original message as text, select this option.

   - **Include and indent original message text**. This option includes the original message as text and indents it for easier reading.

4. Click **OK** to save the new settings and return to Outlook.

You can also change the style of the text used in your reply by clicking the **Font** button and selecting a new font, style, size, or color.

Forwarding Messages

Occasionally you receive email that would be of interest to a third party. You could create a new message addressed to that third party and retype all the information from the original message. Or, you could forward the original message and save yourself a lot of time and effort.

Using Forward to pass messages along

1. Double-click the original message to open it.

2. Click the **Forward** button on the message form Standard toolbar. As with the Reply feature, Outlook creates a new message form with all the information from the original (except the recipient).

3. Add the intended recipient(s) in the **To**, **Cc** and **Bcc** fields.

4. Type any additional information that you want to include above the original message.

5. Click the **Send** button to place the forwarded message in the Outbox.

As with the reply feature, you can change the way forwarded messages are formatted. Return to the **Reading** tab of the Options dialog box and select a new format from the **When forwarding a message** drop-down list. The effects of the available choices match the corresponding choices in the reply options.

Dealing with Attachments

When you receive a message with an attachment, you have a couple of options for dealing with the attachment, depending on what it is. If it's an email message included as an attachment, you can double-click it to open it. If it's a file, you may be able to open it by double-clicking it. If it's a file type associated with a specific program in Windows 95, the program opens automatically and reads the file. For example, if you double-click a Word document attachment (a file with a .doc extension), Word starts and opens the attached document.

If double-clicking doesn't work, you'll have to save the attachment to your hard disk, start the associated program, and then open the file from within the associated program.

Saving an attachment to your hard disk

1. Open the email with the attachment.

2. Right-click the attached file and select **Save As** from the shortcut menu (see Figure 19.26).

FIGURE 19.26

You can do quite a few things with an attached file.

3. Use the Save Attachment dialog box to indicate the file name and location.

4. Click **Save** to return to the open email message.

In addition to saving the attachment, you can print, cut, copy, and paste it. You may even be able to view the file contents by using the **Quick View** option, if there is a viewer installed for the particular file type. You can find all these commands on the shortcut menu when you right-click the attachment.

Printing Messages

As convenient as electronic information is to use and store, there are times when nothing less than hard copy will do. Therefore, when you need or want a printed copy of an email message, it's yours for the asking. You can print a copy with a couple of quick mouse clicks (if you have a printer installed).

Converting electronic messages into hard copy

1. Open the appropriate folder and highlight the message you want to print.

2. Open the **File** menu and choose **Print** to open the Print dialog box shown in Figure 19.27.

3. Choose the printer to use from the **Name** drop-down list.

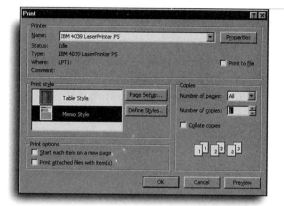

FIGURE 19.27

Customize your hard copy with the Outlook print options.

4. Set the remaining print options.

Print options you can set in Outlook include

- **Print style**. To print an individual email message, select **Memo Style**. **Table Style** prints the contents of the folder as it appears in the Information viewer. You can even create your own style by clicking the **Define Styles** button.

- **Print options**. If you've selected more than one message to print, you can have them printed on separate pages by selecting **Start each item on a new page**. Otherwise, they are printed one right after the other on the same page. Selecting **Print attached files with items(s)** opens the program associated with the file (if there is one) and prints the attachment. This only works if there is an associated program.

- **Copies**. Select the pages to print (**All, Odd, Even**), the number of copies to print, and indicate whether or not you want them collated.

5. Click **OK** to print the selected message(s).

You can also print a message (using the default settings) by highlighting the message and clicking the Print button on the Standard toolbar.

SEE ALSO

➤ *To learn more about printing, see page 215*

Sorting Email

If you retain a lot of email in your Inbox or other folders, you may find it easier to search for a particular piece if you change the sort order of the folder. Occasionally, I find myself looking for something that I know came from a certain person, but I can't remember the date or the subject. When this happens, I re-sort the folder by the From column and find that person's name so I can review everything she sent.

Reorganizing your email by changing the sort order

1. Open the folder you want to sort.

2. Click the header of the column by which you want to sort the folder. An engraved down arrow indicates a descending sort (from A to Z); an engraved up arrow indicates an ascending sort (from Z to A).

3. Click the column header a second time to change the sort from ascending to descending, or vice versa.

You can sort on multiple columns by holding the Shift key down while clicking the column header. In other words, if you want to sort the Inbox by sender, you would click the From column. If you then want to sort the messages from each sender by date, you would hold the Shift key and click the Received column header.

Grouping Messages

Outlook has another handy feature for organizing your folder contents—grouping. *Groups* are containers for items, based on the column headers. If you group your messages by the From column, you create a group for each sender of messages in the current folder (see Figure 19.28).

Creating item groups

1. Open the folder in which to create groups. It must be a folder that appears in table form, such as the Inbox, the Tasks folder, or the Active Appointments view of the calendar.

2. Right-click the column header of the field you want to use to create groups.

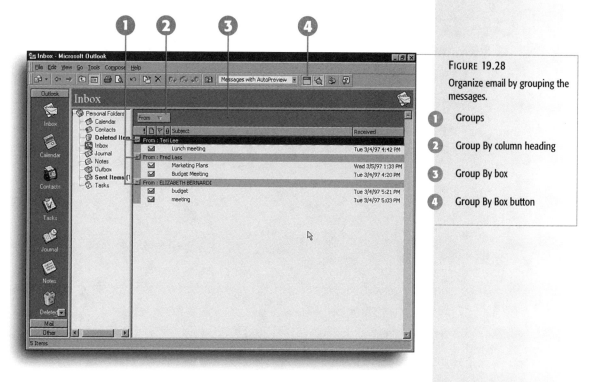

FIGURE 19.28

Organize email by grouping the messages.

1. Groups

2. Group By column heading

3. Group By box

4. Group By Box button

3. Select **Group By This Field** from the shortcut menu.

4. Click the + icon to the left of the Group name to expand the group and view the group contents.

You can create subgroups of the original group(s) by repeating the above steps and selecting a different column header.

You can also create groups by dragging the column header into the Group By box and dropping it. If the Group By box is not visible, click the Group By Box button on the Standard toolbar.

Managing Your Time and Information

Staying on Schedule with Calendar

If you haven't noticed yet, Outlook is not just another email program. It's a full-functioned Personal Information Manager, providing you with plenty of tools to get organized. The old cliché "Time is money" may be tired and worn out, but it's still true. To ensure that you get the most out of your time and your information, utilize all the tools Outlook has to offer. The Calendar will keep you on schedule.

Keeping track of appointments can be a full-time job if you don't have a good system. Writing appointments on the back of notepads, the edges of your desk blotter, or on scraps of paper is a great system if you have nothing better to do than search for them when you lose them. Using a daily planner or other appointment book is certainly a lot better. However, using the Outlook Calendar feature beats them all—it lets you schedule, change, move, copy, print, and even forward (via email) appointments with a couple of mouse clicks. Now let's see your daily planner do that.

The first thing to do is familiarize yourself with the various components that make up the Calendar (see Figure 20.1). To open the Calendar folder, click the Calendar shortcut on the Outlook Bar.

The section of the Outlook Calendar that most of us are familiar with is the Appointment Book, where you record and track your appointments. The *Date Navigator* provides a pair of calendars, plus a few neat scheduling tricks. Finally, the *TaskPad* offers a handy notepad for jotting down tasks that need doing.

Using the Appointment Book

To get the most out of the Appointment Book, you should be aware of how it works. As you can see in Figure 20.1, it resembles a regular appointment book, with the date at the top of the page and time slots along the left margin. If you use the scrollbar to move the page up and down, you'll notice that the hours before 8am and after 5pm are gray, not white. That's because Outlook assumes your work day is from 8 to 5. If you change the date to a Saturday or Sunday, the whole day is grayed out because Outlook assumes you work a Monday-through-Friday job. You can change your work week, as well as some other Calendar settings, by opening the **Tools** menu, choosing **Options**, selecting the **Calendar** tab of the Options dialog box, and modifying the appropriate options.

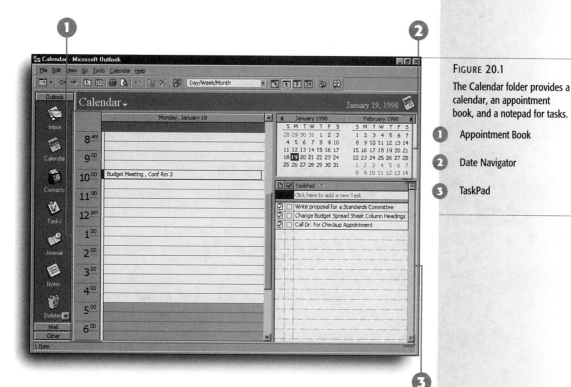

FIGURE 20.1

The Calendar folder provides a calendar, an appointment book, and a notepad for tasks.

①   Appointment Book

②   Date Navigator

③   TaskPad

For easy viewing of your appointments, the following four buttons appear on the Standard toolbar to the right of the Current View drop-down list:

Go to Today 📅. Takes you to today's date (according to your computer's clock), no matter what date you're currently viewing in the Calendar.

Day 📅. This is the default view for the Appointment Book.

Week 📅. Turns the Appointment Book into a weekly calendar with large blocks for workdays and small blocks for non-workdays.

Month 📅. Converts the information viewer into a monthly calendar with blocks for each day of the current month.

Using the Date Navigator

The Date Navigator is the small pair of monthly calendars in the top-right corner of the Calendar information viewer. So you don't think they're there just for ornamentation, let me fill you in on a couple of things you can do with them in addition to checking the date.

By highlighting a series of dates on the monthly calendars (you are limited to 42 adjacent dates), you can transform the Appointment Book into a view of the selected dates (see Figure 20.2).

FIGURE 20.2

Make your own custom Day/Week/Month view by selecting dates from the Date Navigator.

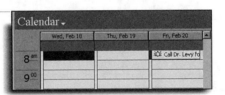

You can even select nonadjacent (limit of 14) days by holding down the Ctrl key while clicking the desired dates. By clicking one of the day headers (S, M, T, W, T, F, S), you can convert the Appointment Book into a monthly calendar without taking up the whole information viewer (which happens when you click the Month button on the toolbar).

To change the date on the Appointment Book, click the new date on one of the Date Navigator calendars. Also, if you look closely, you can see that the dates with appointments appear in bold, enabling you to tell at a glance which days are free.

Finally, to move a month forward or back, you can click the left- or right-pointing arrows. Or you can jump to a different month by clicking the month header to access a pop-up list of months.

Using the TaskPad

The TaskPad, which is really a part of the Tasks folder, appears in the Calendar to provide a quick and easy to-do list. Any tasks you enter on the TaskPad also appear in the Tasks folder. Modifying a task in one place produces the same results in the other.

To enter a simple task, click the first line of the TaskPad (**Click here to add a new Task**) and type in the to-do item. To create a more complex task item, double-click a blank line in the TaskPad to open a new task form.

Some of the other things you can do with the TaskPad include

- *Sorting*. Click any of the headers to sort by that column. Click a second time to reverse the sort order.

- *Marking a completed task* Done. Place a check mark in the Done column (the column with the checked-box header).

- *Accessing the shortcut menu*. Right-click any task or blank line to open the shortcut menu. From the shortcut menu, you can open a new task form, preview notes you've included with an existing task, change the TaskPad view, and modify the TaskPad settings. To learn more about creating tasks, see "Recording Tasks" later in this chapter.

Making Appointments

If you've got a job, a business, or a life, you probably have things to do, places to go, and people to meet. In other words, you've got appointments. If you want to keep your appointments, I know of no easier way than by recording them in the Outlook Calendar.

Scheduling appointments in the Outlook Calendar

1. Click the Calendar icon in the Outlook Bar to switch to the Calendar folder.

2. Open the **File** menu, point to **New**, and choose **Appointment** to open and fill in a new appointment form. You can also click the New Appointment button on the Standard toolbar.

3. Enter the appropriate information in the appointment form fields, using the Tab key to move between fields.

The following fields are available in the appointment form:

- **Subject**. Enter a description of the appointment in the Subject field. This information will appear in the Appointment Book.

- **Location**. Indicate where the appointment is to take place.

- **Start time**. Enter a date and time for the appointment, or click the down arrows and select a date from the pop-up calendar and a time from the drop-down list.

- **End time**. Enter a date and time for the end of the appointment. As with the Start time, you can use the calendar and drop-down list to set the date and time.

- **All day event**. Check this option if the appointment is going to consume the whole day (an out-of-town meeting, for example).

- **Reminder**. If you want to be alerted prior to the start of the meeting, place a check mark in this box. From the drop-down list, select how long before the meeting you want to be notified. Click the speaker icon to turn on (or off) a sound alert and to choose which sound file to use. The sound alert is turned on by default.

- **Show time as**. This option is handy if you're on a network and others can access your schedule. It indicates that you are busy for the time you allocated to the appointment.

- **Notes text box**. Enter information about the appointment. You can even insert files or other Outlook items in the text box.

- **Categories**. Great for organizing Outlook items—you can assign a category and later view all your appointments by category. It's an easy way to see at a glance your business schedule in contrast to your personal schedule.

- **Private**. Check this option to hide this appointment so others who have access to the folder can't see it.

4. Click **Save and Close** to add the appointment to your schedule and return to Outlook.

Your new appointment appears in the Appointment Book in the appropriate date and time slot. By the way, you can also open a new appointment form by double-clicking the desired time spot in the Appointment Book (on the correct date, of course).

Setting Recurring Appointments

Some appointments just won't go away, no matter how much you try to ignore them. You know what I'm talking about—doing the weekly payroll, attending the boss's Monday morning pep talks, taking the kids to Scout meetings. These are the appointments that occur on a regular basis—every Monday at 8 am, the third Friday of each month, every other Tuesday. Rather than creating an appointment for each occurrence, you can create one recurring appointment. When you create the appointment, click the Recurrence button on the Appointment Form toolbar to open the Appointment Recurrence dialog box shown in Figure 20.3.

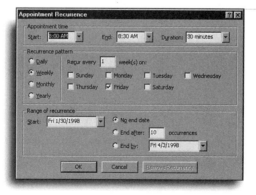

> **Adding a recurring appointment**
>
> You can also create a recurring appointment by right-clicking on the Appointment Book and selecting **New Recurring Appointment** from the short-cut menu—or by selecting the **Calendar** menu and choosing **New Recurring Appointment**.

FIGURE 20.3
You can set the frequency, days, and even the end date for a recurring appointment.

Enter the correct settings and then click **OK** to save them and return to the appointment form. Click **Save and Close** to return to the active folder.

Creating Appointments from Tasks

Outlook also provides you with a quick, minimum-fuss way to turn a to-do item (a task) into an appointment. For example, if you have a to-do item that says Make a doctor's appointment you'll want to create an appointment when you finally make the call and are granted an audience with the doctor (also known as a doctor's appointment).

Using an Outlook task to create an appointment

1. Click the Calendar shortcut in the Outlook Bar to open the Calendar folder.

2. Drag the item from the TaskPad to the Date Navigator and drop it on the appointment date to open a new appointment form with the task information filled in (see Figure 20.4).

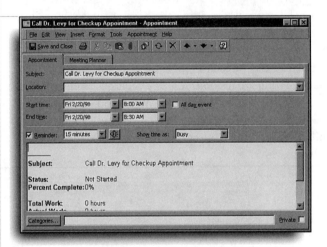

FIGURE 20.4
Outlook does most of the work for you when you use drag and drop to create an appointment.

3. Fill out the necessary information in the appointment form.

4. Click **Save and Close** to record the new appointment and return to Outlook.

Before you drag an item to the Date Navigator, make sure the correct month is showing. If you have the correct date showing in the Appointment Book, you can drag a task directly to the time slot and open a new appointment form with the subject, date, and time filled in correctly.

Editing Appointments

You might have any number of reasons for changing an appointment. Appointment dates, times, and locations have been known to change. Also, if you're entering notes in the Appointment

Book to remind yourself of things you want to discuss, you'll be adding and possibly deleting items. Whatever the reason, you will undoubtedly find yourself wanting to edit an appointment at some time or another. Fortunately, with Outlook that's not a problem.

Changing an appointment

1. Click the Calendar shortcut in the Outlook Bar to open the Calendar folder.

2. Select the date of the appointment you want to change.

3. Double-click the appointment you intend to modify. Its appointment form opens.

4. Make the necessary change(s).

5. Click **Save and Close** to save the changes and return to the active folder.

By the way, don't make the mistake of closing the form by any means other than the **Save and Close** button, or your changes won't be saved. If, on the other hand, you reconsider and don't want to save the changes, close with Alt+F4 or the Close button (x) in the upper-right corner of the form window.

If the only change you want to make to an appointment is its time or date, the process is even simpler. To change the time, drag the appointment from the original time slot to the new one. Changing the date is almost as easy—drag the appointment to the correct date on the Date Navigator. Then, when the appointment appears on the new date page of the Appointment Book, drag it to the correct time slot.

Viewing Appointments

One of the nicest things about the Outlook Calendar is that you can manipulate your appointment information in so many different ways. How you look at your appointments can tell you a lot about your schedule. Viewing the details of a single appointment gives you very specific information about that item, but doesn't tell you much about how your time is allotted for the day, week, or month. The truth is, depending on the information you need, each of these views can be extremely helpful.

Deleting an appointment

Some appointments get canceled entirely. All you have do when that happens is select the appointment and click the Delete button ⊠ or press the Delete key.

Changing your perspective as well as your view

1. Click the Calendar shortcut on the Outlook Bar to open the Calendar folder.

2. Click the down arrow at the end of the Current View field in the Standard toolbar to open the drop-down list of available views (see Figure 20.5).

FIGURE 20.5

Outlook provides a variety of ways to view your appointments.

3. Click a view from the list to change from the current view to the selected view.

With the exception of the Day/Week/Month view, all the preset views are in a table format (rows and columns) and take up the entire information viewer. If you're feeling creative and adventurous enough, you can even create custom table views by adding, deleting, and moving columns and by changing the formatting of an existing view or creating an entirely new one (open the **View** menu, choose **Define Views**, and then click the **New** button).

Adding an event to the Calendar

To add an event to the calendar, open the **Calendar** menu and choose **New Event**. Enter the subject and location in the Event dialog box and then click **Save and Close**.

Managing Your Tasks and To-Do Lists

The TaskPad in the Calendar folder provides simple task management, but you'll want to switch to the Tasks folder for your more sophisticated task needs. The Tasks folder is the TaskPad enlarged to take up the entire information viewer. Anything you enter or change in the Tasks folder appears or changes in the TaskPad as well.

The real power of the Tasks folder lies in the extensive selection of views it provides. By changing the view, you can reorganize your tasks in a variety of ways that enable you to determine how to best accomplish the jobs at hand.

Recording Tasks

Although new tasks can be created in an infinite number of ways, the simplest in my book (no pun intended) is to just double-click a blank line in the view. Okay, so an "infinite" number may be stretching it, but there *are* six different ways to create a new task in the Tasks folder.

Creating a new task in the Tasks folder

1. Click the Tasks icon on the Outlook Bar to open the Tasks folder.

2. Double-click a blank line in the current view to open and complete a new Task form, as shown in Figure 20.6.

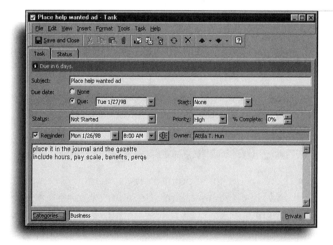

FIGURE 20.6

You'll find a lot more to a task than first meets the eye.

3. Fill in the necessary information. You can include as little or as much as you need.

   The available options include

   - **Subject**. Make this brief and informative so you can easily identify the task at a glance.

   - **Due date**. Select **None** if this has to be done eventually but doesn't yet have a specific due date. For tasks that must be done by a particular date, click **Due** and enter the date. If the task will require a certain amount of time, enter a **Start** date.

* **Status**. Indicate what stage the task is in and its priority.

* **Reminder**. To set an alarm for this task, click **Reminder** and select a date and time for the alert to appear.

* **Notes**. Add whatever information will be required to complete the task.

* **Categories**. For an easy way to organize tasks, use Categories.

4. Click **Save and Close** to add the new task and return to the active folder.

Changing task information

If you find that you need to change some of the task information, all you have to do is double-click the task to open the Task form, make whatever changes are needed, and click **Save and Close** to save the changes and return to the active folder.

The new task appears in the current view, in the position dictated by the sort conditions. You can sort tasks by clicking the header of the column by which you want to sort. Click again to change the sort order from ascending to descending or vice versa.

To delete a task, select it and click the Delete button on the Standard toolbar (or press the Delete key).

Creating Recurring Tasks

Like recurring appointments, some jobs keep coming back time and time again—taking the monthly inventory, servicing the equipment, or even taking out the garbage (I can never remember which day is Garbage Day and which is Recycle Day). The easiest way to handle this is by creating a recurring task.

Creating a recurring task

1. Click the Tasks icon in the Outlook Bar to open the Tasks folder.

2. Double-click a blank line in the current view to open a new Task form.

3. Fill in the necessary task information.

4. Click the Recurrence button on the Task Form toolbar to open the Task Recurrence dialog box shown in Figure 20.7.

5. Set the recurrence options and click **OK** to return to the Task form.

FIGURE 20.7

Select when and how often you want the task to recur by setting the appropriate options.

6. Click **Save and Close** to add the new task and return to the current view.

Now when the task appears in any of the Tasks folder views, it has a small Recurrence icon attached, indicating that it's a recurring task.

Tracking Tasks with Task Views

Having a to-do list is handy, but being able to turn it upside down and rearrange it in a multitude of ways is even handier. What if you want to see only the tasks for the upcoming week? Or perhaps you want to see just how far behind you are by checking out all the overdue tasks.

Whatever the need, one of these Tasks folder views will probably meet it:

- **Simple List**. This default task view lists the task and the due date.
- **Detailed List**. Similar to the **Simple List**, this one adds a Status column as well as % Complete and Categories columns.
- **Active Tasks**. Shows all tasks that have not been completed.
- **Next Seven Days**. Shows only tasks coming due in the next week.
- **Overdue Tasks**. Shows tasks whose due dates have come and gone, but which remain unfinished.
- **By Category**. If you're using categories, this list organizes all tasks by category.

- **Assignment**. Shows only tasks that have been assigned to others.

- **By Person Responsible**. This one is different from **Assignment** in that it is sorted by the person who originated the task.

- **Completed Tasks**. My favorite. This is the one you can look at with pride and relief (as long as there's something there to look at). All the tasks you mark as completed appear here.

- **Task Timeline**. Displays a timeline that arranges tasks chronologically.

To change views, click the down arrow at the end of the Current View field in the Standard toolbar and select a new view from the drop-down list that appears.

As with Calendar views, you can customize existing Tasks views or create new ones. And you can change some basic settings (as with the Calendar view again) by opening the **Tools** menu, choosing **Options** to open the Options dialog box, and then selecting the **Tasks/Notes** tab.

Using Notes

Notes are useful for jotting down information that has no other logical resting place. Because I can never figure out where I put the manuals for things (they're in a safe place, I'm sure), I find notes useful for recording stuff like instructions on presetting the channels on the VCR, unjamming the copy machine, and determining what my modem settings really are supposed to be. You know, I should probably use a note to record the place I store the manuals. Nah . . . that would be too easy. Anyway, Notes are a great way to keep track of miscellaneous information that doesn't fit anywhere else.

Creating Notes

Creating a note is one of the simplest tasks you'll perform in Outlook.

Creating an Outlook note

1. Click the Notes icon in the Outlook Bar to open the Notes folder.

2. Double-click a blank spot on the information viewer to open and complete a new Note form.

3. Create a short title for the note by typing it on the first line and pressing Enter. This text appears under the icon in the Icons view or next to the icon in the other views.

4. Continue to type, filling in the body of the note with as much information as you need. To create more space, press Enter when you reach the bottom of the note.

5. Close the note by clicking the Close button (x) in the corner of the note or pressing Alt+F4.

Anytime you want to view an existing note, just double-click it.

Customizing Notes

If you find notes convenient enough to use frequently, you'll want to take advantage of the capability to customize them and thereby make them even more useful. You can change their color or size, change the way they appear, and even assign them to categories.

Colorizing notes is a handy way to categorize them without having to use categories. Not only are they more easily identified, but you don't have to create new categories (sorry, standard Outlook categories don't include New Neighbors Names, Directions for Using Power Tools, or Where Are Those Darn Manuals?).

Changing the color of an Outlook note

1. Right-click the note you want to colorize. A shortcut menu appears, as shown in Figure 20.8.

2. Select **Color** to open the submenu of color selections.

3. Pick a new color for this note.

What you end up with is not only a colorful screen, but also an easy way to identify different types of notes (see Figure 20.9).

FIGURE 20.8

You can perform a number of note operations from the shortcut menu.

FIGURE 20.9

Color coding sets different types of notes apart.

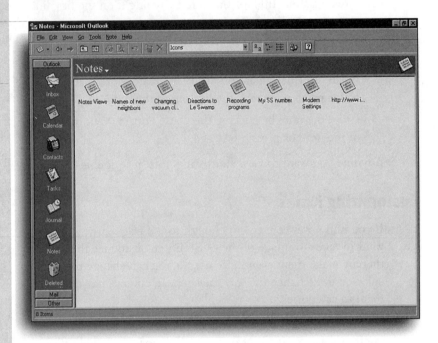

Another way you can customize notes is by resizing them. When a quick note overflows the bounds of the default note box, you'll be able to see all the text if you change the size of the box. This is particularly useful because Outlook notes don't have scrollbars. Alternatively, you can use the up- and down-arrow keys to scroll.

Changing the size of an Outlook note

1. Double-click the note to open it.

2. Move your mouse pointer to any of the four sides or corners of the note until the pointer changes to a double-headed arrow.

3. Drag the side or corner until the note reaches the desired proportions.

Resizing a note

You can resize a note by double-clicking its title bar. Actually, that is a misnomer in this case because nothing appears in the so-called title bar (the blue bar at the top of the note). Double-click the bar once to maximize the note (full screen) and again to minimize it (back to normal).

Viewing Notes

For such a simple feature, Notes offers a variety of different views. As a matter of fact, you even have several choices about how notes appear in the default view, Icons.

To change the way notes are displayed in the Icons view, click one of the three buttons to the right of the Current View drop-down list on the Standard toolbar.

- *Large Icons*. This is the default, with the large note icon above the text label.

- *Small Icons*. Tiny note icons spread across the information viewer, with the text label appearing to the right of the icon.

- *List*. A list with tiny icons to the left and text labels to the right.

Then there are the rest of the Notes folder views, which can be found on the Current View drop-down list:

- **Notes List**. A listing of all notes, with columns for date created and associated categories as well as a short preview of the note contents.

- **Last Seven Days**. Identical to the **Notes List**, except only those notes created in the last week are included.

- **By Category**. If you're using categories, this view groups the notes by individual category.

- **By Color**. Similar to **By Category**, this view groups notes by color.

As with other Outlook folders, you can customize existing views and create new ones by accessing the Define Views for [*folder name*] dialog box (open the **V**iew menu and choose **Define Views**).

You can also change some of the basic settings in the Notes folder by modifying the options in the Notes defaults section of the **Task/Notes** tab in the Options dialog box (open the **Tools** menu and choose **Options**). There you can change the way reminders work, assign different colors to overdue and completed tasks, and more.

In the event that you need to modify a task, simply double-click it to open the Task form, edit the information as needed, and then click **Save and Close** to save your changes and return to the active folder.

If, on the other hand, you've come to the realization that cleaning up your office is really a waste of time because it's only going to get messy again, you may want to delete that task that says "clean up office." Nothing to it—select the task and click the Delete button on the Standard toolbar (or press the Delete key).

Keeping the Outlook Journal

Everyone knows what a journal is—it's a place where you record important events and information. An Outlook Journal is no different. It's a folder that allows you to keep track of activities associated with contacts (phone calls and appointments, for example), as well as all Outlook items and even documents created in other Office applications.

As far as I'm concerned, being able to record and track phone calls is the Journal's best feature. Although you can open a new Journal form by double-clicking any blank spot on the Journal folder's information viewer, I find it handiest to start in the Contacts folder because that's where I keep my phone numbers.

Using the Journal to track phone calls

1. Click the Contacts icon in the Outlook Bar to open the Contacts folder.

2. Find the contact you plan to call and dial the number. Even if you haven't set up your contacts database, you can try this by using the contact record that Outlook automatically creates for your personal information during the installation.

3. Drag the contact onto the Journal icon on the Outlook Bar and drop it to open a new Journal form (see Figure 20.10).

4. Click the **Start Timer** button as soon as the party answers if you want to track the amount of time spent on the phone call. This is great for anyone billing for phone time.

5. Enter notes about the conversation in the text box.

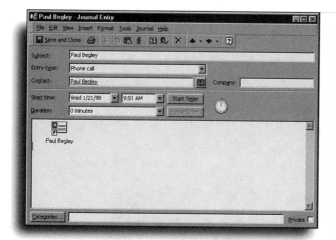

FIGURE 20.10

The contact information is already filled in for you.

6. Modify any other necessary information when the phone call is concluded.

7. Click **Save and Close** to save the new journal entry and return to the active folder.

If you use the timer, the duration field is automatically filled in for you when you save the journal entry. If you forget to start the timer, you can approximate the time and enter it manually in the **Duration** field.

I also find it helpful that Outlook automatically places a shortcut to the contact in the notes area of the Journal form. The short-cut makes viewing the contact information for that individual very easy if you happen to be reviewing the phone call journal entry.

SEE ALSO

➤ *To learn more about maintaining contact information, see page 482*

Setting AutoJournal Options

There are even some Outlook items for which you can have Outlook automatically record journal entries, the most useful of which (to the average, non-networked user) is email. Every time you send an email message to a contact for whom automatic journaling options are set, the email is automatically recorded in the Journal under the contact name. When this is combined with recording phone calls as journal entries, you can review all your communication with a particular contact with a couple of mouse clicks.

Setting Journal options

1. Open the **Tools** menu and choose **Options** to open the Options dialog box.

2. Click the **Journal** tab to view the Journal options, as shown in Figure 20.11.

3. Set the Journal options to suit your needs.

FIGURE 20.11

You can select an automatic Journal option to set and a specific client to set it for.

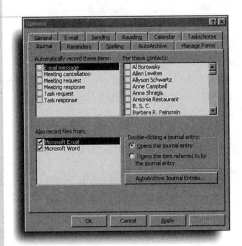

The available Journal options include

- **Automatically record these items**. A Journal entry for all items with a check mark is automatically recorded each time an item of that type is created for any of the contacts selected in the **For these contacts** section.

- **For these contacts**. Check off all the contacts for whom you want to automatically record the items selected in the **Automatically record . . .** option.

- **Also record files from**. To automatically record a Journal entry each time you create, open, or close a document in one of the listed applications, place a check mark in the box next to the application.

- **Double-clicking a journal entry**. Indicate whether you want a double-click (on a Journal entry) to open that Journal entry or to open the item associated with it. For example, double-clicking an email Journal entry will open either the Journal entry that includes the email or the email itself, depending on the choice you make here.

- **AutoArchive Journal Entries**. Click this button to set the options for AutoArchiving Journal entries.

4. Click **OK** to return to the active folder.

The new Journal options take effect immediately.

Attaching Items to Journal Entries

Even those items for which you don't (or can't) set automatic Journal options can be included in a Journal entry. Actually, the procedure is identical to inserting an item in an email message.

Inserting an Outlook item, file, or other object in a Journal entry

1. Click the Journal icon on the Outlook Bar to open the Journal folder.

2. Double-click to open the Journal entry in which you want to insert the item.

3. Select one of the following attachment types from the **Insert** menu. For this example, we'll attach an **Item**.

- **File**. You can attach any computer file, including a text, graphics, or spreadsheet file, just to name a few.

- **Item**. This selection enables you to insert an Outlook *item*, such as a contact, an existing email message, or an appointment, in an email message.

- **Autosignature**. If you've created an autosignature, you can use this selection to include it in the message at the cursor location. An *autosignature* is text that you create to end messages. Many people include their name and company information, or sometimes a personal quote.

- **Object**. Objects can be Office documents, clip art, WordArt, or video or sound clips. The selection is extensive. You can even create new objects to include in your email.

4. Locate and select the item in the Insert Item dialog box shown in Figure 20.12.

FIGURE 20.12
Highlight the folder to view its contents.

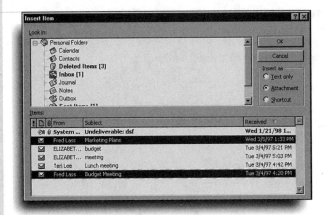

5. Highlight the appropriate folder in the **Look in** box, and select the item(s) from the **Items** list box. The **Insert As** option enables you to choose the format of the inserted item. The default is **Attachment**, which includes the item as an attachment. The other options are to include the item as a text entry or to include a shortcut to the item.

6. Click **OK** to insert the selected item(s) in the Journal entry.

7. Click **Save and Close** to save the Journal entry and return to the active folder.

Inserting an item, file, or other object attaches a copy of the item to the Journal entry. The original item remains intact, no matter what you do to the Journal entry or the inserted item.

Sorting and Viewing Journal Entries

Like most other Outlook folders, you can sort and view the contents of the Journal folder in a variety of ways.

Sorting in Outlook is the same from folder to folder—click the header of the column by which you want to sort. Click it again to reverse the sort order. Changing the Journal Folder view is even easier.

Taking another look at your Journal entries

1. Click the Journal icon on the Outlook Bar to open the Journal folder.

2. Click the down arrow at the end of the Current View dropdown list.

   The Journal folder provides the following preset views:

   - **By Type**. This timeline view groups entries by item type.

   - **By Contact**. Another timeline view, this one organizes Journal entries by the contact associated with the entry.

   - **By Category**. If you're using categories, this timeline view shows you all your entries grouped by category.

   - **Entry List**. If the timeline drives you to distraction, check out this view. It's a nice simple list of all the journal entries.

   - **Last Seven Days**. Here's another list view, which includes only those entries created within the—you guessed it—last seven days.

   - **Phone Calls**. A listing of all the phone call entries.

3. Select the view of your choice to change the current view to the selected view.

If you get a notion to customize the Journal views or create one of your own, all you have to do is open the **V**iew menu and choose **D**efine Views to open the Define Views for [Journal] dialog box. Pick a view and click **M**odify to change it. Click **N**ew to create your own Journal view.

Getting Organized with the Contacts Database

A Quick Tour of the Contacts Folder

In addition to scheduling, sending email, and journaling, Outlook also provides an easy way to organize all those phone numbers and addresses that are accumulating on post-it notes, scraps of paper, and business cards thrown in a drawer. If you find yourself crawling under the desk frequently to search for Post-It note phone numbers that used to be stuck to your monitor, it's probably time to put the Contacts folder to work for you. Before jumping into the nuts and bolts of building a Contacts database, you might want to review the components that make up the Contacts folder. The best way to do that is to click the Contacts icon on the Outlook Bar to open the Contacts folder, and take a look (see Figure 21.1).

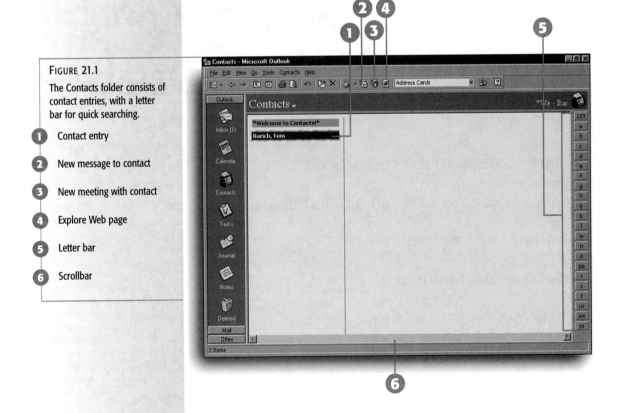

FIGURE **21.1**

The Contacts folder consists of contact entries, with a letter bar for quick searching.

1. Contact entry

2. New message to contact

3. New meeting with contact

4. Explore Web page

5. Letter bar

6. Scrollbar

To provide you with a sample contact, Outlook creates an entry from the name and organization information you entered during installation. As you add contacts, they appear in the information viewer in alphabetical order. That's where the letter bar on the right comes in. When you have more than a screenful of contacts, you can move to the first contact of a letter group by clicking the appropriate button on the letter bar. In addition, the scrollbar at the bottom of the information viewer becomes active at this point, so you can then use it to move backward and forward through all your contacts.

The three new buttons on the Standard toolbar are specific to the Contacts folder and provide a quick way to utilize certain portions of the contact information:

- *New message to contact.* Highlight a contact and click this button to create a new email with the contact's email address inserted in the **To** field.

- *New meeting with contact.* Clicking this button opens a new Meeting form and inserts the highlighted contact's email address in the **To** field and in the **All Attendees** list on the **Meeting Planner** tab.

- *Explore Web page.* For this button to work, you need three things: a contact with a valid Web page address entered in the Contact form Web page field, a Web browser, and an Internet Mail service installed in Outlook. With all these items present, clicking this button opens your default Web browser and Connect To dialog box for the Dial Up Connection associated with your Internet Mail service.

Hidden toolbar buttons

Some of the buttons may be hidden if the Outlook window is too narrow. If you don't see some of the buttons mentioned here, either maximize the Outlook window or drag the right or left border to widen the window.

Adding Contacts to the Contacts Database

Of course, the first thing you have to do to get any use out of the Contacts database is enter your contact information. As with most Outlook features, you can do this in several ways. You can add items individually by entering the information in a Contact form, you can create a contact entry from an incoming email message, or you can import contact information from an outside source (such as another Personal Information Manager [PIM], a database, or a spreadsheet).

Using the Contact Form

If Outlook is running and you've got your scraps of paper, your business card collection, and your Rolodex handy, you're ready to begin adding entries to the Contacts database. The new Contact form provides fields for standard contact information such as name, address, phone number, and quite a bit more.

Adding contact entries with the Contact form

1. Click the Contacts icon in the Outlook Bar to open the Contacts folder.

2. Click the New Contact button 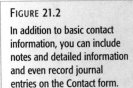 on the Standard toolbar or press Ctrl+N to open a new Contact form and fill it out (see Figure 21.2).

FIGURE 21.2

In addition to basic contact information, you can include notes and detailed information and even record journal entries on the Contact form.

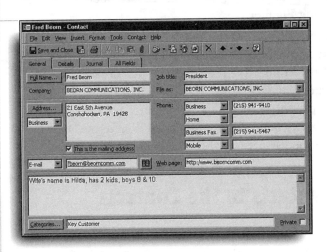

The new Contact form offers four tabs to enable you to keep track of more than just name, address, and phone number:

- **General**. This is your basic name, address, and phone number information.

- **Details**. More specific information about the contact, including such things as assistant's name, birthday, spouse's name.

- **Journal**. Journal options, plus a listing of Journal entries for this contact.

- **All Fields**. Select the type of Outlook field (with a lot to choose from) and see the values for this contact.

3. Enter as much contact information on the **General** tab as you want.

Although entering basic contact information on the form is pretty straightforward, you should take note of a couple of things:

- **Full Name**. If you enter only a first name, the Check Full Name dialog box appears, offering you the opportunity to add a title, middle name, last name, and suffix. You can access this dialog box at any time by clicking the **Full Name** button.

- **Address**. Use the drop-down list below the **Address** button to enter a home address and even a third address for the contact if necessary.

- **E-mail**. Outlook allows you to enter up to three email addresses for the contact. Use the drop-down list to enter the second and third.

- **File as**. Outlook gives you quite a few options for the way you want the contact listed. No matter what your choice, make sure you are consistent. If you file some contacts under "FirstName, LastName" and others under "LastName, FirstName", you'll go crazy trying to find them as your Contacts database grows.

- **Phone**. Your selection of phone numbers to record is extensive. Use the drop-down list in each phone number field to enter additional numbers.

4. Click **Save and Close** to add the new entry to the Contacts folder, as shown in Figure 21.3.

FIGURE 21.3

Each new entry is listed alphabetically according to the **File as** selection you made in the Contact form.

Welcome to Contacts!

Barich, Tom

Fred Beorn
21 East 5th Avenue
Conshohocken, PA 19428
Business: (215) 941-9410
Business Fax: (215) 941-5467
E-mail: fbeorn@beorncom...

Adding Multiple Contacts from the Same Company

Even if you're a good typist, entering a lot of contacts can be time-consuming and tedious. Thankfully, Outlook provides a handy little shortcut for making the job easier if you are entering several contacts from the same company.

Creating entries for contacts from the same company

Save time with Save and New

If you're adding more than one contact entry at a sitting, you'll find yourself creating each entry, saving and closing it, and then opening a new form for the next. Why not save yourself a mouse click or keystroke and use the **Save and New** command? When you're ready to save a contact, open the Contact form **File** menu and select **Save and New** to save the current contact and open a new Contact form at the same time. Better yet—use the Save and New button, which is right next to the **Save and Close** button on the Standard toolbar.

Shortcut to adding more contacts for the same company

After entering a contact, right-click the selected contact and choose **New Contact from Same Company** from the shortcut menu.

1. Click the Contacts icon in the Outlook Bar to open the Contacts folder.

2. Highlight the first contact from the desired company.

3. Open the **Contacts** menu and select **New Contact from Same Company** to open a new Contact form with the company name, address, business phone, and business fax numbers already entered. Of course, only those pieces of information present in the original contact will appear in the new Contact form.

4. Enter the necessary contact information.

5. Open the **File** menu and select **Save and New in Company** to save the contact and open a new form with company information filled in.

6. When you get to the last new entry for this company, click **Save and Close** to return to the active folder.

You can utilize the same feature for non-business contacts by entering a unique word or phrase in the **Company** field (for example, Williams family or Sternberg clan).

Because people tend to move around a lot these days, you may find yourself having to change the contact information at some point or another. Simply double-click the contact whose information has changed, and edit the appropriate information as soon as the Contact form opens.

Creating a Contact from an Email Message

I often find that my first contact with many people is through email. If it's someone I plan to continue communicating with, I usually want to include him or her in my Contacts database. I could switch to the Contacts folder, open a new Contact form, and enter the information, but I've found a simpler way. And since I'd rather be on the beach catching a few rays instead of stuck at the computer entering data, I take every shortcut I can find. After I'm through reading the email, I use it to create a contact entry for the individual.

Using email to create contact entries

1. Open the email message you want to use.

2. Right-click the name/email address in the **From** field to open the shortcut menu shown in Figure 21.4.

FIGURE 21.4

You can do quite a few things with an incoming email message by right-clicking the address.

3. Select **<u>A</u>dd to Contacts** to open a new Contact form with the **Full Name** and **E-mail** fields already filled in with the information from the selected email message.

4. Fill in the rest of the information and click **<u>S</u>ave and Close** to add the new contact and return to Outlook.

You can also easily include the contents of the message at the same time you create a new contact from an email message. Simply open the Inbox, drag the message to the Outlook Bar, and then drop it on the Contacts icon. A new Contact form opens with the **Full Name** and **E-mail** fields filled in and the contents of the message inserted in the text box at the bottom of the form.

Deleting obsolete contacts

If you stop doing business with a vendor, or an ex-employee moves and leaves no forwarding address, you'll probably want to clean up your Contacts folder and delete the obsolete information. Just select the contact and click the Delete button or press the Delete key.

Importing Contact Information

If you already have your contact information organized in a program other than Outlook, you can switch it to Outlook with a minimum amount of inconvenience. Depending on which program you're currently using, you may be able to import your existing data into Outlook. You can import from Schedule+, an existing Personal Address Book, another set of Outlook personal folders, several Personal Information Managers, and even database or spreadsheet files.

Using the Import and Export Wizard to convert contact information from another source

1. Open the **File** menu and choose **Import and Export** to open the **Import and Export Wizard** shown in Figure 21.5.

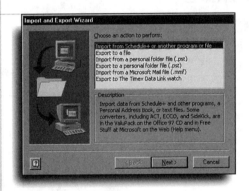

FIGURE 21.5

The Import and Export Wizard provides a wide variety of import and export options.

2. Select the type of import you want to perform from the **Choose an action to perform** list.

   The imports you can execute include

   - **Import from Schedule+ or another program or file**. Use this option to import from Schedule+ (I'll bet you already figured that one out), a Personal Address Book, an Access or FoxPro database, an Excel spreadsheet, or a comma- or tab-delimited file. These last two (*delimited files*) come in handy if Outlook doesn't have a direct data converter available for your PIM. You might be able to export data from your PIM to a comma- or tab-delimited file and then import it to Outlook by using this option.

- **Import from a personal folder file (.pst)**. Use this operation to import from a different set of Outlook folders (from a friend or coworker who has a lot of the same contacts).

- **Import from a Microsoft Mail file (.mmf)**. If you want to include contacts from your Microsoft Mail file, choose this option.

3. Click **Next** to proceed. At this point, the screen that appears depends entirely on the selection you made in step 2.

4. Follow the remaining steps in the wizard until the import is complete.

The Import and Export converters are not automatically copied from the CD during installation. Therefore if you want to use one of them, you may have to copy them onto your hard drive.

Retrieving the Import and Export converters from the Office 97 SBE CD-ROM

1. Insert the Office 97 SBE CD into your CD-ROM drive. If the opening screen doesn't appear in 5-10 seconds, open Windows Explorer and double-click the autorun.exe file on the CD.

2. Click the ValuPack icon to open the **Welcome to the Microsoft Office 97 Small Business Edition ValuPack** Help topic.

3. Scroll down the **What do you want to know about?** list and click the icon to the left of **Microsoft Outlook import and export converters**.

4. Click the icon in the sentence that describes the type of operating system you're using (see Figure 21.6).

5. Click **Yes** when the dialog box appears asking if you want to install the translators.

6. Accept the End User License agreement (if you agree) to install the converters.

The next time you open the Import and Export Wizard, you'll see the new converters when you select **Import from Schedule+ or another program or file,** and click **Next**.

FIGURE 21.6

Click the icon for your operating system (Windows 95, NT 4.0, 3.51).

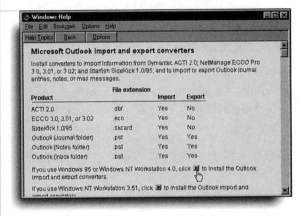

Using the Contact Information

Okay, so you've expended a lot of energy inputting all this contact data into Outlook. What do you do with it now? Well, you can sit back and admire it, or you can put it to work for you.

Creating an Email Message from a Contact

The beauty of becoming computerized is that you can enter information once and use it over and over again without any additional effort. You can take advantage of this feature by using your Contacts database to create new email messages. What makes it even handier is that you don't have to be in the Contacts folder; you can create email from anywhere in Outlook.

Using the Contacts database to create a new message from any folder

1. From any folder you're in, press Ctrl+Shift+M to open a new message form.

2. Click the Address Book button on the Standard toolbar to open the Select Names dialog box.

3. From the **Show Names from the** drop-down list, select **Contacts**, as shown in Figure 21.7.

4. A list of names appears on the left. Select names from the list and click the **To, Cc,** or **Bcc** button to place them in the appropriate message recipient field.

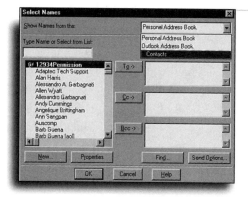

FIGURE 21.7

The **Show Names from the** drop-down list contains all the address books installed in Outlook.

5. Click **OK** to close the Select Names dialog box and return to the message form.

6. Fill in the rest of the information and click **Send** to send the email and return to the active folder.

If you happen to be in the Contacts folder and decide to create an email message, simply drag the desired contact (must have an email address) to the Outlook Bar and drop it on the Inbox icon. A new message form immediately opens with the contact's email address in the **To** field.

Viewing Contact Information

Getting your contact information into Outlook is the work, and viewing and using it is the fun. Okay, so maybe fun is stretching it a bit. Let's say viewing and using email is the part that makes all the work worthwhile. The Contacts folder is like its sibling folders in that it offers you a number of different ways to view its contents.

If you check out the Current View drop-down list on the Standard toolbar, you'll see what I mean:

- **Address Cards**. This default view shows individual cards for each contact, including only basic address, phone, and email information.

- **Detailed Address Cards**. The same as **Address Cards**, but with additional information displayed.
- **Phone List**. This is a table view (rows and columns), listing all your contacts alphabetically and displaying **Full Name**, **Company**, **File As**, **Business Phone**, and more.
- **By Category**. Another table view that groups contacts by the category to which they are assigned.
- **By Company**. This option creates a table view that groups contacts by company name. I just had occasion to use this one as a result of not following my own advice. I entered a contact but paid no attention to the **File as** field. When I went to look for the contact, it was nowhere to be found. The company name was the only thing I could remember, so I switched to the **By Company** view and found the contact immediately by checking the appropriate group.
- **By Location**. If you have a lot of international contacts, this view will come in handy. It creates groups of contacts based on the **Country** field.

Switching views in the Contacts folder is as easy as opening the Current View drop-down list and selecting the desired view. You can even customize the views by adding, removing, and rearranging the fields that are displayed.

Modifying Contact List Views

No matter how many preset views Outlook provides, you're sure to want to see something that nobody else requires. Everyone runs into unique situations or has special needs that the Outlook programmers could not have anticipated. They did, however, anticipate that such needs would arise. To that end, they provided a way for Outlook views—including the Contacts Folder views—to be customized. To get started, open the Contacts folder by clicking the Contacts icon in the Outlook Bar.

Customizing the Contacts Folder views

1. Open the **View** menu and select **Define Views** to open the **Define Views for "Contacts"** dialog box (see Figure 21.8).

2. Select the view you want to customize.

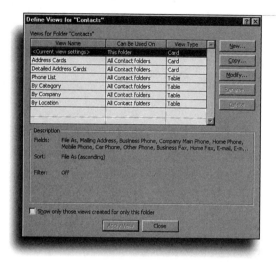

FIGURE 21.8
You can change an existing
view or create your own new
view.

3. Click **Modify,** make your changes, and return to the **Define Views for "Contacts"** dialog box.

4. Click **Close** to save the changes and return to Outlook.

If you'd like to create an entirely new view, click the **New** button instead of the **Modify** button.

Changing the Table Views

In addition to adding and removing fields with the Modify feature, you can also change a table view (rows and columns) by rearranging the fields and creating groups. Rearranging the fields enables you to display the fields in the order in which they are of most use to you. By grouping contacts, you can separate them into distinct collections based on the most relevant data.

Moving fields around in a Contacts table view

1. Click the Contacts icon in the Outlook Bar to open the Contacts folder.

2. Select a table view (**Phone List, By Category, By Company,** or **By Location**) from the Current View dropdown list on the Standard toolbar. For this example, we'll use the **Phone List** (see Figure 21.9).

3. Place your mouse pointer over the header of the field you want to move. Then click and hold down your left mouse button.

FIGURE 21.9

The Phone List provides a
straightforward listing of all
your contacts.

FIGURE 21.9

The Phone List provides a
straightforward listing of all
your contacts.

4. Drag the field header to a new location on the header bar
   and drop it as soon as the red arrows appear above and
   below the field header (see Figure 21.10).

FIGURE 21.10

The red arrows indicate an
insertion point for a moved
field.

1. Field header

2. New location

3. Original location

4. Header bar

5. Repeat until all fields are arranged to suit your needs.

If you make a change to an existing view, you will be reminded
of the fact the next time you start to switch views. You will then
have to either save the modified view as a new view, replace the
existing view, or lose the changes.

Creating groups can be very useful if you have a lot of contacts
with a certain field in common, such as Company, Category, or
Country. These just happen to be the Group By views that come
standard with Outlook. But what if you have a different field

that would provide a good basis for a group? That's easy—create your own Group By view. In the event that the field you want to group by doesn't appear, you can add it on-the-fly as we'll do in the next example.

Using an existing view to create a new Group By view

1. Click the Contacts icon on the Outlook Bar to open the Contacts folder.

2. Select **Phone list** from the Current View drop-down list on the Standard toolbar.

3. Click the Group By box button ▣ on the Standard toolbar to display the Group By box above the header bar of the Phone List.

4. Place your mouse pointer over any field header and right-click.

5. Select **Field Chooser** from the shortcut menu to open the Field Chooser shown in Figure 21.11.

FIGURE 21.11

The Field Chooser is aptly named because it enables you to choose from all the available fields in Outlook.

6. Select the field type from the drop-down list (**Address Fields** for this example).

7. Drag the field of your choice to a spot on the header bar and drop it as soon as the red arrows appear.

8. Click the Close button (x) in the upper-right corner or press Alt+F4 to close the Field Chooser.

9. Drag the field header by which you want to group the contacts to the Group By box and drop it. The contact list is immediately grouped by the selected field (see Figure 21.12).

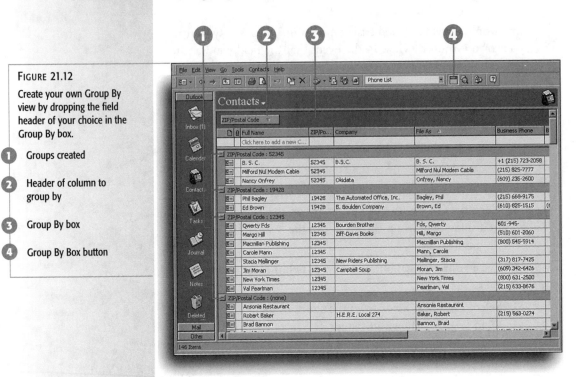

FIGURE 21.12

Create your own Group By view by dropping the field header of your choice in the Group By box.

① Groups created

② Header of column to group by

③ Group By box

④ Group By Box button

Missing contact information in table views

Outlook has a nasty habit, when displaying table views, of not showing all the contact information it imports from an outside source. This is a bug. After you perform an import, the information shows up in the correct fields in the Contact form and in the card views, but not in the table views. **Zip/Postal Code** is one field that failed to display for me. Unfortunately, the only workaround for this is to open the Contact form, re-enter the information manually, and click **Save and Close**. From then on, the missing information appears in all views.

The default sort is ascending by the new group, which means you may have to scroll down to see the groups. This is generally the result of having a number of contacts with no information in the Group By field. If you want to create subgroups, you can do so by dragging as many field headers as you want into the Group By box.

Sorting and Filtering Contacts

Another way to change the way you look at your contact information is to sort it and filter it. Sorting rearranges a table view alphabetically, either in ascending (A to Z) or descending (Z to A) order, using the sort field you choose. Filtering, on the other hand, is a method of including or excluding certain contacts based on a set of conditions that you impose on the entire Contacts database. Both sorting and filtering can be applied to both table and card views in the Contacts folder.

Sorting is so easy that even those of us who occasionally confuse ascending and descending can do it and get it right at least half the time.

Sorting a table view the easy way

1. Open the Contacts folder by clicking the Contacts icon in the Outlook Bar.

2. Select a table view from the Current View drop-down list on the Standard toolbar.

3. Click the field header of the field you want to sort by. If the field has not previously been used in a sort, the sort is ascending by default. For example, if you click the Company field header, the contacts will be sorted alphabetically by the contents of the Company field.

4. Click the field header again to change the sort order from ascending to descending, or vice versa. The engraved triangle that appears indicates the sort order (upward pointing indicates ascending, downward pointing indicates descending).

You can create secondary sorts by holding down the Shift key and clicking additional field headers.

To sort a card view, right-click a blank spot on the information viewer (between, under, or over cards) and select **Filter** from the shortcut menu. Set the sort and click **OK** to return to the sorted card view.

Filtering is a whole different ball game. This is where you get the opportunity to decide who's in and who's out, temporarily. In addition, it works in both table views and card views.

Applying a filter to the Contacts database

1. Click the Contacts icon in the Outlook Bar to open the Contacts folder.

2. From the **View** menu, select **Filter** to open the Filter dialog box as shown in Figure 21.13.

3. Select the tab on which to enter the filtering conditions.

    The Filter dialog box provides the following tabs containing filtering choices:

- **Contacts**. Here you'll find basic filtering conditions, such as words or phrases to search for and fields in which to find them. For example, if you enter IBM in the **Search for the word(s)** field and company field only in the **In** field, you will end up with only those contacts that include "IBM" in the **Company** field.

- **More Choices**. This tab has more specific conditions, such as whether or not contacts have attachments or categories.

- **Advanced**. This is where you get down to the serious filtering. Here you can select one or more fields and enter very specific conditions for each. For example, you could search for those contacts whose Business Phone number begins with 212 only, or whose Title is Dr., or whose email address is not blank.

FIGURE 21.13

The Filter options available in the Filter dialog box are quite extensive.

4. Enter the conditions you want to use.

5. Click **OK** to apply the filter.

You can always tell when you have a filter applied by the (Filter Applied) message that appears at the right side of the folder banner. Another thing to keep in mind is that you don't have to use the correct case for words you're filtering on when setting the conditions (unless you select the **Match case** check box on the **More Choices** tab).

Chances are you'll probably want to remove a filter at some point. It's pretty simple, but you have to return to the Filter dialog box to do it.

Removing a filter from the Contacts folder

1. Open the <u>V</u>iew menu and choose **Fi<u>l</u>ter** to open the Filter dialog box.

2. Click the **Clear <u>A</u>ll** button to remove all previously set conditions.

3. Click **OK** to remove the filter and return to the active folder.

If you like having choices, let me tell you that you can also access the Filter dialog box by right-clicking a blank record (row) in a table view or a blank spot in a card view and selecting **Fi<u>l</u>ter**.

Remember, filtering contacts out does not remove them; it hides them from view until you remove the filter.

Printing Contact Information

Because you switch to an electronic contact management system to get better organized, you should take advantage of everything it has to offer. At first blush, putting electronic information back on paper may seem kind of crazy after all the trouble you went to transferring it from the paper; however, at times, printing a hard copy of your Contacts database makes very good sense. If you don't have a laptop and you're going on the road, you certainly don't want to be without your contact information. Even if you have a laptop, you may be going into an environment that makes hard copy more practical than a laptop computer. Whatever the reason, you will undoubtedly find times when you want to print out some or all the contents of the Contacts folder. To get exactly what you want with a minimum amount of time and effort, you need to take care of a couple of things. You have to set your print options, select the style, and set up the page before you print.

Printing involves more than just selecting a printer. You have to decide what to print, how to print it, and how many copies to print. In addition, you can even set special options that apply to your particular printer. If you're not already in the Contacts folder, click the Contacts icon in the Outlook Bar to open it.

Setting the Contacts folder Print options

1. Select **Address Cards** from the Current View drop-down list on the Standard toolbar.

2. Open the **File** menu and choose **Print** to open the Print dialog box shown in Figure 21.14.

FIGURE 21.14

Select your printer, decide what and how to print, and you're home free.

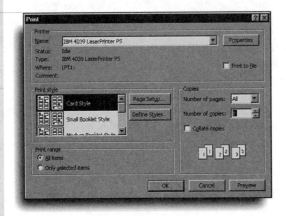

3. Select the printer to use from the **Name** drop-down list.

4. To set special options for your particular printer, click the **Properties** button. After setting the options specific to your printer, click **OK** to return to the Print dialog box.

5. Select **Print Style**.

   The **Print Style** list offers you several choices for the format in which the printed version will appear:

   - **Card Style**. This prints the contact information that appears in the card view, as it appears in the card view.

   - **Small Booklet Style**. Use this style to print a small booklet with eight booklet pages per standard paper page. The contact information appears as in the card view, but reduced in size to fit.

   - **Medium Booklet Style**. Identical to **Small Booklet Style**, except it prints four booklet pages per sheet instead of eight.

   - **Memo Style**. Prints one contact per page, set up in a style similar to an interoffice memo.

- **Phone Directory Style**. For a quick phone directory, you can't beat this style. Printed alphabetically, it includes only names and phone numbers.

6. Click **Page Setup** to change **Format**, **Paper**, and **Header/Footer** options for the selected print style. When you're finished setting the options, click **OK** to return to the Print dialog box.

   Page Setup options include the following:

   - **Format**. This tab includes such items as number of columns (except **Memo** style, which has but one column), fonts and font attributes for the body, and more.
   - **Paper**. Use this tab to select the paper size, source, margins, and booklet page dimensions.
   - **Header/Footer**. Here you can add headers and footers to appear at the top and bottom of each page.

7. Set the print range. If you highlighted one or more contacts before opening the Print dialog box, you can select **Only selected items** to print just those contacts that are highlighted.

8. Select an option in the **Number of pages** drop-down list. Your choices include **All**, which prints every page; **Even**, which prints only the even-numbered pages; and **Odd**, which prints only the odd-numbered pages.

9. Enter the number of copies you want to print.

10. Place a check mark in the **Collate copies** check box if you're printing multiple copies of a multipage contact list and want the copies collated (printing one set of sequential pages for each copy rather than all copies of page one, then all copies of page two, and so on).

11. Click **Preview** to see what the print job is really going to look like.

12. Click **OK** when you're ready to print.

If you find yourself doing a lot of printing, you may find it irksome to have to keep setting the same options each time you're ready to print. If that's the case, you can easily change the defaults for each print style.

Changing the default setup of a print style

1. Open the **File** menu, select **Page Setup,** and then choose **Define Print Styles** to open the Define Print Styles dialog box shown in Figure 21.15.

FIGURE 21.15

You can modify an existing print style or create a new one of your own.

2. Select the print style to modify and then click the **Edit** button to open the Page Setup dialog box.

3. Set the options to suit your needs. You can change the layout, the type of paper to use, and even the header and footer information to include.

4. Click **OK** to save the new settings and return to the Define Print Styles dialog box.

5. Click **Close** to return to the active folder.

The next time you use the modified style, the settings will appear just as you set them. You can even create a new style by using the **Copy** button in the Define Print Styles dialog box. Set the options as you want them, enter a new name, click **OK**, and you have a new style.

Using Publisher to Get Your Message Out

Designing a New Publication

Welcome to Publisher

Do you have your marketing strategy all thought out? Is it time to create a brochure for your products or services? Perhaps you need a letterhead, some business cards, or a flyer. Or maybe you're just tired of spending a fortune on greeting and birthday cards at the stationery store. Whatever your needs, Publisher enables you to create graphical publications like a pro in no time. As soon as you install it and start it up, you're ready to begin.

To open Publisher, click the **Start** button on the Windows 95 taskbar and select **Microsoft Publisher 98** from the **Programs** menu. The first time you start Publisher, a warm and friendly welcome greets you, along with an invitation to take the Publisher tour. If you want a quick overview of all the features available in Publisher, take a few moments to complete the tour. If you're eager to get started, however, choose **Done** so you can begin creating your first publication.

Publisher offers several methods for getting started with a new or existing publication (documents are called publications in Publisher). A catalog (see Figure 22.1) opens with the following choices available on the tabs:

- **Publications by Wizard**. A large selection of wizards that walk you through the steps of creating commonly used publications such as newsletters, flyers, and more.

- **Publications by Design**. A set of designs (colors and styles) you can use to create matching items. This is useful for designing the office stationary because you can have a uniform design for everything from business cards to letterhead, envelopes, and special forms.

- **Blank Publications**. Here you'll find predesigned page formats for special paper needs (such as folded paper or special sizes).

- **Existing Publications**. You can use this to open publications that either you or someone else previously designed.

Each method has advantages for particular types of publications, and you'll find that over the course of time you'll use all the methods.

Creating Publications by Wizard

Each time you open Publisher, a colorful, crowded catalog displays, with the **Publications by Wizard** tab in front (see Figure 22.1).

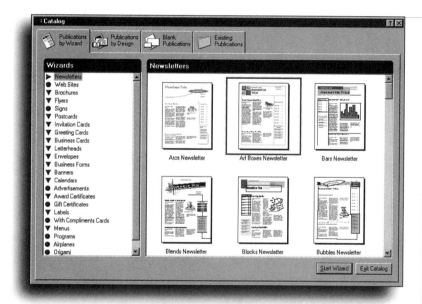

FIGURE 22.1
The Wizard has so many pre-configured templates that you're bound to find the type of publication you need.

The wizard is a helpful publishing expert who can walk you through all the steps needed to create a slick, professional publication. Each type of publication is prebuilt with layout and formatting options.

Choosing the Type of Publication

Scroll through the wizard's list to find the type of publication that matches the task you face. The choices are broad and varied, and if nothing seems to match your needs exactly, you're sure to find something that comes close enough to work with. Then scroll through the styles for that publication type to select the one you want to use.

Bringing the catalog up when you need it

The catalog only appears automatically when you first start Publisher. If you're already working in Publisher, you can reopen the catalog by opening the **File** menu and choosing **New**.

The wizard is a guide, not a dictator

Nothing the wizard does is etched in cement. You can make changes to the format, the layout, and the general look of the publication to your heart's content. The wizard merely provides a template.

Because there's a great deal of wisdom in the adage "a picture is worth a thousand words," it seems best to demonstrate what the wizard can do by producing a publication.

A newsletter is a common and popular publication, so the wizard and I will create one (I'll use the Box Newsletter style). You can follow along or just watch—the choice is yours.

Making Design Decisions

A great many decisions face you when you decide to create a publication, and many people discover them after they've already invested a lot of time and energy in creating the publication. There's something terribly disheartening about spending hours making pretty designs, writing inspiring text, and placing everything on the pages just so, and then having someone ask, "Did you remember to leave room for a mailing label?"

To make sure this doesn't happen, the wizard takes you through a process that covers all the things you should be thinking about.

Configuring Your Publication

Don't worry about two-sided printing

Many of the publication types offer styles that are described as "designed to print on both sides of the page." If your printer doesn't support duplex printing (the technical term for printing on both sides of the paper), don't worry about it. You can handle the job manually by printing one side and returning the paper to the printer to print the other side. Or, you can prepare the job on separate pages and turn it over to a quick-print shop. Don't avoid the perfect template just because it requires two-sided printing.

1. Click the style of newsletter that strikes your fancy. Then choose **Start Wizard** (or double-click the picture).

2. The left side of your Publisher window displays the wizard for this publication type. The preformatted publication is next to it (see Figure 22.2). Choose **Next** to get started.

3. Answer the questions the wizard asks about the way you want to prepare your publication. The questions differ, depending on the type of publication you're creating. Choose **Next** as you finish each wizard dialog box.

4. Enter any information required for the publication. A title or an address is needed for many types of publications. Choose **Next** when you have entered the information that's needed.

5. To change information you've already entered, click the **Back** button to move to the previous dialog box.

6. When you've answered all the questions and made all the decisions, choose **Finish** on the final wizard dialog box.

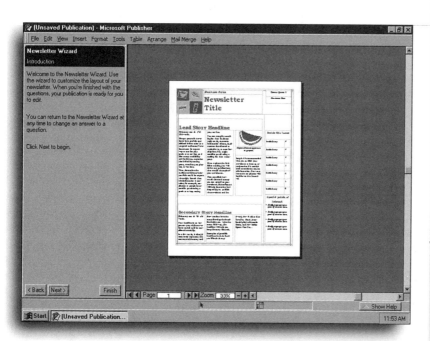

FIGURE 22.2

The wizard stays with you as you design your publication.

Skip the questions

Instead of moving through all the questions and answers, you can click **Finish** at the first wizard pane and move directly to the publication. If you find something you want to change, choose **Show Wizard** and click the appropriate category in the wizard list. When you change the design specification, Publisher immediately changes the publication.

7. The wizard displays a list of all the decisions you made (see Figure 22.3). You can click any category and change your answer.

FIGURE 22.3

The wizard is very flexible and willing to go along with any changes you want to make.

1 List of configuration categories

2 Hide Wizard button

Hiding Help

If you don't want to view the Help window that appears when you create a publication, click the **Hide Help** button in the status bar.

8. If you don't need the wizard, say goodbye by choosing **Hide Wizard**. (To bring the wizard back, choose **Show Wizard**.)

Your publication layout is ready for your own input. It's a good idea to click the **Show Help** button because Publisher is smart enough to bring up Help topics that are directly related to this type of publication (see Figure 22.4).

FIGURE 22.4
The basic design is established, and help is at your fingertips.

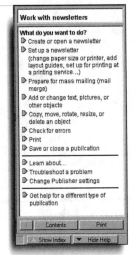

Help versus the wizard

If you open the Help window, make sure you close the wizard. If you don't, the two panes cover almost all of your publication, and you won't be able to get any work done.

Now, of course, you have to tackle the difficult task of creating the content. Publisher has lots of tools to help you, which we'll cover in the next few chapters.

Using Publications by Design

Think about all the different forms you need in your business. Cards, stationary, envelopes, invoices, purchase orders—the list goes on and on.

Re-opening the catalog

Normally, the catalog is displayed only when you first start Publisher. If you're already working in Publisher, you can display the catalog again by opening the **File** menu and choosing **New**.

To achieve a slick, professional image for your business, everything should match. Luckily, Publisher has a feature that was invented to help you do this.

Click the **Publications by Design** tab on the catalog to see a vast number of options (see Figure 22.5).

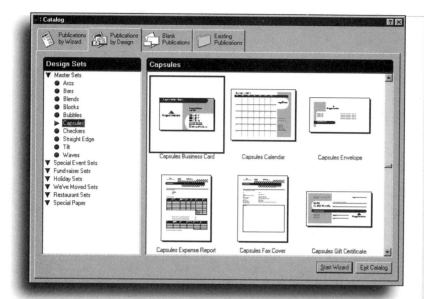

FIGURE 22.5
Pick a design set and then create all the different publications you need— everything matches!

Choose a design set and then choose the publication type you want to create. It all works just like the Publications Wizard.

Incidentally, in addition to the Master Sets, which are designed for businesses, Publisher includes a number of special design sets.

Using a Blank Publication Design

The Publications Wizard is great for many tasks; however, sometimes the layout isn't terribly complicated, but just needs to fit onto an unusual paper size. Or perhaps you need paper that's folded a certain way, and you don't want to worry about crossing the fold as you place elements on the publication. The **Blank Publications** tab provides you with a variety of paper formats to start you off on the right foot (see Figure 22.6).

These page types are useful for those odd-job publications that require special paper sizes or a publication that has to be folded in a special way. These jobs arise from time to time, and the selection on the **Blank Publications** tab offers a way to do-it-yourself without fretting over the details. The page size is set, and any paper-folding that might be required is premarked.

FIGURE 22.6

It's easy to create a special type of publication if the basic layout is preset for you.

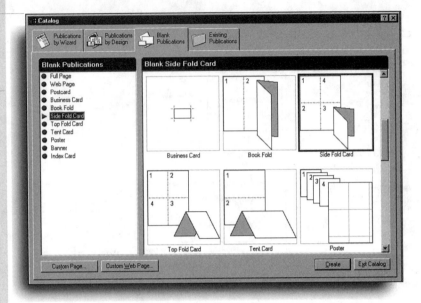

You just have to select the type of page that's needed for your publication, and Publisher takes care of the mathematics of margins and the placement of contents.

Designing special page types

1. Click the **Blank Publications** tab of the catalog to view the paper format types.

2. Click the icon for the page type you need, and then choose **Create**.

3. If you don't see exactly what you need, choose **Custom Page** to design your own format in the Page Setup dialog box (see Figure 22.7).

4. Specify the layout for a Custom Page by using these guidelines:

   - **Normal**. Choose this option if your page needs no folds or special margins.

   - **Special Fold**. This is the one for you if your publication has a specific fold that's different from the typical fold on regular-size paper.

   - **Special Size**. Use this option if your publication has a size that is different from the paper it will be printed on. For example, a banner uses multiple pieces of paper (you have to glue or tape them together to read the banner), and a business card uses only a corner of the paper (although you duplicate it all over the paper and then cut the cards out).

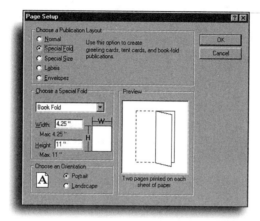

FIGURE 22.7

Design exactly the page type you need for your publication.

- **Labels**. Yep, you guessed it. Use this one to create labels.

- **Envelopes**. This is the way to customize the layout for printing your envelopes. You can choose among the common sizes for envelopes or design a custom size.

5. If you selected **Special Fold**, choose a type of fold from the **Choose a Special Fold** drop-down list.

6. If you selected **Special Fold** or **Special Size**, specify the **Width** and **Height** of the page. This is not necessarily the width and height of the paper (see the discussion on pages versus paper later in this chapter).

7. If you selected **Labels**, a list of Avery label types appears. Choose the label you're planning to use.

8. Choose either **Portrait** or **Landscape** orientation, observing the effect in the **Preview** window.

9. Choose **OK** to close the Page Setup dialog box.

Most of the special paper types are preconfigured for a specific number of pages. For example, a folded card actually has four printed pages (even though there is only one sheet of paper).

Publisher knows how many pages you'll need to complete your project and offers to create the layout before you start (see Figure 22.8). It's a good idea to accept the offer by choosing the **Yes** button. Incidentally, you can add or remove pages manually whenever you want to.

FIGURE 22.8

Let Publisher complete the layout for you.

When the layout displays (see Figure 22.9), it's the right size, with the right margins. All that remains to do is provide the content (which is, of course, the hardest part of creating a publication).

FIGURE 22.9

Publisher has preformatted your special paper size, and the folding scheme is built into the layout.

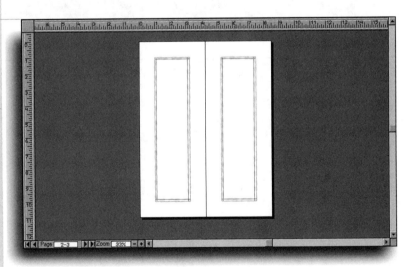

As you enter the content, you can be confident that everything will print at the right place on the page. If there's a fold involved, each side of the fold is treated as a separate page. If you're designing a card, nothing will print upside down.

SEE ALSO

➤ *To learn more about page orientation and previewing your publication before printing, see page 602*

➤ *To learn more about entering text, see page 528*

➤ *To learn more about inserting graphics, see page 536*

Starting from Scratch

If you have some knowledge and experience, you can make your publication a total do-it-yourself project. In fact, even if you don't have expertise, you might want to have the fun of creating your own design and layout.

Choose **E**x**it Catalog** from the catalog window to say "Thanks, but I'd rather do it myself." A blank page appears in the Publisher window (see Figure 22.10). Publisher has many of the same types of onscreen elements as the other Office programs.

If you're already working in Publisher, click the New button ▯ on the Standard toolbar to bring up a blank page.

That's all you have to do to set everything up. Now you have to enter the content, using the tools we'll be discussing throughout the ensuing chapters.

SEE ALSO

➤ *To learn more about entering text, see page 528*

➤ *To learn more about inserting graphics, see page 536*

Working with Pages

Not all publications are single-page products. In fact, if all you need is a fancy memo or a cleverly formatted letter, your word processor would probably serve just as well.

When you work with publications, the concept of a page becomes a bit complicated.

Understanding What a Page Is

A page is not a piece of paper; it's an area you have to fill with content. For example, picture the following publications, all of which are printed on one piece of paper.

FIGURE 22.10

A blank page can be a daunting sight when you have to produce something creative and professional.

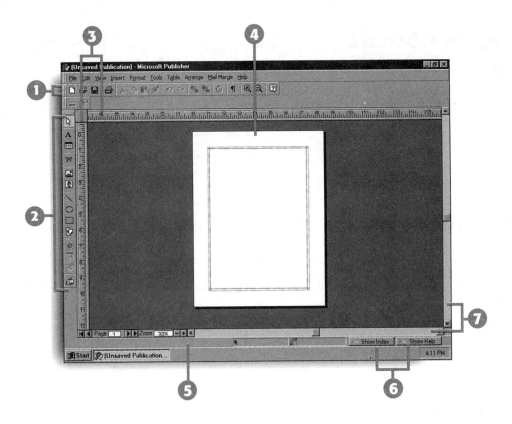

① Standard toolbar

② Formatting toolbar

③ Rulers

④ Blank presentation

⑤ Status bar

⑥ Help buttons

⑦ Scrollbars

- A greeting card has four pages.
- A place card has two pages.
- A folded flyer has four pages.
- A flyer that is folded in thirds (the way you fold a letter) has six pages.

Publisher knows how to handle multiple pages that may or may not be printed on the same piece of paper. As you develop your publication, you may have to add pages (and you may also have to delete pages occasionally). The rules to remember are

- Any publication with a fold must have pages added (or deleted) in groups of four.
- Any publication for which you are printing on both sides of the paper must have pages added (or deleted) in groups of two.
- Odd-numbered pages are always on the right, even-numbered pages on the left.
- You do not have to supply content for every page, but you must include the page in the layout so you don't interfere with the "groups of two" or "groups of four" schemes.

Viewing Pages

Publisher offers two ways to view the pages in your publication: Single Page and Two-Page Spread.

Select a view by opening the **View** menu and then toggling the choice called **Two-Page Spread**. A check mark appears to indicate when the Two-Page view is invoked.

The Single Page view is straightforward—the page is in the Publisher window. However, viewing a publication in the Two-Page Spread view is a little more complicated.

Figure 22.11 shows a Two-Page Spread view of a publication that is four pages long. It's pretty much impossible to avoid noticing that only one page is seen in the software window. That happens because the currently selected page is Page 1, and in a Two-Page Spread view, the odd-numbered pages are always on the right. Because there is no page in front of Page 1, there's nothing on the left in the software window.

> **Blank pages aren't unusual**
>
> There are plenty of times when you'll leave the first or last page of your publication blank (or both of them). If you have preprinted paper stock that you use as a cover page, or paper that has a graphic on it that is used for either the cover or back page, you won't want to add content to those pages. However, you must keep all the pages intact as you work in Publisher so you don't lose the odd/even (left/right) alignment of your publication.

FIGURE 22.11

The first page of a publication is always on the right when you view the Two-Page Spread.

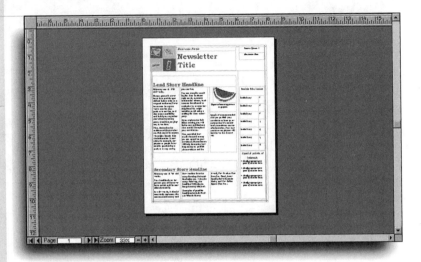

On the other hand, Figure 22.12 shows pages 2-3 of the same publication and represents the way the Two-Page Spread view looks when you're working on any page except the first or last.

FIGURE 22.12

You can view two pages at a time when you're working on a multiple-page publication.

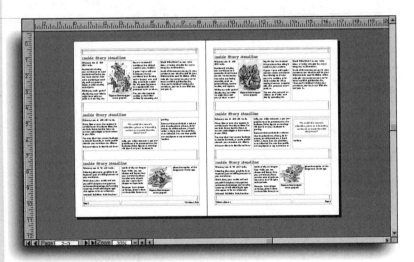

Moving Through the Pages

The view you're using stays consistent as you move through your publication. If you're applying the Two-Page Spread view, advancing a page advances you to the next spread because you move two pages at a time.

To move through your publication, use the page controls on the status bar at the bottom left of your Publisher window (see Figure 22.13). The controls are for changing pages and also for zooming in on pages.

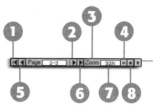

FIGURE 22.13

Use the page controls to navigate through your publication.

1 Move to the first page

2 Move to the next page

3 Select a zoom percentage

4 Zoom out one step

5 Move to the previous page

6 Move to the last page

7 Current zoom percentage

8 Zoom in one step

Zooming In

Because layout and page appearance are so important in a publication, the default view for working in Publisher is Full Page. However, when you're entering or editing text, that view is impossible to work with because you can't really read anything except large headings. Zooming in is a necessity.

Publisher uses percentages to control zooming and provides several ways to move in and out.

The quickest way to get to a close-up view is to press F9, which toggles between the current zoom setting and 100% zoom, moving you back and forth as needed (see Figure 22.14).

You can also use the zoom controls on the status bar to move in and out a bit more precisely:

- Click the Zoom percentage box to choose a percentage from the pop-up list (see Figure 22.15).

- Click the plus and minus buttons to move in or out in steps (the steps are the percentages indicated in the pop-up list).

Adding Pages

Before you add a page, you should be viewing your pages appropriately, which means that multiple-page publications should be viewed in the Two-Page Spread view. The results of adding pages depend on the current view: if you're in Two-Page Spread view, two pages are added at a time. Single-Page view means that one page is added.

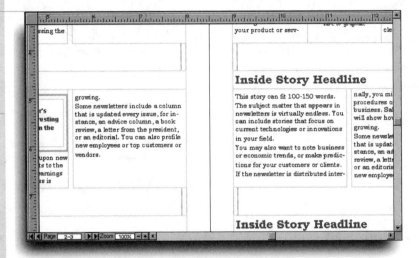

FIGURE 22.14

Press F9 to zoom in and do what you have to do. Then press F9 again to zoom out so you can inspect the impact of your work.

FIGURE 22.15

Move in or out to the percentage level that works best for your current task.

Sometimes you see a dialog box

If you use Ctrl+Shift+N to add blank pages when you're working in some predesigned publications, you see a dialog box offering layout options (for text frames and picture frames) for the additional pages. The choices vary according to the type of publication, and you merely select any options you want to place on your new blank page.

Here are two quick ways to add a page:

- Press Ctrl+Shift+N to add a blank page immediately after the page that's currently in the window. If you're viewing two pages, two blank pages are added, and they become the next two pages.

- If the last page of your publication is in the window, click the Next Page arrow. A message appears, asking if you want to add another page. Click **OK** (or choose **Cancel** if you clicked the arrow by mistake).

A better method for adding pages is to take advantage of the choices available in the Insert Page dialog box, which you see by opening the **Insert** menu and choosing the **Page** command.

If you choose this command when you are working in Two-Page Spread view, the dialog box looks like Figure 22.16. The choices on the dialog box give you a wide range of options:

FIGURE 22.16

You can accomplish a lot more than just adding a page when you use the Insert Page dialog box.

- Specify the number of pages to add (use multiples of two).

- Indicate where the pages should be inserted. The default is immediately after the currently displayed pages, but you can change that to immediately before or between the pages.

- Decide whether you want blank pages, pages with a text frame, or duplicates of an existing page.

    The last choice is useful when you're creating special layout elements that you want on all or some pages. Just select the page number that has the objects you want to duplicate, and the new page will have those objects.

The Insert Page dialog box looks slightly different if you are working in Single-Page view (see Figure 22.17). There is, of course, no option to place the new page between any existing pages. All the other options are the same as with the Two-Page Spread view.

FIGURE 22.17

The choices are narrowed slightly when you're viewing one page at a time.

Deleting Pages

To delete a page, first be sure that page is in the Publisher window. Then open the **Edit** menu and choose **Delete Page**. If there are two pages in the window, the Delete Page dialog box asks you to be more specific (see Figure 22.18).

If you make a mistake, you can undo your action by opening the **Edit** menu and choosing **Undo Delete Page**.

FIGURE 22.18

Which page are you
referring to?

Getting Help

If you've been using Windows and Windows software for a
while, you're probably feeling quite confident about accessing
Help files. After all, everything in Help in Windows works the
same.

Opening the Help Windows

Sorry, Publisher doesn't follow the rules. The way this Help system works is unique to Publisher.

The following two Help windows are available in Publisher:

- An Index window, which displays topics in alphabetical order
- A Help window, which displays the actual Help pages for the
topics

At the bottom right of your Publisher window are two buttons:
Show Index and Show Help.

Don't get excited about the logic yet; it doesn't quite work as it
seems. Here's how the buttons work:

- Click **Show Index** to see both the Help index and the last
Help page you viewed (even though the button says "Index,"
it means "both windows"). The button names change to
Hide Index and **Hide Help**.

- Click **Show Help** to see the last Help page you viewed
(the Index stays hidden). The button name changes to
Hide Help.

- If both windows are open, choose **Hide Index** to close the
Index—the Help page remains on the screen.

- If you choose **Hide Help** when both windows are open,
both windows close.

Using the Index

The fastest way to get information from the Help system is to find a topic in the index.

Finding Help on a topic

1. Click the **Show Index** button to open the Help windows.

2. Enter a word or phrase in the text box at the top of the index. Any matching Index entry is automatically selected in the list of index entries, and the Help page offers specific assistance (Figure 22.19).

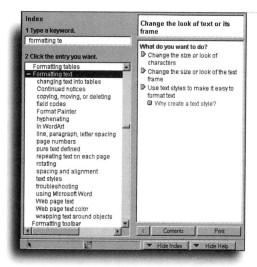

FIGURE 22.19

As you type, the Help Index matches your characters against its entries.

3. Select the sublisting (sublistings are indented) that matches your query.

4. The Help page displays either a paragraph of explanation (sometimes in a separate box) or a list of specific topics.

Using the Help Pages

After you've located the section of the Index you need, you can view the information that appears on the Help page. However, some Help pages have only additional topics listed (these are the contents of the Help section connected to your query). Click the topic of interest to move to the next Help page. If the next page has nothing but more listings, select the one you need.

Sometimes you have to keep doing this through a number of pages, choosing topics from contents listings in page after page until you've narrowed down your query enough to see a real Help page.

When a Help page finally shows up, it's usually a set of instructions that explains tasks in a one-step-at-a-time method. Some of the instructions have an icon named "How?" beneath them— you can click the icon to learn how to do that particular task (see Figure 22.20).

FIGURE 22.20

If you have trouble performing any step, just ask how.

You'll run across a slew of additional features in Help pages:

- Click the **Print** button below the Help page window to print the Help page that's currently displayed.

- Click the **Contents** button to return to the first Help page (the page that appeared first, containing a list of contents).

- Click any blue listing to see a definition of a feature or terminology.

- A listing that has a color arrow to the left is a demo, which takes you through pages that are filled with information about the topic. Click **Next** to move from page to page through the demo, or choose **Cancel** when you've seen enough to understand the topic.

- A listing named **Click for Web tip** indicates that the contents contain help about the current topic related to publishing on Web pages.

- Some Help pages have a **More Info** tab on which you'll find some additional information related to your primary topic.

Using Tippages

Publisher uses Tippages to tell you in a very polite way that something you're trying to do won't work or just isn't a very good idea. For instance, a dialog box might open to explain that you cannot fit ten inches of text in a five-inch box. Even more polite is the offer to show you instructions on how to resolve your error. This is much better than sending a rude beep through your speakers.

Opening, Saving, and Closing Publications

Publisher has some slightly different approaches to the commonplace tasks of opening and closing publications. Things don't work exactly the same way they do in your other Windows software.

Working with One Publication at a Time

You can only have one publication open at any time. If you are working on a publication and open a different one, Publisher closes the first publication. If you've modified that publication since the last time you saved, you'll be given an opportunity to save it.

Opening Publications

If you're already working in Publisher and want to open an existing file, you can open the **File** menu and then choose **Open** to access the **Existing Publications** tab of the catalog (see Figure 22.21).

FIGURE 22.21
A picture of the publication is a good reminder.

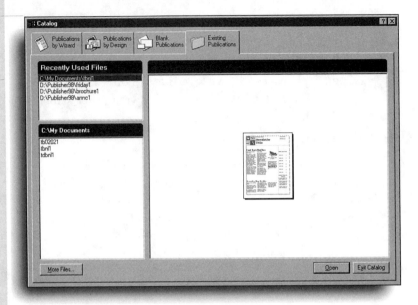

This dialog box is unlike the Open dialog box you encounter in most Windows software:

- The upper box lists the last four files you opened in Publisher (the same list exists at the bottom of the **File** menu just as it does in your other Windows programs). The paths are included with the filenames.

- The lower box lists all the publications in the currently selected document folder.

- Choose **More Files** to see a regular Windows Open dialog box so you can open files that are in different folders.

- As you select a publication, a picture of its first page displays in the preview box to jog your memory.

After you make your selections, choose **Open** to open the publication. Unlike other Windows Open dialog boxes, this one won't let you manipulate the files. If you want to delete, copy, or rename a file, you must use a standard Open dialog box.

You can also click the Open button on the Standard toolbar to see the standard Windows Open dialog box.

Saving Publications

A certain scenario is acted out constantly in offices all over the world. If you have participated in it, you'll recognize it as I describe it. Here's a short version of the plot:

Scene 1—a typical day in an office: A computer consultant or trainer tells users to save their work early and often. The vast majority of users pay no heed.

Fade to black, scene 2, the next month: The consultant's phone rings, and the caller is a wildly hysterical user. After the user spent seven hours on a document, the computer burped or the user closed the document and inadvertently said "No" to the dialog box that asked "Do you want to save this document?" Now the user is demanding that the consultant help get the document back because it's due in twenty minutes.

Guess the ending. If you guessed that nothing can be done, you're correct. If you guessed that the user demanded to have the consultant fired, you're probably correct. If you guessed that the user saw the light and is now saving documents religiously and frequently, you're probably wrong. The panic wears off—ask any trainer or consultant.

The people who wrote Publisher must have been involved in that scenario many times because they've invented a nifty device: dialog box nagging.

Every fifteen minutes, a dialog box appears to remind you that you haven't saved your publication recently (see Figure 22.22). Publisher offers to save it for you. Whether you reply with **Yes** or **No**, fifteen minutes later, it's back.

You can change the nagging interval to suit your own work habits.

Changing the Save Reminder interval

1. Open the **Tools** menu and choose **Options**.
2. Click the **Editing and User Assistance** tab.
3. In the **Remind to save publication** section of the dialog box, specify a different interval for the reminder.
4. Choose **OK** to save your new settings and close the dialog box.

Guidelines for adjusting the Save Reminder interval

If you type fast, insert pictures rapidly, and generally get things done "faster than a speeding bullet," you might want to shorten the interval. After all, you have a lot to lose in fifteen minutes. If you don't work quite so swiftly, you can probably afford to set the interval for a longer time, perhaps twenty-five minutes. The trick is to balance the annoyance of the reminder with the risk of losing work if something happens.

FIGURE 22.22

Just say **Yes**. Always say **Yes**.

Of course, there is also a standard Save icon on the Publisher toolbar and a **Save** command on the **File** menu.

Closing Publications

Sometimes you have a good reason to close a file instead of saving it. If you saved your publication and then started making radical changes you regret, the easiest way out of your dilemma is to close the file without saving it. Then you can open it again so you can work on the version that existed the last time you saved it.

To close a publication, open the **File** menu and choose **Close**. If you've modified the publication since the last time you saved it, you'll be asked if you want to save before closing. Your answer depends on the condition of the publication at the moment.

Adding Text and Graphics

Entering and formatting text

Creating styles

Adding graphics

Adding WordArt

Manipulating frames

Using bullets and numbers

Using tables

Adding Text in Publisher

Here comes the hard part of creating a publication—you have to write the words. No matter how much help the Wizard offered, you have to invent the words yourself.

The placement and appearance of the words you use are as significant as the words themselves. A headline that's brilliantly clever won't work well if it's too small.

Adding Text to a Wizard Publication

When you work with a publication that the Wizard designed, there are text boxes preset for you. Your own words must be substituted for the "words" being used as a placeholder.

Replacing placeholder text

1. If you've just started Publisher, click the **Existing Publication** tab on the opening dialog box to open a publication. Otherwise, click the Open button 📂 on the Standard toolbar and open the publication on which you want to work.

2. Click anywhere inside the text box you want to use to select it. The text is highlighted and the text box frame appears (see Figure 23.1).

FIGURE 23.1

The text box is alive and active, waiting for your words.

3. It's impossible to see text from the default Full Page view, so zoom in by pressing F9. Then use the vertical and horizontal scroll bars to position the text frame exactly where you need it.

4. Because the text is selected (highlighted), the first character you enter replaces all the existing placeholder text. Just continue to type, entering all the text that belongs in this text box. (Or enter as much as you want to—if you don't fill the text box or you have too much text to fit in the text box, you can adjust everything later).

5. Move to another text box and enter the content that belongs there. The type of text box determines the content (see Figure 23.2).

FIGURE 23.2
Headlines and headings should be attention-getting.

6. Continue to enter text until you run out of things to say or run out of space for all the things you want to say. Don't worry, you can make adjustments to the layout for either problem.

7. Zoom out to see a Full Page view so you can determine the effect of your work on the publication.

The preset text boxes are formatted automatically by the Wizard, so when you enter your own text, it's in the font and style that the automatic design created. You don't have to live with it—this is your creation. See the section on formatting text later in this chapter.

You can save this publication now, or you can close it without saving it. If the automatic save feature is enabled, you will be prompted periodically to save the publication.

SEE ALSO
➤ *To save a publication, see page 525*

Adding a Text Box

If you're creating your publication from scratch, or you added a new page to a predesigned publication, you can't enter text until you create a text frame. Most of the time, you add your own text frames when you are creating a publication from scratch.

Adding a text frame

1. Click the New button 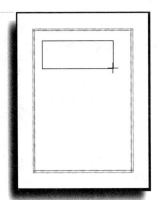 on the Standard toolbar to open a blank publication.

2. Click the Text Frame tool on the Objects toolbar.

3. Position your mouse pointer on the page where you want the upper-left corner of the text frame to appear. Then hold down the left mouse button while you drag down and right until the text frame is approximately the size you need (see Figure 23.3).

FIGURE 23.3
Size the text frame so the contents will fit nicely.

4. Release the mouse button. The text frame appears on your page. If you look carefully you can see a cursor pulsating in the upper-left corner of the text box; it's waiting expectantly to see what you're planning to say.

You can tweak the position and size of the text frame later, after you've entered the content. Now it's time to use the text frame to enter all the magnificent prose that will give your readers insight into your brilliant ideas.

SEE ALSO

➤ *To resize or position a text frame, see page 545*

Entering and Formatting Text

Entering text is just a matter of typing, of course. However, there are some guidelines for newsletter-type publishing you should keep in mind:

- Sentences are separated by a single space (you probably use two spaces after a period in the correspondence and reports you produce in your word processor).

- New paragraphs have no indents.

- Body text is justified full (meeting both margins).

Entering text in a text frame

1. Zoom in (press F9) so you can see what you're typing as you enter characters.

2. Use the tools on the Formatting toolbar to change the look of the text (see Figure 23.4). You have to select existing text before you can apply any format changes.

   You also can apply formatting before you type and then turn it off when you are finished with it. For example, you can choose Bold, then type text (which appears in boldface), and then choose Bold again, which toggles that format off so that subsequent typing is not boldface.

3. To change the font, select the text you want to change (or press Ctrl+A to select all the text in the text frame). Then click the arrow to the right of the Font box and choose a new font from the drop-down list.

4. To change the font size, select the text you want to change. Then click the arrow to the right of the Font Size box and choose a new size from the drop-down list.

5. To format text for special attributes (bold, italic, and so on), select the text and click the appropriate icon (see Figure 23.5).

Publisher provides specialized toolbars

There are several Formatting toolbars in Publisher, one for text and several for different types of graphics. The appropriate toolbar appears when you select a frame. If no text frame or graphics frame is selected, no Formatting toolbar appears in your window.

Put a text frame in a text frame for headlines

I learned a good trick for text frames that have headlines. Don't just change the font size and attributes to make the headline stand out—give the headline its own text frame. Create a text frame inside the text frame you're working with, and enter the headline in the new text frame. You can format the text frame itself by adding color, adding a border, or making other changes to ensure the headline grabs attention.

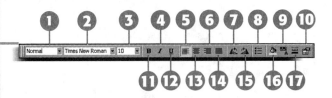

FIGURE 23.4

Use the tools on the Formatting toolbar to change the look of your characters.

1. Create or apply a style.
2. Change the font.
3. Change the font size.
4. Italic
5. Align left
6. Align right
7. Rotate left
8. Bullet and number lists
9. Text color
10. Text frame properties
11. Bold
12. Underline
13. Align center
14. Justify full
15. Rotate right
16. Fill color
17. Line/border styles

6. To apply formatting for which there is no icon on the toolbar, select the text, open the **Format** menu, and choose **Font**. Then choose the formatting you need from the Font dialog box (see Figure 23.6). Use the Sample area to preview any selections you make. Choose **OK** to close the dialog box.

7. After you've applied the changes, click anywhere outside the selected text to remove the highlighting (or press an arrow key to move past the highlighted section).

Creating Styles

Publisher doesn't come out of the box with a list of styles the way your word processor does, but you can create a style quite easily. Then, every time you want to format text a certain way, you can choose the style you created.

The ideal approach is to format text in your publication until it's absolutely perfect (perhaps you created a terrific headline) and save it as a style. After that, instead of going through all those steps the next time you enter a similar type of text, you can tell Publisher to use the style. All the formatting you labored over is applied in an instant.

The following attributes can be used in a style:

- Alignment
- Character spacing
- Font
- Font size
- Indents
- Line spacing
- Lists
- Tabs

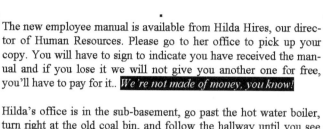

The new employee manual is available from Hilda Hires, our director of Human Resources. Please go to her office to pick up your copy. You will have to sign to indicate you have received the manual and if you lose it we will not give you another one for free, you'll have to pay for it.. *We're not made of money, you know!*

Hilda's office is in the sub-basement, go past the hot water boiler, turn right at the old coal bin, and follow the hallway until you see the black steel door. Bang on the door (there's a hammer on a rope next to the door for your convenience). If Hilda is there, she'll open the door. If she is away from the office, come back another time.

This manual contains information about the following items:

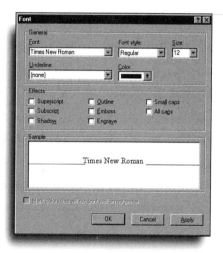

FIGURE 23.6

The Font dialog box offers additional formatting options.

Creating a style

1. Select the text you've formatted to absolute perfection.

2. Open the **Format** menu and choose **Text Style** to open the Text Styles dialog box. Choose **Create a New Style** to get started with the Create New Style dialog box shown in Figure 23.7.

3. Type a style name in the **Enter new style name** text box. By the way, notice that information about the font and alignment of the selected text appears in the dialog box. You

FIGURE 23.7
Use a name for the style that
reminds you of the type of text
or formatting it represents.

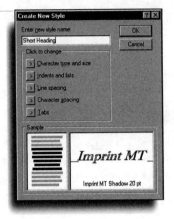

can view any other formatting you applied to the text by
choosing the appropriate button.

4. Choose **OK** to return to the Text Style dialog box. Choose
   Close to save your work, and now your new style is listed in
   the Style box on the Formatting toolbar.

Editing Styles

That headline style you created looked magnificent—it just
jumped off the page. However, when you applied it to another
headline, it didn't work quite so well. The second headline had
two lines instead of one, and now you realize you want to make
some changes so the two-line headline will be easy to read. For
consistency, you want all your headlines to look the same, so
editing the style is the only way to go.

Changing styles

1. Open the **Format** menu, choose **Text Style,** and then select
   the style you want to change.

2. Choose **Change this style** to open the Change Style dialog
   box.

3. Choose the format option that needs attention—**Line
   Spacing**, for example—and make the necessary changes
   (see Figure 23.8).

4. Choose **OK** twice to return to the Text Style dialog box, and
   then choose **Close** to save your changes.

FIGURE 23.8

This style needs more space between the lines of text.

5. Return to every place in your publication with text using this style and select that text. Reapply the style by choosing it from the Style box on the Formatting toolbar.

Importing Styles

Most of us use word processing software. If you're like me, you have the same fussy approach to the appearance of those documents as you do for your publications. That means you may have created or tweaked some styles in your word processor that you'd like to use in Publisher. Well, you can because you can import a style.

Importing a style

1. Open the **Format** menu and choose **Text Style**.

2. In the Text Styles dialog box, choose **Import new styles** to bring up the Import Styles dialog box.

3. Click the arrow to the right of the **Files of type** drop-down list box and select your word processor (see Figure 23.9). If your word processor isn't listed, you cannot import styles.

FIGURE 23.9

If your word processor is supported, you can use a style from any document.

4. Move to the folder that holds the documents for the word processor and select a document that you know contains the style you're after. Choose **OK**.

5. Publisher churns away for a few seconds and then returns you to the Text Style dialog box, where all the styles that existed in your document are now listed (see Figure 23.10).

FIGURE **23.10**

This is certainly easier than building styles from scratch.

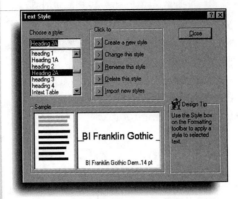

6. You can delete, change, or rename any of the styles with the tools on the dialog box. Choose **Close** to return to the Publisher window.

All the styles are now also listed in the Styles box on the Formatting toolbar so you can use them as you format text.

Adding Graphics

Graphics can make a point, amuse your readers, or draw attention to important text. However, one of the best reasons to use graphics is that they're so much fun to work with.

Adding a Graphics Frame

Before the fun starts, however, you have to put a frame on your page, because like most great art, graphics images are designed to exist in frames. (If you're working in a predesigned layout, a frame already exists on your page, unless you're adding additional art).

Publisher provides two graphics frame tools on the Objects toolbar:

- *The Picture Frame tool.* Use this for a picture you've scanned, imported, or created in a graphics program.

- *The Clip Gallery tool.* Use this for clip art you can select from the enormous assortment of clip art available with your Publisher software.

Because it's far more common to use clip art for graphics images, we'll use the Clip Gallery tool. The process for picture frames is similar, and if you have a scanned image you want to place in your publication, you can use a picture frame.

Creating a clip art frame

1. Click the Clip Gallery tool on the Objects toolbar.

2. Click the page where you want the clip art to appear.

3. The Clip Gallery window opens and presents an almost overwhelming assortment of images, as shown in Figure 23.11.

Keep the Office SBE CD-ROM in its drive

Publisher has an enormous collection of clip art, and the assortment is so large that you'll almost always find something that fills the bill. By default, the majority of the clip art files are kept on the Microsoft Office Small Business Edition CD-ROM instead of being transferred to your hard drive. When you want to use clip art, be sure the CD-ROM is in the CD-ROM drive.

FIGURE 23.11
This art gallery has an enormous collection, but you can reduce the confusion by browsing specific sections.

4. The best way to view the collection is to select a category, which reduces the number of images you have to browse. Choose the category that seems pertinent.

5. Browse through the images until you find one that appeals to your artistic and creative senses. Select it and choose **Insert** (or double-click the image).

6. The clip art is placed in its frame on your page (see Figure 23.12).

FIGURE 23.12

After your clip art is on the page, you should think about writing a caption or some introductory text to explain it.

SEE ALSO

➤ *For help in arranging your clip art, see page 563*

➤ *To resize or move a graphics frame, see page 545*

Adding Pictures

Clip art isn't the only type of graphics available for your publication; the Clip Gallery also has photographic images.

The steps to add an image are the same as the steps required for adding clip art (click the Clip Gallery tool and then click on your page).

When the Clip Gallery window opens, click the **Images** tab (see Figure 23.13).

Get more clip art on the Internet

If the selections available in the Clip Gallery fail to satisfy you, click the **Clips from Web** button in the lower right corner of the Clip Gallery window. This opens your browser and heads for `http://www.microsoft.com/clipgallerylive`, where you can find additional clip art. The clipart you download becomes part of your gallery.

FIGURE 23.13

When line art doesn't seem appropriate, you can insert a photograph instead.

Adding WordArt

If you have to make an important point or draw attention to a subject, you can use either a graphic or a snappy short headline. Sometimes it's hard to decide whether pictures or words will work best. Stop pondering and use both at once! Use WordArt.

WordArt is a hybrid element, both text and art. It's fun to work with, and it's a major attention-getter.

Creating a WordArt frame

1. Click the WordArt Frame tool on the Objects toolbar.
2. Position your pointer on the page where you want to place the upper-left corner of the WordArt frame.
3. Drag down and right to create a frame that's the right size for your WordArt element. When you release the mouse, the WordArt window opens, and the Enter Your Text Here dialog box awaits your text entry (see Figure 23.14).

FIGURE 23.14

Replace the placeholder text with some snappy, clever words.

4. Enter the text you want to use as art. WordArt works best if you keep the number of words to a minimum (try limiting WordArt to four words).
5. Choose **Update Display** to move your text into the WordArt frame, and then click the x in the upper-right corner to close the dialog box.

After you put your text into the WordArt frame, the frame itself looks like hash marks, which indicates it's in editing mode. Now you can use the toolbar shown in Figure 23.15 to manipulate the WordArt.

WordArt has its own software window

WordArt is a separate software program with its own menu bar and toolbar. When you finish working with your WordArt frame, your Publisher window returns automatically.

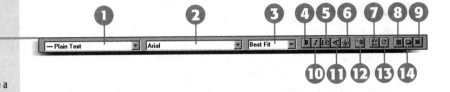

FIGURE 23.15

The toolbar has lots of clever devices you can use to create a visually arresting element.

1   Shape

2   Font

3   Font size

4   Bold

5   Upper/lowercase same height

6   Stretch

7   Spacing between characters

8   Shading

9   Borders

10 Italic

11 Stack

12 Alignment

13 Special effects

14 Letter shadows

The fun of using WordArt starts with changing the shape and font. After you've established these settings, you can continue to use the toolbar gadgets to play with your WordArt until it's as prominent, obtrusive, or outrageous as you want.

Shaping up WordArt

1. Click the arrow on the Shape box to see the available shapes, and select the one you want to use (see Figure 23.16).

2. When the WordArt is twisted and gnarled perfectly, pick a font by selecting one from the Font box. It's usually best to skip the Font Size box—the default selection, **Best Fit**, almost always works.

3. When you finish tweaking, click anywhere outside the WordArt frame to return to the Publisher window.

Editing WordArt

WordArt frames behave a little differently—they have two edit modes:

- Click the frame to select it and see the sizing handles. The mouse pointer is a moving van when it's positioned inside the frame or on the frame border (this works the same as all graphics frames because WordArt is a graphic, not text). Use this edit mode to move or resize the WordArt frame.

- Double-click the frame to see the hash-mark frame border and bring up the WordArt window. Use this edit

FIGURE 23.16

The shapes themselves don't appear on your publication. Your text assumes the shape as if it were poured into the shape.

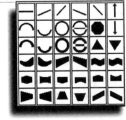

mode to change the text or settings of the WordArt graphic.

Adding More Effects to WordArt

You can apply lots of effects to WordArt in addition to the shape and font. Try some of the toolbar icons to see the special effects that work best for you. Figure 23.17 is an example of a WordArt graphic that's been treated with the Text Shadow effect.

Trial and error is unavoidable

You'll probably try one shape after another, and one font after another, as you manipulate your WordArt. This is one element that has no logical approach and no "natural" configuration. Just keep playing with the settings until something works for you.

FIGURE 23.17

WordArt makes a headline more interesting.

Using the Graphics Formatting Toolbar

When you select any graphics frame, including WordArt, the Formatting toolbar appears in the Publisher window. The tools are specific to manipulating graphics and the frames that enclose graphics (see Figure 23.18).

WordArt font choices are special

Many of the WordArt fonts aren't letters, they're symbols. For example, the Holiday font is a collection of special symbols representing holidays (there's a font with food symbols, too). In addition, Wingdings fonts are available, which contain lots of useful symbols.

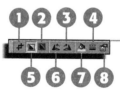

These tools are occasionally handy, and you'll use some of them more than others. Figure 23.19 is a two-page spread that shows what you can do with clip art. The top graphic on the left page is the original art work; below it you can see the effect of rotating the graphic. The right page has a frame with fill color applied and another frame containing a cropped version of the graphic.

FIGURE 23.18

The Formatting toolbar for graphics specializes in graphics frames.

1. Crop Picture
2. Wrap Text to Picture
3. Rotate Right
4. Line/Border Styles
5. Wrap Text to Frame
6. Rotate Left
7. Fill Color
8. Object Frame Properties

FIGURE 23.19
Play around with the tools on
the Graphics Formatting toolbar to see the effects on a
graphics frame.

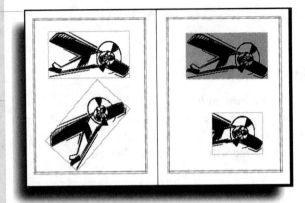

Adding Shapes

Publisher provides a robust collection of graphics that don't
require frames. These are graphic shapes, and they're available
on the Objects toolbar.

Inserting Shapes

Two methods are available when you want to add shapes to your
publication:

- Click the shape and then click on the page. When the shape
  appears, you can resize it to fit.
- Click the shape and then click and drag on the page.
  The shape takes its form and size from the dragging
  action. For example, the square box can be dragged to
  create a rectangle.

The Objects toolbar provides four Shape tools:

- Straight line
- Oval
- Rectangle
- Custom Shapes (see Figure 23.20)

Editing Shapes

After a shape is on the page, you can apply a number of manipulations to alter and improve it.

FIGURE 23.20
Abstract and symbolic shapes are available for those attention-catching graphics you want to add to your publication.

When you select a shape, the Shapes Formatting toolbar appears in the Publisher window (see Figure 23.21).

FIGURE 23.21
Shapes have their own Formatting toolbar.

Table 23.21 describes how to use the various shape-formatting tools.

Table 23.1   Shape-formatting tools

Toolbar	Command	Description Button
<img>	Rotate Left	Click to rotate the object 90 degrees to the left.
<img>	Rotate Right	Click to rotate the object 90 degrees to the right.
<img>	Flip Horizontal	The object retains its vertical position while it flips horizontally. To see the effect of a horizontal flip, place your right hand palm down on a flat surface. The thumb is on the left. Flip it horizontally (turn it palm up) and the thumb is on the right.
<img>	Flip Vertical	In this case, the object retains its horizontal position while flipping vertically.
<img>	Fill Color	Click this button and select a color from the drop-down palette to fill the object with the selected color.
<img>	Line/Border Style	Use this tool to add, remove, or change the object's border.

You can also using the sizing handles to manipulate the shape of the shape, which can produce just the startling effect you need (see Figure 23.22). Place your mouse pointer over one of the handles until it becomes a resize pointer. Press and hold the left mouse button while dragging the handle to resize and reshape the object.

No shape properties available

The Object Properties tool appears on the Formatting toolbar, but it is inaccessible.

FIGURE 23.22
Try resizing to achieve a weird, twisted, warped effect.

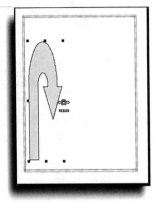

Adding Text to Shapes

Using a shape as the background for a headline or a short paragraph is a slick way to present information. Just create a text box on the shape, and enter the text. Then choose an appearance scheme for the text frame on the shape:

Use Ctrl+T to toggle transparency on and off

You can select any text box and press Ctrl+T to make the frame transparent to any background, whether the background is a shape, a graphics image, or just your page. Press Ctrl+T again to remove the transparent attribute.

- Do nothing to the text frame, so it is a plain black-on-white text box.

- Colorize the text frame in a contrasting or complementary color.

- Use Ctrl+T to make the text frame completely transparent, so it appears as if the text is directly on the shape.

Figure 23.23 shows an example of each of the options for placing text on a frame.

FIGURE 23.23
Apart from the difference in the text, notice that these graphics were created by combining shapes from the Custom Shape palette.

Manipulating Frames

The text and picture frames you've placed in your publication can be manipulated to make the frame contents look better, creating a more attractive, effective page.

Sizing and Moving Frames

You'll find that the most common correction you make is changing the size or position of frames. Lots of reasons can exist to change the size, position, or both:

- To make the page more attractive.
- To make one item on a page stand out from the other items.
- To ensure that a text frame holds all the text of that particular story.
- To make room for an additional element that must be added to the page.

Changing the size of a frame is easy because Publisher provides tools in the form of sizing handles.

Resizing a frame

1. Click the frame you want to resize. Sizing handles appear on the sides and corners of the frame.

2. Place your pointer over a sizing handle, which causes the pointer to change to a Resize pointer (see Figure 23.24).

FIGURE 23.24
Use the sizing handles to enlarge or reduce a frame.

3. Drag the sizing handle in the appropriate direction to change the size of the frame.

Here are some tricks for making resizing easier and more effective:

- Keep the proportions of the frame intact by holding down the Shift key while you drag a corner handle.

- Keep the center of the object cemented in place while you resize by holding down the Ctrl key while you drag a sizing handle. This means if you drag the right-side sizing handle, the left-side sizing handle automatically moves too.

- Keep the frame proportionate and the center locked in place by holding down both the Ctrl and Shift keys while you drag.

- Always release the mouse button before you release the Ctrl or Shift keys.

- Resizing text frames causes the text to rewrap to fit the new size.

- Resizing graphics frames can cause distortion in the graphics image (unless you use the Shift key).

Moving a frame is even easier than changing its dimensions, but there is a small difference in the way text and graphics frames work.

Moving a text frame

1. Click anywhere in the text frame to select it and see the sizing handles.

2. Position your pointer on the frame between any two sizing handles until the pointer changes to a moving van.

3. Drag the mouse in any direction—the frame goes along (see Figure 23.25).

Moving a graphics frame

1. Click anywhere in the frame to select it.

2. If your mouse pointer is located inside the frame or on the frame border, the pointer changes to a moving van.

3. Drag the frame to its new location.

FIGURE 23.25
You can move when the moving van shows up.

Moving a Frame to Another Page

Publisher provides several methods for moving frames from one part of your publication to another.

You can use the familiar Windows Cut, Copy, and Paste commands, of course, using the Windows Clipboard:

- Right-click a text frame and choose **Cut** or **Copy** from the shortcut menu. Then right-click in the new page and choose **Paste**.

- Right-click a graphics frame and choose **Cut** or **Copy** from the shortcut menu. Then right-click in the new page and choose **Paste** .

Moving frames with the Clipboard involves a special twist, however—if you're working in Two-Page Spread view, you can only paste a graphic to its odd/even counterpart. This means you cannot cut or copy a graphic from an odd page and paste it on an even page—it automatically jumps to the odd page. Use Single Page view if you're using the Clipboard.

You can also drag frames by using the Moving Van pointer.

- In Two-Page Spread view, drag frames from one page to the other.

- In Single Page view, drag a frame off the page and into a blank spot on the Publisher window (the area next to the page is called the *scratch area*). Then move to the target page and drag the frame back onto the publication (see Figure 23.26).

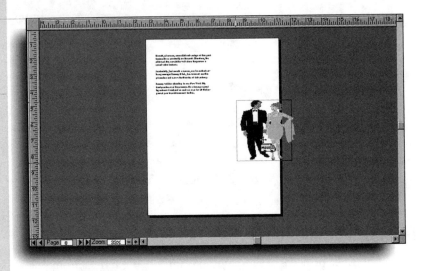

FIGURE 23.26

After you park the frame in the scratch area, you can move it back onto a different page.

Formatting Frames

Frames are handy because they offer a way to enclose text or pictures, giving you a lot of control over the way these elements appear.

But that's just the beginning. The frames themselves can also be an attractive and effective component of your publication. You can embellish the frames in your publication to create additional eye-catching effects.

Colorizing Frames

Graphics frames and text frames can both benefit from the extra pizzazz provided by color. You can fill the frame with color or add even more punch by using a texture along with the color.

Filling frames with color and texture

1. Select the frame you want to change, which causes a Formatting toolbar (either text or graphics) to appear in the Publisher window.

2. Click the Fill Color tool ⬙ to display the color palette (see Figure 23.27).

3. Click a color swatch to flood the frame with that color.

4. Choose **More Colors** to see the Colors dialog box, where you can manipulate values and settings to create your own colors.

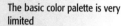

FIGURE 23.27

Select a color to fill the frame, or choose a more advanced option.

5. Choose **Fill Effects** to see the Fill Effects dialog box, where you can fine-tune the frame filler:

- Select **Tints/Shades** to tweak the hue a little bit at a time. Tints make colors a bit lighter, and shades make them a bit darker.

- Select **Patterns** to see an assortment of patterns you can use to give the frame a look of depth.

- Select **Gradients** to choose a background pattern that resembles an airbrushed painting. The intensity of the background color changes in a graduated format (see Figure 23.28).

The basic color palette is very limited

Publisher 98 uses design sets for publications, which means that colors are coordinated. The original display of the Fill Color tool is limited to your color scheme, and you must choose **More Colors** to see a full range of hues.

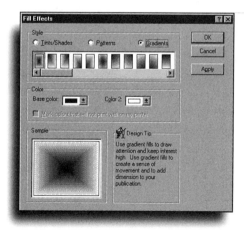

FIGURE 23.28

A gradient pattern gives a sense of depth to a frame.

6. Choose **OK** when you've made your selection to exit the Fill Effects dialog box.

Adding Borders to Frames

Another way to enhance a frame, which also enhances its contents, is to put a border on the frame. This is another decorative effect for which Publisher offers a slew of options.

Framing a frame

1. Select a frame (either text or graphics) to put the Formatting toolbar in the window.

2. To apply a plain border quickly, click the Line/Border Style tool  and select one of the four border widths offered on the drop-down list (see Figure 23.29).

FIGURE 23.29

A quick click of the mouse puts a border around the frame.

3. To approach this design with more alternatives, choose **More Styles** on the drop-down menu to see the Border Style dialog box shown in Figure 23.30.

FIGURE 23.30

The choices are more numerous, and more creative, when you use the Border Style dialog box.

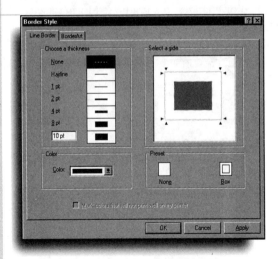

4. Choose a border thickness and color to put the border around the frame.

5. To put a border on selected sides of the frame, first select the sides by clicking the light gray border line that represents the side you want to border. To select additional sides, hold down the Shift key while you select.

6. Select the border thickness for the sides you've chosen.

7. Choose **OK** to close the dialog box and apply the border you've designed.

If that's not enough, you might want to put fancy artwork around a frame. Your choices are incredibly broad, and they're available in the same Border Style dialog box, on the **BorderArt** tab (see Figure 23.31).

Create a 3D effect

You can make two adjacent sides thin and the other two sides thick to create a 3D drop-shadow effect on your frames.

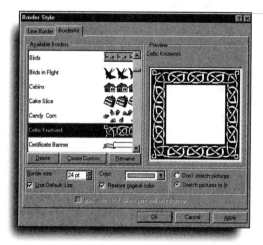

FIGURE 23.31
If I choose the right border, do you think I might be able to have the artwork from my newsletter hung in the National Gallery?

You can use the options on the **BorderArt** tab to fine-tune your decorative efforts:

- Use the **Border size** box to change the width.
- Click the arrow next to the **Color** box to choose a color from the palette.

The options for stretching or not stretching the pictures in the border vary, depending on the border, and it's best not to change them.

When you choose **OK**, the border is applied to the frame (see Figure 23.32).

Adding Special Text Elements

Publisher supports a couple of ways to enhance text that you'll find useful in many different types of publications: Bulleted/Numbered Lists and Tables.

FIGURE 23.32

The border adds a decided flair, and this page is beginning to look very slick.

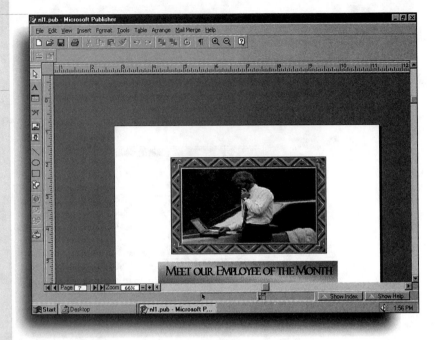

Using Bullets and Numbers

A list of items is just as boring to look at as to hear while a speaker drones through it. You can make each item in the list stand out and appear interesting by using bullets or numbers.

Applying bullets or numbers to a list

1. Select the text you want to convert to a bulleted or numbered list.

2. For a quick bulleted list, click the **Bullets** tool on the Formatting toolbar and choose a bullet character (see Figure 23.33).

FIGURE 23.33

Pick a character to use as a bullet.

3. For a more robust range of choices, select **More Bullets** from the drop-down menu to open the Indents and Lists dialog box shown in Figure 23.34.

FIGURE 23.34

You can impose total control on the formatting of your list

4. Choose **Bulleted List** to see those options, or select **Numbered List** if you want to enumerate each item in the list.

5. Select the options you need to make your list look professional and slick.

6. Choose **New Bullet** to scroll through the Publisher fonts and find a symbol font that has the character you want to use for a bullet.

7. Choose **Line Spacing** to change the amount of blank space between items on the list.

8. Choose **OK** to close the dialog box and apply the bullets or numbers to the selected text (see Figure 23.35).

Using Tables

Tables are incredibly useful because they make it easy to keep track of a lot of information without losing your place on the page.

Creating a table

1. Click the Table tool on the Objects toolbar.

2. Position your mouse pointer where you want the upper-left corner of the table to appear, and drag down and to the right to create a table of the right size.

FIGURE 23.35

This list won't get lost in the middle of all the text in the article.

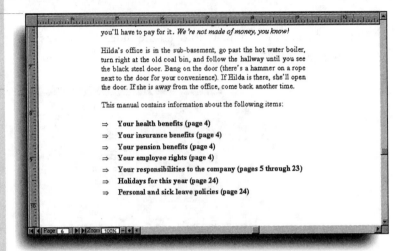

FIGURE 23.35

This list won't get lost in the middle of all the text in the article.

3. When you release the mouse, the Create Table dialog box appears (see Figure 23.36). Choose a style from the **Table format** listing, and then specify the settings you need for **Number of rows** and **Number of columns**.

FIGURE 23.36

Configure the settings for the table before you begin to enter data.

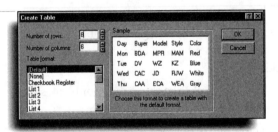

4. Choose **OK** to exit the dialog box and begin entering data in the table.

Data entry for a table is straightforward. Enter text and then use the Tab key to move to the next cell. Here are some guidelines you'll probably find helpful:

- You can format the table, any individual columns or rows, or any text with the normal text-formatting tools.

- As a shortcut, you can select an entire column or row by clicking its gray button (the top of a column or the left edge of a row). Formatting changes apply to the selected column or row.

- To repeat text in the top row of a column all the way down that column, select the column, open the **Table** menu, and choose **Fill Down**.

- To repeat text in the first column of a row all the way across that row, select the row, open the **Table** menu, and choose **Fill Right**.

- Choose **Insert Rows or Columns** from the **Table** menu to see a dialog box that offers options for expanding the size of the table.

Publisher tables grow with you

By default, the table expands to fit your text as you enter characters. You can turn that feature off by opening the **Table** menu and clicking **Grow to Fit Text** to deselect it. However, characters you type that don't fit in the cell will not be seen until you select that option again.

Adding Professional Touches to Your Publication

Grouping and Ungrouping Frames

As you design the elements in your publication, you spend a lot of time on each individual object to ensure it meets your standards of perfection.

The process involved in building an element frequently involves multiple objects. For example, a picture has a caption or a graphic has several shapes. Working with multiple elements can be difficult and time-consuming unless you know the tricks and shortcuts. Of course, this chapter covers those tricks and shortcuts or I wouldn't have mentioned them.

Understanding Layers

Many pages that contain multiple objects also have objects that overlap in some fashion. You might put an illustration in a story text box. You might have several graphics elements combined to create a snazzy eye-catching graphic.

When objects overlap, they have a pecking order imposed by Publisher—start at the bottom. That means the first object you place on the page is on the bottom layer, the next object is one layer up from the bottom, and so on.

As an example, look at the two pages shown in Figure 24.1. The left page contains the individual elements for building a graphic house (the house, a window, and a door). The right page contains the results when the window and door were dragged onto the house.

FIGURE 24.1

The door disappeared—there's no way to enter this house.

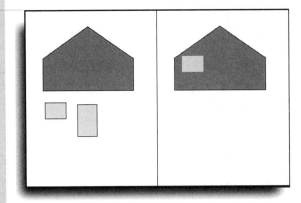

I can look at the right page and determine the order in which the elements were created on the left page. It's obvious that—from first to last—the order was door, house, window.

Big deal—I can figure it out, but can I fix it? I certainly don't want to re-create the elements. More important, I don't want to have to worry about the order in which I create elements when I'm working with text, pictures, headlines, shapes, and so on.

Luckily, Publisher has a fix. You can change the order in which objects are layered.

Changing the order of layered objects

1. Select one of the objects that is layered incorrectly (you probably can't see what's on the bottom so you must use one of the objects on the top and move it down). This is what I had to do to make the missing door appear on the house.

2. Choose **Ar̲range** from the menu bar to see the menu choices shown in Figure 24.2.

FIGURE 24.2

Publisher provides four ways to move an object to a different layer.

3. Choose the command that matches the manipulation you need, using the following guidelines:

   - Choose **Bring to Fron̲t** to make the selected object the top-most object.

   - Choose **Send to Bac̲k** to place the selected object on the bottom layer.

   - Choose **Bring F̲orward** to move the selected object one layer up from its present location.

   - Choose **Send B̲ackward** to move the selected object back one layer from its present location.

After selecting the door in Step 1, I would use **Bring to Front** to make the door appear.

If you have only two layers, making an object jump from front to back is sufficient, of course. The command options that allow you to move objects up or down through the layers by degrees are used for multiple layers. Sometimes you have to repeat a command to move closer or farther more than once; for instance, you may need to move an object from the fifth layer to the third layer.

Grouping Objects

There are frequently elements on a page that belong together and, in fact, can't live without each other. Some of them are obvious, such as a set of graphics elements you arrange in an interlocking manner. Others are not so obvious, such as the relationship between a picture and its caption or a headline and its accompanying illustration. Figure 24.3 shows a spread with an example of both types of interrelated arrangements.

Shortcuts for changing layer position

Press F6 to bring an object to the top, and use Shift+F6 to send an object to the back.

FIGURE 24.3
The elements on the left page are obviously interdependent, but less obvious is the interdependency between the headline and illustration on the right page.

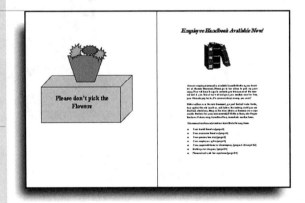

Suppose you have to move interdependent objects. Or, even worse, suppose you have to make them smaller to make room for more text or another element. Making each part of an element smaller (or larger) by the same amount is a time-consuming, tedious, nerve-wracking job.

Grouping makes it possible to get the job done and keep your sanity. Grouping is a way to "marry" elements so whatever you do to one element, you do to all.

Creating a Group

You can tell Publisher which items you want to place in a group by either of two ways:

- Draw a box around all the elements you want to include (see Figure 24.4). First, place your mouse pointer at the top left edge of the area to encompass. Then press and hold the left mouse button while dragging the box over all the items you want to include in the group.

- Select the elements one at a time by holding down the Shift key as you click each element.

FIGURE 24.4
Throw your lasso and tighten it around all the elements you want to group.

Publisher creates the group with the following characteristics (see Figure 24.5):

- The Group Objects button is placed at the bottom of the group.

- When you move your mouse over any individual element in the group, the pointer is a moving van.

- A light gray line and sizing handles appear around the entire group.

- Sizing handles appear around each individual element in the group.

FIGURE 24.5
Each element and the group itself are delineated with sizing handles.

Working with a Temporary Group

When you create a group, it's a temporary group. As soon as you left-click your mouse anywhere (including on an element in the group), a divorce is issued and this marriage no longer exists.

You can perform the following manipulations on the group:

- Drag it to a new location (the mouse pointer is a moving van whenever it's positioned over any element).
- Right-click any element in the group and choose **Cut** or **Copy** from the shortcut menu. Then right-click and choose **Paste** at the target location.

Note that you cannot resize the group (those sizing handles are grayed out, meaning they're inaccessible).

Making a Group Permanent

Most of the time you'll want to retain the group in case you have to move or resize it again, so make the group permanent by clicking the Group Objects button. The two puzzle pieces on the button now fit together.

When a group is permanent, the sizing handles around the group are accessible and you can resize the group—every element in the group changes in size proportionately.

To ungroup a permanent group, click the Group Objects button to separate the puzzle pieces. Then click anywhere outside the group. (You can also select a group, open the **Arrange** menu, and then choose **Ungroup Objects**.)

Arranging Objects on a Page

Neatness counts. In fact, neatness is one of the rules when you're creating a publication. The elements of a page have to line up properly or your publication screams "an amateur prepared this."

Lining Up Objects

When you have a group of objects on a page that are positioned sloppily, you can line them up by using any of several schemes.

However, the procedure works only on a group of objects that is arranged either horizontally or vertically. You can't do two things at once. For example, Figure 24.6 shows two pages with objects that need to be lined up.

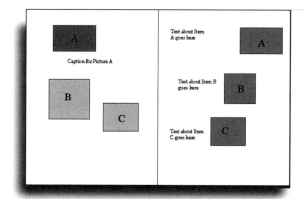

FIGURE 24.6
Neither page is ready for prime time.

On the left page, box A needs to be in the center of its row. Boxes B and C must be aligned neatly side by side below box A. This page requires two separate actions; you can't accomplish everything at once.

On the right page, all the boxes need to be aligned properly in a vertical manner. It only takes one process to accomplish that.

Let's look at the steps required to make these two pages look more professional.

Lining up objects

1. Select the objects you want to work on by clicking the objects one by one while holding down the Shift key (or by dragging a box around the objects). When you release the mouse button, the objects are grouped (see Figure 24.7).

FIGURE 24.7

The first group of objects is selected, ready to be lined up properly.

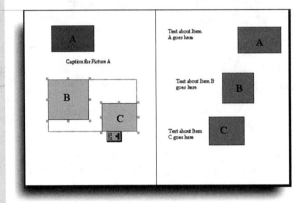

2. Open the **A̲rrange** menu and choose **A̲lign Objects**.

3. When the Align Objects dialog box appears (see Figure 24.8), select the alignment scheme you want to impose, using these guidelines:

FIGURE 24.8

The dialog box offers plenty of choices for making your page shipshape.

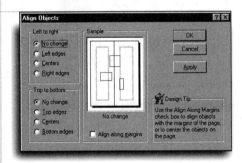

- The objects are lined up in relation to one another unless you check the **Align along m̲argins** check box.

- Choose a horizontal alignment (left to right) if the objects are arranged one under another on the page. They'll line up neatly, using the scheme you chose.

- Choose a vertical alignment (top to bottom) if the objects are next to each other on the page.

4. For the selected objects in this example, select an option from the **Top to Bottom** section of the dialog box:

- Choose **Top Edges** to place the tops of the frames on the same imaginary line. The position of the sides and bottom edge of each frame is dependent on its size.

- Choose **Centers** to draw an imaginary horizontal line through the center of each frame and line them up. The other edges are positioned depending on the individual sizes of the frames.

- Choose **Bottom Edges** to place the bottom of each frame on the same imaginary line.

- Select **Align Along Margins** to align the top, center, or bottom of each frame along the appropriate margin.

5. Choose **OK** when you have made your selection. The objects are aligned to match your choice. If you don't like the results, click the **Undo** icon on the toolbar and start again.

6. Select the next set of objects and repeat the process, choosing the appropriate options.

There are no rights and wrongs—this is really a matter of preference. When you finish aligning all the objects, however, there should be some sense to the scheme. The most important reason for neatness is to arrange things so that readers can understand and follow the information. The results of this exercise are shown in Figure 24.9. For the group on the left, I chose **Bottom Edges** from the Top to Bottom options; for the group on the right, I chose **Right Edges** from the Left to Right options.

Nudging Objects

Sometimes I want two objects to be lined up in a very precise way, but what I mean by *precise* is "exactly the way I envision it, not necessarily along some guideline." I move each object a bit at a time, getting closer and closer. The closer I get, the harder it gets. It seems that whenever I have to drag a very tiny distance

FIGURE 24.9

This alignment pattern is orderly enough to ensure that reading the assortment of information won't be difficult.

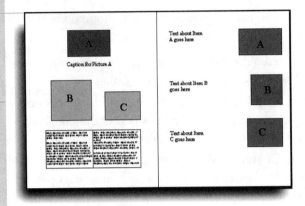

with my mouse, I lose control a little bit and overshoot the mark. The process of adjusting both objects can go on for a very long time.

Publisher provides a feature that allows you to nudge objects along a path without using your mouse, which is a real boon.

The quickest way to nudge an object is to select it and then hold down the Alt key as you press the appropriate arrow key. The object moves 0.13" each time you press the arrow key, which is a very small step.

You can, however, change the measurement for the size of the move if you want to move in larger or smaller increments. The default measurement is set in the Nudge Objects dialog box, and I've found it's a good idea to test the new measurement while I'm in the dialog box. That way I can keep adjusting until I get the right movement.

Nudging objects

1. Select the object you want to nudge.

2. Open the **A<u>r</u>range** menu and choose **Nudge**.

3. When the Nudge dialog box opens, drag it to a position on your window where it doesn't hide the object you're trying to nudge (see Figure 24.10).

4. Select the **Nudge by** check box to make the text box available, and specify a new measurement.

5. Click the appropriate arrow on the dialog box and watch the effect on the selected object.

The nudge factor

Although you can change the default **Nudge by** number, you can't reset it unless you remember what it was (0.13"). When you change the number, it remains that way until you change it again. Neither opening a new publication nor closing and reopening Publisher will reset the number.

FIGURE 24.10
You can keep an eye on the results as you use the dialog box.

6. Continue to adjust the measurement and watch the results until the nudging factor is satisfactory to you.

7. Choose **Close**. The measurement you specified becomes the new default measurement for Alt-key nudging.

Using Snap To

The Snap To feature is a way to force objects to line up against a guideline. I've found this feature to be invaluable for publications in which some objects must be in a specific position on every page.

For example, if you're doing a newsletter or an annual report where the top of each page has a heading and a picture under the heading, it's much slicker if the heading and pictures always line up the same way. Even if these objects vary in width or height, putting the top of the heading and the top of the picture in the same place on every page looks extremely professional.

In effect, you make this happen by inserting a guideline. Then the edge of an object and your guideline become magnetized. As soon as they get close to each other—SNAP!—they line up. You can use guidelines or ruler marks as your magnetic guides.

There are three Snap To options available on the **Tools** menu, each representing a different type of guide:

- **Snap to Ruler Marks**
- **Snap to Guides**
- **Snap to Objects**

By default, the Ruler Marks and Guides features are enabled, but you must create the marks and guides to make the feature operational.

Using Ruler Marks

Ruler marks (also called ruler guides, which is a better description) are created for individual pages. There's no such thing as a global ruler guide. If you're using the Two-Page Spread view, the ruler guides cover both pages.

Use ruler guides for those pages where objects must be snapped into place at exactly the measured positions you require.

Creating ruler guides

1. Hold down the Shift key and move your mouse pointer to either ruler.

2. When the mouse pointer changes to an Adjust pointer, press the left mouse button and drag the ruler onto your page (see Figure 24.11).

FIGURE 24.11

Drag the ruler guide to exactly the position you need (use the other ruler as a measurement reference).

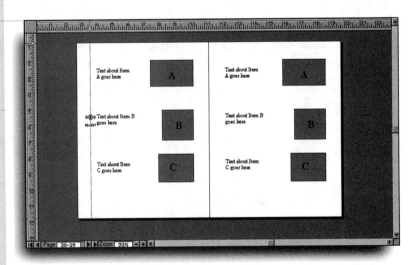

3. Release the mouse button at the position where you need the guide (check the measurement on the other ruler).

4. If you need both horizontal and vertical ruler guides, repeat the process with the other ruler.

The ruler guide is visible on the page as a green line, but don't worry—it doesn't print.

- Adjust the position of the ruler guide by holding down the Shift key and placing your pointer on the guide. Then drag the guide to the new position.

- Remove the ruler guide by holding down the Shift key and placing your pointer on the guide. Then drag the guide back onto the ruler.

After you've created the ruler guide, you can move objects to it without worrying about the need to move too precisely. When an object gets near the ruler guide, it snaps to it (see Figure 24.12). Check the **Tools** menu first, to make sure the **Snap to Ruler Marks** option has a check mark indicating it's enabled. (If it doesn't, click the command to put a check mark next to it; this command is a toggle—click once to turn it on, click again to turn it off.)

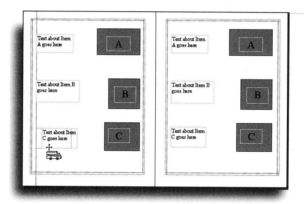

Figure 24.12
The virtual magnets take over as soon as an object gets close to a ruler guide.

You're not limited to one ruler guide in each direction—you can insert as many as you need. Multiple ruler guides are a great way to align a lot of objects on a page, because you can separate the objects by using ruler measurements instead of eyeballing them.

As an example, the group of objects on the left side of Figure 24.13 was created without any attention to the placement of each object (which is a much faster way to work). The group on the right is the result of placing ruler guides that are mathematically correct for the number of rows and columns on the page.

If you have the Snap To option enabled, you won't be able to position any object near the guide. When the object gets close, it will snap to the guide. You either have to move the object a good distance from the guide or turn off the option.

FIGURE 24.13

The choice is yours—quick and disorderly (left) or picture-perfect by using ruler guides (right).

Using Layout Guides

Layout guides work the same as ruler guides, except they're global to the publication. When you create a layout guide, it appears on every page. To force anything to appear on every page, whether it's a guideline or a real object, you must work on the background page. The background page is actually a layer that appears behind every page in a publication.

SEE ALSO

➤ *To learn more about using the background page, see page xx*

Creating layout guides

1. Press Ctrl+M to move to the background page.

2. Open the **Arrange** menu and choose **Layout Guides** to bring up the Layout Guides dialog box (see Figure 24.14).

3. Change the page margins by specifying new numbers. (See the next discussion in this section, "Why change margins?")

4. Break up the page or create a grid by indicating the number of columns and rows you need. The lines for columns and rows are applied equidistantly in the dialog box, but you can change them later. See the discussion on "Using Layout Guide Grid Lines" later in this section.

5. Mirror the left and right pages by selecting the **Create Two Backgrounds With Mirrored Guides** option.

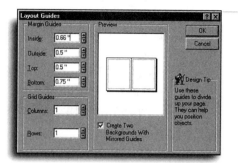

FIGURE 24.14
Create guides to ensure
precision placement of
all the objects throughout
the publication.

6. Choose **OK** when you have finished filling out the dialog box.

7. Press Ctrl+M to leave the background page and return to your publication page.

Why Change Margins?

Changing margins with layout guides isn't the same thing as changing the margins for the paper you're using when you print your publication. All you're doing with layout guide margins is restricting the placement of objects on the publication pages. In addition, you use the guidelines for the Snap To feature to make your pages neat and consistent.

The answer to the question "Why change margins?" is "Because there's an element on the background you don't want to hide." If there's no background element, don't change the margins.

I've seen lots of publications that used background elements on every page, and I'll mention some of the common ones so you can steal the ideas for yourself. At the same time, you can visualize the margin you'd have to change to make use of these ideas:

- *A decorative wide stripe of color running down the outside edge.* Remember that "outside edge" means the left edge for even-numbered pages and the right edge for odd-numbered pages. Visualizing this should also help you understand mirrored pages. The outside margin of your page must be moved toward the center of the page so there are no objects on top of the background stripe.

- *A logo in the outside bottom corner of each page.* This requires bringing in the outside and bottom margins with layout guides.

- *A running header or footer with titles or other text (perhaps combined with a small graphic).* Apply the appropriate margin change for your layout guides.

Remember that, in addition to acting as a boundary, layout guide margin lines also are your magnets when you want to use the Snap To feature on the objects you're placing on the page.

Using Layout Guide Grid Lines

Using the **Columns** and **Rows** options in the Layout Guides dialog box provides a way to indicate placement rules as you add elements to your publication. For example, consider the following approaches for a publication:

- *There is a consistent design that requires a graphic on the top of each page and text for the remaining portion of the page.* Set yourself up with a grid line at the separation point.

- *Your publication requires a section at the bottom of each page for notes or citations or other "small type" elements.* Establish a grid line to keep that separation consistent.

- *The background page contains a color stripe about a third of the way down from the top (a creative device when every page has a headline or art work at the top). The stripe offers consistency in separating the element at the top from the text at the bottom.* Set a layout guide grid line for the top of the stripe and another for the bottom of the stripe so you don't place objects within the stripe area.

Of course, in addition to providing a boundary, the grid lines are used for the Snap To feature, making your pages neat and professional.

Adjusting Layout Guides

When you set your options in the dialog box, you have no opportunity to specify the placement of column or row lines. After the dialog box closes, your background page displays evenly placed guides; however, you can manipulate the lines to match the placement you need.

Moving layout guides

1. Check the Status bar to make sure you're working on the background page. If you're not, press Ctrl+M.

2. Hold down the Shift key and move your mouse pointer to the line you want to reposition.

3. When the mouse pointer changes to an Adjust pointer, drag the line to a new location (see Figure 24.15).

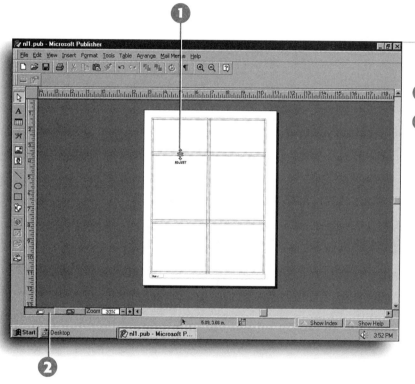

FIGURE 24.15
Take control of your guide!

1 Adjust pointer

2 Background page indicator

4. Repeat the process for each grid line you want to move.

5. Press Ctrl+M to return to the publication page and continue your work.

To use layout guides while you're working in your publication, make sure the **Snap to Guides** feature is selected in the **Tools** menu. Then just move an object near the guide, and it will Snap To.

Using Snap to Objects

Sometimes you need to make sure objects are positioned right next to each other, or one atop the other, with no space between them. You could drag or nudge the objects for a very long time, trying to accomplish this.

It's easier to let the objects use the Snap To feature. When you use this feature, you need only get the objects close enough to feel the attraction for each other. They'll take care of the rest all by themselves.

All you have to do is turn on the feature by opening the **Tools** menu and then choosing the **Snap to Objects** command.

Using Word Wrap

One of the most professional touches you can add to your publication is *word wrap*. This isn't the same concept used in word processing to describe the way a sentence moves to the next line automatically. In Publisher, word wrap means wrapping text around graphics.

Wrapping Text Around Picture Frames

Wrapping text around a graphics frame

1. Create a graphics frame within a text frame (put a picture in it), or move an existing graphic onto a text frame.

2. If the graphics frame isn't on top, press F6 to bring it to the front.

3. Click the graphics frame to select it. The Formatting toolbar (specialized for graphics) appears, with the Wrap Text to Frame tool enabled by default. You can see the automatic text wrapping in Figure 24.16.

Adjusting the Text Wrap Margins

You can push the text away from the figure if everything seems a bit crowded. This is accomplished by adjusting the margins inside the picture frame. By default, pictures can touch the frame—there are no margins. However, if you create margins for the picture frame, the picture moves away from the edge and creates some empty space between itself and the frame. The effect creates space between the picture and the text that's wrapping around it.

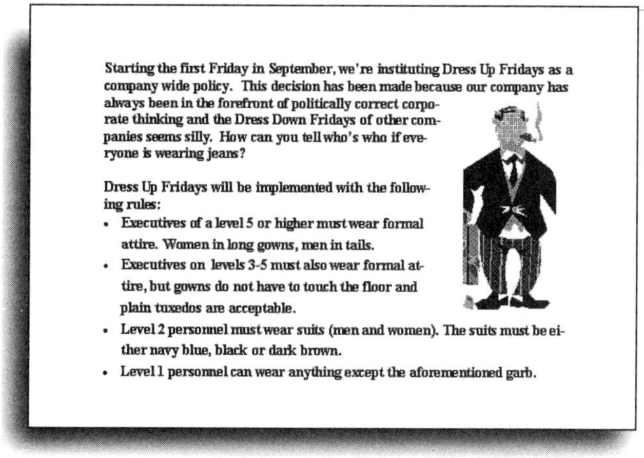

Starting the first Friday in September, we're instituting Dress Up Fridays as a company wide policy. This decision has been made because our company has always been in the forefront of politically correct corporate thinking and the Dress Down Fridays of other companies seems silly. How can you tell who's who if everyone is wearing jeans?

Dress Up Fridays will be implemented with the following rules:

- Executives of a level 5 or higher must wear formal attire. Women in long gowns, men in tails.
- Executives on levels 3-5 must also wear formal attire, but gowns do not have to touch the floor and plain tuxedos are acceptable.
- Level 2 personnel must wear suits (men and women). The suits must be either navy blue, black or dark brown.
- Level 1 personnel can wear anything except the aforementioned garb.

FIGURE 24.16
The frame of the graphic acts as a barrier, and text cannot get past it.

Adjusting the margins for a picture frame

1. Click the graphics frame to select it, and choose the Object Frame Properties button on the Formatting toolbar.

2. When the Object Frame Properties dialog box appears (see Figure 24.17), increase the size of any margin that has text too close to its edge.

3. Choose **OK** to save your changes and close the dialog box.

Move the frame to make the text readable

If your frame interrupts the text and you end up with text on both sides, move the frame to an edge to put all the text on one side. You could also center the frame to balance the text on both sides, but that's frequently difficult to read.

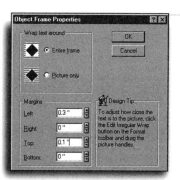

FIGURE 24.17
You can fine-tune the space between the frame and the text.

Wrapping Around the Picture

Sometimes it's more effective to wrap text around the picture instead of around the frame. This gives an interesting irregular margin to the text that abuts the picture. Instead of a boring straight line, the text margin dips and waves.

However, as you'll see, this frequently presents some minor problems, so you'll probably have to tweak the arrangement a bit.

To wrap the text around the graphic itself instead of around the frame, click the Wrap Text to Picture button on the Formatting toolbar. The text snuggles up to the picture, wrapping itself around all sides of it (see Figure 24.18).

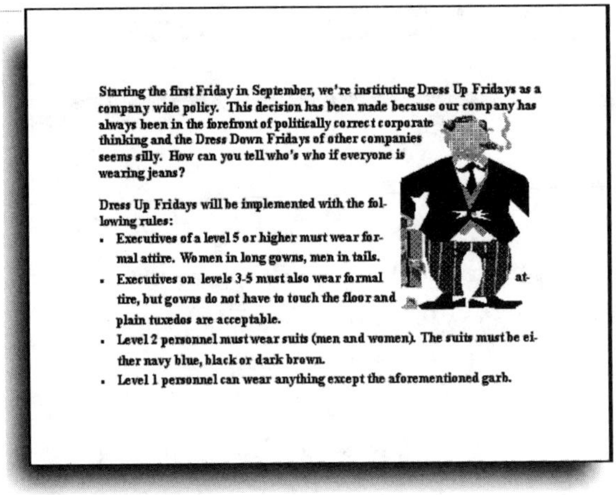

FIGURE 24.18
Without the frame, the text wraps irregularly.

Wrapping text around the graphic doesn't always work particularly well. Sometimes moving the picture fixes the problem. Sometimes it's necessary to adjust the text frame to change its word-wrap properties (select the text frame and then use the sizing handles to narrow or widen the frame).

Editing Irregular Wraps

When you choose to wrap text around a picture instead of a frame, Publisher provides a new tool to help you tweak the appearance of the wrap. As soon as you select the Wrap Text to Picture tool, the Crop tool on the toolbar disappears, and a new tool, Edit Irregular Wrap, is available. You can use this tool to change the position of the text that surrounds the picture.

If neither of those remedies make the result more attractive, you can try one more thing before deciding your page is too ugly to print—you can change the way the text flows around the picture. One thing to keep in mind—this doesn't work with WordArt objects.

Editing the flow of wrapped text

1. Select the picture by clicking anywhere on it.
2. Click the Edit Irregular Wrap tool on the Formatting toolbar. The outline around the picture changes to display multiple sizing handles (see Figure 24.19).

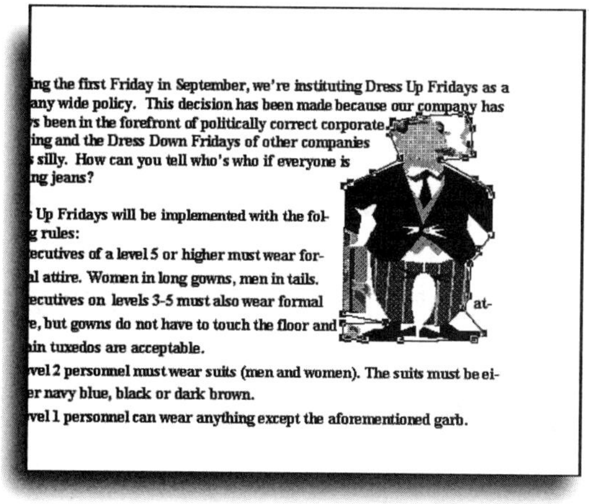

FIGURE 24.19
Use the sizing handles to move the outline that the text is using to determine its wrap.

3. Place your mouse pointer over a sizing handle, which turns the pointer into an Adjust pointer.
4. Drag the sizing handle in the appropriate direction, either forcing text away or bringing it closer.
5. Continue to move the outline until the text wraps in the proper fashion.
6. Click anywhere outside the figure to deselect it and see your results.

The trick to this maneuver is that if you push text far enough away, it rewraps itself to the other side of the picture. To make this even easier, decrease the margin between the picture and its outline boundary on the other side, creating more room for text wrap on that side.

For example, the picture displayed in Figure 24.19 originally had small bits of text wrapped on the right side of the figure. Editing the right and left edges of the outline forced all that text to rewrap on the left side of the picture (see Figure 24.20).

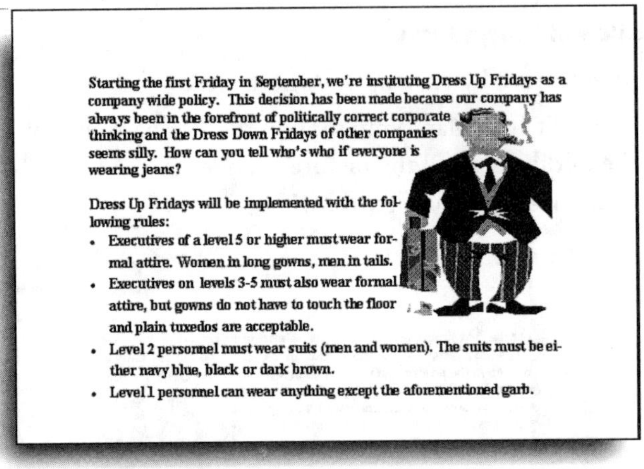

FIGURE 24.20

Now the right text margin is nicely irregular, and no text spills over to the right side of the picture.

Starting the first Friday in September, we're instituting Dress Up Fridays as a company wide policy. This decision has been made because our company has always been in the forefront of politically correct corporate thinking and the Dress Down Fridays of other companies seems silly. How can you tell who's who if everyone is wearing jeans?

Dress Up Fridays will be implemented with the following rules:

- Executives of a level 5 or higher must wear formal attire. Women in long gowns, men in tails.
- Executives on levels 3-5 must also wear formal attire, but gowns do not have to touch the floor and plain tuxedos are acceptable.
- Level 2 personnel must wear suits (men and women). The suits must be either navy blue, black or dark brown.
- Level 1 personnel can wear anything except the aforementioned garb.

Continuing Text in Other Frames

Okay, you're typing merrily in a text frame and all of a sudden you can't see what you're typing. There are no beeps or error messages and you can continue to type, but you can't see what you're doing, because your text is being displayed below your line of vision. No scroll bar is available for moving down, and the arrow keys don't take you to your last line of typing.

You've run out of text frame.

Publisher allows you to continue to type because there's an assumption that you'll probably adjust everything to make sure all your typing appears somewhere in your publication. And, of course, Publisher provides the features to make that assumption a reality.

Your text is in a holding area. Publisher provides a holding area so you can create the text for your publications without worrying about placement.

- Newsletter stories can begin on the front page and continue on another page inside the newsletter.

- Two-page publications can be designed without worrying about fitting the complete text for a subject on one side.

- Multiple text frames can be sized to fit a design plan without worrying about cutting text to fit into each frame. You can use a second frame of a different size to finish your article.

Being able to move text among frames to preserve the design makes it possible to create professional-looking publications.

Working with Overflow Text

As you continue to type and run out of room in the frame, Publisher stores the text you can't see. It indicates that there are characters being held in the overflow area by displaying a Text in Overflow indicator (see Figure 24.21).

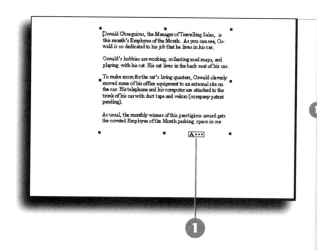

FIGURE 24.21

I'm typing below the bottom of the frame and the Text in Overflow indicator tells me that my text is being saved for me.

1 Text in Overflow indicator

When text is held in the overflow area, you have to find someplace to put it. You can use another text frame on the same page or another text frame on a different page, or you can create a new text frame on any page.

Work around the "hidden typing" feature

You can expand the text frame you're working on so you can see what you're typing (even beyond the bottom of the page), or you can change the font to a very small size. When your text is complete, you can resize the font or the text box and take care of the overflow text.

This feature works very well if you like to create your text outside of Publisher and then copy and paste it into Publisher text frames.

Moving overflow text to a new frame

1. Create a new text frame to hold the text. If you want to create a new page for the overflow text, open the **Insert** menu and choose **Page**. In the Insert Page dialog box (see Figure 24.22), select **Create one text frame on each page** and then specify the number of new pages and where they should be placed.

2. Publisher moves you to the new page, so use the Page Control arrow to move back to the page with the overflowing text frame. Select the text box.

3. Open the **Tools** menu and choose **Text Frame Connecting** to bring up the Connect Frames toolbar. Then click the Connect Text Frames button (it looks like a chain link). Your mouse pointer turns into a pitcher (see Figure 24.23).

FIGURE 24.22

Create the text box you need while you're creating the page you need.

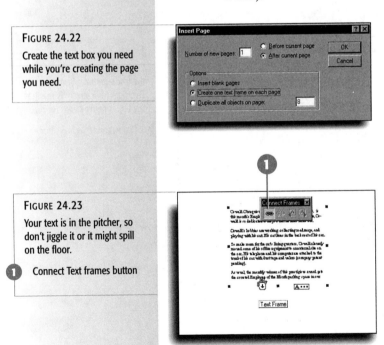

FIGURE 24.23

Your text is in the pitcher, so don't jiggle it or it might spill on the floor.

① Connect Text frames button

4. Move to the text frame you want to use for the rest of the text. The pitcher is ready to pour your text into the frame (see Figure 24.24). Click anywhere in the frame to have it accept the text.

FIGURE 24.24
The overflow text and the empty frame merge as soon as you click your mouse.

The top of the new frame displays a connect button with an arrow pointing left, indicating that this frame is connected to a previous frame. The connect button on the first frame has a similar connect button, with the arrow pointing right. You can click these arrows to move quickly between the frames.

Check the bottom of the new frame to make sure the bottom connect button displays a diamond. If the button has three dots, there is still overflow text you have to take care of.

Adding Continued Notices

When you create a multipage publication such as a newsletter, it's common to have an article or story overflow its text frame. Usually these publications have multiple columns and each column contains a separate story, instead of dedicating the entire page to one story.

It's traditional to tell the reader where to find the rest of the story, using the phrase "Continued on . . .." Standard practices for publishing also include the phrase "Continued from . . ." at the beginning of the continuation.

You can insert these features into your publication.

Adding Continued notices

1. To add a "Continued On" notice, move to the first text frame and click the Text Frame Properties button on the Formatting toolbar.

Other solutions for overflow text

If the amount of overflow text is minimal, it's probably just as easy to adjust the frame size, make the font smaller, or cut some copy.

2. In the Text Frame Properties dialog box (see Figure 24.25), select the **Include "Continued on page"** option.

3. Move to the connected frame and repeat the process, selecting **Include "Continued from page"** in the dialog box.

4. Click **OK** to save the changes.

FIGURE 24.25

It's easy to insert a Continued notice in a connected frame.

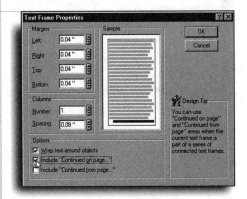

Publisher adds the correct page numbers automatically and places the special text properly (see Figure 24.26).

If you have more than two connected frames on separate pages, remember to add both notices to all but the first and last frames.

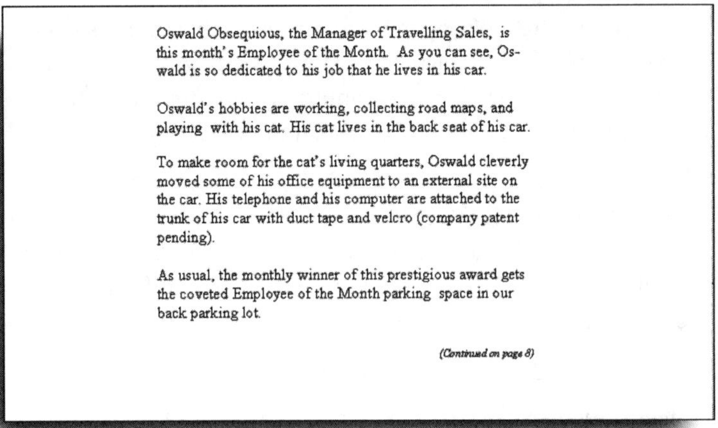

FIGURE 24.26

Continued notices are formatted and positioned professionally, matching the style used by magazines and newspapers.

Oswald Obsequious, the Manager of Travelling Sales, is this month's Employee of the Month. As you can see, Oswald is so dedicated to his job that he lives in his car.

Oswald's hobbies are working, collecting road maps, and playing with his cat. His cat lives in the back seat of his car.

To make room for the cat's living quarters, Oswald cleverly moved some of his office equipment to an external site on the car. His telephone and his computer are attached to the trunk of his car with duct tape and velcro (company patent pending).

As usual, the monthly winner of this prestigious award gets the coveted Employee of the Month parking space in our back parking lot.

(Continued on page 8)

Changing the Continued Notices

You can edit the wording or formatting of the Continued notice if you want something unique.

Editing Continued notices

1. Select the text of the notice, but don't select the page number (it's not really text, it's a code). Note that the Style box on the Formatting toolbar displays the style **Continued-On Text**.

2. Change the text to whatever you want it to be.

3. Change the formatting of the text if you want to enlarge it, change the font, or make any other formatting changes.

4. If you want your formatting changes to be permanent for all Continued On notices instead of applied only to this instance, choose the **Continued-On Text** style from the **Style** text box.

5. The **Change Or Apply Style** dialog box opens (see Figure 24.27). Select **Change the style using the selection as an example**. Then choose **OK**.

6. Repeat the process for the Continued From notice if you want to make changes there.

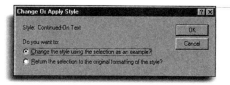

FIGURE 24.27
Make the formatting changes permanent by applying them to the style.

If you accidentally delete the page number from a Continued notice while editing, place your pointer in the appropriate position, open the **Insert** menu, and choose **Page Numbers**. The correct number is automatically placed in the text.

Adding Special Effects

Using the Design Gallery

Need a sparkling centerpiece to liven up a page filled with technical information? How about a terrific piece of abstract art to add zing to a headline? Fancy borders, backgrounds for titles, forms for customer replies, and even prebuilt tables of contents are waiting for you in the Publisher art museum, the Design Gallery.

To pay a visit, click the Design Gallery Object button on the Objects toolbar (see Figure 25.1).

FIGURE 25.1

Welcome to the world of doodads, fancy borders, and spiffy graphics.

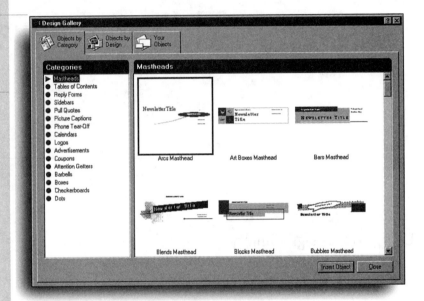

Before you scroll through the categories, take a moment to get acquainted with the other gallery wings. Move to the **Objects by Design** tab to see the available design sets (see Figure 25.2).

Placing Designs in Your Publication

When you need an eye-catching design for that blank spot on your page, add it to your publication. Perhaps you need a form that readers can use to fill out credit card information, or just a fancy graphic for a headline.

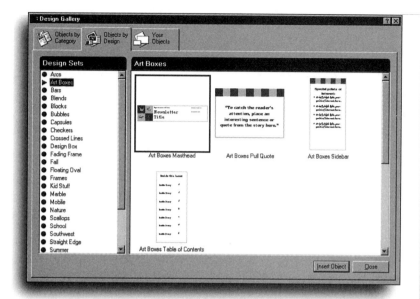

FIGURE 25.2
You can choose objects with styles and colors that match.

Inserting a design object

1. Be sure the page that needs the object is in the Publisher window and then click the Design Gallery Object tool on the Objects toolbar.

2. On the **Objects by Category** tab, select a category and then use the scrollbar to move through the available designs for that category. When you find the one you want to use, select it and choose the **Insert Object** button.

3. The design is placed into your publication and you can position it exactly where you need it (see Figure 25.3).

Creating Your Own Gallery Designs

Once in a while, either because you're a good designer or because you just had a great accidental stroke of luck, you create a design from scratch that's really nifty. It took forever to do, so you don't want to do all the work again if you ever need it in the future. Don't worry, you can put your design into the Design Gallery and bring it out again when you need it.

FIGURE 25.3

This order form can be edited to remove any credit cards you don't accept.

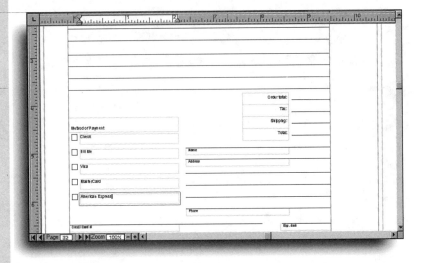

Adding your own design to the gallery

1. Use your imagination, with clip art or a WordArt frame or a shape, to create a magnificent design. Then click the design to select it.

2. Choose Design Gallery Object from the Objects toolbar.

3. Move to the tab named **Your Objects** and choose the **Options** button to see the Options menu (Figure 25.4).

FIGURE 25.4

There are several options for manipulating designs you place in your own gallery wing.

4. Choose **Add Selection to Design Gallery**. The Add Object dialog box appears, with the object you selected in your publication displayed in the preview box (see Figure 25.5).

5. In the **Object name** text box, type a name for your design. In the **Category** text box, choose the category you want to assign to the design, and then choose **OK**. If this is the first design you're adding to this gallery, there are no existing

categories, so you must invent a category name before you can assign the design to a category.

6. Your creation is inserted in your gallery (see Figure 25.6).

FIGURE 25.5

Name your creation and assign it to a category.

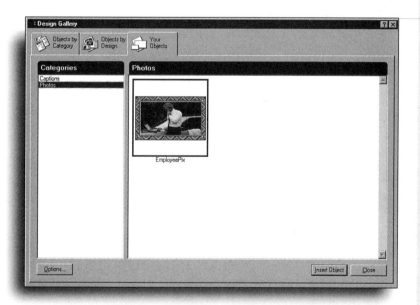

FIGURE 25.6

As you add more designs and categories, your gallery wing begins to look like the main wings.

7. Choose **Close** to return to your publication.

You can add as many designs as you please to the gallery for this publication. Any time you're working in this publication, you can choose an element from the **Your Objects** tab of the Design Gallery.

You can repeat this process for every publication you create; however, the objects that display include only the objects for the current publication. There is no way to see a list of all the objects you've created across all your publications.

Of course, that makes you ask, "What if I need a design from one publication when I'm working with a different publication?" And, of course, I have the answer: "It's easy."

Using a design from a different publication

1. Choose the Design Gallery Object tool from the Objects toolbar.

2. Move to the **Your Objects** tab.

3. Choose **Options** and then choose **Browse** from the pop-up **Options** menu.

4. The Other Designs dialog box opens so you can view a list of all your publications (see Figure 25.7).

FIGURE 25.7

The Other Designs dialog box works just like a traditional Windows Open dialog box.

5. Double-click the name of the publication that has the gallery you want to visit. You are returned to the Design Gallery, where styles from that publication's design set are displayed. If the publication you chose does not have a design set, Publisher displays a message informing you that no design set was found.

6. Select the design you need to import into your current publication and choose the **Insert Object** button.

7. Your selection is placed in the current publication.

Adding a Calendar

You can add a calendar to a publication to inform your readers about events or special dates. To help you configure your calendar, a wizard asks questions and offers choices.

Designing a calendar

1. Open the Design Gallery and select **Calendars**. Choose a style from the available offerings. You might prefer something more bold than formal, or you might want to go out on a limb and pick something really splashy.

2. Choose the **Insert Object** button to place the calendar in your publication. Then click the Wizard button to start the wizard (see Figure 25.8).

FIGURE 25.8
After the basic design is placed in your publication, use the wizard to configure it.

3. The wizard opens and you can choose whether you want to work on the design or the dates. If you opt to change the **Design**, you see the same choices you saw in the Design Gallery (just pick a different design). If you opt to change **Dates**, choose the **Change Dates** button to select the month and year for your calendar.

4. Close the wizard by clicking the x in the upper-right corner.

Other special elements

In addition to the calendar, the Design Gallery includes several other elements that are more useful than decorative. Take the time to check out Coupons, Advertisements, and Logos.

Using Background Pages

The only way to understand and use *background pages* in Publisher is to absorb two important facts:

- The pages you work on as you create your publication are transparent.
- All your pages share the same background page (although you can create mirrored background pages to enhance any odd/even page layout or margin differences you create).

Because the pages you work on are transparent, anything you put behind them shows through. It's like that kids' toy where you draw on plastic with a stylus and then pick up the plastic to make everything disappear so you can start drawing again. If you were to paint a big red dot on the cardboard behind the plastic, you'd see the big red dot whenever you draw on the plastic.

Because all your pages share the same background page, anything you want to appear on every page of your publication can be placed on the background page. If you're using mirrored pages, it means your page numbers will be on the left for even-numbered pages and on the right for odd-numbered pages. If you create a graphic designed to run down the side, it will appear on the outside edge (the left of even pages, the right of odd pages).

This all works extremely well and efficiently, providing a place to add page numbers, descriptive text, or graphics.

You can use your imagination as you decide on the various ways you can make use of the background page. The two common uses are page numbers and watermarks. *Watermarks* are usually pale objects that are not designed to be dominant, very much like watermarks on good bond paper.

Move to the background page by pressing Ctrl+M (and move back to your working page with the same key combination—it's a toggle). You can also open the **View** menu and select **Go to Background**. You can't tell the difference between a background page and a blank regular page when you look at them, so Publisher keeps you informed by removing the page controls and replacing them with the background page symbol (see Figure 25.9).

FIGURE 25.9

The status bar shows a background page symbol when you're working in the background.

1   Background page symbol

Adding Page Numbers

Page numbers are necessary for certain types of publications, such as newsletters or annual reports. They're placed on the background page because they appear on all pages (you can remove them from the first page if you want, which is quite common).

This example creates page numbers on facing pages, assuming the publication is printed on both sides. If you're not printing your publication as a two-sided document, you can omit the steps for the other page.

Adding page numbers to your publication

1. Move to the background page by pressing Ctrl+M.

2. Open the **View** menu and choose **Two-Page Spread**. The status bar displays two background symbols to indicate you're working on left and right background pages.

3. Create a small text box on the left page, positioning it where you want the page number to appear (usually the upper- or lower-left corner or the center of the bottom edge).

4. Type the text you want to appear with the page number in the text box. (For example, type the word Page and then press the Spacebar). Don't enter a page number.

5. Open the **Insert** menu and choose **Page Numbers**. A pound sign appears where the page number will display on the real page (see Figure 25.10).

6. Repeat the process on the right page. Remember that if you are using a corner instead of bottom center, you should use the opposite corner on this page (you're creating a mirrored background page).

7. Press Ctrl+M to return to your working pages. The correct page numbers appear on every page.

FIGURE 25.10

The pound sign is translated to a page number when you return to work on your publication pages.

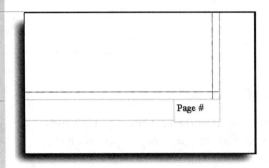

Troubleshooting Page Numbers

There's a good chance that after you inserted the page number text box on the background and switched back to your publication pages, you can't see your page numbers, or, perhaps you see your page numbers on some pages but not on others. This happens a lot.

The problem is that you placed your page number in a position where text or graphics reside on your publication. These items are hiding the page number.

The important fact is that although your publication page is transparent, the items you place on it aren't. Anything you place on the background is hidden by any text or graphic image on top of it.

When you enter your page number on the background page, use the guidelines to ensure you're working below the bottom line of real elements (or above the top line if you're placing your page numbers on the top of the page). The guidelines on your regular pages don't represent the edge of the paper you'll use when you print—they're guidelines representing the margins of your pages.

SEE ALSO

➤ *To learn more about using guidelines, see page 570*

Adding a Watermark

Watermarks are clever, slick, and professional. You can use them to repeat a graphic or text (such as "For Your Eyes Only," "Confidential," or "First Draft").

Watermarks are graphics elements, so if you want to use text as a watermark you must create a WordArt element.

Adding a text watermark

1. Press Ctrl+M to go to the background page.

2. Create a WordArt frame and enter the text you want to use for the watermark.

3. Click anywhere outside the WordArt frame and then click once in the frame to select it.

4. Open the **Fo**rmat menu and choose **Recolor Object**. The Recolor Object dialog box appears (see Figure 25.11).

FIGURE 25.11
For a watermark, think "drab."

5. Click the arrow next to the **Color** box and select a shade of gray. Choose **OK** to close the dialog box.

6. If you're creating separate left and right backgrounds, copy the WordArt box to the other background page by right-clicking the box and choosing **Copy** from the shortcut menu. Then move to the other page, right-click, and choose **Paste**. The object is pasted on top of the original, so drag it to the other page.

7. Press Ctrl+M to return to your regular publication page and check the results (see Figure 25.12).

If you want to use a picture as a watermark, the process is the same except that you have to create a picture frame and add clip art to it instead of using WordArt. Be careful to choose a picture that maintains its clarity and definition when it is recolored gray.

You can manipulate the text watermark

Remember that WordArt isn't really text. It's a graphic; therefore, you can rotate it to make the text more interesting or attention-getting.

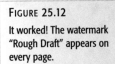

FIGURE 25.12

It worked! The watermark "Rough Draft" appears on every page.

SEE ALSO

➤ *To learn more about creating WordArt, see page 539*

Troubleshooting Watermarks

If you can't see your watermark when you return to your publication page, the problem is the same one I mentioned earlier for page numbers—something is hiding it.

The fix, however, is different, because you don't move a watermark to a position outside your working margins.

Instead, you must make the elements in front of the watermark transparent. Go to the page where the watermark isn't showing and select the text or graphics box that is hiding it. Press Ctrl+T to make the box and its contents transparent and let the watermark show through.

Hiding the Background

You might find you want to hide one or more background elements on a specific page of your publication. For example, it's common to hide the page number on the first page if it's a true cover page (and the last page if you've designed a back cover).

Hiding the background for a specific page

1. Display the page you want to change.

2. Open the **View** menu and choose **Ignore Background**. A check mark appears next to the command.

3. Repeat for each page you need to change.

If you have multiple elements in your background, you can hide the page number and keep the other items (a watermark, for example).

Hiding only the page number on a specific page

1. Move to the page you want to change.

2. Draw a text box that covers the page number.

3. If you can still see the page number, the text box is transparent. Make it opaque by pressing Ctrl+T.

4. Repeat this for each page you want to print without a page number.

This is limited to page numbers because these are usually the only background objects placed outside the working margins. You wouldn't place a blank text box in the middle of a page.

Creating Publications for Marketing and Fun

Publisher has provided some terrific diversions for you (as you create them) and for your readers and customers. With a little imagination, you can use these publications for marketing or advertising.

Start by creating a paper airplane. You can put the company logo on it and sail it in a crowded mall as a marketing device.

Creating an airplane

1. If you're already working in Publisher, open the **File** menu and choose **New** to access the catalog. If you're just launching Publisher, the catalog appears automatically.

2. Select the Airplanes Wizard and choose a type of airplane (see Figure 25.13). Then click the **Start Wizard** button to begin.

3. Choose **Next** in the Airplanes Wizard dialog box to begin making selections (the important decision is about the aerodynamics of the wings).

FIGURE 25.13
What would you like to fly?

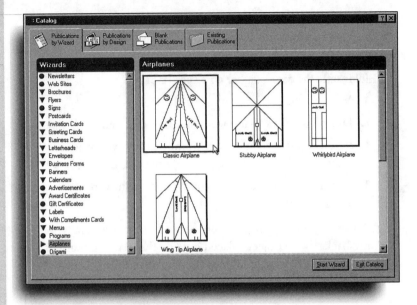

FIGURE 25.13
What would you like to fly?

4. Choose **Finish** and hide the wizard. Then click the text placeholder frames so you can type in your company name or add graphics frames for your company logo (see Figure 25.14)

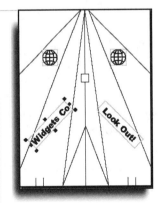

FIGURE 25.14
Customize your creation to suit your purpose.

5. Move to the next page to see the instructions. If you're an aerodynamics wizard, you could change the text on the instructions (if you think there's something that isn't clear).

6. Save your publication. Then print it, fold it, and fly it.

SEE ALSO

➤ *To review how to enter text, see page 531*

➤ *To learn more about printing your publication, see page 602*

You might also want to think about printing a slew of origami creations for your customers. Use them to distribute an offer on a special discount or product. Origami is an ancient art that uses a single piece of paper to form intricate shapes (frequently animals or birds). It's breathtaking to watch a real origami artist, but you can imitate the ancient experts with Publisher. Figure 25.15 shows the two pages that print for an origami cup that won't leak if it's folded correctly. The left page is the origami, the right page contains the instructions.

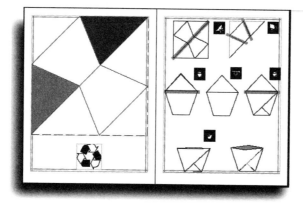

FIGURE 25.15
It's a puzzle, a customer gift, and an advertisement.

Don't forget that the wizard also provides quick procedures for producing banners, signs, and flyers. You'll never run out of marketing and advertising paraphernalia.

Publishing Your Work

Print your publication

Use a professional printer

Publish to the Web

Printing Your Work

As wonderful as it looks on your 256-color monitor (or perhaps your system is configured to display even more colors), the acid test for your publication is the way it looks on paper.

Previewing the Printed Publication

Most of your other Windows software offers a **Print Preview** command so you can peek at the final printed version of the document you're creating. When you work in Publisher, how-ever, you really work in print preview mode all the time.

The only difference between what you see on your screen and the final printed product is that the boundaries and guidelines that appear onscreen don't print. To see a true print preview, turn them off by using one of these methods:

- *Press Ctrl+Shift+O*. Use the same key combination to turn them on again—it's a toggle.
- *Open the* **View** *menu and choose* **Hide Boundaries and Guides**. To turn everything back on, return to the **View** menu, where the command has changed to **Show Boundaries and Guides**.

Figure 26.1 is a view of a page with the boundaries and guides hidden from view. It gives you an accurate preview of the printed page.

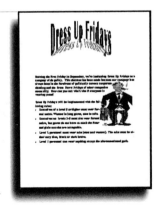

FIGURE 26.1
You can preview the printed product by eliminating the Publisher guidelines.

Preparing to Print Without Color

If you don't have a color printer, you have to do some test printing. That's because the colors you see on your monitor translate to a variety of shades of gray when you print. If your graphics have a lot of contrast, everything should print perfectly well; however, it's best to test each page to see if you have to tweak the colors.

Printing a test page

1. Display the page you want to test.

2. Open the **File** menu and choose **Print** to open the Print dialog box (see Figure 26.2).

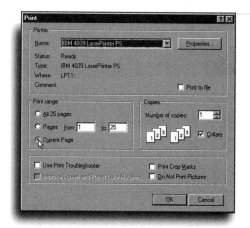

FIGURE 26.2

Print the page for a quick check on black and white printing.

3. Choose **Current Page**.

4. Choose **OK** to send the page to the printer.

Graphics and drop shadows that have a lot of contrast should print perfectly well. For example, Figure 26.3 is the printed page for a company announcement. Nothing got lost in the translation to a noncolor printer.

However, you might find that color combinations that look terrific together onscreen melt together on the printed page. The beautiful color combinations you struggled with print without any real contrast (see Figure 26.4).

FIGURE 26.3
This printout looks just fine.

Starting the first Friday in September, we're instituting Dress Up Fridays as a company wide policy. This decision has been made because our company has always been in the forefront of politically correct corporate thinking and the Dress Down Fridays of other companies seems silly. How can you tell who's who if everyone is wearing jeans?

Dress Up Fridays will be implemented with the following rules:

- Executives of a level 5 or higher must wear formal attire. Women in long gowns, men in tails.
- Executives on levels 3-5 must also wear formal attire, but gowns do not have to touch the floor and plain tuxedos are acceptable.
- Level 2 personnel must wear suits (men and women). The suits must be either navy blue, black or dark brown.
- Level 1 personnel can wear anything except the aforementioned garb.

FIGURE 26.4
The coral door between the green windows on my lilac house disappeared when I printed.

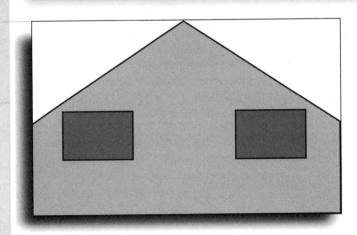

If you are printing without color, don't spend a lot of time selecting colors as you work on your publication, and, of course, test-print each page before you declare it finished.

Printing Your Publication

When you're ready to print, the publication format determines how much work you have to do with printer settings. For example, if your publication requires a nonstandard paper size, you have to tell the printer about it (actually, you have to tell the printer how you plan to feed it into the printer).

You can make all the configuration adjustments you need from the Print dialog box.

Printing your publication

1. Open the **File** menu and choose **Print** to open the Print dialog box. Figure 26.5 shows the Print dialog box for a color printer—if you have a non-color printer, options relating to color aren't accessible.

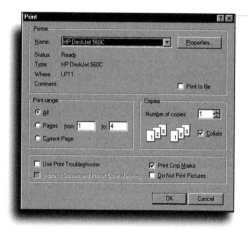

FIGURE 26.5

Select the configuration options you need to print this publication.

2. Set the basic options for this print job, using these guidelines:

   • **Print range**. Specify the pages you want to print. You can print the entire publication, a specific range of page numbers, or the page that's currently in the Publisher window.

- **Copies**. Specify the number of copies you want to print. If you are printing multiple copies, select **C**ollate to print each copy from the first page to the last page. Deselect the **C**ollate option to print multiple copies of page one, followed by multiple copies of page two, and so on.

- **Use Print Troubleshooter**. Select this option if you want Publisher Help files for printing to display on your screen when you print. The Print Troubleshooter asks questions and provides suggested solutions if you indicate that the printing went awry.

- **Improve Screen and Printer Color Matching**. If your printer and monitor support it, you can use the Image Color Matching (ICM) feature available in Windows 95 and Windows 98. ICM tweaks colors to give you the closest possible match between your monitor display and the color your printer produces. (If this option is not grayed out, you can assume that ICM is enabled).

- **Print Crop M**arks. Use this option if your publication has a page size that differs from the paper size you're using to print. The crop marks tell you where to cut to make sure all the pages match.

- **D**o Not Print Pictures. Select this option to speed up printing if you're doing a draft copy for approval. You should also select this option if you are using a separate process for the final printing and the graphics will be part of a *paste-up* that's used for outside printing.

3. Choose **P**roperties to set the paper and graphics options in the Printer Properties dialog box (see Figure 26.6).

4. Choose a standard for graphics quality. This may be called resolution on another tab in your printer settings, or you may see specific graphics choices as in Figure 26.6. Remember that the higher the quality of graphics printing, the slower the printing. If you're printing a draft copy, you may want to lower the quality.

FIGURE 26.6

Every printer has specific properties, so your dialog box may look different.

5. Choose a paper type and size (which may be located on another tab). Some printers offer choices between paper or transparencies; others just offer tray choices and assume you'll place whatever you want in the tray. All printers offer a choice between Portrait (vertical) and Landscape (horizontal) page layout. (Well, dot matrix printers don't, but you wouldn't be printing a publication on a dot matrix printer).

6. Choose **OK** to return to the Print dialog box when you have finished setting these options.

7. Choose **OK** on the Print dialog box to begin printing.

Printing Odd-Size Publications

Some publications are very tiny, such as a single business card. Others are enormous, such as a banner. When you print one of these publications, the Print dialog box offers an additional button named **Page Options**.

Printing Small Publications

If you used Publisher to create a business card, the Page Options dialog box offers you some handy choices (see Figure 26.7). Incidentally, the same principles are at work if your publication is a place card, a small sign, or any other small publication.

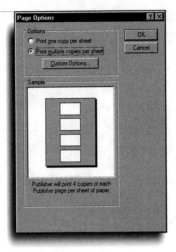

FIGURE 26.7

You can tell Publisher to fill the paper with duplicates of a small publication.

- **Print <u>o</u>ne copy per sheet**. Use this option if you're sending your business card to a professional printer.

- **Print <u>m</u>ultiple copies per sheet**. Select this option if you want to print your business cards yourself (and you have a good cutting machine).

Opting for multiple copies makes the **Custom Options** button accessible, and choosing the button produces the Custom Options dialog box shown in Figure 26.8.

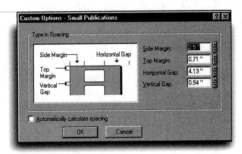

FIGURE 26.8

Set the spacing for printing duplicate items.

The default settings are usually exactly what you need, so unless you have some special situation, leave them alone. If you make changes and they don't work, return to this dialog box and select **Automatically calculate spacing**. Publisher will use the same formula that created the original defaults and return everything to those settings.

Choose **OK** twice to return to the Print dialog box.

Printing Very Large Publications

Two of the nifty choices offered by the Publisher's wizards are banners and posters. You can use these publications for signs or for special occasions (see Figure 26.9).

 Welcome Back Hepzibah

FIGURE 26.9

This banner is six feet long—if her name were Liz, I might not have a printing problem.

The problem with banners is, of course, printing them. I don't know of any office printers that use continuous paper without breaks or perforations. Therefore, you have to print across multiple pages and then put the papers together with glue, tape, staples, Velcro, or whatever you come up with.

When you print a banner or oversized poster, the Print dialog box offers assistance by adding an option named **Tile Printing Options**. Choose it to see the Poster and Banner Printing Options dialog box shown in Figure 26.10.

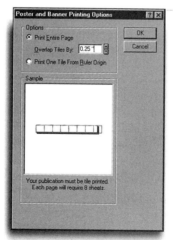

FIGURE 26.10

These printing choices are really "pasting" choices, because they help you configure printing to make pasting easier.

The dialog box gives you quite a bit of information so you can make intelligent choices. It considers each piece of paper a "tile" in the publication page. The **Sample** section of the dialog box indicates how much of the last tile is needed to print the entire publication, and if there seems to be leftover paper, you can try increasing the overlap (giving you more room for glue). Most of the time, however, the default choices are the optimum choices.

Select the single tile with the Publisher ruler

When you want to print one tile, Publisher chooses the tile that is lined up with zero markings on your ruler. You must drag one of the rulers to make sure a zero mark is on the corner of the element you want to check.

- **Print Entire Page**. Select this option to print the page (publication).

- **Overlap Tiles By**. If you don't want to use the default settings, specify a different overlap area. This might change the way each tile prints and will probably also increase the number of tiles.

- **Print One Tile From Ruler Origin**. Use this option to print a single tile so you can check a specific element in your publication. This is handy for seeing what happens if a graphic or a WordArt box is split between multiple tiles during printing. (You can change the overlap options to force a change in the split).

Choose **OK** to return to the Print dialog box.

Using a Professional Printer

Unless you have an incredibly powerful, expensive printer in the office, your important publications are probably sent to an outside printing service. That could mean a copy shop, a high-end printing company, or anything in between.

To avail yourself of outside printing services, you must go through the setup procedures for a printing service. Depending on your decisions, you have either two or three steps to complete. We'll go over the procedures in detail, but here's a quick overview of what to expect:

- Decide on the print method, choosing among color, black and white, or spot color.

- Choose a printer type (Publisher provides printer types for outside printing).

- Provide instructions to the printing company.

Deciding on a Printing Method

Start the setup process by opening the **File** menu and choosing **Prepare File for Printing Service.** Then choose **Set Up Publication** from the submenu. This brings up the Set Up Publication dialog box (see Figure 26.11).

FIGURE 26.11

Select the type of printing you want to set up.

Deciding on a Printing Process

The first decision you must make is the type of printing you want to send out. Here are some guidelines to help you understand the options on this dialog box:

- **I've decided not to use a commercial printing service, thanks.** The only reason to select this option is if you've already set up the publication for outside printing but changed your mind.

- **Black, white, and shades of gray.** Select this option to have the printing service print the publication without color. This selection is for those offices that don't have a high-resolution black-and-white printer available.

- **Full color.** Use this option to send the publication to a printer that supports color. If you have a color printer but it isn't very powerful and perhaps prints only at 300 or 600 dpi resolution, this option gains you better printing.

Publisher does not support in-house full-color printing at a resolution greater than 1200 dpi resolution.

- **Spot color(s)**. Choose this option to use spot colors in addition to black, white, and shades of gray. Selecting this option brings up additional choices on the dialog box because it requires some additional configuration. See the spot colors discussion in the next section for instructions.

Configuring Spot Colors

If you've selected the **Spot Color(s)** option, you have some additional selections to make in the Set Up Publication dialog box. A **Select spot color(s)** section appears in the dialog box (see Figure 26.12).

FIGURE 26.12

Decide on a color for special elements in your publication.

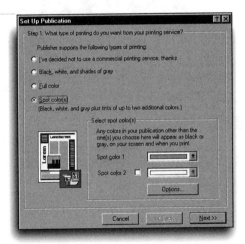

Setting up spot colors

1. Select a color from the palette that displays when you click the arrow next to the **Spot color 1** text box.

2. Select the **Spot color 2** check box if you plan to spend the money for a second color. Then choose the second color.

3. Choose **Options** to tell the printer how to handle elements that overlap each other (see Figure 26.13).

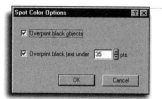

FIGURE 26.13
Control the way black elements are printed when they overlay colored elements.

- **Overprint black objects**. Select this option to have black objects that overlay colored objects printed on top of the color. It means the color is laid down first, and then the black is laid down on the appropriate section. If you deselect the option, the color will not be laid down where black is planned, which sometimes produces gaps.

- **Overprint black text under *XX* pts.** Select this option to lay down the color object first and then overprint black when the point size is less than the size specified in the dialog box. Deselecting this option could also cause gaps. When the type size is very large (36 points or above), the risk of gaps pretty much disappears.

4. Choose **OK** to return to the Set Up Publication dialog box.

Choosing a Printer

Regardless of which option for printing you select (except the "No thanks" option), you must choose **Next** on the Set Up Publication dialog box to continue your setup. The next dialog box is for selecting a printer (see Figure 26.14).

When you installed Publisher, special printers were installed to handle outside printing. One of those printers is the default selection on this dialog box, and the only reason to change it is if you have a printer installed that matches the printer your outside service uses. Of course, if you did, you wouldn't need the outside service.

If you chose either black-and-white or spot-color printing, the **MS Publisher Imagesetter** is probably the displayed printer. If you chose full color, the **MS Publisher Color Printer** is listed.

FIGURE **26.14**

Choose the device that will print your publication.

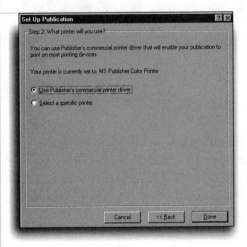

Configuring Printing Instructions

If you selected full-color printing, you're now finished with setup. Choose **Done** and say **Yes** when you're asked if you want to update your publication. Then move on to the next section, "Printing to the Outside Printer."

If you selected black/white/gray printing or spot color, you have a bit more to do.

Filling out printing instructions

1. Choose **Next** to move to the printing options configuration page (see Figure 26.15).

2. Select options, depending on your outside printing service's instructions:

   - **Automatically choose "Extra" paper sizes**. If your printing service uses paper larger than the size of your finished publication, choose this option.

   - **Show all printer marks**. If your printing service wants crop marks and registration marks printed, select this option also.

3. Choose **Done** when you have made your selections.

4. When Publisher asks if you want to update the publication to match the outside printer, choose **Yes**.

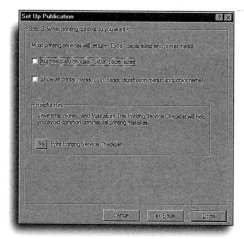

FIGURE 26.15

Ask your printing service how to configure these options.

Do yourself a favor while you're at this dialog box and choose **Print Printing Service Checklist**. A multipage document prints (to your regular printer—this isn't an outside job), providing a robust list of questions to ask and preparations to make. It covers folding, bleeds, crop marks, and all sorts of other important details. After you finish filling out the questions and discussing the options with your printing service, you'll be confident you haven't missed any important points.

Printing to the Outside Printer

Now that your setup is complete, it's time to take all the steps necessary to have your publication printed outside.

Numerous options are available for these final steps, and some of them depend on the instructions from your printing service.

- Print a proof copy (a rough draft) on your own printer for your printing service to use as a guide. To do this, open the **File** menu and choose **Print Proof**.

- Print information for your printing service. To do so, open the **File** menu, choose **Prepare File for Printing Service**, and then choose **Print Publication Information**.

- If your printing service needs a PostScript file, open the **File** menu, choose **Prepare File for Printing Service**, and then choose **Create File in PostScript**.

Your publication changes to match the printer

If you chose black/white/gray or spot color, your publication changes to match the printing. All the colors are gone. You might want to save the publication under a different name by opening the **File** menu and choosing the **Save As** command before updating it for the outside printer.

- If your printing service uses Publisher 98, give them a copy of your publication file.

- If your printing service has specific requirements for setting up the print job, follow those instructions.

Publishing to the Web

If you're in charge of the company Web site, you might want to use Publisher to prepare Web pages. You have two options for accomplishing this:

- Design the publication for the Web, using one of the wizard Web formats.

- Convert an existing publication for use on the Web.

Creating a Web Publication

The best way to create a publication for the Web is to start with the Publications by Wizard tab on the catalog. The catalog appears automatically when you start Publisher, but if you're already working in Publisher, open the **File** menu and choose **New**.

Creating a Web publication

1. On the **Publications by Wizard** tab of the catalog, select the **Web Sites** listing.

2. Scroll through the Web site choices and select the one you want to use. Then choose the **Start Wizard** button.

3. Make choices in the wizard as you're asked to, choosing **Next** to move along.

4. Choose **Finish** in the last wizard dialog box, and then choose **Hide Wizard** to begin working on your Web publication (see Figure 26.16).

Converting a Publication for the Web

You can convert an existing publication for use on your Web site. This is not usually as effective as preparing a Web page from scratch, but sometimes it works well enough to give it a try.

FIGURE 26.16

The Web page layout is complete, and text and graphics need to be added.

Converting a publication to a Web page

1. Open the **File** menu and choose **Create** **W**eb **Site from Current Publication**.

2. Choose **Y**es when you're asked if you want to run the Design Checker. The Design Checker searches for potential problems with the conversion, looking for elements in your publication that might cause trouble.

3. Tell the Design Checker to check **All** pages and choose **OK**. As problems are found, take note of them, and when the Design Checker finishes, fix whatever problems you care about.

4. When the Design Checker is finished, it displays an announcement that the check is complete. Choose **OK**.

5. Open the **File** menu and choose **We**b **Site Preview**. Publisher does a little work on the file, and then your browser opens with your publication in the browser window (see Figure 26.17). At this point, your publication is converted.

If you don't like what you see, tweak your publication and go through the process again. If everything is dandy, you can publish it.

Some Design Checker problems aren't problems

It's impossible to guess the problems you might see in your publication, but there are two common ones you might safely ignore. One is that a picture isn't in its original proportions. This only occurs when you deliberately change the proportions, so it's safe to ignore. Another common problem is that when graphics and text overlap, the entire section is treated as a graphic. It's okay to ignore that if you don't plan to edit the text on the Web page (you'll probably replace text more often than you'll edit it).

FIGURE **26.17**

Here's what the publication looks like in a browser.

Publishing Your Web Publication

Three methods are available for publishing your Web publication:

- Publish it directly to your Web page.
- Publish it to your company intranet server.
- Publish it to a folder on your computer (useful if you don't have access to a modem). Then you can either transfer it later or give it to the company Webmaster.

Publishing Directly to Your Web Page

Open the **File** menu and choose **Publish to Web** to begin. The first time you choose this command, you see a message from Publisher about obtaining the necessary tool.

To publish your Web publication directly to your Web page, you must have the Microsoft Web Publishing Wizard, which you obtain by downloading it from the Microsoft Web site. When you installed Publisher 98, an icon named Setup for Microsoft Web Publishing Wizard was installed on your desktop. Double-click this icon to open your browser and fetch the software.

After you download the Web Publishing Wizard, it will walk you through all the steps to access your Web page and publish your work.

Publishing to the Company Intranet

If you have an intranet server on your network, you can publish your Web page to it and thus distribute your publication to all employees.

Publishing to a company server

1. Open the **File** menu and choose **Save As HTML**.

2. In the Save as HTML dialog box, choose **Network**. The Map Network Drive dialog box opens (see Figure 26.18) so you can select the computer and folder that holds intranet publications. Use the next available drive letter (unless that folder is already mapped).

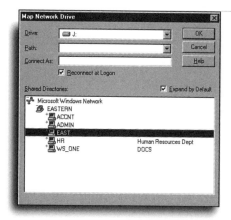

FIGURE 26.18

Store your publication as an HTML document on your company's intranet server.

3. You're returned to the Save as HTML dialog box. Choose **OK**.

Publishing to a Local Folder

To publish your Web publication to a folder, you don't need a modem.

Publishing to a folder

1. Open the **File** menu and choose **Save As HTML**.

2. Choose a folder from the Save as HTML dialog box or choose **New Folder** to create one. Then choose **OK**.

When you're ready to publish to the Web (you put a modem on your computer), open the Web publication from the folder and publish it, or, copy it to your Webmaster's computer.

Using SBE Extras

Using the Small Business Financial Manager

Import accounting data

Build reports

Create what-if scenarios

Getting Started

If you use accounting software to keep your books, you're probably well aware of its limitations. Try creating a customized report or a what-if scenario, and you'll see what I mean. Excel has the power to take your accounting data and whip it into any shape you want, but you face two big challenges—getting the data into Excel and building the reports and scenarios. Well, those challenges just got a little easier to handle.

The Small Business Financial Manager is an Excel add-in that converts accounting software data into an Excel format and uses it to create reports and what-if scenarios. Although it is an add-in, you cannot install it from the Excel **Tools** menu's **Add-ins** submenu. You must install it from the Office 97 SBE CD-ROM.

After you install the add in, it appears on your Excel menu bar as a new menu titled **Accounting**. As you can see in Figure 27.1, the menu contains a variety of offerings, including several wizards.

The Small Business Financial Manager also adds a shortcut to the desktop. You can launch Excel and start the Small Business Financial Manager by double-clicking the shortcut icon. The

FIGURE 27.1

The Small Business Financial Manager becomes a part of Excel after you install it.

first thing you see is a dialog box warning you that the workbook you're about to open contains macros (see Figure 27.2).

The truth of the matter is, most macros are time-saving shortcuts that automate tasks for you by condensing multiple keystrokes into a single shortcut key or toolbar button. Every time you use a shortcut key in an SBE application, you are using a macro. For example, by pressing Ctrl+V or clicking the Paste button on the Standard toolbar, you are activating a macro that opens the **Edit** menu and selects **Paste**. This is a very simple macro, but you can build extremely complex macros that execute hundreds of keystrokes. That is exactly what makes the Small Business Financial Manager perform its magic—it consists of a multitude of complex macros that automatically analyze your accounting data.

FIGURE 27.2

Caution: Some macros may be hazardous to your data's health.

Like many things in life, macros can be used for both good and not-so-good purposes. If programmed with malice aforethought, macros can be turned into computer viruses that may destroy your data. This is the reason for the warning. Unfortunately, all the warning tells you is that macros are present, but not whether they are of a harmful type. However, the Small Business Financial Manager came directly from the Microsoft CD, which is thoroughly tested before being created, so you can choose **Enable Macros.** (If you choose **Disable Macros**, you eliminate all the power of the Manager.) The Small Business Financial Manager worksheet opens (see Figure 27.3).

To start a wizard, click one of the worksheet buttons (Import, Analyze, Report, or Chart) or open the **Accounting** menu and choose a wizard.

What if Excel is already running?

If you are already working in Excel, you don't need to return to the desktop to start the Small Business Financial Manager. The wizards are available on the **Accounting** menu.

FIGURE 27.3

You can get started right away with the Small Business Financial Manager by clicking one of the buttons on the screen.

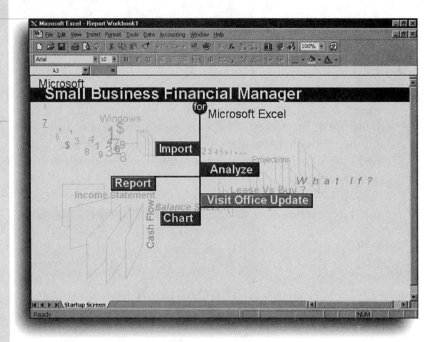

Importing Accounting Data

Before Excel can effectively utilize your accounting data, you've got to turn it into something that Excel can recognize and work with. No problem—as long as you're using one of the accounting software packages listed in Table 27.1.

TABLE 27.1   **Accounting packages supported by the Small Business Financial Manager**

Accounting Package	Version
ACCPAC Plus Accounting for DOS	v6.1a
BusinessWorks for Windows	V9.0
DacEasy Accounting for DOS	v5.0
Great Plains Accounting for DOS	v8.0, 8.1 and 8.2
MAS 90 Evolution/2 for DOS	v1.51
MYOB Accounting for Windows	v7.0
One-Write Plus for DOS	v4.03

continues . . .

TABLE 27.1   **Continued**

Accounting Package	Version
Peachtree Complete Accounting for DOS	v8.0
Peachtree Complete Accounting for Windows	v4.0
Peachtree for Windows	v3.0 and 3.5
Platinum Series for DOS and Windows	v4.1 and 4.4
QuickBooks for Windows	v3.1, 4.0 and Pro 4.0
Simply Accounting for Windows and v4.0 (Canada)	v3.0 (U.S. and Canada)
Timeline MV Analyst/Server	v2.3, 2.4, and 2.5

If your accounting package isn't listed in the preceding table, you can log on to Microsoft's Web site to see if there are any new filters, or call customer support (1-800-426-9400). Also, you can refer to the Small Business Financial Manager Help system—you'll find a list of accounting packages with details involving each one and how it works with Small Business Financial Manager.

If your accounting software appears in Table 27.1, you're halfway home. However, before you start using the Small Business Financial Manager to import your data, you should tend to a couple of matters.

- Make sure you're set up for 12 accounting periods.
- Close out the current period in your accounting software.
- Make sure your accounting system is on an accrual basis, not a cash basis.

Importing your accounting data into the Small Business Financial Manager

1. Open Excel 97.

2. Open the **Accounting** menu and choose **Import Wizard** to start the Import Wizard (see Figure 27.4).

3. Select **Import** and click **Next** to continue.

Avoid import problems with QuickBooks 4.0 data

Intuit's insistence that all its users register their software after purchasing it, has resulted in a potential problem when using the Small Business Financial Manager. If you attempt to import QuickBooks 4.0 data into the Small Business Financial Manager from an un-registered copy of QuickBooks, you may encounter import errors and file corruption problems. You should also remove all password protection from the files before importing.

Import before closing

You should import the data before closing out fiscal periods, or Financial Manager will not import transaction details.

Accessing the Import Wizard from the startup screen

If you are opening Small Business Financial Manager from the desktop icon, you can click **Import** from the startup screen.

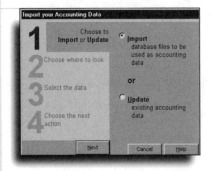

FIGURE 27.4
The Import Wizard walks you through the import process.

4. Use the **Choose where to look** drop-down list to find the folder containing your accounting data files (see Figure 27.5). Click the **In specific folders** option to activate the list.

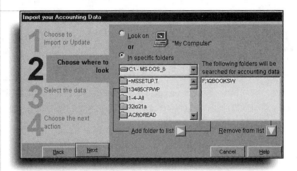

FIGURE 27.5
The first order of business is to locate your accounting data.

5. Select the folder that contains your accounting data and click the **Add folder to list** arrow. Then click **Next** to continue.

6. In the third Import Wizard dialog box, select the accounting data you want to import (see Figure 27.6) and click **Next**.

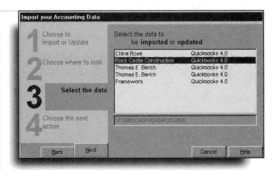

FIGURE 27.6
You can import accounting information from as many data files as you want.

7. If you're ready to begin the import, click **Yes** when asked to confirm that you want to start. When the import finishes, you have several choices for your next action (see Figure 27.7).

FIGURE 27.7
After you finish importing, you can get right to work creating reports and scenarios.

You actually have three choices after your data has been imported:

- **Create a Financial Report**. Use this option to create a balance sheet, cash flow report, income statement, or other report.

- **Perform a What-If Analysis**. This is great if you want to peer into the future and see what would happen if certain factors were to change. You might use it to project sales for the next year if you increase prices or expand your line.

- **Remap your Accounting Data**. Remapping ensures that your accounting data has account categories with which the Small Business Financial Manager can work. This should be your selection after importing data for the first time.

8. Select **Remap your Accounting Data.** You should always make this selection the first time you import a data file.

9. Click **Finish** to perform the mapping and display the Map Your Accounts dialog box shown in Figure 27.8.

10. Check the Import Wizard's mapping job, make the necessary changes by dragging and dropping or cutting and pasting, and click **OK** when you're satisfied that all accounts are properly mapped.

Deciding when to perform the import operation

If you have an extremely large accounting data file and this is your initial import, you may want to do it at a time when you plan to be away from your computer. Importing and converting a large amount of data can take as much as a couple of hours, and during that time all of your computer's resources are used for the import. In other words, you can't work on anything else. Just to give you some idea of import time, an 842KB QuickBooks 4.0 data file took me about four minutes to convert. Times will vary, depending on many factors.

Print your chart of accounts first

To head off potential errors that may result if the Import Wizard mismaps some of your accounts, you should consider printing a copy of your chart of accounts from your accounting software. Use the chart of accounts to check the Wizard's mapping job before moving on.

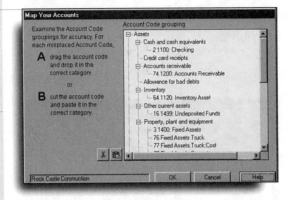

FIGURE 27.8

The Import Wizard offers its best attempt at placing your accounts in the right Small Business Financial Manager categories.

After you finish with the import, the Wizard returns you to the active spreadsheet. You're then ready to utilize the data you've just imported.

Building Reports

Excel excels at producing sophisticated reports from raw financial data. To make it even easier for you to coax that kind of reporting from Excel, the Small Business Financial Manager provides a Report Wizard that practically makes *you* a report wizard in your own right.

Accessing the Report Wizard from the startup screen

If you are opening Small Business Financial Manager from the desktop icon, you can click **Report** from the startup screen to get started.

Creating accounting reports with the Report Wizard

1. Open the **Accounting** menu and choose **Report Wizard** to open the first step of the Report Wizard, as shown in Figure 27.9.

FIGURE 27.9

You can choose your report type and your data source.

2. Select the report type from the **Financial Reports** list. Then, from the **Company Name** drop-down list, choose the company for which to run the report. For the purpose of this example, we are using a **Cash Flow** report.

3. Click **Next** to proceed to step 2 of the wizard, in which you indicate more narrowly the type of report you want to create (see Figure 27.10). The choices here depend entirely on the choice you made in the preceding step.

Try the sample database

The sample accounting database that comes with Small Business Financial Manager (Volcano Coffee Company) gives you a good way to practice using the Small Business Financial Manager features without messing up your own data.

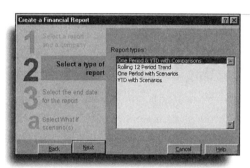

FIGURE 27.10
Each main report type has several subreports to choose from.

4. Select the subreport to use and click **Next** to move on to step 3 of the Report Wizard.

5. Choose an end date for the report and click **Finish** to create a report like the one seen in Figure 27.11.

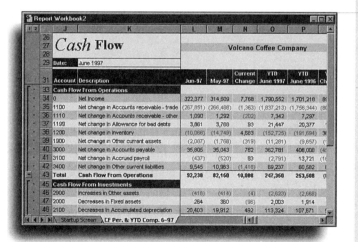

FIGURE 27.11
For professional-looking reports, you can't beat the Report Wizard.

Graph it with the Chart Wizard

If you're at the startup screen, click the **Chart** button to start the Chart Wizard. Or you can open the **Accounting** menu and choose **Chart Wizard**. Choose from the available financial charts and continue selecting options in the wizard to create a chart.

Use the Analyze button

If you're at the startup screen, click the **Analyze** button to open the Select a Financial Manager Analysis Tool dialog box.

Although the Report Wizard has only a handful of basic reports, the numerous subreports available provide you with fairly extensive reporting capabilities.

Using the Analysis Tools

The Small Business Financial Manager toolbox contains a number of handy tools to help you scrutinize your accounting data. From comparing your business with the industry averages to projecting future performance, the analysis tools can help you keep your business on track.

Creating a Business Comparison Report

Ever wonder how you stack up against the competition? Well, here's your opportunity to stop wondering and find out where you stand. You can build a set of Business Comparison Reports that take your financial data and compare it against related industry average numbers compiled by Robert Morris Associates.

Building a Business Comparison report

1. Open the **Accounting** menu and choose **Select Analysis Tool** to open the Select a Financial Manager Analysis Tool dialog box (see Figure 27.12).

FIGURE 27.12

The Financial Manager analysis "toolbox" contains some handy gadgets for putting your financial house in order.

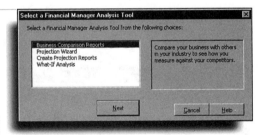

2. Select **Business Comparison Reports** and click **Next** to start the Business Comparison Wizard.

3. From the first drop-down list, select the company on which to report. Then from the second drop-down list, choose a date range you want the report to cover (see Figure 27.13).

4. Click **Next** to open the industry classification list shown in Figure 27.14.

5. Choose the classification that most closely matches that of your company. The list initially displays general classifications. Click the plus sign (+) to the left of the parent classifications to expand the list of subclassifications. To be used in the report, the classification must be at least four digits and appear in the text box below the classification list (see Figure 27.14).

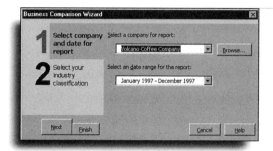

FIGURE 27.13

Use the Business Comparison Wizard to see how you measure up to the competition.

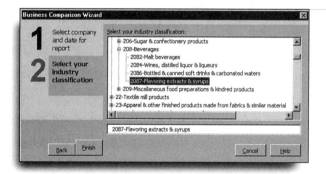

FIGURE 27.14

Data for a wide range of industries is included for use in Business Comparison reports.

6. Click **Finish** to create a comparison report like the one shown in Figure 27.15.

7. To see income and balance sheet comparisons, click the worksheet tabs at the bottom of the screen. You can also access these comparisons by clicking the Income Statement or Balance Sheet hyperlinks at the top of the Business Comparison report.

8. Because the Business Comparison report is an Excel worksheet, you can close it by opening the **File** menu and choosing **Close**. If you want to save the report for future reference, answer **Yes** when asked; otherwise, answer **No** to return to the Small Business Financial Manager opening workbook.

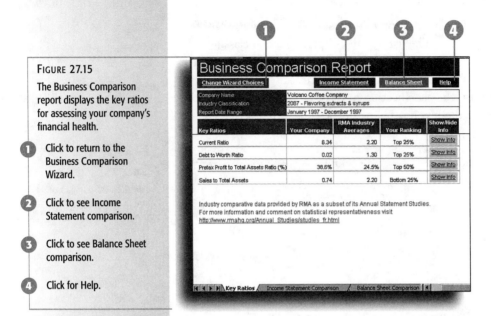

FIGURE 27.15

The Business Comparison report displays the key ratios for assessing your company's financial health.

1 Click to return to the Business Comparison Wizard.

2 Click to see Income Statement comparison.

3 Click to see Balance Sheet comparison.

4 Click for Help.

Looking Ahead with the Projection Wizard

If you're running a business, you've got two major responsibilities— keeping your business running smoothly today and planning ways to grow it and keep it running smoothly in the future. Some of the Small Business Financial Manager features can help you run your business today, and the Projection Wizard can offer you a glimpse into the future. By analyzing your historical data and adding some assumptions about the future, you can come up with a reasonably accurate picture (as long as your assumptions hold true). You start by creating a projection with the Projection Wizard, and then you produce reports from the projected data by using the Create Projection Reports tool.

Creating growth forecasts with the Projection Wizard

1. Open the **Accounting** menu and choose **Select Analysis Tool** to open the Select a Financial Manager Analysis Tool dialog box (shown in Figure 27.12).

2. Highlight **Projection Wizard** and click **Next** to start the Financial Manager Projection Wizard (see Figure 27.16).

3. Select the company from the **Company** drop-down list and enter a name for the new projection in the **New** text box. You can modify an existing projection by selecting it from the **Existing** drop-down list.

Another way to open the dialog box

Don't forget the startup screen method for choosing an analysis tool–click the **Analyze** button to bring up the Select a Financial Manager Analysis Tool dialog box.

FIGURE 27.16

Use the Financial Manager Projection Wizard to peer into the future.

4. Click **Next** to proceed to step 2 of the Financial Manager Projection Wizard (see Figure 27.17).

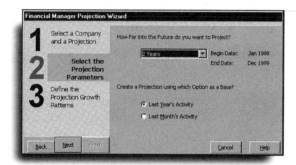

FIGURE 27.17

In step 2, you decide how much historical data to use and how far into the future you want to look.

5. From the drop-down list, select an amount of time into the future for which you want to forecast data. The dates covered by your selection appear to the right of the drop-down list.

6. You can use company information from the previous year or the previous month to create your projection. Click the appropriate option to select which data set you want to base your forecast on.

7. Click **Next** to move to the final wizard dialog box, shown in Figure 27.18 and choose whether you want to enter your growth projection as a percentage or as a fixed dollar amount.

8. Enter the amounts or percentages by which you estimate your income and expenses will change over the period of time for which you're forecasting.

FIGURE 27.18

Try not to overestimate future income or underestimate future expenses.

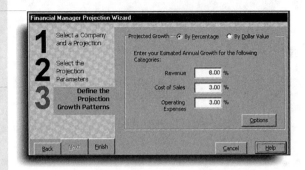

This is where you make your assumptions about the future by entering the following information:

- **Revenue**. This is your income derived from sales of products or services.

- **Cost of Sales**. This figure represents the direct cost of the products or services you sell. Labor and materials are two of the most common expenses included in cost of sales.

- **Operating Expenses**. All expenses not directly related to the cost of your sales fall into the operating expenses category.

- **Options**. Clicking the **Options** button displays a dialog box that enables you to change the growth rate numbers for any given month within the projected time period. This is ideal for seasonal businesses in which there are periods of high activity followed by periods of substantially lower activity.

9. Click **Finish** to create your projections. Depending on your system and how far into the future you're projecting, it may take several minutes to create the projections.

10. When the projections are complete, a dialog box appears to notify you of the fact. Click **OK** to return to Excel.

Now that you've got your projections in hand, you can see what the future holds for you if your growth estimates are correct. So without further ado, it's time to create a report based on the new projections.

Creating a Projected Income Statement report from Projection Wizard forecasts

1. Open the <u>A</u>ccounting menu and choose **Select Analysis Tool** to open the Select a Financial Manager Analysis tool.

2. Choose **Create Projection Reports** and click <u>N</u>ext to open the Create a Projection Report Wizard shown in Figure 27.19.

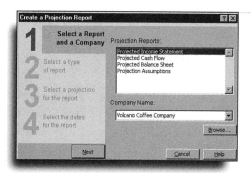

FIGURE 27.19

You can create a variety of financial reports from your forecast data.

The available reports include

- **Projected Income Statement**. This report summarizes your income and expenses to present you with a detailed look at future performance.

- **Projected Cash Flow**. Is there cash in your company's future? This report will let you know.

- **Projected Balance Sheet**. To see the state of your general financial health, the Projected Balance Sheet is your best bet. This report takes assets, liabilities, and equity into consideration.

- **Projection Assumptions**. Choose this report to see a list of the estimates you entered for the selected projection.

3. Choose the type of report to create and the company whose data you want to use. Then click **Next** to proceed to the report type screen.

   Keep in mind that depending on the report you choose, the remaining steps may differ from those appearing here.

4. Choose a report type. **One Period & YTD with Comparisons** shows you the results for a particular period along with year-to-date figures and the amounts and percentages of change. The **Rolling 12 Period Trend** displays the previous 12 months' performance for the company selected. We'll use the **Rolling 12 Period Trend** report for this example.

5. Click **Next** to move to the next step of the wizard and choose a projection to use as the basis of your projection report.

6. Click **Next** to proceed to the next step and choose a start date and end date for the report (see Figure 27.20).

FIGURE 27.20

The dates you choose appear to the right of the start date list.

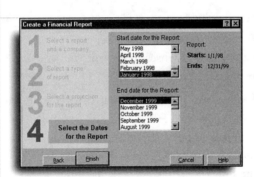

7. Click **Finish** to create a projection report like the one shown in Figure 27.21.

8. To save the report, click the Save button on the Standard toolbar or open the **File** menu and choose **Save**. To return to Excel without saving the report, open the **File** menu and choose **Close**.

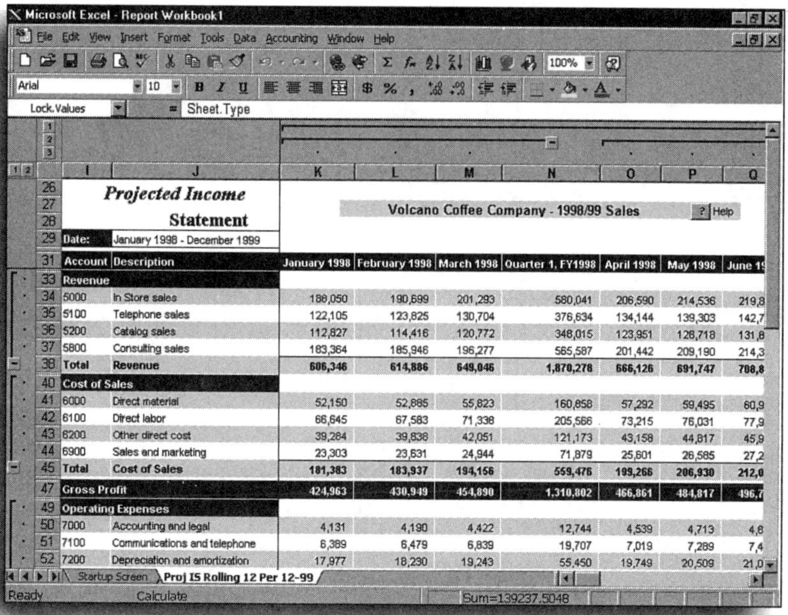

FIGURE 27.21
The Projected Income
Statement report gives
you a detailed picture of
future performance based
on your forecast data.

Creating What-If Scenarios

Running a business involves making decisions for the future
based on more than one possible scenario. If you find yourself
with a surplus of cash at the end of the year, should you spend
it on beefing up your marketing campaign or adding that new
equipment you've been eyeing? What would happen if you
expanded your operation and hired more people? These are all
questions that you need to assess before making a final decision.
Using the Small Business Financial Manager What-If Wizard
can make those decisions a lot easier. The What-If Wizard
enables you to set up different scenarios and plug in the information to see the outcome for each of your alternatives.

Using the What-If Wizard to create what-if scenarios

1. Open the **Accounting** menu and choose **Select Analysis
   Tool** to open the Select a Financial Manager Analysis Tool
   dialog box shown in Figure 27.12.

2. Select **What-If Analysis** and click **Next** to start the Perform
   a What-If Analysis Wizard shown in Figure 27.22

**Accessing the What-If Wizard
from the startup screen**

If you are opening Small
Business Financial Manager
from the desktop icon, you can
click **Analyze** from the startup
screen to open the Select a
Financial Manager Analysis Tool
dialog box. Then highlight
What-If Analysis and click
Next to continue.

FIGURE 27.22

Start by selecting the company to work with.

3. Select a company from the list and click **Next** to continue.

4. Enter a name for the scenario in the **New** text box. As soon as you begin typing, the Begin and End Dates become enabled (see Figure 27.23).

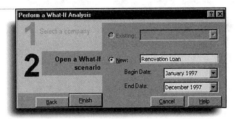

FIGURE 27.23

After you give your scenario a name and set the date parameters, you're ready to create the what-if analysis.

5. Set the Begin and End Dates for the data to be used for this scenario. Then click **Finish** to open the Save Scenario Workbook As dialog box shown in Figure 27.24.

6. Select a folder from the **Save in** drop-down list, enter a name (or accept the default) in the **File name** text box, and then click **Save**. As soon as the scenario is saved to disk, it opens in an Excel workbook (see Figure 27.25).

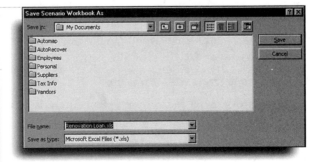

FIGURE 27.24

The Import Wizard walks you through the import process.

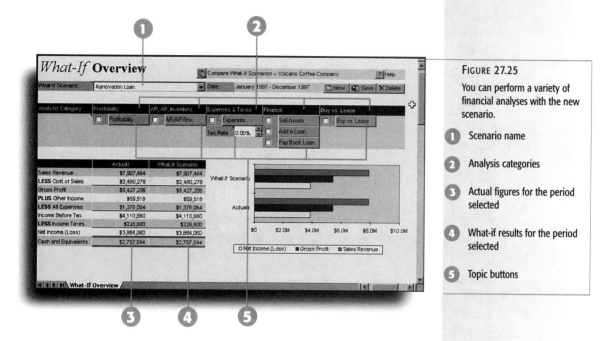

FIGURE 27.25

You can perform a variety of financial analyses with the new scenario.

1 Scenario name

2 Analysis categories

3 Actual figures for the period selected

4 What-if results for the period selected

5 Topic buttons

7. Select an Analysis Category and then click a topic button to enter hypothetical data (see Figure 27.26). Click **OK** to close the dialog box and continue with the analysis.

FIGURE 27.26

You can get as wild as you want, but the more realistic your hypothetical numbers are, the more valid your analysis will be.

8. Enter the hypothetical information to see the effect it would have on your financial data (see Figure 27.27).

9. Repeat the process for all the variables you want to test.

10. Press Alt+F4 to close the scenario when you're finished.

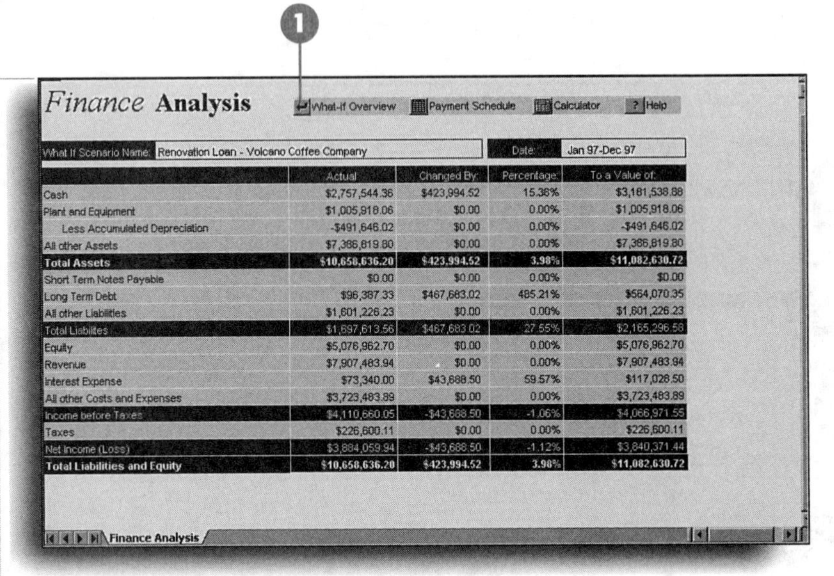

	Actual	Changed By:	Percentage:	To a Value of:
Cash	$2,757,544.36	$423,994.52	15.36%	$3,181,538.88
Plant and Equipment	$1,005,918.06	$0.00	0.00%	$1,005,918.06
Less Accumulated Depreciation	-$491,646.02	$0.00	0.00%	-$491,646.02
All other Assets	$7,386,819.80	$0.00	0.00%	$7,386,819.80
Total Assets	**$10,658,636.20**	**$423,994.52**	**3.98%**	**$11,082,630.72**
Short Term Notes Payable	$0.00	$0.00	0.00%	$0.00
Long Term Debt	$96,387.33	$467,683.02	485.21%	$564,070.35
All other Liabilities	$1,601,226.23	$0.00	0.00%	$1,601,226.23
Total Liabilites	$1,697,613.56	$467,683.02	27.55%	$2,165,296.58
Equity	$5,076,962.70	$0.00	0.00%	$5,076,962.70
Revenue	$7,907,483.94	$0.00	0.00%	$7,907,483.94
Interest Expense	$73,340.00	$43,688.50	59.57%	$117,028.50
All other Costs and Expenses	$3,723,483.89	$0.00	0.00%	$3,723,483.89
Income before Taxes	$4,110,660.05	-$43,688.50	-1.06%	$4,066,971.55
Taxes	$226,600.11	$0.00	0.00%	$226,600.11
Net Income (Loss)	$3,884,059.94	-$43,688.50	-1.12%	$3,840,371.44
Total Liabilities and Equity	**$10,658,636.20**	**$423,994.52**	**3.98%**	**$11,082,630.72**

FIGURE 27.27

Review the changes to your financial picture caused by the new data.

1. Click to return to the opening what-if screen.

Need a handy calculator?

Click the Calculator button on the worksheet to open the Windows Calculator, which functions like a standard calculator. You can click the calculator buttons or type to enter numbers and operators. Transfer numbers to and from the Calculator window by using the **Edit** menu's **Paste** and **Copy** commands.

You can create as many scenarios as you want, and even compare different scenarios to one another. Play with what-if for a while, and you'll find how much it can do.

The two remaining options on the **Accounting** menu allow you to perform a couple of simple operations. The **Insert Balance** command inserts the balance of the account you select into the current worksheet. If you are working on a report for which the financial data has recently been updated, you can choose **Recalculate Reports** to update the report with the new data.

One last thing. For help with the Small Business Financial Manager, go to the **Help** menu and select **Financial Manager Help Topics**, which is added during installation.

Making Travel Plans with Expedia Streets 98

Introducing Expedia Streets 98

Whether you travel for business or pleasure, taking a trip is a lot easier if you plan ahead. With Expedia Streets 98, you can plan your entire trip right from your computer. From checking distances and locating points of interest, to mapping a route and printing it out, Streets 98 makes travel plans a snap. It's great for locating competitors, vendors, friends, or even vacation spots.

Streets 98 provides a comprehensive map of the continental United States that includes most U.S. cities, villages, and towns, as well as major cities of neighboring countries. The detail is so great that you can view individual streets within even the smallest communities.

Installing Expedia Streets 98

Before you can put Streets 98 to work, you've got to install the program. It will require approximately 5MB of hard disk space, so be sure you have enough room before starting. To begin the installation process, insert the Streets 98 CD in your CD-ROM drive. If you have Auto insert notification turned on for your drive, the installation program starts automatically. If the installation doesn't begin automatically, open Windows Explorer, select the CD-ROM drive, and double-click setup.exe.

Installing Expedia Streets 98

1. Click **Continue** on the initial Welcome screen to begin the install.

2. Enter your name in the Name Information dialog box and click **OK** to continue.

3. Double-check the name information in the confirmation dialog box and click **OK** if it is correct. Click **Change** if it's not correct.

4. Write your Product ID number in a safe place and click **OK**. The Setup program begins a search for any previously installed components. When it finishes the search, it opens the End User License Agreement dialog box.

5. Click **I Agree** to accept the license terms and continue or **I Do Not Agree** to reject the license terms and exit the

installation. If you want to review a hard copy of the license, click the **Print License** button.

6. As soon as you click **I Agree**, the Folder dialog box appears as shown in Figure 28.1.

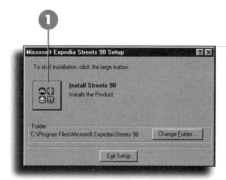

FIGURE **28.1**

Select the folder in which you want to install Streets 98.

1   Click to install.

7. To accept the default installation folder, click the large **Install** button in the mid-left section of the dialog box. To designate another folder, click **Change Folder**.

8. Select a program group in which to add the Streets 98 items, or type in a name to create a new one. **Microsoft Expedia** is the default selection. Click **Continue**.

9. The setup program checks to see if you have a current version of Internet Explorer. If you have a current version, a dialog box informs you. Click **OK** to continue. If you have a version of Internet Explorer that is older than the one on the Expedia Streets 98 CD-ROM, you are asked if you want to update to the more recent version. If you want the updated version, click **OK;** otherwise, click **No**. Setup now begins to copy files from the CD-ROM to your hard drive.

10. When all the files are copied, a final dialog box appears, informing you that setup was successful. Click **OK** to finish the setup or click the **Online Registration** button to go online and register Streets 98.

Running Streets 98

To run Streets 98, insert the CD (the CD must always be inserted to run Streets 98). If you have **Auto insert notification** turned on, the program starts automatically. If you have **Auto insert notification** turned off, you'll have to go to the **Start** menu and select **Programs**, **Microsoft Expedia Streets 98** (or whatever Program Group name you selected during install).

Whichever way you start the program, the first thing you see is the Start Screen shown in Figure 28.2.

FIGURE 28.2

The Start Screen gives you access to basic Streets 98 functions.

Skipping the Start Screen

If you want to bypass this Start Screen whenever you open Streets 98, click the **Don't show this screen again** check box before choosing a feature button.

To use any of the Streets 98 features, click the appropriate button on the Start Screen. All the features found on the Start Screen are also accessible as toolbar buttons or menu choices after you're in the map view. Move your mouse pointer over each choice to discover the button you need to click.

Viewing the Map

Using some of the more sophisticated Streets 98 features will be easier if you familiarize yourself with the map view and some basic tools for navigating and viewing the map.

Without further ado, click the **Close** button on the Start Screen. The first time you open the map view, Streets 98 presents you with a map of the entire United States—minus Alaska and Hawaii (see Figure 28.3). Although a good deal of Mexico and Canada are included in the map, there is no detailed information available for either country.

FIGURE 28.3
The map view starts out with
an overview of the continental
United States.

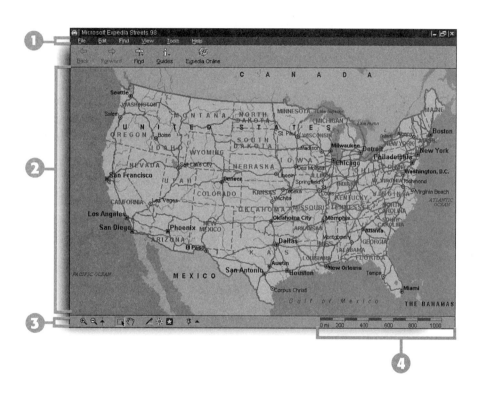

1 Menu bar

2 Map area

3 Menu toolbar

4 Distance scale

The first task you should master is zooming. Even if you're taking a trip from New York to Los Angeles, you'll want to get a closer look at the route. The quickest way to zoom in to a specific area is to use the Selector tool, which is the default pointer tool that the map view opens with. As soon as you access the map view, your pointer acquires a square frame around the point. This indicates that the Selector tool is active.

Zooming in to a specific area on the map

1. Position your mouse pointer above or below the area you want to zoom, and to one side.

2. Click and hold the left mouse button. When a rectangle appears, drag it over the area you want to zoom in on. When the area is enclosed in the rectangle, let go of the mouse button.

3. Click the rectangle with the mouse pointer, which becomes a magnifying glass with a plus sign as soon as you place it within the rectangle (see Figure 28.4).

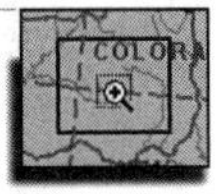

FIGURE 28.4

To zoom in to an area, enclose it and click the rectangle with the magnifying glass/mouse pointer.

You can continue to zoom in, using the Selector mouse pointer, until you are close enough to view individual city streets. You can also use the Zoom in button on the toolbar to get a closer look, or the Zoom out button to get a broader picture. Both of these buttons are good for zooming in and out gradually. If you want something a little more powerful, click the Zoom Slider button on the toolbar to activate the Zoom tool shown in Figure 28.5.

To use the Zoom tool, move the slider (the downward-pointing white triangle) up to zoom out and down to zoom in. The mileage number that appears at the bottom of the tool indicates the distance above the chosen location you would have to be to view it as it appears on the screen. You can also zoom in or out by clicking the up or down arrows located to the right of the slider bar.

FIGURE 28.5
The Zoom tool shows you the map view as seen from the indicated distance above the earth.

While viewing an area of the map, you can narrow your view by clicking the map to see a selection of specific zoom sites. You will typically find the city and state closest to the point you click listed as choices. Click one of the selections to zoom to it.

For moving the map around, you have two choices. When you move your mouse pointer to any of the four edges of the screen, the pointer turns into an arrow. If you click, the map scrolls in the direction of the arrow. If you want more control over moving the map, use the Panning button on the toolbar. Place the hand pointer on the map and drag it in any direction you want.

Another tool that comes in handy, no matter what you're doing with Streets 98, is the Map Legend. It is a lot easier to use the map effectively if you understand what the symbols in the legend mean. Open the **Tools** menu and choose **Map Legend** to open the list shown in Figure 28.6.

Quick zooming is just a right-click away

For quick access to several zoom features, right-click anywhere on the map and select **Zoom** from the shortcut menu. The **Zoom** submenu lets you zoom in, out, to the entire U.S. map or just the 48 states, or to a highlighted route. To return to the default map view of the continental United States, click **To 48 States**.

FIGURE 28.6
The Map Legend explains the symbols used throughout Streets 98.

The symbol categories found in the Map Legend include Populated Places, Boundaries, Points of Interest, Transportation, Water Features, and Physical Features. Scroll through the legend to find the category or symbol you're looking for.

Planning a Travel Route

One of the handiest features of Streets 98 is the Route Highlighter, which enables you to mark a route on the map, print it out, and even save it for future use. Anytime you're planning a trip into unfamiliar territory, it's a good idea to highlight your route and print it out so you have easy-to-follow directions at your fingertips. No matter whether you're going across town or across the country, your chances of arriving on time and with your sanity intact will be greatly improved.

Before you actually highlight your route, you should examine all the possibilities and determine the route that will best satisfy your needs. Highlighting a route is easy after you decide whether you want to find the shortest, quickest, or most scenic route.

Finding the Shortest Route

Obviously, to determine the shortest route you need to be able to measure distances between points. It just so happens that Streets 98 includes a handy measuring tool so you can quickly and easily calculate distances between points on the map.

Measuring the distance between two points

1. Use the selector tool to enclose your starting and destination points in a selection rectangle.

2. Position the mouse pointer within the rectangle and click to zoom in.

3. Open the **Tools** menu and choose **Measuring Tool** (or press Ctrl+E) to activate the Measuring tool pointer. An information box with instructions and a distance indicator appears, and your cursor turns into crosshairs with a yellow ruler. To move the information box out of the way, drag it by its title bar and drop it in another location.

4. Position the crosshairs (not the ruler) at your starting point and click once.

5. Drag the pointer to the first bend in the proposed route and click again. With each click, the Measuring tool anchors itself. As you move the tool, the distance indicator shows the distance from the original starting point.

6. Continue this process until you reach your destination point.

7. If you want to record the distance, write it down and then right-click to close the Measuring tool.

Taking the Scenic Route

Very often, the best part of a trip is the journey itself. Some of my best traveling experiences have been little side trips and adventures in "getting lost." If time is not the major factor in determining your route, you can let Streets 98 help you figure out the most interesting way to get from here to there. In addition to tourist attractions, the Points of Interest feature can also help you locate hotels, motels, bed and breakfasts, and restaurants.

Finding points of interest

1. Open the **Find** menu and choose **Nearby Points of Interest**, or click the Points of Interest button ⭐ on the toolbar.

2. Move the mouse pointer—which now looks like crosshairs with a rotating star within a circle—to any spot along your route and click to open the Find Nearby Points of Interest dialog box shown in Figure 28.7.

3. Slide the distance indicator to the right to increase the radius you're willing to travel from the selection point. As you move the distance indicator, Streets 98 searches for more sites and lists them in the window below.

4. Click a category to expand it and see the list of sites found. Then click the desired point of interest to locate it on the map.

Finding the quickest route

Although Streets 98 does not provide a specific tool for the purpose, you can usually determine the quickest route by first measuring the distance of all your potential routes. Then calculate the driving time by dividing the distance by the approximate speed you will be able to maintain on each route.

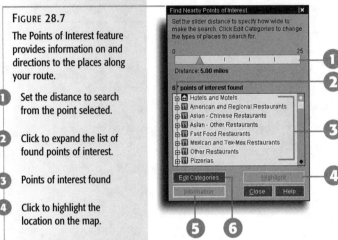

FIGURE 28.7

The Points of Interest feature
provides information on and
directions to the places along
your route.

1 Set the distance to search
from the point selected.

2 Click to expand the list of
found points of interest.

3 Points of interest found

4 Click to highlight the
location on the map.

5 Information on highlighted
place

6 Click to add or remove
categories from the list.

5. Highlight a point of interest in the list and click the
Information button to see the phone number and address
of the selected place. Press Alt+F4 or click the Close (x) button to close the information box and return to the Points of
Interest dialog box.

6. To highlight a point of interest on the map, select the point
in the list and click the **Highlight** button.

7. Click **Close** to return to the map view.

To determine the most interesting route to take, you have to
move to various points along each possible route and use the
Points of Interest feature. After you add points of interest to
your map, you can click one of them to display an information
dialog box again.

Creating a Route

After you decide on a route, the next step is to mark it out—
by using the Streets 98 Route Highlighter feature—and save it.

Using the Route Highlighter feature

1. Click the Route Highlighter button ![icon] on the toolbar
(or press Ctrl+H) to open the Route Highlighter dialog
box shown in Figure 28.8.

FIGURE 28.8

In addition to tracking the distance of your route, you can also change the color and line style used for marking it.

2. Choose the color and line style for your route from the drop-down palettes in the Route Highlighter dialog box.

3. Place the crosshairs mouse pointer on the starting point of the route and click to anchor the first point.

4. Move the pointer to the first bend in the road and click to anchor the next point. The line between the points is highlighted in the color and line style selected.

5. Continue along the entire route, laying down a point at each bend in the road until you reach your destination.

6. Press Esc to turn the Highlighter tool off.

7. Press Ctrl+S to save the route. Be sure to give it a unique name so that you can find it easily in the future. You can also save a route by opening the **File** menu and choosing **Save Map**. Either method opens the Save As dialog box.

8. Select a location for the saved route from the **Save in** drop-down list, and type the new name for the route in the **File name** text box.

9. Click **Save** to save the route to disk and return to the active map view.

The next time you want to see the route, open the **File** menu and choose the **Open Map** command (or press Ctrl+O). To highlight a different route, click the **New Route** button in the Route Highlighter information box. To clear a route, open the **Edit** menu, click **Clear Highlights**, and choose **Last Route**. After you save a route, you might want to clear it to keep the view uncluttered.

While mapping out a route, you may come to a city with a number of alternate routes around or through it. To zoom in for a closer look, you can use the Zoom Slider. As soon as you get a

Using Undo to delete a leg of your route

If you lay a point on the route and change your mind, all you have to do is click the Back (undo) button ⬅ on the menu toolbar. If you then change your mind again and decide to put the point back, click the Forward (redo) button ➡ next to it.

bird's-eye view of the city, you can resume highlighting your route through the city. When you finish with the city, you can use any one of the zooming tools to zoom out and continue highlighting.

Finding Locations

Ever wonder where Tryon, Florida, is? Have you heard about the great sandwiches at Fat and Skinnies Sandwich Restaurant but have no idea where it is? What do you do when you make a date with the person of your dreams to meet at the Hide A Way Café somewhere in Oregon, and then lose the cocktail napkin you wrote the address on? Well, if you have Streets 98, the answer to all these questions is easy—fire it up and use the Find a Place feature. If the town or place is in the Streets 98 database, you're home free.

Finding a location

1. Open the **Find** menu and choose **A Place** (or click the Find button 🔲 on the menu toolbar) to open the Find Place dialog box shown in Figure 28.9.

2. Type the name of the place or location in the **Place** text box. The more complete the information you enter, the better your chances of pinpointing the location will be.

3. Type a state in the **State** text box or select one from the drop-down list.

4. Click **Find** to search the database and open the Found Places dialog box, which displays a list of matches like the one in Figure 28.10.

5. Click a place on the list to locate it on the map. Double-click the name to locate it and highlight it at the same time. If it's a point of interest, double-clicking it also opens its information box.

6. If the Found Places dialog box is still onscreen when you finish, click **Cancel** to return to the map view.

The Find a Place feature zooms in as close as possible to the location, so you might have to zoom out to get a clear picture of exactly where the site is in the overall scheme of things.

Travel advisory

One thing you want to keep in mind is that the maps may not always be accurate. Even map-makers make errors, and roads sometimes change. You can receive regular updates to Streets 98 by ordering a subscription. Open the **Help** menu and choose **Contents** to open the Help dialog box. On the bottom of the screen, you should see a note that says `CLICK HERE FOR STREETS SUB-SCRIPTION INFORMATION`. Click that note to sign up for the annual subscription program.

Acceptable abbreviations

For a list of abbreviations you can use in the Find a Place or Find an Address features, open the **Help** menu and choose **Search For**. In the **Click the index entry** list box, double-click either **Abbreviations on maps** or **Abbreviations, addresses** to view a list of acceptable abbreviations.

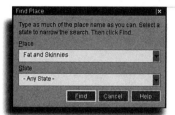

FIGURE 28.9

Type in the name (and state—optional) of the place you're looking for.

FIGURE 28.10

The results of your search include a selection of items containing all or part of the name you typed.

Finding a Street Address

I love this feature. If you know the exact street address of a person or business, Streets 98 pinpoints it for you if the street is part of the Streets 98 database. This beats using a city map that shows you the street but leaves you guessing about which section of that street holds your destination.

Locating an address

1. Open the **Find** menu and choose **An Address** (or click the Find button on the menu toolbar) to open the Find Address dialog box shown in Figure 28.11.

2. Enter as much of the address as you have, using the Tab key to move from text box to text box. The more detail you can supply, the more accurate the findings will be.

3. Click **Find** to search the database and locate the address. If there is more than one such address, Streets 98 creates a list of matches like the one in Figure 28.12.

4. If you click the address, Streets 98 zooms in to the exact location. If you double-click, Streets 98 highlights the address, inserts a pushpin, and creates a label (see Figure 28.13).

FIGURE 28.11

Enter as much address information as you possess.

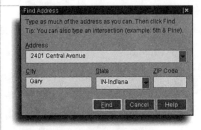

FIGURE 28.12

The more detailed your address information, the fewer matches you have to sort through.

FIGURE 28.13

Finding a street address is a breeze with Streets 98.

To close a location label, click the close button (x) in the top-right corner of the label.

Finding Web Links with Expedia Online

Streets 98 has another feature that will be of interest to all travelers who happen to be surfers—World Wide Web surfers, that is. There is an abundance of information available on the Internet, and Streets 98 has decided to tap into it to provide you with information on potential travel destinations.

To utilize the Web Links feature, you must have a modem (or other Internet connection), an account with an Internet Service Provider, and a Web browser. Office 97 SBE provides Microsoft Internet Explorer 4.0 as its Web browser.

Using Expedia Online to find travel information

1. Click the Expedia Online button ![Expedia Online] on the menu toolbar to open the Expedia Online dialog box shown in Figure 28.14.

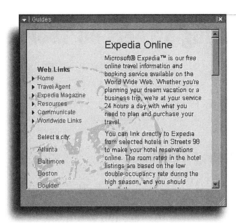

FIGURE 28.14
You'll find most major U.S. cities listed here.

2. Select a Web link or a city from the list to open the Web Link Connect to the Web dialog box.

3. Establish your Internet connection and then click the link or city name to launch your default Web browser and locate the link you selected (see Figure 28.15).

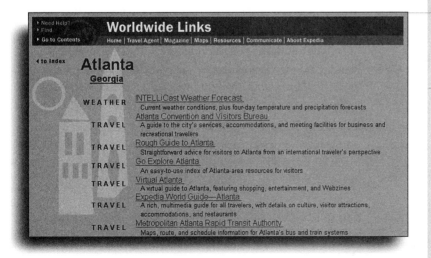

FIGURE 28.15
The Web site contains additional links for the destination you selected.

4. Click the links of interest to view additional information.

5. When you finish with Expedia Online, close your Web browser and click the Microsoft Expedia Streets 98 button on your taskbar to return to Streets 98.

Using Streets 98 Tools and Options

Streets 98 comes with a number of tools and options that enable you to perform a variety of functions and customize the program to suit your needs. From viewing longitude and latitude to managing your pushpins, Streets 98 puts you in control.

Using Tools

We've already seen some of the Streets 98 tools in action—for example, the Map Legend and the Measuring tool. Now, we'll cover the rest and give a few examples of how to use them. All the tools can be accessed from the **Tools** menu on the menu bar. Here's what you'll find in the Streets 98 tool chest:

- **Pushpin Explorer**. These handy little markers look and act just like their counterparts in the real world. When you find a spot on the map that you want to mark, insert a pushpin so you can find the location again.

- **Locator Map**. The Locator Map is a small map window that provides an overview of where the main map location is in relation to the surrounding area. The Locator Map can be used for navigation as well. Clicking a spot on the Locator moves both the main map and the Locator Map to bring the spot to the center of both maps.

- **Location Sensor**. When you select the Location Sensor, an information box appears on screen. As you move the pointer over the map, the information box displays the name, longitude, latitude, and time zone of the location under the pointer. Point to the down arrow in the Location Sensor information box title bar to open a drop-down menu where you can change the way latitude and longitude are displayed.

- **Map Legend**. A list of descriptions for all the symbols used in the map displays.

- **Measuring Tool**. A device for measuring the distance between points on the map.

- **Route Highlighter**. A marking tool that enables you to highlight a route anywhere on the map for easy reference.

- **GPS**. If you have a GPS (Global Positioning System) receiver, you can use Streets 98 to pinpoint your exact location at any given time. Chances are, if you're at home, you already know where you are. However, if you're on the road, this can be quite handy when used on a laptop or other mobile computer.

- **Export Map for HPC**. If you have a handheld personal computer (HPC)—also referred to as a personal digital assistant or PDA—you can install Pocket Streets 98 from the CD-ROM and export maps from your desktop computer to your handheld device.

- **Options**. The Street Options dialog box provides several options that enable you to modify the way Streets 98 works and looks.

The Locator Map and the Location Sensor are pretty simple and don't require any detailed instructions. Just select them from the **Tools** menu to use them (see descriptions in previous bulleted list).

Using Pushpins

The pushpins are a little more sophisticated than the other tools and provide some additional options that you might find useful. There are several ways to insert a pushpin on the map:

- Use the **Find A Place** or **Find An Address** command to automatically insert a pushpin when you pinpoint the location.

- Click the Pushpin button ▣ on the toolbar and click anywhere on the map.

- Double-click anywhere on the map.

To change the label or pushpin type, right-click the pushpin and select **Properties** from the shortcut menu to open the Pushpin Properties dialog box shown in Figure 28.16.

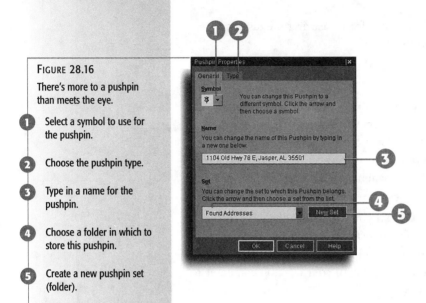

FIGURE 28.16

There's more to a pushpin than meets the eye.

1 Select a symbol to use for the pushpin.

2 Choose the pushpin type.

3 Type in a name for the pushpin.

4 Choose a folder in which to store this pushpin.

5 Create a new pushpin set (folder).

Fill out the information in the Pushpin Properties sheet and click **OK** to return to the map.

As soon as you begin to use pushpins, you'll want to be able to get back to them without having to search the entire map. That's where the Pushpin Explorer comes in handy.

Locating existing pushpins with the Pushpin Explorer

1. Open the **Tools** menu and choose **Pushpin Explorer** to open the Pushpin Explorer shown in Figure 28.17.

2. Click the folder in the **Sets** list (left pane) that holds the pushpin you want to see.

3. Highlight the pushpin in the right pane.

4. Click **Open** to see the location on the map. The Pushpin Explorer closes and you are immediately whisked away to the pushpin location. To exit without selecting a pushpin, click the Close (x) button in the upper-right corner. You can also locate a pushpin by double-clicking it in the right pane of the Pushpin Explorer.

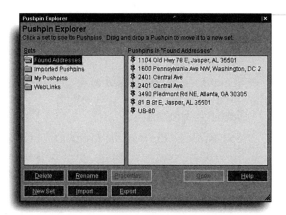

FIGURE 28.17
You can use the Pushpin Explorer to manage your pushpins.

You can also use the Pushpin Explorer to move pushpins from one folder to another by dragging and dropping. Click a pushpin in the right pane. Then, while holding the left mouse button, drag the pushpin to a folder in the left pane (**Sets**). Release the left mouse button to drop the pushpin in the new folder.

You can also manipulate pushpins by right-clicking a pushpin on the map and selecting one of the items on the shortcut menu:

- **Open**. If you included a note when you created this push-pin, click open to view the note.

- **Show Name/Hide Name**. If the pushpin label is not show-ing, click this item to display it. If the label is showing, click this to hide it.

- **Move**. You can relocate the pushpin by selecting this item and clicking on a new location for the selected pushpin.

- **Delete**. If you want to remove the pushpin permanently, click this menu item.

- **Hide set [*pushpin set name*]**. To hide all pushpins of the set to which this pushpin belongs, use this option.

- **Close All Balloons**. If you have note balloons displayed for any of your pushpins, selecting this menu item closes all the open balloons at once.

- **Properties**. Use this selection to rename the pushpin or change its symbol, type, or set.

Options

The options available in Streets 98 enable you to customize the way the program works. You can change the way the menus operate, the method used to display distances, and more.

Setting Options

To customize the way the program functions, you can use the Streets Options by opening the **Tools** menu and choosing **Options** to open the Streets Options dialog box shown in Figure 28.18.

FIGURE 28.18

Make Streets 98 work the way you want it to.

The following Streets Options are available:

- **Menus fly out automatically**. If you prefer to have the menus appear only when you click a selection, remove the check mark from this option.

- **Always show tooltips**. To hide the small white and yellow text boxes that appear to explain Streets 98 features, deselect this option.

- **Play button and menu sounds**. If you like the sounds that result from using menus and buttons, leave this option selected. To turn off the sounds, remove the check mark.

- **Show distances in**. Choose the measurement standard you're most comfortable with—**Miles** or **Kilometers**.

After you set your options, click **OK** to save the new settings and return to the map. If, after changing these options, you decide you'd like to put them back to their original settings, return to the Streets Options dialog box and click the **Reset** button to restore the defaults.

Copying Maps into Other Documents

The next time you create your own invitations to a gala event at your home, business, church, or school, why not include a map as well? Instead of drawing it by hand or using a drawing program, you can simply zoom in to the location of the event, copy the map, and paste it into your word processor.

Copying a map to a document

1. Use the **Find an Address** feature (covered earlier in the steps for locating an address) to pinpoint the location on the map and insert a pushpin.

2. Zoom out until you have the proper amount of detail in the map.

3. Open the **Edit** menu, choose **Copy**, and then choose **Map** (or press Ctrl+C) to copy the current map to the Windows Clipboard.

4. Switch to the document in which you want to include the map.

5. Use the document's paste command (most Windows 95 programs use Ctrl+V) to place a copy of the map at the insertion point (see Figure 28.19).

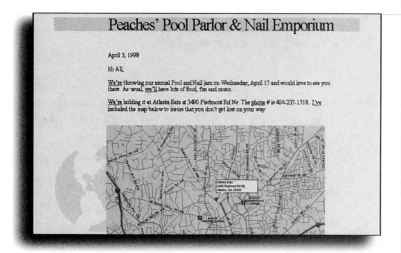

FIGURE 28.19

Inserting a map in your document is easy and will be greatly appreciated.

In many applications, including Word 97, you can resize the map after you insert it in your document.

Printing Your Map

After you plan your trip, find all the hot spots along the way, decide on the route, and mark it out, the only thing left to do is print it. To produce hard copy (a printout) of your map or route, follow these steps:

Printing a map

1. Set up the map view to display the location or route you want to print out.
2. Open the **File** menu, choose **Print,** and then choose **Map** (or press Ctrl+P) to open the Print dialog box shown in Figure 28.20.

FIGURE 28.20

Give your printout a title, set your printer options, and you're ready to go.

3. Enter a title for the printout so you'll recognize it when you need it. On the road, at night, with one eye on the road and the other trying to distinguish between a bunch of map printouts, you'll appreciate a clear, concise title.
4. Select your printer. If it doesn't appear in the box, click **Change** to pick the printer to use.
5. Click the **Print simpler maps** check box if your printer has difficulty printing the selected map.
6. Click the **Print** button to print a hard copy of the current map.

If you have a large route and wish to print out the entire route in detail, you will have to print each leg of the route separately.

Glossary

Active document   The document that is currently selected in your software window.

Add-ins   Programs that are independent of, but work with, a larger program.

Alignment   The way text lines up against the margins of a page.

Argument   In Excel, the value placed in a formula or function, as in SUM(A1:B5) where A1:B5 is the argument.

AutoRecover   The capability of recovering a document after a power failure or other unexpected mishap that shuts down your computer. Automatic backup copies must be enabled, and the last backup is presented when you return to the software.

Autosignature   Text that you create to use as a signature in email messages. Many people include their name and company information, or sometimes a personal quote.

AutoText   Text that is corrected automatically. You can invent a string of characters that will "correct" itself to a word or phrase.

Axes   The lines that establish the frame of reference for plotting data on a chart. Usually charts contain an x-axis that is vertical and a y-axis that is horizontal.

Background page   In Publisher, a virtual page that holds elements you want to repeat on every page of your publication.

Browser   Software that's used to access the Internet.

Cell   An area in a worksheet or table that holds a specific individual piece of information.

Cell data   Any information, including numbers, text, and formulas, that is contained in a worksheet cell.

Chart   A graphic representation of a selection of workbook cell data.

Clip Gallery   A program that contains clip art, pictures, sound files, and video clips that can be used to spruce up Office documents.

Date Navigator (Outlook)   A calendar on the Outlook window that has arrows for easy navigation through months and years.

Delimited file   The result of exporting data from a worksheet or table in which a character represents the end of the contents of each cell (usually a comma).

Design Gallery   In Publisher, a gallery of predesigned and preformatted special elements you can add to a publication.

Dialog box   Any of the information boxes that appear during the installation or use of an application and require input from the user.

Docked toolbar   Any toolbar that is attached to one of the four sides of an application window (or to another toolbar attached to one of the sides).

Document Map   A vertical display of the headings in a Word document. Click an entry to move quickly to that part of the document.

Drop-down list   A list of choices presented when you press the arrow to the right of a field in a dialog box.

Endnotes   A two-part feature in which a note number is placed within the document and reference information about the numbered word or phrase is automatically placed at the end of the document.

Fields   Placeholders for data that changes, such as a date, a mail-merge field, or a page number.

Filter   A set of criteria for including or excluding data that is to be viewed or printed.

Find Fast   A utility that indexes Office documents for quick retrieval.

Floating toolbar   A toolbar that is not anchored to the edge of the window, but instead displays in the document window for easy access.

Footnotes   A two-part feature in which a note number is placed within the document and reference information about the numbered word or phrase is automatically placed at the bottom of the page.

Gutter   The space on a page left blank for binding (the left edge of a right page, the right edge of a left page).

Hard copy   Computer jargon for a printed copy of a document file.

Highlight   Adding a band of color to text by using the Highlight tool on the Word toolbar.

ICM   (Image Color Matching)   A feature available in Windows 95 and Windows 98 that uses profiles f or printers and monitors to provide you with the closest possible match between your monitor display and the colors your printer produces.

Justification   Aligning text so that it fills the area between the left and right margins.

Layout guides   In Publisher, guidelines you put on the background page, representing boundaries for all pages in your publication. You can also use these guidelines to align objects.

Macro   A method of recording keystrokes and mouse clicks so that you can play them back automatically. This is a way to automate frequently repeated tasks.

Notes   A feature in Outlook that enables you to write notes to yourself on electronic "sticky notes."

Office Assistant   Animated Office Help system that provides interactive help, tips, and other online assistance.

Paste-up   In Publisher, a method of laying out individual parts of a document to prepare for professional printing. For instance, you might print the text and paste photos.

Path   The name of the folder (or multiple folders) needed to locate a file, separated by the backslash character. For example, My Documents\Letters\Mom.doc.

PIM   Personal Information Manager software (such as the Contacts folder in Outlook) in which you track information about contacts and keep notes on your interaction with those contacts.

Placeholder text   Text that is inserted automatically in a field or a Publisher text frame. You replace it with your own text.

Pushpin   In Expedia Streets 98, a marker for a location on a map.

Replace   A command on the Edit menu that you can use to replace text with different text automatically. This feature can also be used with codes, such as tabs and paragraph marks.

Ruler guides   In Publisher, guidelines (representing ruler positions) that you place on a page to help you line up objects. Also called *ruler marks*

Scratch area   The portion of the Publisher window outside the page display. Use the scratch area to "park" frames you want to move to another page.

ScreenTips   Notes that display on your screen to explain a function or feature. These were called ToolTips in earlier versions of Office software.

Shortcut keys   Keyboard combinations that provide shortcuts for menu commands. For example, Ctrl+S is a shortcut key for the File menu's Save command.

Shortcut menu   The menu that appears when you right-click an object.

Snap To   In Publisher, a feature that forces objects to a specific position on a page.

Spike   In Word, a feature that permits you to remove multiple elements one at a time and place them in an AutoText file. After you collect the elements, you can place them in a new location in your document.

TaskPad   In Outlook, a list of tasks that displays when you use the Calendar folder.

Template   Available in Word, Excel, and Publisher, templates provide predesigned patterns on which Office documents can be based.

Text Overflow icon In Publisher, a button at the bottom of a text frame that appears when the text in the frame is continued in another connected text frame.

Watermark A pale element placed in the background of a document page. Used for graphics or special text such as "Confidential."

Workbook An Excel document that contains one or more worksheets, chart sheets, or VBA modules.

Worksheet The workbook component that contains cell data, formulas, and charts.

Index

Symbols

* (asterisks) Excel multiplication operator, 310

^ (carets), Excel exponentiation operator, 310

$ (dollar signs), Excel cell references, 311-312

= (equals signs), Excel formulas, 309-310

/ (forward slashes), Excel division operator, 310

- (minus signs), Excel subtraction operator, 309

( ) (parentheses), Excel formulas, (AVERAGE function), 333

. (periods), worksheet cell names, 317

+ (plus signs), Excel addition operator, 309

 # (pound signs), Excel worksheets, 261, 334-335

_ (underscores), worksheet cell names, 316

4clipart.com Web site, 173

A

absolute cell references, Excel, 310-316
    changing reference types, 312-313
    copying formulas, 314-316

accent marks, 243

accounting data, 626. *See also* Small Business Financial Manager; Excel 97
    creating charts (Chart Wizard), 632
    creating reports (Report Wizard), 630-632

    importing data, 626-630
      creating reports, 629
      remapping data, 629-630
      supported accounting packages, 626-627
      using Import Wizard, 627-629

Accounting menu commands (Excel), 253, 624
    Import Wizard, 627
    Insert Balance, 642
    Recalculate Reports, 642
    Report Wizard, 630
    Select Analysis Tool, 632

Add Service to Profile dialog box (Outlook)
    adding Internet Mail service, 427
    adding Personal Address Book, 430

adding data, Excel. *See also* formulas (Excel 97 worksheets)
    AutoCalculate, 306-307
      calculating filtered records, 393
    SUM function, 326-327
      AutoSum, 306-308

adding (inserting). *See* inserting

addresses
    finding street addresses, 655-656. *See also* Streets 98
    Outlook. *See* Contacts (Outlook); Personal Address Book (Outlook)

advertising, creating marketing publications, 597-599

Airplane Wizard (Publisher), 597-598

alignment
    Excel
      chart data labels, 359-360
      worksheet text, 293-294
    publication objects, 563-570. *See also* arranging objects, publications (Publisher)
      nudging objects, 565-567
      ruler guides, 568-570
      Snap To, 567. See also guides, publications (Publisher)
    Word text
      indents, 90-92
      page numbers, 84-85
      setting tab stops, 98-101
      tables (toolbar buttons), 149-150
      vertical alignment, 81, 92-93

alphabetizing. *See* sorting

analysis tools
    Business Comparison Reports, 632-634
      income/balance sheet comparisons, 633
      industry classifications, 632-633
    Projection Wizard, 634-639
      creating Projected Income Statement reports, 637-639
      estimating income/expenses, 635-636
      selecting dates, 635
    What-If scenarios, 639-642
      entering hypothetical data, 641
      saving, 640

AND operator, filtering Excel lists, 389-392

animation, Word
    menus, 241
    text, 109-110

blank pages, publications (Publisher), 515

Blank Publications (Publisher), 509-512

blank workbooks/ worksheets, opening (Excel), 255-257

blue row numbers, Excel lists, 392

bold text
Excel chart titles, 363
Publisher, 531, 533
Word, 104

borders
publication frames, 549-552
tables (Word), 158-162
worksheet cells, 296-297

boxes. *See* frames (Publisher)

breaks, Word documents
lines (soft returns), 95-96
pages (pagination options), 96-98
inserting manual breaks, 98
setting automatic break options, 97
sections, 72-76
changing types, 79-80
copying/moving, 75-76
deleting, 75
inserting, 72, 74-75

bringing objects forward, Publisher, 559-560

browsing Word documents
Browse function, 45-46
Document Maps, 46-47

bulleted lists
publications (Publisher), 552-554
Word, 166-170

business analysis. *See* Small Business Financial Manager; analysis tools

buttons. *See* toolbars; dialog boxes

C

calculations
Calculator, 642
Excel worksheets, 306-308
AutoCalculate, 306-307
AutoSum, 306-308
calculating filtered records (SUBTOTAL function), 393-396
cell names, 316-321
cell references (addresses), 308-313
column/row labels, 322
formulas. See formulas (Excel worksheets)
functions. See formulas (Excel worksheet), functions
recalculating reports, Small Business Financial Manager, 642
tables (Word), 165-166

Calendar (Outlook), 456-457
adding events, 464
appointments, 459-464
Appointment Book, 458
creating from tasks, 461-462
deleting, 463
recurring appointments, 461
rescheduling, 462-463
scheduling, 459-461
viewing, 463-464
Date Navigator, 458
notes, 468-472
coloring, 469-470
creating, 468-469
icon size, 471
sizing, 470
viewing, 471-472
tasks, 464-468
creating, 459, 465-466
creating appointments, 461-462
deleting, 466
editing, 466
recurring tasks, 466-467
TaskPad, 459
viewing, 467-468

calendars, inserting into Publisher publications, 591

canceling print jobs, Word, 216

capitalization, Word AutoCorrect, 129-131

carets (^), Excel exponentiation operator, 310

catalogs, creating. *See* Mail Merge (Word)

cells
Excel worksheets. *See* worksheets (Excel)
Word tables
borders/shading, 158-162
changing height/width, 156-158
formatting text, 163
merging/splitting, 154-155

centering. *See* alignment

Change Style dialog box (Publisher), 534-535

characters. *See* text

charts (Excel), 339
axes, 345-346
formatting, 368-370
setting data. See also charts, creating, editing/selecting data ranges
titles, 345-346, 362-363
turning labels on/off, 346
copying, 350
creating (Chart Wizard), 338-350
axes. See charts, axes
data labels. See charts, data labels
editing/selecting data ranges, 343-345
financial charts. See Small Business Financial Manager
gridlines. See charts, gridlines
legends. See charts, legends
Office Assistant, 340
placing charts in workbooks, 348-350
selecting chart types, 340-342
selecting data sources, 339-340
showing data tables, 348-349
starting wizard, 339
titles, 345-346